RB. £12.60

A PORTRAIT OF
LENI RIEFENSTAHL

A PORTRAIT OF
LENI
RIEFENSTAHL

Audrey Salkeld

JONATHAN CAPE
LONDON

First published *1996*

1 3 5 7 9 10 8 6 4 2

© Audrey Salkeld 1996

Audrey Salkeld has asserted her right
under the Copyright, Designs and Patents Act, 1988
to be identified as the author of this work

First published in the United Kingdom in 1996 by Jonathan Cape,
Random House, 20 Vauxhall Bridge Road, London SW1V 2SA

Random House Australia (Pty) Limited
20 Alfred Street, Milsons Point, Sydney,
New South Wales 2061, Australia

Random House New Zealand Limited
18 Poland Road, Glenfield,
Auckland 10, New Zealand

Random House South Africa (Pty) Limited
PO Box 337, Bergvlei, 2012 South Africa

Random House UK Limited Reg. No. 954009

A CIP catalogue record for this book
is available from the British Library

ISBN 0-224-02480-9

Typeset by Deltatype Ltd, Ellesmere Port, Cheshire
Printed and bound in Great Britain by
Mackays of Chatham PLC

Contents

Preface

I was drawn to the story of Leni Riefenstahl through a deep interest in mountaineering films and a curiosity about the highly individual *Bergfilme* which were popular in Germany between the wars and which made a movie star of this former dancer. With their emphasis on loyalties and rivalries, heroism, homeland and combatting raw elements, these mountain films have often been likened to Hollywood westerns. The genre, however, unlike its American counterpart, more or less died out soon after the end of the Second World War.

Posterity remembers Leni Riefenstahl for the documentaries she directed at Hitler's invitation in Nazi Germany during the years 1933–1936. In sifting contemporary evidence and the verdicts of later historians, I hoped my researches would resolve – in my own mind at least – whether she was player or pawn in the murky world of propaganda politics. What is clear to me now is that motivations can rarely be so neatly apportioned. Still, I am grateful to the many literary sources, listed elsewhere, that helped me to build up a picture of this horrific period, among them Riefenstahl's own written works. I owe her my thanks for patiently answering my questions.

My friend Jill Neate, who has since died, was extraordinarily helpful in the early days of this project, finding out-of-print books for me and in particular translating some of Riefenstahl's early writings as well as extracts from the autobiography of Hans Ertl. Hans-Jürgen Panitz of Omega Film, Munich, kindly produced videocopies of almost all the early *Bergfilme*, while Channel 4 supplied an English-language tape of the perceptive and award-winning television portrait of Leni Riefenstahl made under the direction of Ray Müller. The British Film Institute allowed me access to Ivor Montagu's papers, which BECTU, the Broadcasting Entertainment, Cinematograph and Theatre Union, has helped to clarify.,

For letters, advice and other assistance I thank: John Boyle, Kevin Brownlow, Ingeborge Doubrawa-Cochlin, Eleonore Cowper, Julia Elton, Roy Fowler, K. G. T. Gladstone of the Imperial War Museum, Duff Hart-Davis, Anderl and Trudl Heckmair, Tom Holzel, Val Johnson, Stefan König, Jane Lilly, Kay Mander, and Gitta Sereny.

My own family − especially by husband Peter − has borne my preoccupation patiently and for far too long.

Finally, and with affection, I acknowledge my great debt to Tony Colwell, my editor and friend, for his support and unfailing good advice over the years.

AUDREY SALKELD
March 1996

I

The Woman in White

She was conspicuous, everywhere at once it seemed, intense, imperiously issuing orders, magnificent, dressed in white. From film goddess she had metamorphosed to Greek goddess or guardian spirit, high priestess of the Olympian Games.

Hélène Bertha Amelie Riefenstahl, 'Leni' as posterity will remember her, was at the pinnacle of her artistic and controversial career in the summer of 1936 at Hitler's Berlin Olympics. She was just approaching her thirty-fourth birthday. The two-part film she made of that year's Games, which ran for almost four hours, set a standard for sports reportage, the influence of which is still felt. Yet in no sense was it mere documentary reporting. Film critics of the stature of the late Leslie Halliwell see it as a brilliant example of film-making in which the artful management of camera movement, editing and music combine to make the experience 'truly Olympian, especially in the introductory symbolic sequence suggesting the birth of the Games.' Here was visual poetry, a paean to the transcendence of the human spirit and the beauty of the human form. Bestowing upon the combined production his exclusive three-star grading, Halliwell declared it among the ten best documentaries ever made. Others unequivocally believe it to be evil, permeated throughout by the worship of fascism. Over many years theirs was the louder voice.

Riefenstahl's awareness of any occasion had less to do with the sequence of images and actions unravelling before her eyes than with the concussion these images made upon her senses. She perceived a *Gestaltung*, a form or shape, an atmosphere of what was happening, and her genius lay in the ability to translate this into film, particularly through her highly individual style of editing. No special sanctity was placed upon precise actuality where the feel or intensity of the

1

moment could be enhanced by a reshoot, or an inserted close up. As with her earlier documentaries of the Nuremberg Rallies, the use of techniques borrowed from feature film-making offended many purists for its apparent blurring of fact with artifice.

She had come to film directing by a roundabout route. As a child Riefenstahl was often lost in make-believe, a daredevil dreamer climbing trees, swimming lakes, building rafts and dens, her head full of fantasies. She wrote poetry and little plays. She loved music and painting, and she longed, as many young girls do, to go on the stage. There were endless family rows as she wheedled and implored her father to let her attend drama school. He was a cultivated man who enjoyed the theatre, indeed had dabbled in amateur dramatics as a youth, but he was fixed in the idea that his daughter would be a fallen woman were she to tread the boards. Though she could wrap him round her finger in some things, Leni knew he would never yield on this, and with her mother's connivance she secretly enrolled for dancing lessons at the late age of sixteen. Her father remained in the dark until one day, after a class concert, a friend innocently congratulated him on his gifted daughter. He was so 'horribly angry', Leni remembered, that she and her mother feared he would have a stroke. For weeks he refused to speak to either conspirator and then only to threaten her mother with divorce proceedings. At last, for the sake of family unity, a worn-out Leni reluctantly promised to give up all dreams of becoming a great dancer.

On leaving school, she spent a few terms at art college before being sent to be 'finished' at a girls' academy in the Harz mountains, where the headmistress was instructed by her father to treat her with utmost firmness. In defiance, the enlightened woman allowed her almost at once to direct and act in school plays and to visit the theatre. Young Leni had packed her ballet shoes and practised assiduously every day. At the end of a year, she struck a deal with her father: she would agree to work in his office if he let her continue with her ballet lessons. He did better than that, signing her up with a Russian ballet teacher and the Jutta Klamt School for expressive dance. In time, Leni made it on to the stage as an interpretive solo dancer, to be received encouragingly in Berlin and beyond, and no one was more proud of her than her father. Reconciled to his stubborn daughter's ambition, he wept with joy at her first recital in October 1923.

After injury threatened her nascent career, Leni switched to films with barely a backward glance, first as an actress, later to work on both sides of the camera. Her maiden production as a film-director in her own right was the delicate *Das blaue Licht* (*The Blue Light*), a tragic fantasy set in the Dolomite mountains, in which she also starred. When the film was released early in 1932, among those to read its parable message of alienation and aspiration was a fellow dreamer and myth-lover, leader of the Nazi Party Adolf Hitler, then entering the final stages of his run-in to the Reich Chancellory.

Hitler's admiration for Riefenstahl's work soon extended to a charged relationship with the film-maker herself, and once he assumed power nothing would satisfy him but that she make films for him personally. Three documentaries about the Nuremburg rallies, including the hypnotic *Triumph of the Will*, preceded his wish for her to cover the 1936 Olympic Games. Money seemed little object, but she did not see eye to eye with Goebbels who, as Minister of Popular Enlightenment and Propaganda, was nominally in charge of all film-making in Nazi Germany. She took her grievances directly to the Führer – and got her own way. In a Germany where women were supposed to content themselves with the three 'K's extolled by Bismark, *Kinder, Kirche und Küche* – children, church and kitchen sink – here was a woman who came and went unannounced and unchallenged through the cordons of guards surrounding the leader. Living in a man's world, doing what was generally considered a man's job, she at the same time exploited all the feminine advantages. She was attractive. An American journalist, convinced this was 'the woman behind Hitler', described her for his readers:

> She is a striking, dark-haired, determined woman, dressed in the simple but effective fashion of Nazi Germany. Her eyes – dark brown and glowing with life and spirit – are heavy-lidded. At times they display a decided squint, as the movie camera has revealed again and again . . . Her beauty is of a type that has a distinctive appeal in Germany. Lithe, spare, and boyish is her figure. Her mouth is wide and suggestive. Collectively, her features radiate youth and verve.

She was 'extremely athletic and rather tall', he continued. It all added up to an appearance that distinguished her at any gathering. A 'swagger and haughtiness' testified to her assertiveness, and her carriage plainly expressed self confidence and a knowledge of her own capabilities.[1]

She was temperamental, passionate and impulsive, impossible in many respects, but generous and intuitive, too, with a gift for knowing how to be a good and loyal friend. Her appetites for work and play were phenomenal. Though at this time she had never married, her name had been linked with many men, particularly colleagues and cameramen involved in her various projects. Sensuous and attractive, she was both desired and desiring. Love was essential to her creativity. Physically she had been a late developer, she told one Sunday paper interviewer in 1992:

> No breasts you know, and my cycle only began when I was 21. Of course, I was always in love, from heaven knows when. The first one was a boy I saw in a street near our home – for a whole year I walked along at the same time every day, just to see him, but it was ten years until I actually met him – and by then, of course, I was quite uninterested.[2]

Her first sexual experience, at twenty-one, seems to have been disappointing, but after that she accepted lovers for what they were, rather than what she wanted them to be, having learned, as she liked to assert, the difference between illusion and reality. Did Hitler number among her lovers? It was well-known that he enjoyed being seen and photographed with glamorous film stars, and anyone could tell that the bond between him and Riefenstahl was particularly close. She herself admitted to being dazzled by the Führer, but always insisted they were never intimate. Their relationship was at a peak in that Olympian summer of 1936 when frequently they were seen sharing a joke together at the Games, jointly greeting athletes or facing the flashbulbs of the world's pressmen. She seemed unassailable.

Surprisingly, there had been little more than scrappy newsreel coverage of preceding Olympic Games. One might have expected something ambitious from Los Angeles four years earlier, but Hollywood had no interest in real-life sport. A modest film of the Winter Olympics of 1928 had been made by Riefenstahl's colleague and mentor Dr Arnold Fanck, but it was a hasty, half-hearted effort, despite employing two of the best outdoor cameramen of the day: Sepp Allgeier and Hannes Schneeberger would both go on to work many times with Riefenstahl. Fanck had embraced the newsreel approach: be there and snatch what you can. At least it left his evenings free for playing roulette in a fashionable St Moritz hotel, but it was not Leni's way.[3]

She had been tempted to include the 1936 Winter Games in her own Olympic film, but it would have doubled the effort, and Goebbels had already commissioned coverage elsewhere. Instead, she went along to Garmisch with some of her best assistants and experimented with camera angles and filmstock. With some satisfaction she would note later that Goebbels' film, directed by Hans Weidemann, was ridiculed by athletes in the Olympic village that summer, despite its one or two 'fantastic shots' – and she took the message. To make a good sports film was never easy, even with the most skilled operators and the best equipment of the day.

To avoid the same trap, Riefenstahl trained a nucleus of her best cameramen and assistants at various sports functions in the months running up to the Games. With and without film in their cameras, they would practise special camera movements designed to give the best shots. From the outset, her favoured cameramen were in on the planning, and helped dream up all manner of ways for achieving unexpected points of view. Critics would afterwards suggest that she rode on the back of others' expertise, usurping all the credit for herself. It is hollow criticism. Most film directors hire the best professionals available, to provide the chemistry likely to assure the best results. Film-making is almost inevitably a communal process, and rarely does a film crew fail to exceed the sum of its component individuals: the oddity is to remark upon the fact. Henry Jaworsky, one of her junior cameramen on the Olympics film, has told how Riefenstahl would assign the day's positions, instructing everyone which lens to use, what focal length, which filters, how many frames a second. She was most certainly in control, and the view is shared by those surviving cameramen – Walter Frentz and Guzzi Lantschner – who appeared in the biographical film of Riefenstahl made in 1993 by Ray Müller. Both paid tribute to her overall vision and her unerring sense of the dramatic. That said, in putting the right man in the right place, Riefenstahl was allowing the cameraman's own talent the freedom in which to flourish. Jaworsky was in no doubt, there were many fine photographers working on the production, but Riefenstahl was 'the motor and brains of the whole thing.'[4]

Her earlier film of the 1934 Nazi rally in Nuremberg had been widely acclaimed as an artistic masterpiece. That this success was achieved by a woman, and one moreover seen to enjoy special privileges within a difficult system, inevitably fuelled the envy of cinema contemporaries, as well as loyal Party workers. With so many eager to see her fall, her position and reputation were precarious. At the Olympic Games she was under enormous pressure to pull something really remarkable out of the hat if she wanted to survive. She knew that.

Gymnastics and athletics had always attracted her; indeed she loved most sports. When she gave up professional dancing, she maintained the discipline of regular training, and she liked to ski every winter. The 1928 Winter Games inspired her to a frenzy of field and track activity when she returned to Berlin, where she dedicated herself to becoming superfit. The prospect of the Summer Olympics in her home town eight years later provoked a similar surge of exercise. She visited the Grunewald stadium three or four times a week, for high jump practice and other light athletics, in pursuit of a state silver medal. Yet, despite her excitement over the forthcoming events, the idea of actually filming the Eleventh Olympiad seems not to have been her own. And in this instance may not have been a direct commission from Hitler either. Her memoirs tell that she was buttonholed while training one day by Dr Carl Diem, the man responsible above all others for bringing the Games to Berlin and ensuring they were the greatest ever. He could see what a publicity coup it would be if the celebrated Leni Riefenstahl could be persuaded to produce an Olympics film to match her *Triumph of the Will*, and in this he had the backing of the International Olympic Committee. He assured her that the IOC, as organisers of the event, could override any attempt Dr Goebbels' ministry might make to disrupt her efforts, and she need fear no competition from the newsreel cameramen: they would be confined to the public stands. As in Nuremberg, where she had contrived towers, trolleys and lifts for special viewing platforms – even commandeering firemen's turntable ladders – she could expect every co-operation in meeting her needs.

Riefenstahl had sworn many times not to make any more documentaries, wanting to return to acting which she still regarded as her real vocation, but Diem was persuasive and the commission certainly attractive. Ways immediately sprang to mind in which novel results might be obtained, although she could foresee tremendous problems, too. Still, no one else had anything like her experience for filming a massive co-ordinated event like this, nor of working in large sports arenas. She knew she could do it – and there was nothing on the stocks which could not be postponed for eighteen months or so. After a token show of reluctance, she gave herself totally to the task. Hitler, when she told him, seemed surprised but was supportive, she says. Goebbels, too, despite the months his own Ministry had spent planning an Olympics film, came round to the idea. Riefenstahl signed a distribution contract with the Tobis syndicate, and Geyer laboratories put editing and screening suites at her disposal. She set up a new production company – *Olympiade-Film GmbH* – to handle project finances and, more important, she secured everyone's assurance that complete artistic freedom was hers. In time she would play the Hitler card, as she had several times before, to maintain that freedom.

Riefenstahl worked intuitively. She has said often that she had the entire film in her head from the beginning, and the editing planned before shooting ever began: 'I treated the whole thing like a vision . . . I was like an architect building a house.'[5] Clearly this is a reference to her *Gestaltung*, her sense of the essence of the Games. Without knowing what dramas would unfold, there could be no exact plot or shooting script from which to work, yet much could be prepared ahead of time. The human struggle was what most interested her, what went on in the heart and mind of the competitor – or at least in the mind and sinews. Not every event would be portrayed in the final work, but she had to take the precaution of covering them all, in heats and finals, and from a variety of angles, to be sure of capturing those special moments when records are broken or rivalries flare. This extremely extravagant method of film-making would leave unused some seventy per cent of the 250 miles of film shot.

From the start she had anticipated dividing the picture into two halves, two self-standing films of up to two hours each, one concentrating on arena events and the second on other sports. Goebbels appears not to have appreciated this fully until Riefenstahl needed more money during the editing, by which time he was trying to wrest the project from her and call back Weidemann to put the film together. In his diary on 6th November 1936, he wrote:

> Fraulein Riefenstahl is pulling hysterical fits on me. It is impossible to work with this wild woman. Now she wants another half a million [Reichsmarks] for her film and to make two out of it. Yet it stinks to high heaven in her shop. I am cool right down to my heart. She cries. That is the last weapon of women. But that does not work on me any more. Let her get to work and keep things in order.[6]

He saw no need for an artistic production, such as Leni proposed. She, on the other hand, could muster no interest in newsreel-type coverage, nor in producing a chirpy little fantasy cut on movement, to music. The drama and ritual significance of the Games had to be described. In a prologue, to which she attached great importance, the modern Games would be linked to their Greek origins. In her mind's eye she pictured Grecian statues dissolving into living athletes

– most notably Myron's famous *Diskobolos*. She saw mists flirting around classical ruins, naked maidens dancing. She would film the Olympic flame being lit and carried on its long path to the Games – the first time this had become part of the Olympic ritual. To help with this prologue she enlisted a brilliant film-maker, Willy Zielke, who had recently completed *Das Stahltier* for the directors of the state-owned German railways. His brief had been to commemorate a hundred years of railway history, but he managed to conjure up such a surreal and terrifying image of The Steel Beast that his patrons, and Dr Goebbels, neither of whom saw the movie until it was completed, demanded all prints and negative be destroyed. Zielke himself was deemed guilty of 'Damaging German Reputation' and was soon afterwards committed to a mental asylum. Riefenstahl pulled strings to have him released for her film work, although he was then committed again until she rescued him once more towards the end of the war.[7]

Heinz von Javorsky (who changed his name in Hollywood to Henry Jaworsky) was one of two cameramen to go to Greece with Riefenstahl for the official torch lighting ceremony. He has told how, when they arrived at Olympia, the programme which had been arranged struck them as utterly drab and uninspired, nothing remotely approaching the image Riefenstahl had built in her mind. Taking in all the cars and crowds and the unforgiving noonday sun, she said, 'This is not for me. We will just have to set up our own lighting of the sacred flame.' And she staged a tableau infinitely more beautiful, setting the pattern for the way she would go on. When it came to filming the relay of runners transporting the brand, and this too fell short of the aesthetic quality Riefenstahl demanded, she improvised once more. Jaworsky remembers how every two kilometres a fresh athlete would light his torch from the one before and then run another two kilometres, before being picked up by a bus:

> That's the way it went all the way to Berlin. The first few were very famous runners – like the winner of the first modern Olympic Games (he was sixty years old by now). Then came the son of the Prime Minister, a modern sportsman, then they had the young Greek students. And I was with Leni Riefenstahl in a beautiful big Mercedes convertible, my camera was tied down and she was telling me 'Shoot this, shoot this!', excited as usual. At one point – I would say, he was within the first twenty – a young Greek was running and taking the torch and he was extremely handsome,

tanned like bronze, beautiful curly hair, well-built. And she said, 'Shoot more of him, shoot more of him! Shoot everywhere more of him, he is beautiful!'[8]

When the young man ended his run and was supposed to be picked up by his bus again, Leni cried, 'Wait, wait! I have to have this man for more, he is too good to be lost out here.' She arranged for him to stay longer, telling Jaworsky, 'He looks like an antique Greek, he looks like a Pericles.'

Riefenstahl had her 'Pericles' dressed (or rather, undressed) as a marathon runner and brought to Delphi where a few hours' work produced the evocative material she was after. He was then taken back to Athens to be kitted out in a beautiful white tropical suit. This perfect Greek – who turned out in fact to be a Russian – was quick to see this as the life he felt born to. Ultimately, young Anatol Dobriansky followed the team back to Germany, where Leni looked after him. When he failed a screen test at Tobis, she helped him to become a film editor. He remained in Germany all through the war, volunteered for perilous one-man submarine missions and survived.

★

In March of 1936 Hitler's troops had reoccupied the Rhineland, that corridor along the Franco-Belgian border demilitarized since 1918. Though this is seen now as perhaps the fundamental step towards the Second World War, the Führer's actions went unchallenged by the rest of Europe, preoccupied as it was with the worsening situation in Spain. Within Germany, the action brought an enormous sense of release from the humiliating constraints imposed by the terms of the Versailles Treaty and the Locarno Pact. There was no alarm that the newly-introduced conscription might lead ultimately to war: Hitler let it be known he was prepared to negotiate individual peace treaties with practically any nation but Czechoslovakia or Austria, and he was not averse to rejoining the League of Nations, which Germany had left soon after the Nazis came to power in October 1933. A plebiscite in 1935 had already returned the Saar to Germany. With rearmament and ambitious construction programmes such as the *Autobahn* network, employment was high (for all but Jews and other minorities unpopular with the Nazis), and the cost of living was kept artificially low. The masses were offered cheap holidays and travel as well as hearty recreation and cultural activities through the *Kraft durch Freude* (Strength through Joy) leisure scheme. Altogether, the mood within the Fatherland was of increasing confidence and national pride. Times were still hard, but there was a general pulling together and Hitler's stock was high. Few railed against increased regimentation or press censorship or the growing curtailment of personal liberties and free speech. Perceptive foreign visitors and pressmen – their activities as yet unrestricted – may have been warning the world of a disastrous collapse in basic humanity under the Nazi system, but their governments were still hoping to reach some modus vivendi with Hitler's new Germany, with which after all there was much to be impressed.

Goebbels saw the Berlin Olympics as one more opportunity for strengthening national morale while putting the Third Reich gloriously on show. Word soon went round that visiting correspondents and dignitories were to be treated like royalty. Hitler, too, appreciated the value of festivity and spectacle. It was after all a cornerstone of his Volk-ish philosophy, essential in keeping the masses untroublesome and industrious. Yet with little personal interest in athletics, the Führer blew hot and cold over the whole Olympics business throughout the preparations. He could have mustered more enthusiasm were there a serious prospect of Germany winning, but even he could see the chances for that were slight. He certainly had no desire to provide hospitality for negro and Jewish contestants and others who did not fit his warped view of racial acceptablilty. If the Americans were shameless enough to allow their medals to be won by blacks, there was no way he wanted any part in congratulating the victors.

On the other hand, the Games provided an excuse to further his grandiose plans for remodelling the capital, and he insisted on personal involvement in all the construction work. A radical seven-mile east-west road development was pushed through to provide an axis across the city from the old royal palace to the new Olympic *Reichssportfeld*, but it was not universally popular. Several much-loved buildings were sacrificed and celebrated linden trees had to be felled in this first stage towards creating a ceremonial boulevard in line with his overblown aspirations. A *Via Triumphalis*, as it was soon dubbed, envisaged more for the return of victorious armies than athletic champions. An impressive complex of stadia, sportsfields and tracks for both competition and training, a swimming pool, ancillary buildings and car parks – and even a theatre – sprang up to the west of the city, with an Olympic village in a birch forest further west still, beyond the suburbs. Other facilities for water and equestrian sports

10

were prepared within easy reach, and the sailing events would take place at Kiel, on the Baltic.

The centrepiece was the cavernous 100,000-seater Berlin Olympic Stadium. Hitler recalled afterwards how he had swept away designs submitted by the Ministry of the Interior for replacing the existing stadium on this site – built for the cancelled 1916 games – with one costing 1,100,000 marks or an alternative at 1,400,000. Confounding his colleagues, Hitler proposed a preliminary grant of 28,000,000 marks for the construction, thoroughly enjoying the look of astonishment on the assembled faces. In the event, the final bill rose to around 77,000,000, but more than 500 million was earned back in foreign currency. Or so he always claimed.

According to Werner March, the architect of the new stadium (and son of Otto March, author of the one it replaced), whenever the Führer came to inspect the building's progress he would observe grumpily that everything was far too small.[9] His dissatisfaction finally spilled over into a pathological aversion, and he regretted not having insisted the design be handled by Albert Speer, who had been responsible for the grand constructions in Nuremberg. Speer has told how he was summoned one day to hear an agitated Führer instructing his State Secretary, Hans Pfundtner, that the Olympics were to be cancelled.

'They cannot take place without my presence,' Hitler stormed, 'And I will never set foot inside a modern glass box like that.'

The concrete structure, with its glass partition walls, was similar in design to the stadium in Vienna, and Hitler could never bring himself to find a good word for anything Viennese. Speer worked through the night on a plan for cladding the skeleton in natural German stone, while at the same time introducing portentous cornices. The offending glass partitions would be done away with. Crisis was averted and Hitler, appeased, proposed decorating the Olympic complex with statues by two approved sculptors, Arno Breker and Josef Wackerle.[10] The episode had convinced him even more strongly that Speer was the one to whom his vision for the new Berlin should be entrusted.

There had been international calls for the Games to be withdrawn from Germany, or to be boycotted. The Amateur Athletic Union of the United States voted by only the narrowest of margins to permit an American team to take part. (For other reasons, neither the Soviet Union nor Spain sent teams at all.) Just before the Winter Games in Garmisch a row had erupted between Hitler and Count Baillet-

Latour, president of the International Olympic Committee, over the countless vicious graffiti and anti-Semitic posters flaunted along the German roads. With some heat Baillet-Latour told the Führer these were completely unacceptable at a festival open to all races and nations, a festival dedicated to peaceful competition. Through his interpreter Hitler made the curt reply that matters of the greatest internal importance could not be altered to suit 'a small point of Olympic protocol.'

Protocol indeed! It was 'a question of the most elementary courtesy' Baillet-Latour retorted hotly, and threatened immediate cancellation of both Winter and Summer Games.

Surprised at first into silence, Hitler soon became very voluble. With his gaze fixed on a corner of the ceiling, he worked himself into a frenzy until seemingly oblivious of the others in the room. It was almost as though he were in some sort of trance. Schmidt, the interpreter, ceased translating and waited for the crisis to pass, clearly all too familiar with such tantrums.

We are told that the Chancellor then fell silent for several tense minutes before blurting out, 'You will be satisfied; the orders shall be given.' The interview terminated, he brusquely left the room. The offensive signs disappeared until the Winter Olympics were over.[11]

Before the Summer Games, orders were given to the press for all reporting on racial issues to be suspended and Berlin was cleared of signs and placards declaring 'JEWS NOT WELCOME' and 'JEWS ENTER HERE AT THEIR OWN RISK', normally commonplace in the city. Persecution not just of the Jews but also of the Catholic church was put on hold to lull visitors into believing that only benign stability was being promoted. The American journalist William Shirer, who had the temerity to file a dispatch reporting this cynical clean-up for the brief period of the Games, was censured and threatened with expulsion.

Meanwhile Leni Riefenstahl had been allocated an old summer castle in a park not far from the stadium in which to house herself and her crew throughout the Olympic fortnight. After a twelve to sixteen hour day, when everyone was nodding off to sleep, she would gather the whole 'gang' together around a big table. And although, like everyone else, she had worked flat out all day, according to Jaworsky she would still be full of energy, would rap the table and tell the assembled company, 'Gentlemen, you can do all the sleeping you like two weeks from now!'

They would talk through the day's results and the rushes seen at the laboratories, and with a model of the sports field in front of them plan their coverage for the next day. They were continually harried by SS men, who appeared bent on making life as difficult as possible for them. Riefenstahl remembers this as highly personalised warfare between Goebbels and herself as she fought to keep her men and cameras in their prominent positions, and he shrieked at her that they spoilt his careful tableaux. Even the Olympic organisers, whom she had been assured would be most accommodating, baulked at some of her gadgetry and were horrified by the number of pits she wanted dug to allow low-angled camera shots of the athletes against the sky. Why, they despaired, did the woman want to turn their lovely sportsfields into marmot warrens? Weeks of preparatory wrangling with what seemed to her every single athletics official finally secured her sanction for two pits at the high jump, and one each for long jump, pole vault, hop skip and jump events – she could have one at start and finish of the 100-metre track. Two or three towers could be erected inside the stadium, but she would not be permitted to have more than six members of the team in there at any one time. The main consideration was to avoid distracting the athletes, and thus further restrictions were placed on what heats and finals could be photographed at all. And, when not up on scaffolding or buried in their pits, cameramen were supposed to operate only from sitting or prone positions.

Although the interpretation of these conditions gave rise to some very public and bitter exchanges in practice, keeping Leni and her immediate colleagues continually alert to ways the rules might be bent, she had won important concessions. Athletic officials still needed convincing that sporting activities had any place in the cinema. Leni herself believed passionately that such a liaison was valid, whether you were a sportsman or a moviegoer. Her spontaneous attraction to 'everything that is beautiful' and 'a concern for composition' were her driving impulses.

Certainly, she was excited by the idea of the domination of the body by individual will, but also by the camaraderie at the heart of contests like this. Accepting that her striving for 'form' could be seen as something very German, she has always strenuously rejected any suggestions that this is fascistic in origin. 'What does it mean, fascist aesthetics?' she has asked on many occasions. Hostile critics pounce at her claims that 'Whatever is purely realistic, slice-of-life, average, everyday does not interest me. Only the unusual, the special excites me. I am fascinated by what is beautiful, strong, healthy, by what is alive. I seek harmony. When that is produced, I am happy.' Such statements carry chilling resonances of superbeings, of a desire for supernatural order if you are looking for them. Yet if uttered by anyone not seen to be associated with the Third Reich would raise few eyebrows. What is a film but a stylised version of life?

'I don't know all these things myself, exactly. It comes from the unconscious and not from my knowledge,' she has said – not in retrospect, with the object of disassociating herself from unhealthy prejudices. She has always said it. At the 1928 Winter Olympics, before anyone knew the Nazis would come to power, she expressed herself in similar vein.

★

Her two Olympia films *Fest der Völker, Fest der Schönheit* (collectively known as *Olympiade* or *Olympia*) were well received in Germany and much of Europe, and quickly earned back the money expended on them. They were not seen in Britain, however, before the War; and when she took them on a publicity tour to the United States at the end of 1938 she was wrong-footed by the infamous *Kristallnacht*, the ruthless Nazi pogrom which destroyed Jewish businesses across Germany, rounding up or killing many of the country's remaining Jews. No German could find a welcome in America at that time, and a crestfallen Leni returned home with her films unsold.

Though exonerated after the War of any punishable offence by a succession of denazification trials, Leni Riefenstahl's detractors saw to it that she never worked freely again during her years of strength and was rarely if ever welcomed at cinematic functions. For half a century her films were scarcely seen publicly, or on television in their entirety, though clips were pillaged for innumerable documentaries by other people. Histories of cinema were written, particularly of the feminine contribution to film-making, in which Riefenstahl received either no mention at all or merely a token dismissive reference. She had been relegated to a footnote, by almost universal complicity. There seemed no way of separating art from propaganda, nor any willingness to attempt to do so. Was this fair?

II

Mountains of Destiny

Hollywood was the centre of the movie industry at the start of the 1920s. American films flooded the picture houses which were springing up in high streets all across Europe, as they were throughout the States. Germany, struggling to revive its film industry after the First World War, and to purge it of a new wave of pornographic productions that followed the abolition of censorship by its young Weimar Republic, introduced quotas for foreign films. The new Reich Film Act controlled what was shown, and tax inducements were given for the distribution and screening of home-produced art and educational films. The aim was to foster higher standards of production, and it was spectacularly successful: quality improved so much that the decade is now known as the Golden Age of German cinema.

In Berlin, in June 1924, Hitler was busy dictating *Mein Kampf* in the Landsberg Prison after his abortive Beer Cellar *Putsch* the previous November. Although Germany's unemployed still stood at 2.6 million, things were beginning to settle after a period of economic, political and artistic upheaval. Berlin, a rapidly growing city, was at this time the cultural capital of Europe, if not the world. Literature, art, architecture, acting, dance, music – all flourished. The impresario Max Reinhardt's vision of drama for the masses played out to packed houses in more than thirty theatres in Berlin. Particularly popular was astringent political cabaret. The film of the year was Fritz Lang's *Die Nibelungen*, and the book Thomas Mann's *The Magic Mountain*. Among painters, the Dadaists were in town; expressionists and cubists were still in their heyday. This was Picasso's abstract period, and the year of the launching of both the Red Group and the Blue Four. Klee and Kandinsky were among the reforming tutors of the Bauhaus,

15

which was on the brink of moving from Weimar to Dessau. In Italy, fascist militia marched into Rome. Lenin had died earlier that year. J. Ramsay MacDonald headed the first (and brief) Labour Government in Britain, and Coolidge was president of the United States. American Indians were granted full citizenship, vestigial television images were transmitted and the first major airline companies launched. Dinosaurs had been found in the Gobi Desert, in Egypt they were still excavating Tutankhamun's tomb. On the highest mountain in the world Mallory and Irvine disappeared into swirling mists.

Leni Riefenstahl was nearly twenty-two. She had been enjoying success as a solo dancer for six months, travelling around Germany and the capitals of Europe, performing recitals of her own choreographed works. Her expressive dance was a development of the style pioneered by Isadora Duncan, and her ambitious programme consisted of ten numbers – which, with encores, frequently swelled to fourteen. During the single short intermission, it was nothing for her to collapse on a couch, exhausted and unable to utter a word.

During her brief stardom she fulfilled more than sixty engagements, her mother and her pianist her most constant companions. She saw next to nothing of her boyfriend, the fading tennis ace Otto Froitzheim who, despite his reputation as a playboy, was pressing her to marry him. It is easy to see that with training, new dances to improvise and learn, and costumes to design, life had become little more than a treadmill of work and travel, with too many nights spent sleeping on trains. Yet her fitness and a natural tenacity combined with sheer youthful exuberance to keep her going and her spirits high. Until, that is, one triumphal performance to a full house in Prague, when Riefenstahl leapt awkwardly and tore a ligament in her knee. Somehow she finished her other engagements, but for most of the time she was in great pain. Then, all the effort and emotion caught up with her. Barely able to walk without a stick, and tired to the core, she was forced to face the possibility that she might never dance again. The specialists she consulted in Germany, Holland and in Switzerland all came up with the same advice: she needed rest, then more rest; and no one could make any promises. It was not what the ever-impatient young lady wanted to hear. She had schemed and plotted and defied her father for years to become a dancer, trained obsessively, overcome earlier illnesses, injuries and self-doubt to read those sweet words of acclaim: 'a marvellously gifted dancer; her artistry utterly authentic and original'; 'a revelation. An almost total realization of the heights of artistic expression which can be achieved in the realm of dance'; 'a dancer who will appear perhaps once in a thousand years, an artiste of consummate grace and unparalleled beauty'. It could not end now! Life without dance was inconceivable. Nothing else mattered. Even the prospect of marriage depressed her. Deeply subdued, Leni Riefenstahl returned to Berlin and with no great optimism made an appointment to see a physician friend of her father's.

Waiting for the *U-Bahn* at the Nollendorfplatz station on a June afternoon, and bracing herself from one spasm of stabbing pain to the next, her attention was caught by a poster advertising the latest of Dr Arnold Fank's mountain films. It showed a man straddling an abyss and there was something so striking and strong, so balletic about his pose that Leni, the dancer, was mesmerised. For a while she could do no more than stare as the trains came and went.[1] The film − *Berg des Schicksals* (*Mountain of Destiny*, or *Peak of Fate* as it was later released in the United States) − was showing just across the square. Impulsively she left the railway station and within minutes she was inside the cinema, her appointment forgotten.

From the very first montages of rock and haunting cloud, she was enthralled. Here was a world absolutely new to her. Mountains, which had belonged hitherto only on postcards, became on screen, as she was later to write in her memoirs, 'alive, mysterious, and more entrancingly beautiful than I had ever dreamed'.[2]

Her excitement soared with every minute she sat there − beauty and strength seemed to cascade towards her. When she left the theatre, it was with a new yearning which kept her awake for hours that night. Was it the wild nature of the mountains which stirred her so, or the artful juxtaposition of the images? She could not decide and when at last she slept it was to dream of ragged summits: 'I saw myself running across scree slopes, hanging from rock walls, but the star of all, the symbol of all the feelings unleashed in me, was that sharp rock needle in the film, the Guglia di Brenta.'[3]

★

Dr Arnold Fanck had been making Alpine films for around four years, films that were characterised by their glorious scenery. There had been amateur attempts to film skiing and other mountain sports from the turn of the century − Frank Ormiston Smith 'bioscoped' the high Alps in 1902 and, in 1913, F. Burlingham climbed the Matterhorn with a thirty pound camera and a twenty pound tripod − but the awkward terrain and bulky equipment were limiting. Most movie

17

action was studio-based until well into the 1920s, enabling professional tricks to be employed and lighting to be more easily controlled.
Fanck was obsessed with Nature in the raw. There could be leeway
for artifice in the way shots were spliced together, but for him the
individual images had to be true. Completely self-taught, Fanck
claimed never to have seen a professional movie until he came to edit
his own. His early films boasted no plots: he wanted simply to capture
the liberating joy of sport in the high Alps – and that was enough for
his audiences, too. It was all very innocent and escapist, even if later
pundits would come to see it as unhealthy fanaticism.

Mountain of Destiny was Fanck's fourth film. By now, though action
was still paramount, he had progressed to a rudimentary plot, and if its
'human interest' did not satisfy all the critics, even the jaundiced
Mordaunt Hall of the *New York Times* found the film 'unquestionably
stirring'. Riefenstahl returned to the theatre every night for a week,
and for her Dr Fanck's vivid images did not pall. It was clear to her that
she had to get into the mountains, and a few weeks later, with her
young brother Heinz, she embarked on a month-long sightseeing
tour through the Dolomites. The reality was all she had imagined:

> . . . red rock fortresses, soaring from green meadows into blue
> skies, dazzling little lakes, iridescent as butterfly wings, shining
> amid the dark and secretive firs, slender soft-green larches arching
> gently in the wind – the whole enchanted landscape brought back
> all those long-forgotten fairy tales of my childhood.[4]

Greeting the mountains as old friends, she sensed with what she
called mysterious certainty that from now on they would never again
be excluded from her life. To her delight, at the end of her holiday,
the hotel where she was staying on the Karersee, or Lake Caro,
advertised a private showing of *Mountain of Destiny*, at which the film's
star, Luis Trenker, would put in an appearance. Destiny indeed!

Ruggedly good looking, Luis Trenker was thirty-two when he
secured this, his first acting role. He came from the disputed territory
of South Tyrol, where his father was an artist and wood carver. As a
young lad he was sent out to look after thirty sheep and a few goats
among the Dolomite precipices and he had been climbing mountains
ever since. During the First World War he was conscripted into
the Austrian army and served in the trenches and cliffside redoubts
of the Alpine front, eventually becoming a mountain instructor
in winter warfare. In charge of a battalion of mountain guides, he
experienced the painful absurdity of having to shoot at young Italians

who had been his boyhood friends. It left him with little love for the narrow-mindedness of extreme nationalism, although accusations of a similar nature would come to haunt him after the next war.

When hostilities ceased in 1918, a much-changed Trenker returned to his native Grödnertal (nowadays the Val Gardena) where – with few alpine tourists – there was little to be earned from guiding. He tried his hand as a timber merchant and international salesman before resuming his interrupted architectural studies in Graz in 1920. At some time during that year he seems to have worked briefly for Dr Fanck as an anonymous skier in the director's first film,[5] when it might be imagined his athleticism and raffish presence would have caught Fanck's eye, to be borne in mind for other projects. Curiously, neither man afterwards acknowledged this early association. In later life, Trenker put down his start in mountain films to a foul day in Graz in 1923,[6] when he went to see Fanck's *Im Kampf mit dem Berge (Struggle with the Mountain)*, as much to get out of the rain as anything else. Though he entered the cinema with scepticism, 'what I saw was my own dream world,' he said. 'The silvery, snowy crowns of the Valais, sparkling crystals of ice, and a sun-drenched summit. My mood brightened and I was overwhelmed by a feeling of inexpressible joy and exhilaration, which grew with each image.'[7]

Trenker immediately contacted Fanck, suggesting the Dolomites of South Tyrol as an ideal setting for his next mountain film. The spectacular Guglia di Brenta would make an exciting backdrop, he told the producer, adding, 'You can count on any assistance you want from me.' Fanck was wary. Very much his own man, he was in no hurry to ally himself with anyone who might get too pushy, and he wrote back brusquely to say the Dolomites lacked sufficient snow or any glaciers. Later, however, after a chance meeting in Bolzano, he relented and invited Trenker to work as his assistant on his next project. Under Fanck, Trenker learned quickly, eventually taking over as leading man when the actor hired for the part found the life too strenuous. *Mountain of Destiny* launched the handsome South Tyrolean on a movie career which kept him a popular public figure until his death at the age of ninety-seven in 1990.

When Leni Riefenstahl introduced herself to Luis Trenker at the film presentation at the Karersee in that summer of 1924, her nervousness swiftly evaporated as she chattered away. She intended acting with Trenker in a mountain film, she told him: he was to put in a word for her with Dr Fanck. Trenker could only laugh: the egotism of this woman was preposterous. She was attractive, to be sure, but a city girl, and hobbling about on an injured leg! In as many words, he told her to run away and forget such things. The mountains were no place for a woman like her. Riled, she retorted that she was perfectly capable of doing anything to which she set her mind – and we can believe it! Maybe she didn't know how to climb; well she would learn. She would show him.

Interviewed in the 1993 television biography, *The Wonderful, Horrible Life of Leni Riefenstahl,* Trenker remembers this first encounter, claiming he told Fanck of this extraordinary aspirant actress who wanted to star in his next film. Leni herself recalls telephoning Dr Fanck after learning he was in Berlin for talks about a new movie, suggesting a meeting. Did he know the Rumpelmeyer Konditerei on the Kurfürstendamm? Fine. She'd see him there.

The café was full when she arrived, but she had no trouble picking out a rather shy-looking, stocky man with a receding hairline. In his mid-thirties, Fanck was only a couple of years older than Trenker, but to Leni he appeared middle-aged. She slid into the empty chair opposite him and introduced herself. With pounding heart, she wrote later, she began at once to talk in her inimitable breathless style – her one wish to convey to the Doctor how much beauty he had shown her with his film, how fresh she found it, how it was impossible to shake off its effect: 'I talk and talk, and Dr Fanck sits in silence, stirring his cup.'

It was impossible to tell what impression her bubbling enthusiasm was having on him. He barely uttered a word during the whole encounter beyond asking what she did for a living. It was clear he took little interest in the theatre and had never heard of her as a dancer. She promised to send him some pictures and her newspaper cuttings.

And then it was over. She was back on the Kurfürstendamm, nursing a sense of deflation. Nothing had been resolved. She had not even confided her burning desire to play in his next production. It was as if a giant hand had reached out and torn her back from the gates of paradise, back into a world that to her had become unreal and empty. Aimlessly, she wandered the streets. Had she got through to Dr Fanck at all? He had given no grain of encouragement – and yet, and yet . . .

Somehow she had the feeling of having taken a decisive step, given fate a chance. 'Then, suddenly,' she wrote, 'it is like a volcano inside me, I feel a glowing determination, like a belief in a certain future. The notion fills my heart.'[8]

One thing was sure: if something were about to happen, she had to be ready. Something must be done about the stabbing pain in the back of her knee. For a month she had hesitated over whether or not to have an operation. Now an idiotic impatience seized her, and walking into the first telephone box, she called the surgeon. Once more we see the measure of her formidable determination: with 'tears and entreaties', she tells us, she begged to be x-rayed that very evening, and when the pictures revealed a cartilage tumour the size of a walnut, with more 'implorings' she elicited the promise of an operation the following morning.

'Ten weeks in plaster, at least, and the result cannot be guaranteed,' the doctor warned her. To Leni it offered the only way forward to the new life she had so set her heart upon. Telling neither parents nor friends what she was up to, she dropped the desired package of cuttings into the mail for Dr Fanck before entering the clinic that same night. By eight o'clock in the morning she was under the anaesthetic. She liked to say afterwards that even as she slipped into unconsciousness the Guglia, the needle of fate, rose up before her to pierce the glowing clouds.

III

The Father of Mountain Films

Arnold Fanck should have been a poker player. If his expression gave nothing away to Leni Riefenstahl, it certainly did not mean he was unconscious of her charms. On the contrary, he was absolutely bowled over by this vibrant young creature who had emerged, as it seemed, out of the blue to seek him out. Shy and unworldly he may have been, but like Trenker and like Riefenstahl herself, Fanck was a man who lived through his passions; and his passions were those of a fanatic. A solitary, sickly childhood had driven him into books and daydreams and forced him to build his own ideas of what could be achieved from life. He knew no half-measures and no admission of defeat.

He was born in Frankenthal near Mannheim in the Rhine Valley, where he spent most of his years between the ages of two and nine confined to bed with chronic asthma, repeatedly having to learn to walk again whenever relapses allowed. In desperation, his parents eventually brought him to Davos, where the mountain air worked its magic. During the four years he spent in the Alpine resort, he was not ill for a single day, and from being a boy who had scarcely ever ventured out of doors, Fanck avidly embraced a world of nature. Mountains became everything to him. In school, the only subject to hold his attention was nature study; outside, he cultivated a passion for photography, which showed no sign of waning when he went on to read geology at university in Zurich as a contemporary of Lenin.

Every free hour was devoted to tramping the mountains with his camera. He was often racked with guilt at the amount of time lost to his studies, and would try to wean himself from his obsession, but to no avail. He kept buying and constructing new cameras. Skiing opened up the realm of higher mountains and became another

22

lifelong passion. In 1909 Alpine touring on skis was still in its infancy, and you seldom if ever crossed another set of tracks on the glaciers. With a Swiss friend, Fanck traversed first the Bernese Oberland and then the whole of Switzerland, east to west, from the Bernina to Arolla, crossing dozens of high passes and ticking off on the way all the peaks which rose above four thousand metres. The pair next set themselves to surmount every Swiss summit between three and a half and four thousand metres that could be reasonably attempted on skis, and were close to fruition in their ambitious programme when interrupted by the First World War. They had taken their skis up more major summits than perhaps any of their contemporaries, and Fanck always maintained that this year before the war was the most glorious of his life.

He had embraced summer climbing with the same zeal and, as a way of sharing his adventures with others, he used to give magic lantern shows of his photographs. Only when he and another of his friends, Hans Rhode, were hired in 1913 as high level consultants for a proposed ski ascent of Monte Rosa did cinematography strike him as a logical progression. For that project, the brainchild of a neighbour Dr Tauern, a professional cameraman had been engaged. Sepp Allgeier also happened to be an outstanding ski-runner and the resulting film, though short, was excellent for its period. It was also the first 'moving' picture the youthful Fanck had ever encountered, but at once he could see how the technique might be improved. As soon as his studies allowed, he determined to shoot a skiing film of his own, a major feature for the cinema – no less! – conveying all the poetry of ski movement against the majesty of the Alps. His long apprenticeship lent him confidence. He could not wait to get to grips with this diverting new medium which reproduced movement in so miraculous a way.

Several years and a world war had to be endured before that moment came. Even when, in the autumn of 1918, 'this storm', as he said, 'had blown over', with inflation soaring he was at a loss to raise the sort of money required for the project. Or indeed enough to purchase his own movie camera. It did not occur to him to look for a backer. Instead, for a year he became a dealer in fine antique Persian carpets, until he had accumulated 9,000 inflation-free Swiss francs.

By the end of 1919 Fanck had the little Ernemann camera he coveted and 3,000 metres of 'off-cut' film, residual lengths from other productions which he carefully spliced into 120-metre rolls in his darkroom. Thus equipped, he arrived at his parents' house in

Freiburg, and began engaging his team. First choice had to be Sepp Allgeier (by now the Black Forest Ski Champion); part of his job description would be to give Fanck a crash course in the technique of ciné-shooting. With his own inborn eye for a picture, Fanck felt sure he could teach Allgeier a thing or two. The film's stars were to be Dr Baader, far and away the best German skier of the time, and another champion, Dr Villinger. 'And so,' wrote Fanck, 'we four ski wizards began the realisation of my dream of many years.'[1]

For several weeks they worked on the Feldberg, Allgeier and Fanck taking it in turns to crank the camera or double as one of the skiers. First rushes showed they had captured the breathtaking scenery in an altogether fresh manner, but the ski action was disappointing. Disparate shots would not edit together well, and were in most cases intrinsically 'ugly'. With the exception of Dr Baader, none of them had passed muster under the inexorable eye of 'that sternest of judges, the slow-motion camera.' He alone had 'such harmonious movement and such control of his skis that it was a delight to watch.'

A string of other well-known skiers were auditioned, but none could be found to match Baader; and Baader alone was not enough for the film. Then Fanck noticed that everyone was talking of a young sportsman from the Arlberg, and he quickly sent him a telegram. Two days later Hannes Schneider joined the little band on the Kreuzeck mountain near Garmisch, and the shoot began all over again.

Though directing off the cuff, Fanck knew exactly what he wanted. Each scene was outlined to Schneider and Allgeier, and Schneider would run through the action time and again, always on unmarked snow, until Fanck was satisfied. And each scene *was* perfect: in his movie-making, Fanck relinquished nothing of the impeccable composition that so characterised his landscape photography. For the first time, film communicated what skiing was about, and showed what a master this Hannes Schneider was, a decade ahead of anyone else:

His every movement had such wonderful certainty that my ever-developing eye could not get enough of the controlled power and beauty of a bending, swinging body on its gliding boards. He placed each turn within a hair's breadth of where I needed it for editing into a sequence. Eleven years later, in my last big ski film *White Frenzy*, I included a wild downhill race with forty of the best cross-country ski-runners of the day. They were streets ahead of the by-then somewhat ageing Hannes Schneider, yet still he proved the undisputed master in front of the camera. Without a Hannes Schneider, all my know-how and all my fermenting aptitude for seeing and filming movement, and all our common enthusiasm for the project, would have been of no use in the end. That is to say, *The Wonder of Skiing* would never have been made and never exerted its magic on so many millions of people.[2]

There were still problems to overcome, not the least of which was the drain on Fanck's personal resources. His slow-motion camera had eaten an enormous hole in the carefully-garnered Swiss francs. In retrospect, he admitted that its purchase was more out of enthusiastic megalomania than necessity. Not even UFA (*Universum Film Ag*) owned such a luxury; they merely hired one from Ernemann when they needed it. But Fanck's heart was lost to the expensive trinket during the War when one of his tasks had been to measure the penetrating power of shells into armour plating. 'The vision of a shell flying slowly through the air and, as it were, leisurely boring its way through the plating made a fantastic impression on me,' he said. 'Something never before seen by human eyes: imagine being able to slow down the lightning-fast movements of skiing – and above all ski jumping – which were scarcely visible to normal vision.'[3]

The day was saved by Dr Tauern who, in return for a partnership, offered to match Fanck's investment. So, in the spring of 1920, the first Freiburg Mountain and Sport Film Corporation was born and filming could continue. In time, members of the little company sat once more up on the Kreuzeck, almost penniless, and were obliged to give ski lessons on bad-weather days to eke out their funds. Here they struck lucky. One of their clients, a Frankfurt food wholesaler, was so delighted to have been taught the double-Christie that he chipped in with two hundredweight of rice and an equal amount of tomato purée. Now decently provisioned, the crew settled into the Concordia Hut among the high glaciers of the Bernese Oberland until the rest of the mountain footage had been shot.

They had lived on skis for almost half a year, working with enthusiasm, during which time the word 'salary' was never once mentioned. If not cheerfully, they endured the monotonous diet, a spate of stomach upsets, and even an outbreak of measles. On the last day's shooting, when Hannes Schneider was required to make a spectacular run from the summit of the Jungfrau, he too awoke racked with fever. But he kept going, the bright sun agony to his weakened eyes. By the end of what had seemed an endless day, his temperature was back to normal, so that ever afterwards, convinced he had sweated the measles away, he would treat every malady with hot water bottles and blankets, a firm convert to the power of enforced perspiration.

Now, for the editing! Fanck bought the latest projection machine on credit and set himself up in his mother's kitchen, casting the image on to the whitewashed wall. (There were no editing tables in those days. Fanck himself would be instrumental in the development of the Steenbeck.) By trial and error he taught himself to cut and join shots, though at first he was at a loss how to shape the material, sitting rather folornly in front of about 2,000 little rolls of film, getting nowhere. 'On each there was a quite wonderful picture,' he said, ' but how oh how to compose them into a harmonious entity?'

Still, the only film he had seen in his life was Dr Tauern's little Monte Rosa epic. What did other directors do? It was time to take himself off to Berlin, which already boasted a number of large cinemas, and embark on some sustained viewing. Film historians have speculated how Fanck's career might have turned out had he then had the good fortune to see, for instance, D. W. Griffith's *Intolerance*. Instead, the first feature he saw was Ernst Lubitsch's expensive costume drama *Madame Dubarry*, starring Pola Negri, a monumental film in its way but quite a different kettle of fish to what Fanck had in mind:

> There was a real dramatic plot, as in the theatre, where in my film nothing happened but that four skiers (becoming sometimes suddenly five, but luckily no one ever noticed) climbed the Jungfrau and then went down again. Furthermore, it was played by real actors, while I had only interested myself in and enthused over the beautiful body movements of my performers, never getting them to mime with their faces.[4]

Looking back, more than thirty years later, Fanck believed his total naïvety had advantages. It led him earlier than most to the realisation that on film – as opposed to in the theatre – emotions could be expressed as much by body language as facial expression. And it struck him also that gestures and expressions need not be exaggerated, as was the theatrical custom, but simple and natural. Nor could he see why this everyday simplicity should not be achieved by inexperienced actors. He admitted that after his first cinema visit it would have been easy to lose his nerve, considering his own apparent lack of plot. Fortunately he did not. When he returned to his film he 'found it just as wonderful how our four skiers climbed through thick snowy woods, through savage icefalls to the summit, high above the cloud-sea, and then descended in playful powder schusses and turns, first through a maze of crevasses, then over long smooth slopes and finally, for good measure, again through the fairyland of the snowy forest down into the valley.' Would not others be equally delighted to see something like this at least once in their lives?

What Fanck learned from watching films that week was an appreciation of their essential rhythm, how shots could be cut together to build an exciting tempo until the high point is reached in the last act, when a short fade-out leads into a conclusion. Armed with this very simplified basic law, albeit for a different type of film, he went home and constructed the simple action in his own film. By late summer *The Wonder of Skiing* was ready.

Dr Fanck – film director now, rather than geologist – packed his six cans of film and returned confidently to Berlin to sell them. The all-powerful distributors – Deulig, Ufa, Decla – shook their heads, telling him that the public would never sit through an hour and a half of skiing. Why, they said, nothing happens beyond going up and down a mountain! But people *had* sat through his lantern slides, he remembered. Wasn't this more exciting? Why let his modern projector languish in his mother's kitchen? Undaunted, he borrowed yet more money and began booking his own cinemas.

The film was given its première in his home town of Freiburg, where the audience applauded at ever shorter intervals throughout the film. 'There was no end to the jubilation,' he declared, satisfied beyond his expectations. He had never once heard clapping during a film in the big Berlin cinemas. Nonetheless, it was clear even to him that this was a novice piece, so why had it been received so enthusiastically? Was it just that they were home town boys?

We got an even better response as we took it from city to city, culminating in Berlin, where no-one knew us and where the audience surely included only a handful of skiers. No – this success, which was to swell like an avalanche year upon year for my subsequent mountain and ski films, was . . . rooted in the longing of the city-dweller for light and sun and snow and mountains and, above all, Nature, which for the most part he has to do without almost continuously.[5]

Evidently Arnold Fanck was above all an idealist, a romantic in his outlook; but he was a realist in his vision. The dramatic effect of this

27

first experimental work, and of successive mountain films, lay in his commitment to landscape and superlative camerawork. When most other film-makers were using elaborately constructed studio sets, with cardboard scenery and painted backdrops, Fanck was sledging five hundredweight of camera equipment high up the glaciers so that his audiences should see the raw elements for themselves. At the same time, he was perhaps the first to employ slow and fast motion as cinematic devices. The respected historian and critic H. H. Wollenberg, analysing Fanck's creative contribution to German cinema, remarked how the German mountain film moved the camera right on top of nature and with the joy of artistic discovery brought the beauty and drama of the visible world to life on the screen. Even without a plot, he said, *The Wonder of Skiing* 'contained more dramatic force than any invented story ever could. It was a drama of nature and the courage of man . . . and it aroused the greatest possible excitement among its audiences.'[6]

In the following year, 1921, Fanck made a mountaineering, rather than a skiing, film. *Struggle with the Mountain* featured Hannes Schneider conducting a young woman on her first Alpine climb. This was followed by the exciting *Foxhunt in the Engadine* and *Mountain of Destiny*. He was improving year by year. At the same time, he was gathering around himself a team of the very best outdoor photographers – the Freiburg School as it came to be known. He firmly believed the loyalty shown by his grateful audiences was in response to genuine beauty and truthfulness: 'namely Nature. And Nature, moreover, as seen through an eye itself drunk with the beauty of it.'

Curiously perhaps, dedicated skiers and mountaineers were still witholding their appreciation for this new genre. In fact, it was from among existing mountain-lovers that the staunchest detractors came, from those who somehow believed that outsiders had penetrated their holy arena, and were desecrating it.

★

Leni Riefenstahl, recovering from surgery in her Berlin clinic, was surprised on the fourth day to be told by the nurse that she had a visitor.

'But nobody knows I am here,' she said.

In walked Arnold Fanck and tossed a wrapped bundle on to her bed. 'I have brought something for you,' he announced awkwardly.

It was a filmscript, and on the title-page were the words: *The Holy Mountain,* written for the dancer Leni Riefenstahl.

She could never put into words what she felt at that moment, Riefenstahl wrote in her first book, which she dedicated to Dr Fanck.[7] She laughed and cried at the same time, marvelling that her deepest wish could so quickly and so completely have been granted. The frustration of her bed-bound weakness was almost too much to bear.

For three nail-biting months she remained in hospital with her leg in plaster, not knowing whether the knee would ever bend again. Fanck, she says, visited nearly every day, going through all the scenes of his proposed film with her, in the supreme confidence that all would turn out well. Otto Froitzheim, her tennis-playing fiancé, bombarded her with loving letters and flowers, but word was abroad that he was having yet another affair, with a colleague on the tennis circuit, and Leni took advantage of the situation to break off their engagement.[8]

At last came the day for the plaster to be removed and she was allowed to stand upright. All was well, thank God. The knee bent without trouble, and it was not long before Leni was as active as before and able to resume her dance training. Just before Christmas she visited Dr Fanck for a screen test, one more hurdle that had to be overcome.

For a start, she would not need all that stage make-up, Fanck told her firmly when she walked into his Freiburg studio: this was not a dance performance. The natural look was what he was after, not glamour: the camera would give her that. Yet, the first rushes, when she saw them, horrified Leni. Who was this strange, plain creature on the screen? She could barely recognise herself, and felt sure this spelt the end of everything. The Doctor was not at all cast down. Different camera angles, different lighting would soon sort things out, he promised. And so it proved. Leni had been given her first lesson in film technique, and as always, she was an avid learner.

It was clear to her by this time that the Doctor's feelings for her were not as paternal as she could wish. She had grown fond of him, too, but not (she maintains) as a lover. She kept him at a friendly yet firm distance, as always perfectly able to compartmentalise the different aspects of her work and private life. Fanck was a cultivated man, a *savant,* and she was greatly impressed by his wide reading and knowledge of modern art, as well as his professional talent. There would be much she could and would learn from him, and it is no exaggeration to call him – as many have – her Svengali. Riefenstahl would have made a mark on her generation whatever she did, by sheer force of personality, whether or not she had met Fanck. As it was, he laid the foundation for her adult thinking, and it is safe to say that without him her career would have taken a quite different course.

By the end of 1924, the contract was safely signed. Leni was to receive 20,000 marks as the film's female lead, playing opposite Luis Trenker, who by then seemed reconciled to the idea. Shooting would begin in Switzerland early in the New Year and was expected to take three months. The generous salary was made possible through Fanck managing to convince UFA that a mountain film with a plot was viable commercially. The studio agreed to back him to the tune of 300,000 marks. Even so, nothing would induce him to work in UFA's huge studio complex near Berlin. All he wanted was to disappear into the mountains with his hand–picked little band. He was still the outsider at heart.

There was just time, before shooting, to learn to ski. Leni had no wish to make a fool of herself on set, even if she had been engaged primarily as a dancer. Without telling Fanck, who was proving very possessive over his new protégée, she took off for the Dolomites where Luis Trenker was collecting some preliminary ski scenes in Cortina with Hannes Schneeberger, another of Arnold Fanck's trusted cameramen. Schneeberger was known to everyone as 'the Snowflea' for his amusing and acrobatic ability to leap around on skis. Both men were more than happy to take time off from their camera work to give Leni tuition, and they trooped off together to the Falzarego Pass.

Telling herself how amazed Dr Fanck was going to be by her dramatic turns, Leni launched herself downhill with gusto. No matter that she landed flat on her face in the snow, it only served to make her more high spirited than ever. Who would have thought speed could be so thrilling? Oblivious to any danger, she took on every slope, however steep, and though her tutors did their utmost to curb her fervour, there was no holding her:

> Skiing downhill was one great jubilation . . . Then, at the height of my delight, misfortune struck. The tip of my left ski caught in the snow, twisted sideways and brought me down. A ragged pain shot through my ankle. Trenker and Schneeberger were on the spot almost at once, helping me, but I could not bear any weight at all on that leg. There was no doubt about it: the ankle was broken.[9]

All three gaped at each other in dismay, their first thought for the film. What on earth was Fanck going to say?

Trenker headed back to Cortina in fading light to fetch a sledge, and as darkness seeped across the mountainside, the Snowflea hoisted Leni on to his back and started the long trudge down to the valley to meet him. A cutting wind had blown up, which whistled across the slopes, whipping whirls of spindrift before it. The overladen Snowflea kept stumbling through the frosty crust, pitching them both headlong into the snow. In the end they could go no further and squatted shivering on their skis to await Trenker's return. Freezing as it was, the cold did nothing to numb Leni's pain.

Next day, with her leg back in plaster, the three drove to catch the train to join Fanck in Switzerland. None of them had found the courage to telephone the director and tell him what had happened.

★

Arnold Fanck was asked later how he came to write a filmscript almost overnight for a dancer, of whom he knew nothing, and with a storyline that had never occurred to him before. 'In the first place,' he replied, 'I was intrigued by the superlative reviews this dancer had been getting':

> . . . and the question I couldn't help asking myself was: what would happen if such a creature of the dance was brought together with a man of the mountains? They may well find themselves strongly attracted, but where would it end? In catastrophe, more likely than not, their two worlds being such poles apart. It prompted me to write *The Holy Mountain*, specifically with the vivacious Leni Riefenstahl in mind, and a typical mountain man like Luis Trenker.[10]

Fanck remarked that when he invited them both to Freiburg, the tragedy was set in motion almost at once: 'After we had finished dinner at my home, I disappeared into the library to fetch a book. When I returned, there was Leni in the corner of my red baroque sofa, and on his knees in front of her, Luis Trenker.'

Act One, he thought to himself, and withdrew discreetly.

It is not quite how Riefenstahl tells the story. She has Fanck, 'his face ashen', discovering Trenker and herself in a joyful embrace, whereupon the Doctor collapses 'sobbing and burying his face in his hands' before running from the house to toss himself into a small river. Once rescued from the water he is taken, 'feverish and delirious', to Freiburg Hospital, where they keep him until morning. Next day, to avert a 'brutal fistfight', it is Leni who threatens suicide. She clambers out on to the windowsill, making as if to jump, and the two men spring apart. Trenker helps her back into the room and all three part in a baleful atmosphere. Back home in Berlin, Riefenstahl needs no crystal ball to tell her that there are going to be tensions when the shooting starts.

Fanck went ahead to Lenzerheide to supervise the construction of a fantastic ice city on a frozen lake, with palaces fifty feet high. This was for a dream sequence in which the two lovers wander in a vast cavern of gleaming icicles. The image is fanciful enough to have been Fanck's own, although its lavish execution demonstrates a certain submission to cinema artifice. Perhaps he was leaned upon by UFA to introduce more visual glamour into his work, as he clearly was to add love interest. For even had he not met Riefenstahl so fortuitously, he surely was going to have to admit a female presence into his previously male-dominated empire if he were to go on making mountain films. Riefenstahl showed up at the right moment, so Riefenstahl it was – and tempestuous as her presence was already turning out to be, things had gone too far into this expensive production to turn back. In any case, the diffident Doctor had little appetite for seeking out, interviewing and testing more young women. Riefenstahl it would have to stay. It wasn't as if he had not foreseen her likely attraction to Trenker. He would just have to live with it. Perhaps in time the little witch would come to regard him as he did her. He nursed the hope.

When the shamefaced trio turned up at the station, the sight of Leni limping in plaster once more may well have tempted Fanck to replace her even yet, had it not turned out to be just the start of an avalanche of disasters descending upon him. *The Holy Mountain* appeared cursed from the start. Hannes Schneider, who would again be playing a skiing role, hit some black ice while touring in the first week of the New Year, sustaining a quadruple fracture to his hip and femur. He was on the danger list for a week and then in traction for six months. Another of the male stars, Ernst Peterson (a nephew of Fanck's), struck a rock while executing a 'wild downhill run' for the camera and, according to Riefenstahl, was tossed fifty feet in the air before he came crashing with a torn tendon in his foot. Snowflea, too, cracked a rib – whether from falling in a ski race or in a quarry is not clear; accounts vary. To cap it all, the weather changed and the expensive ice city melted away.

IV

Climbing the Heights

'So our film camp gradually turns into a field hospital,' Leni Riefenstahl recorded, 'with the despairing Dr Fanck as its principal.' UFA was having serious misgivings as well, threatening to withdraw backing from the project, but none of the team wanted to believe the film was doomed. Riefenstahl did her utmost to keep up everyone's spirits, but in six miserable weeks all they were able to shoot was a few feet of film as the warm *Föhn* wind cleared ever more snow. It was a wretched winter.

Then at last the weather changed. Things froze over once more, the ice sets were rebuilt, Leni was freed from her plaster, and filming resumed. For the important night scene on the Lenzerheide, giant searchlights illuminated the frozen snow and lit up the snow-burdened fir trees:

> It is shockingly cold up there. Then the electric cable gives out – the ice must have fractured the sockets – all the lights are extinguished and the cameras freeze solid. Despite everything, I find the whole business fascinating. Filming is a whole new world to me, a new possibility, which I struggle to fathom. I want to understand everything about it.[1]

Fanck was always ready to explain everything about his method, which borrowed nothing from established theories, any more than it was a fossilised collection of notions. He was forever discovering new effects, new angles, new ways to portray people, animals, clouds, water, ice. From the basis that every single shot had to be a good one, he wanted to show his audiences the natural world through ever-fresh eyes. To this end, every cameraman he employed was a master: Allgeier was experienced before he came to Fanck; the Snowflea

(Hans Schneeberger), Richard Angst, Kurt Neubert and Albert Benitz were all products of Fanck's 'Freiburg school'. The American film historian, David B. Hinton, once remarked that if Fanck had been as good a film theoretician as he was an intuitive film-maker, and committed his thoughts to paper in the manner of Sergei Eisenstein, then his anti-Expressionistic beliefs would have made a far greater impact on German film history. He might have escaped the oblivion to which he is now more or less consigned.[2] All the same, since Fanck was always generous in passing on his knowledge to those with whom he worked, his influence carried widely, if anonymously. It is ironic that most of his protégés – Riefenstahl, Trenker, Angst, Hans Ertl, Sepp Rist – are better known and remembered than their patient mentor.

The troubled shoot of *The Holy Mountain* dragged on throughout 1925 and into the following year. The little crew leap-frogged around the Alps to find the best snow conditions, taking over pensions out of season, and effectively barricading themselves off from the rest of the world in their dedication to the film. Leni found she enjoyed this seclusion, welcomed the 'peace' it gave to 'follow the theme like hunters':

> Often we have to wait a day, or even a week, but ultimately we reap some beautiful scenes. Sometimes after many hours of strenuous climbing, we just get the equipment set up ready when the sun, which has been shining clear in a blue sky, disappears behind the clouds. Then we wait and freeze, feet stuck deep in the snow and with no hut or habitation for miles around in which to warm ourselves. We hold out as long as we can, the sun often playing games with us, coming out for a few moments, then vanishing again. So it goes on for hours until we give in, pack up all the gear, and frozen stiff, with blue noses and ears, descend the crusted snow to the valley.[3]

Fanck was delighted with the way Riefenstahl adapted to the hardships of altitude without complaint. She relished hard work, encouraged the others and was always ready for adventure. True, she was also a distracting influence: her affair with Trenker flared, then faded, with inevitable tensions all round. So much could have been expected, given two such obsessively egocentric and competitive individuals, vying with each other both before and behind the camera. Fanck remained devoted and hopeful, though even he by now ought to have recognised that winning Riefenstahl was a lost cause. Hannes Schneider found her profoundly disturbing, and was convinced she was making a play for him. Years later, when her name carried the taint of Nazi sympathiser, he bitterly regretted having been inveigled into this film at all.[4]

Schneeberger became the friend she turned to increasingly for consolation, and the one who finally undertook the task of teaching her to ski. After the Cortina episode she was a nervous student, 'strutting around stiff as a stick', her heart pounding with anxiety even on gentle slopes. But the Snowflea was patient and understanding, and very good company. He was a great storyteller, and no stranger to narrow squeaks. During the evenings spent in isolated huts or Alpine *Stuben* he could be relied upon to entertain his fellows with adventurous tales.

Into this already volatile mix was introduced a further dynamic with the abrupt and rather curious appearance of one of Leni's old flames. Harry Sokal, a dark-haired young banker from Innsbruck with what she describes as a narrow aristocratic face, became a frequent visitor at Lenzerheide during the early part of the shoot, where he was soon on good old-boy terms with Fanck and Trenker. The story is that he first lost his heart to Leni Riefenstahl in the summer of 1923 when he found her practising dance routines on a Baltic beach. He offered to secure professional engagements for her in Austria and, when that gambit brought little response, followed it up a few days later with a proposal of marriage. Sokal was nothing if not persistent. Taking matters into his own hands, he arranged for her first public dance performance in Munich, launching her on her road to success.[5] In her memoirs, she claims (a little implausibly) not to have known of his involvement in securing further venues, and to have been surprised to meet him again in Zurich some months later, when he showered her with expensive gifts.

'Armfuls' of fur coats began arriving in her hotel room – later she remembered wistfully two minks, an ermine and a sporty little leopard number trimmed with black leather – as he wanted her to look the star, he said, on her forthcoming dance tour. But the realisation that the offers from Paris and London, which had so delighted her, were secured by Sokal, Riefenstahl says, came 'like a slap in the face'. The cost was too great. Returning the pelts with a polite note, she fled back to Berlin.

'Whatever happened to the banking?' Leni asked when Sokal showed up on set.

'Movie-making turns out to be infinitely more interesting,' he told her. It appeared he had a financial stake in *The Holy Mountain*, although he claimed later to have pulled out on learning of the tangled rivalries behind the scenes. They were bound to affect the finished film. He started his own production company, which one day would go into partnership with Leni Riefenstahl's own. With part-Jewish ancestry, Sokal was one of the many to leave Germany when the Nazis took control of the film industry in 1933. By that time, he was not only a rejected suitor, but ideologically polarised from Riefenstahl who, by staying and working for the Third Reich, was seen to be at one with the despised Nazi regime. Unresolved legal and financial affairs between the two soured the relationship further – so that it is now hard to tell how much this colours their remembrances of one another. Certainly, Sokal and his wife, Charlotte Seer-Sokal, have been among the most vociferous Riefenstahl detractors of postwar years.[6]

The storyline of *The Holy Mountain*, as those of all Arnold Fanck's movies, was somewhat fanciful and overblown, not unusual for the mid-1920s. Yet to pronounce its starcrossed love-triangle as melodramatic carries a certain irony, given the tempestuous love-polygon being enacted behind the scenes. The film's mountaineer-hero, 'Carl' (Trenker), while climbing with his friend 'Vigo' (Ernst Peterson), is made jealous on learning that Vigo covets 'Diotima', the love of his own life. This young woman is a dancer – and a flirt (Riefenstahl, of course) – but her heart truly belongs to Carl. High on the mountainside, the honest alpinist, in his torment, challenges his companion. Caught off guard, Vigo steps backwards off the ledge. The sight of his friend dangling helplessly at the end of the rope immediately restores our hero to his senses. He hangs on grimly; all night he clutches the rope, his face turning dark with cold, in the end sacrificing his own life to save the other.

The opening sequence of the film has Diotima performing a lone 'Dance of the Sea' on a rocky ledge in Heligoland, with the wild surf crashing. Fanck's intention was to have the dancer symbolise the ocean, and her lover the mountains, the two as opposite forces of nature ultimately irreconcilable.

Though this was a silent film, Riefenstahl had choreographed the dance to Beethoven's Fifth Symphony and a hapless violinist was lowered on a rope down the slippery rocks to play on her Dancing Ledge, even though she could pick up only the occasional note above the pounding waves. She was, she says, washed several times into the ocean. Being a film star was proving a chancy business. Another time she had her face badly scorched by a magnesium flare. She spent days storm-bound without food or fuel in a high Alpine shelter, and one scene called for her to be buried in an avalanche. Dr Fanck did not believe in doubles or stuntmen.

On top of everything, they seemed never to finish. The studio had all but given up hope. Even during their first spring, Fanck had been summoned to Berlin to be warned the film was proving too expensive and would have to be cancelled. It was saved, in his absence, when Riefenstahl dragged the camera crew up into the flower meadows above Les Avants to shoot some of the missing scenes on the last remaining filmstock. This was her first venture into direction, and the rushes were sent off to Berlin with trepidation. Instead of the reprimand she and the others were half-expecting, back came a telegram from Fanck: CONGRATULATIONS! UFA WILD ABOUT THE MATERIAL. WE'LL GET OUR MONEY!

There were more delays even after that. The film ended up costing in the region of 500,000 marks, a princely sum, even if only half of what Fritz Lang was spending at the time on his *Metropolis* with the same studio.

The Holy Mountain received its Berlin première at the UFA Palast am Zoo in the middle of December 1926, where it ran for several weeks, with three or four showings a day. Riefenstahl performed her 'Dance of the Sea' live at the opening and an improvisation to Schubert's Unfinished Symphony before each evening performance. Audiences were enthusiastic, as were most of the reviews. *Paris Midi* and London's *Westminster Gazette* both declared the film the most beautiful ever made. In Vienna, the *Wiener Neueste Nachrichten* felt that Fanck had clambered into the ranks of the master-directors; Antwerp's *Le Metropole* praised it as a work of great art and humanity, while *La Tribune* of Lausanne saw it as a divine and grandiloquent mountain poem. Dr Günther Dyhrenfurth (later to become a famous expedition leader and mountaineering chronicler), in the newsletter of the German and Austrian Alpine Clubs welcomed it as the best work to date by 'an acknowledged master'. Leni Riefenstahl, he said, was 'a truly enchanting newcomer, moreover a great artiste with the richest and finest expressiveness, completely at one with her role.'[7] The *New York Times* found the plot 'forced' with too much 'shrieking and shouting', and not going anywhere, but Fanck was to be congratulated on his photographic feats. The performances of Trenker and Peterson were described as 'intelligent' and Riefenstahl was 'an actress with no little charm.'

There were more strident critics, of course. The *Weltbühne* swam against the tide, presaging the proto-Nazi allegations that would one day be levelled retrospectively by Siegfried Kracauer and his followers. *The Holy Mountain* it described as 'a highly unholy hill, a quite profane heap of banality and virulent misconceptions.' How much money had UFA squandered on this insistent propaganda for a super race and noble blondness, it wondered.

Fanck took the slur hard, but the bitterest blow of all came when Luis Trenker, fed up to the back teeth with the protracted claustrophobia of the shoot and its attendant histrionics, spilled his grievances to the press. Left with little patience for either Fanck or Riefenstahl, Trenker contested the director's immutable conviction that Nature had to be the central character to the detriment of the human players, whose interplay was invariably neglected. Neither could he stomach the way the action in Fanck's films always had to be accompanied by cataclysmic storms, or avalanches, or plummets into crevasses. In his opinion, Fanck's judgement was suffering under the influence of Leni Riefenstahl. Trenker dubbed his erstwhile lover an 'oily goat' for her nimble-footedness on mountain terrain, a phrase gleefully seized upon by the newsmen, most notably the critic Roland Schacht.

The film certainly represented a considerable departure in style for Fanck, the dyed-in-the-wool realist, with its expressionistic prologue, and the mystical sequence in which Diotima wanders the icy caverns with her lover, a sequence which struck David Gunston, writing some three decades later, as confused and doom-laden and 'worthy of any of the early German pictures of Fritz Lang'. All right for Lang, was the implication, but showing signs of dangerous overreaching in a Fanck opus. Yet these do not appear to be the episodes against which Trenker was railing: like the *New York Times*, he would prefer the story was not always subordinated to the camera studies, and there seems no doubt that his opinion carried some weight with UFA. Little is known of the project Fanck hoped to do next beyond its working title – *A Winter's Tale* – and that it was even more ambitious, and potentially more expensive. Alarmed, UFA – already financially stretched with Lang's *Metropolis*, the biggest budget film it had ever underwritten – quickly pulled the plug on the idea.

Once more Fanck showed his ability to turn out a new screenplay almost overnight when stung to action. *Der Grosse Sprung* (*The Great Leap* – known also as *Gita, the Goat Girl*), was a short slapstick farce, poking fun at the efforts of inexperienced tourists in the mountains, at the same time cocking a snook at Fanck's critics with some artful self-parody. In effect, it was sending up the whole mountain myth business, mountain films included, and casting Leni Riefenstahl as a goat girl could be seen as a direct retort to Schacht. Remarkably Fanck and Trenker were able to patch up their differences long enough for Trenker to play one of his handsome, clenched-teeth heroes in the film, though it was the last production on which he, Fanck, and Riefenstahl would work together.

Fanck had plans for Snowflea, too. As the company's best skier, he was to relinquish his cameraman role for the main comedy lead, something that took a lot of persuasion, since it involved being enveloped in a grotesque inflatable suit. As a supposed ski novice, much flying and crashing was called for, including landing on top of a cow from a great height. We are told that required several takes to get in the can, and we can only hope the Michelin suit cushioned the cow. Snowflea complained he was black and blue by the end of it, and a stone lighter in weight from sweating away inside his hermetically sealed rubber. But he did get the girl for a happy-ever-after ending..

By now Schneeberger is quite definitely the leading man in Riefenstahl's life, and she has no complaints when Fanck disappears back to the editing suite to cut the winter sports footage, telling her and the Flea to take off for the Dolomites and get in some rock climbing practice.

'Oh, and you might rehearse your love scene with him, too,' Fanck adds sarcastically. 'He is going to have to get over his terrible shyness before we start shooting. Just as you must learn to toughen up the soles of your feet!' It appears he wanted her barefoot in all her climbing scenes, but first things first. She needed to get some serious routes behind her before she could contemplate taking off her boots.

After scrambling around the Langköfel Hut, Schneeberger selected a line on the Vajolet Towers for Leni's debut, not what one would generally consider a beginner's route. Like rockets of stone, shooting skywards, these towers had been described only a decade before by the renowned alpinist Guido Rey as 'skeletons of mountains, fantastic, grotesque, yea terrible; but mean and evil.' He went on to ask, 'Who, in cold blood, could imagine a man clinging to the sharp edge of that knife-like ridge and crawling up it to its pointed summit, or, once there, daring to descend?' Riefenstahl says she stood under the high vertical walls, which seemed to sway with the moving clouds, and would have sworn they were quite impossible were it not for two figures up there, as small as ants, climbing the brown Delago

Arête with hundreds of feet of empty space beneath their bootsoles. Schneeberger promptly tied a rope round her waist and set off up the wall, giving her no time to change her mind. Soon he was bringing her, pitch by pitch, up the steep rock, and Leni found it wasn't as hard as she had imagined. The holds were firm, and seemed perfectly secure. As her confidence grew a feeling of tremendous pleasure infused her and she told herself, 'This! – this! is the right sport for me!'[8]

They climbed slowly and steadily, stopping for a short rest when at last they came to a narrow ledge. For the first time, Leni allowed her gaze to sweep down the steep wall, and was surprised not to feel at all dizzy, though her heart was beating faster than normal. A few more short chimneys and traverses and they were halfway already. She cast another glance to where her heels were overhanging their little hold and could not resist joyfully spitting into the void. 'For a split second my head span as I watched it drop over a thousand feet, but the sensation soon passed and I swarmed smoothly up the last few feet of the summit wall. Immensely proud and happy, I stood on "my" first mountain summit. I can scarcely describe how beautiful it was – so free, so far, so near to the clouds and stars.'

The pair next climbed the south face of the first Sella Tower (presumably by the Trenker-Pescosta route of 1913), a much harder proposition. One pitch, in particular, in the middle of the face, was a long chimney. The Flea led off up it and was some sixty feet above Leni's head, straddling the two walls of the chimney, when he called down to say there was nowhere there to belay while he brought her up. She could hardly bring herself to watch as he left the relative security of the chimney and delicately picked his way across one of the side walls to disappear from view. She felt very alone suddenly on this alien wall, and was relieved to hear him call a few minutes later, 'Okay, come on up! But be careful! I'm on a rotten belay. Don't dare come off, whatever you do!'

This was harder than anything Leni had attempted before, and she had half a mind to yell up for Snowflea to come back down but, ashamed at her weakness, she began levering herself cautiously upwards.

As the groove grew wider, she was forced to start bridging. Legs on opposing walls, she straddled up another thirty feet before the chimney became too wide even for that. Now, like the Snowflea, she had to pull herself slowly across on to one wall and creep round the airy edge, to where he waited on his tiny perch. Now she could see

40

just how perilous their position had been. He was taking in the rope through his hands: one fumbled move, a second out of balance and, with no firm belay, they would both have been off. With great delicacy, he moved on so that she could take over the spot while he struggled with an overhang above. Leni could not stop herself shaking, worried that his strength might fail, but she had underestimated the Flea. Finally he scrambled over the top and called for her to follow.

Above the overhang, they caught their breath, but still they had put only half the face behind them, albeit the most difficult half. If there were harder climbs than this, Leni thought, they were out of the question for her. In fact, she coped well and the next day, revived and with all terrors forgotten, she was already looking forward to more peaks and faces.

The barefoot training was painful from start to finish. The sharp Dolomite rock cut her feet to ribbons and she never grew accustomed to it. Even after weeks of running over scree and clambering about without shoes or stockings, Fanck would have to keep interrupting the shooting to allow her feet to stop bleeding.

In the film she was required to clamber about on the Fensterle towers, not high, but very brittle and loose, and as a goat-girl, of course she could have no safety ropes. Other scenes required splashing around in mountain streams all day, when she would swear Fanck had gone out of his way to find the coldest water possible. She felt sure he would have preferred solid ice if he could have had it, and more than once in her writings Riefenstahl (and others) remarked upon the sadistic streak Fanck exposed towards those trapped in his power.

Ignoring her protestations, he would make her swim in the Karersee for what seemed hours, wearing nothing more than a flimsy shift, promising her, 'You'll be delighted with the effect when you see it.' And she had to admit the waters were beautifully clear right down to the bottom. It did make for a highly erotic scene.

Floating there in the icy green water, Leni couldn't help but remember that this same Karersee was where her new life had begun two years before, where she had first come face to face with Luis Trenker. His sarcastic laughter, when she told him of her ambitions, still echoed in her mind. Well, she had shown him. She played opposite him in his next movie, just as she said she would. And she was upstaging him in this one. But had she really achieved her heart's desire? Was film work what she wanted to do from now on?

Giving up dancing had been a terrible wrench, and not something she ever intended. That first film was supposed to have taken no more than three months, after which she always meant to resume her dance career. She had brought her pianist on set whenever it could be arranged, to put in hours of practice when not before the cameras, and even before *The Holy Mountain* was finished she had taken on a number of outside engagements. She had danced at the film's Berlin run, but she did not feel that her dancing was progressing and, at twenty-four, she might never make up for those two years lost through her accident and the filming. When she signed the contract for *The Great Leap*, it was the symbolic ending of her dance career. She accepted that.

She loved the film life, enjoyed this close-knit company, adored the mountains . . . If only the process could be less lengthy. With dancing, she had always felt she lived every moment God sent. Could one say the same of filming? As an actress – not really. She was ready for another great leap of her own, but was unsure yet in which direction.

The Great Leap, released towards the end of 1927, was unlike anything else Fanck produced, and in the age of Chaplin and Keaton was clearly his attempt at slapstick comedy. It proved a modest success, though is seldom seen now. David Gunston – writing in *Film Quarterly* (Autumn 1960) – clearly saw Riefenstahl and Schneeberger as the film's great strengths, considering the stolid, pipe-smoking Trenker rather out of place among the comedy capers. Riefenstahl, as Gita, was 'jaunty, provocative, and self assured'. She had visibly developed as an actress as, 'clad in an extraordinary costume of the combined peasant styles of half a dozen lands, . . . she romped through this little farce with her flock of goats, partnering Schneeberger quite delightfully.'

He praises, too, the surreal humour and the 'Kafkaesque' climax in which the inflated hero, twice the size of life, defies gravity and soars on skis to win the race and carry off the voluptuous goat girl:

> The epilogue is worthy of Sennett, whose influence has never been felt in a stranger context. After an appropriate interval in the mountain cabin (portrayed by stop-motion photography) as the seasons give place one to another, the considerably deflated Schneeberger and the glowing Leni emerge once again into the light of day accompanied by a sparkling brood of miniature Michelin men about two feet tall. Fanck was never to achieve anything like this again.[9]

★

With two successful films behind her, Leni Riefenstahl could consider herself established as an actress. She was comfortably off and happy in her relationship with Schneeberger, which we are told lasted for two years. But artistically she remained unsettled. Fanck's next commission was a documentary of the 1928 Winter Olympics, for which he had no need of actors. Leni was anxious to widen her experience and, with German cinema at its apogee, there were acting jobs around at all grades, despite the fierce competition. Even though she now had contacts within UFA, and Schneeberger was getting outside camera work, nothing much turned up for her. She had become typecast, seen only as a dancer or a mountaineer.

Brief references are picked up of her playing the lead in an obscure Austrian film about the Mayerling tragedy, *Die Vetsera* (*Fate of the House of Hapsburg*, 1928), but this is omitted from both her memoirs, *The Sieve of Time* and her earlier *Kampf in Schnee und Eis* (*Struggle in Snow and Ice*, 1933). The film gets so few mentions in books on the history of cinema that one is forced to conclude it was a production she and others preferred to forget.

No one knew better than Leni Riefenstahl the value of getting one's face known, and she kept up a manic social life, attending parties and premières, making it her business to be on good terms with producers, directors and others of influence in the industry. G. W. Pabst, Abel Gance, Walter Ruttman, Harry Sokal of course, and Alexander Tairov all feature in her reminiscences of this time. It must have been particularly galling, in such a climate, not to find the right outlet for her aspirations. The biggest prize to slip through her fingers was the coveted role of the cabaret singer Lola-Lola in Josef von Sternberg's *The Blue Angel*. She had not auditioned for the part, but appears to have gained the impression that it was hers for the asking.

Sternberg was one of those she had made it her business to know. Impressed by his Paramount silent *The Docks of New York* (1928), and on learning that he was in Berlin for his next project, she dressed up to the nines and gatecrashed a planning meeting for the new film at UFA headquarters. Sternberg's curiosity was sufficiently aroused to invite her to dine and from such improbable beginnings a real friendship appears to have developed – 'a deep but unsexual friendship', as Riefenstahl has always maintained. Marlene Dietrich clearly felt there was sufficient in it to be jealous, yet Sternberg himself makes no mention of Riefenstahl in his memoirs.

Dietrich's biographer Steven Bach has told how almost every German actress remotely suitable was rumoured to be in the running for this plum Lola-role. He said names flew like confetti at a parade. After Marlene's transfiguration with this film, all sorts of people were claiming credit for having 'discovered' her – Riefenstahl among them. However, by the time Sternberg and Dietrich forged their fruitful union, Marlene had already played bit-parts in some seventeen pictures, opportunity enough for plenty to 'spot' her latent talent. Surprisingly, she was still promoting herself as the 'ingénue type'. Riefenstahl claims to have pointed Sternberg in her direction over dinner one evening, but Bach interprets their conversation differently. He believes Leni misread the character of the part Sternberg was trying to fill, and has her saying:

> Marlene Dietrich? I've seen her only once, but I was struck by her. She was in a small artists' café on Rankestrasse with some young actresses, and my attention was drawn by her deep, throaty voice . . . very sexy, but a bit *common*. Maybe she was a little tipsy. I heard her say quite loudly, 'Why must we always have beautiful bosoms? Why can't they droop a little?' upon which she lifted up her left breast and amused herself with it, startling the young girls sitting around her. Yes, she might be a good type for you.[10]

Bach is sure Riefenstahl was trying to put Sternberg off, and supports this assertion by an interview conducted in 1990 with a former editor of *Film-Kurier*, Hans Feld, who claimed to have been in Riefenstahl's apartment for a supper engagement on the evening the telephone rang with news that Marlene had landed the part. Leni's jaw 'dropped to the floor' when she heard the news, Feld had claimed. She was so upset she 'cancelled' him and the goulash she had been preparing.

Schneeberger had more luck with Sternberg's venture. He was hired as one of two cameramen on the film, and his work was highly praised. Leni remembers visiting the *Blue Angel* set, and makes a point again of mentioning Marlene's 'vulgarity'. Sternberg rebuked her for it, she said, whereupon Marlene threw a tantrum and threatened to walk out if Leni ever showed her face in the studio again. Arnold Fanck's memoirs recall this incident, too, and Marlene's daughter remembers her mother always referring to Leni Riefenstahl as 'that well-poisoner'.

In Ray Müller's filmed biography of her, Riefenstahl as an old lady still exhibits the flare of rivalry when mentioning Marlene Dietrich.

They were almost exact contemporaries, both coming into show business through Max Reinhardt and both trying to impress the same people. At one time, both lived in the same apartment block. The observation has often been made that Riefenstahl envied Dietrich for getting out of Germany while there was still time.

In her search for work, Riefenstahl visited film company after film company to no avail and smarted under the rejection:

> Above all things there burns in me an artistic creativity which must be expressed, or else I cannot exist. I will fight this prejudice with all my strength, but as the weeks and months pass, I seem to be battling in vain – rejection everywhere. Nobody will believe in me. I am in despair – it seems so hopeless.[11]

She needed a distraction, but above all she was missing the intimacy and companionship of the film crew who had been like a family to her for so long. She enjoyed teamwork and the sharing of problems. With everyone away, filming without her, she felt bitterly excluded. When she could bear it no longer, she took herself off for a couple of weeks to see what was happening with Fanck and his team at the Winter Olympics in St Moritz.

Even before the opening ceremony, Leni was captivated by the pageant of colours against the snow and the excitement of 'so many beautiful people together. Men with bronzed faces, girls sweet as film starlets. Everybody meeting up at Sunny-Corner, at Bo's or Hanselmann's for cocktails. Everything so cheerful, merry, competitive, with the famous Engadine sun shining out of a blue winter sky.' With no film duties, she could soak up the atmosphere, ski a little, flirt a little, dance a lot.

It is interesting, in the short account of this interlude written for her 1933 book (and for some reason not carried into the later memoirs), how so much of Riefenstahl's character is revealed: her impetuosity and ability to be completely taken over by mood and events of the moment, the eye for spectacle, athleticism and the human form, as well as for drama and competitiveness, the embracing of talent and the inspiration all these give her to carry on afterwards.

The most powerful moment of all, for her, was the opening parade when teams from the twenty-five participating nations entered the stadium in a dramatic snowstorm. Fanck could not have planned it better. 'What is it all about?' she asks herself rhetorically, to respond:

This is the moment which gives the Olympiad its meaning.

Twenty-five nations united in brotherhood. It is electrifying. Take a good look at them, the crowd, they sense the sparks, are warm and glowing despite the snowstorm and cold, they are jubilant, they shout with joy and stride out. Among the competitors the sports heroes – how proudly they carry their flags, proud to be their country's chosen.[12]

Leni's spirits were quite restored, though when she left the blinding whiteness of the upper Engadine behind, Berlin seemed drearier and more pointless than ever. Even the faces of her friends appeared distorted to her. She found herself beginning to loathe the city, her city, and, inspired by the Olympics, she channelled her energy into track and field athletics, at the same time making serious efforts to improve her mind. 'While I can jump and run, throw javelin and enjoy discussions, I feel free and strong enough to banish my low spirits,' she wrote, and picking up the ethos of the moment, added, 'The joy of a healthy body gives me back the strength to hang on, and to hope.' She read voraciously and haunted the cinemas, analysing what she saw. Soon, she began writing her own film scripts.

V

White Hell and Black Despair

Leni's lover, Hannes 'Snowflea' Schneeberger, came originally from the Zillertal in the Austrian Tyrol. He was seven years her senior, slight, agile, with dark hair and a mountain tan. He had that Latin look and dash of many from the Eastern Alps. Leni describes theirs as an idyllic, even cosy partnership, insisting that they were at their happiest when at home alone together. Over the long months on location, she had come slowly to appreciate his dependability. Whatever the crisis, there was the Flea with his good humour and good sense. 'He liked being led,' she would often recall – and playing the leader was something she was always more than willing to do. With her ready ideas and his unruffled competence, it made for an extraordinarily creative and harmonious relationship. At the end of 1928 there were no visible signs that the idyll was about to end.

Like Luis Trenker, Schneeberger had studied architecture before making the move into films through his love of mountains. Like Trenker, too, he had served on the Dolomite front in the First World War; and although in different regiments, the two were at times colleagues in arms, once sharing a narrow escape while making a rock climbing raid on an Italian stronghold. The Snowflea's most dramatic wartime experience – as a lieutenant with sixty men in his charge – he found himself having to defend Castaletto. Despite the heaviest odds, his detachment held its ground, only for the position to be blown up by the enemy. In the massive explosion all but Schneeberger and eight of his men were buried alive and, with these pathetic few, Schneeberger held out gallantly until help arrived. He was decorated for the achievement.

Naturally, the Flea's war experiences were common knowledge among the film crew and, sensing the potential this Castaletto story had as a plot for a movie, Fanck had Schneeberger write down everything he could remember about his time at the front. Then, marrying this with another dramatic tale of wartime heroism, the director produced what Riefenstahl believes was his best film script ever, *The Black Cat*. It included a meaty part for her as the Black Cat of the title, the heroine Fraulein Innerkofler, a climber working as a spy who perishes in the explosion.

By this time the great flowering of the German film industry was fading. In a worsening economic climate, cinematic exploration – with the exception of a few great names – was increasingly curtailed in favour of populist films that would appeal to the American market. Moreover, American cinema interests were gaining financial stakes in German studios. There was little appetite for war films, and certainly no belief in the export potential of any in which the heroes were fighting on the German side, however valiantly.[1] *The Black Cat* was dismissed out of hand by UFA. Of the several other producers Fanck approached, only Harry Sokal exhibited any interest. Sokal was now well established; his studio's ambitious remake of *The Student of Prague* in 1926, with Conrad Veidt, had been a great success. He was living at this time in the same apartment block as Riefenstahl. Fanck, too, Riefenstahl tells us, had moved in the wake of his UFA successes from Freiburg to Berlin, where he now owned a beautiful villa on Kaiserdamm with a garden and a tailor-made editing suite, not far from where she lived.

Although Sokal could see the potential of *The Black Cat*, he was not prepared to put up all the money himself. Since finding a co-investor could take time, Fanck, pragmatic as ever, reluctantly pushed the project to one side, burnt the midnight oil once more and produced a script more in line with his earlier offerings. This he outlined to Sokal a few days later over a glass of wine in a Berlin café. With the much safer box office bet, Fanck was given the green light. 'We roughed out a contract on a paper napkin which we signed the same afternoon,' Sokal recalled in a 1974 interview. The film, *The White Hell of Piz Palü*, was to become a classic, in no small part due to the intervention of the great German director G. W. Pabst.

Riefenstahl had been following Pabst's career with interest. She was particularly taken in 1925 by his second film, *Die Freudlose Gasse* (*The Joyless Street*), greatest of the so-called German 'Street Movies', to which she had dragged along Fanck and Sokal to see its new female star, Greta Garbo, whom Riefenstahl insisted Sokal should sign up. *The Joyless Street* has since become a cult film, but at the time it was not a box office success. Pabst's sixth film, however, *Die Liebe der Jeanne Ney* (*The Love of Jeanne Ney*), released in 1927, was altogether more subtle, better paced and dynamic, and easily seen as a masterpiece. A year later he began shooting the notorious *Die Büchse der Pandora* (*Pandora's Box*) with Louise Brooks. By this time Leni Riefenstahl had made a point of making his acquaintance, hoping against hope to be invited to star in one of his films, for he was known to draw a sensuous quality from his actresses that other directors failed to reveal. Then she had the sudden brainwave to give fate a hand.

Although she was to play the female lead in Fanck's *Piz Palü*, Sokal struck a very hard bargain: she would receive only a fifth of what she had been paid for earlier films. There were a number of changes Sokal wanted to impose to make this production more 'professional'. In particular, he was aware – as indeed was Riefenstahl – of the essential truth of Trenker's accusations that Fanck was inept in his handling of the human element in his productions, and it was Leni who came up with the brilliant solution to the problem. Why not buy in help for the direction of the emotional scenes? Why not invite Pabst to do them, leaving Fanck free to concentrate on the mountain filming he was so good at?

Pabst greatly respected Fanck's earlier work, recognising his commitment to realism long before the *Neue Sachlichkeit* ('New Objectivity') made it fashionable; and the prospect of working with such an individual master appealed to him. Sokal needed no persuasion either. But what of Fanck? He had always shied away from collaborations. Interpreting events from a personal viewpoint, as she always did, Leni declared that, because of his fondness for her, Fanck would be more than willing to fall in with her ideas. Perhaps Fanck's co-operation did owe something to a sense that rifts were developing between Riefenstahl and Schneeberger, but it is hard to escape the conclusion that, in the event, he was leaned upon heavily by Sokal. Pabst, besides supervising the scenes of human drama, secured overall control of the picture by bringing in his own scriptwriter, Ladislaus Vajada, to assist with the final screenplay, as well as his set designer, Erno Metzner.

In *Pandora's Box*, which had yet to be released, Pabst had cast the Viennese actor Gustav Diessl as Jack the Ripper. Now he wanted him to play the mysterious, brooding Doctor Krafft in *Piz Palü* – a prospect that certainly did not appeal to Leni Riefenstahl. She came into the room while he was being interviewed and slipped Sokal a note predicting the direst consequences were he to be taken on. The whole picture would be ruined. The others were willing to take Pabst's word that Diessl would be fine in the part, as indeed he proved. Leni got her way in another matter, however. Coming out of the studio one day to find it raining heavily, and trying in vain to hail a taxi, she was both flattered and delighted when a chivalrous gentleman leapt forward with an umbrella. Asking if she were the celebrated Fraulein Riefenstahl, he introduced himself as Ernst Udet and offered to drive her home, an invitation she quickly accepted.

Now there was a name to conjure with! Ernst Udet had been an outstanding fighter pilot in the War, one of Baron Richthofen's elite *Jagdgeschwader*. With sixty-two victories in the air, he was the highest scoring air ace to survive through to the armistice. Afterwards – like his colleague Hermann Goering, who ended the war in command of the Flying Circus – he capitalised on his folk hero status by becoming a touring stunt pilot. Everybody had heard of Udet's bravery and panache. Leni was captivated and, while later sharing a cognac with him, suddenly had another of her wild flashes of inspiration. 'How would you like to star in a film?' she asked.

'Sounds fine to me,' he replied. Fanck's scenario was adjusted to accommodate some swashbuckling flying scenes, and Udet joined the team.

To fit in with Pabst's busy schedule, it was decided to shoot his scenes first, as quickly as possible, and so the cast and crew took up quarters near to the Mörteratsch Glacier in the Engadine at the end of January 1928. The valley was in the iron grip of an unprecedented Siberian winter. Some years later, Pabst's assistant director, Mark Sorkin, recalled this frigid assignment:

> Most of the cast and the help came down with pneumonia. But Pabst and Fanck, they must have had a secret sadistic drive: and you can see that in the picture . . . We really froze. All night long we were drinking hot wine and punch, just to keep on breathing. That is why the film is so good: you can see all the harshness of the weather on the faces of the people. And I must say that Riefenstahl was wonderful; never mind what she did later in the Third Reich, but in this picture she was driving herself as hard as anybody, and more. She worked day and night. Schneeberger was in love with her – and she with him, by the way – and they were a good team. She worked harder than anybody. Even Pabst had to admire her. 'It's terrible,' he said. 'What a woman!'[2]

For four weeks Pabst had them in the open, sitting about on the icy 'ledge' they had constructed or lying half-buried in snow, the savage wind whipping sharp ice crystals into their faces. Clothes would freeze as stiff as boards. At the end of each session they would need to thaw themselves out over little cooking stoves. Riefenstahl suffered severe frost damage to her upper thighs, which required several weeks of radiotherapy, besides contracting a bladder disorder which would dog her for the rest of her life. Despite the rigours, she was thrilled with the performance Pabst was able to coax from her. 'I felt for the first time that I, too, was an actress,' she said afterwards, an opinion shared by film journalists and historians. Under Pabst's 'directorial hands of iron, compared with Fanck's arty clay', Riefenstahl was here a 'real actress' wrote David Gunston later, adding how fervently one wishes she could have been a Pabst actress many more times than just this once.[3]

Udet proved charming and punctual, and with almost reckless enthusiasm performed the required aerobatics, skimming past mountain walls with the merest breadth of clearance. Straight away he took to Schneeberger, who had been designated as his special cameraman to shoot from the plane. The Flea had always been interested in flying. In fact, one of Trenker's books mentions how he and Schneeberger had gone off to Vienna together in 1916 to become airmen. 'We had both had enough of snow, ice and gales,' Trenker recalled, but once in the Austrian capital, 'the old longing came over me and I had to go back to the mountains . . . to the Sella group, to my native valley, which lay just behind the front. Schneeberger was shot down and badly wounded on the Isonzo. We met again in hospital at Innsbruck . . .' Udet and Schneeberger would spend all day in the little biplane, and at sundown abandon their film colleagues for the high nightlife of St Moritz, flying back to the location next morning. Once Udet's scenes were safely in the can, not only did he disappear from the set for good, but Schneeberger, too, was recalled to Berlin by UFA. It was, says Riefenstahl wistfully, the end of the happy days.

The remainder moved up first to the Boval, so that Fanck could film the mountain scenes, and then to the old Diavolezza climbing huts, which gave access to Piz Palü. To make the most of the short days, the regime was: up before sunrise, a sip of hot coffee, then out into the cold morning. Leni never learned to feel easy on the glacier. To her, it was always a malicious, voracious beast. You were ever at its mercy, she said. One slight movement and it would open its gullet and swallow you whole. No matter how seductive the smooth white surface, tempting you to ski and cavort upon it, there was always the fear you were skating over chasms concealed by only centimentres of snow. It was sheer chance that this thin skin did not break beneath them, she was sure. On one day, as ten of the team crossed the snow in a sort of caravan at midday, they heard a deep booming from inside the ground. The snow slumped beneath their feet. Leni thought then she was doomed, especially as they had dispensed with ropes to be able to work more quickly. Rooted to the spot, she was too terrified to take another step for fear of disappearing forever. One of their Swiss guides had to speak to her quite roughly to get her to move on. Later, she may have managed to get used to the uncanny voices of the glacier, but she never trusted them.

Fanck wanted to do another of his amazing torchlight scenes – this time from right inside the belly of the glacier. Cameraman Angst was suspended in an abyss 'between heaven and earth', the camera strapped to his body, while David Zogg and Beni Führer, two of the ablest and bravest guides, scrambled down 150 feet into the maze of crevasses, peering into fissures, rope in one hand, blazing magnesium flares in the other. It was galling afterwards when some otherwise well-informed critics thought these dramatic scenes must have been faked in the studio.

One vital shot called for Leni to be hauled by rope up a steep ice wall while an avalanche poured down upon her. A suitable cliff some seventy feet high was selected on the upper glacier, and quantities of loose snow and ice piled on top to be pushed down when the moment came. There were no stand-ins on any of Fanck's films and his actors would frequently complain of his cavalier attitude to their safety once his heart was set on a particular shot. Leni had been caught like that before and she grew increasingly edgy as the preparations were made. Her fears were groundless, Fanck soothed: she would only be pulled a little way up and then let down again. The rope was tied around her waist and on the signal 'Action!' up she went like a sack of cement. Almost immediately, the man-made cornice above crumbled away and a massive cloud of icy debris fell upon her, blotting out the light. Her eyes, ears and mouth filled with powder snow.

Far from being lowered gently down again, her screams were ignored as she was hoisted the full height of the cliff, to be landed like a fish over its sharp rim. Through angry tears she vowed never, never to forgive that man. More than satisfied with the result, Fanck could only laugh at her frustration. That was it, she would never again believe a word he said. But inevitably she would find herself once more falling backwards into crevasses, swinging wildly at the end of a rope, cracking her head against the icy sides of some chasm or other.

For a week they were imprisoned in the cabin by blizzards, the wind so strong that it seemed as if the roof would be carried away. Heavy, avalanche-pregnant slopes separated them from the green of the valley, which beckoned between squalls like some lost paradise. It became almost unbearable, knowing that spring was going on down there without them. Unable to stand it a minute longer, Leni and a disconsolate young guide at length made a break for freedom, slipping soundlessly out of the hut into a snowstorm. Before long they had lost their way and become very frightened. Only chance led them to be discovered and rescued from their personal 'white hell' by an experienced Engadine guide. Against such experiences, were the rest days in the hut, when someone would play an accordian or a guitar and they would all sing songs and tell stories. These were when strong bonds of friendship were forged, bonds which could be expected to withstand years of separation.

Piz Palü was the most famous and successful of Fanck's mountain films, widely acclaimed as the best German film of its year. Again, it had an uncomplicated plot, although as the *New York Times* pointed out perceptively, such surface simplicity concealed 'a swift undercurrent of tenseness and anticipation that carries one along.' A young engaged couple (Leni Riefenstahl and Ernst Peterson), off to climb Piz Palü, meet up with a half-crazed lone alpinist, Dr Krafft (Gustav Diessl), whose young wife was lost in a crevasse here on their honeymoon years before. Ever since, he has searched for her obsessively. They join forces for an attempt on the North Wall, where they are struck by an avalanche. All three mountaineers are stranded on an icy precipice, the younger man badly injured. In echoes of *The Holy Mountain*, Krafft nobly sacrifices his life to save the young lovers, whose rescue is effected by the timely arrival of the renowned pilot, Ernst Udet (playing himself).

Popular reviews at home and abroad were generally good and even the serious critics were impressed. The specialist magazine *Close Up* reported:

> . . . here, as never before, is the living spirit of the mountains, vivid, rarified, terrifying and lovely. Other mountain films we have had, but we have never had mountains – almost personifiable, things of wild and free moods, forever changing. The glorious rush of

avalanches punctuating silence, warnings of greater, more terrible torrents. Snow blown up in a bright fringe on the ridges. Sun, cloud, the never ending revelations of light. Nobody who loves the hills could fail to be held by this tribute to their splendour.

For the hero Diessl, the 'Alleingänger' – with a commanding sullen beauty, and heroic attributes. For the heroine, Leni Riefenstahl, renewed and unexpectedly fresh, unexpectedly charming. A flowing rhythm, breath-catching beauty, genuine alarm. Not blatant or manufactured, but sensed with authenticity. The star remains the mountains. No greater success has been accorded to a German film.[4]

'Trask', one of the regular correspondents for *Variety*, applauded the first class performances 'from the sporting angle', and considered Diessl 'undoubtedly a leading man who would appeal in Hollywood'. He was more grudging when it came to Leni Riefenstahl, telling his readers the former dancer was 'a typical German sporting type but too buxom for the average American taste.'

Curiously, once again, the biggest resistance came from mountaineers themselves, who resented the popularising – and as many saw it, de-sanctifying – of their mountain environment. Nowhere was this antagonism more trenchantly expressed than through the pages of the British *Alpine Journal* and the pen of its editor, Colonel E. L. Strutt. This formidable old warhorse, who saw himself as a lone crusader against 'the monkey-tricks of the young' and an unhealthy death-or-glory cult which was perverting traditional mountaineering standards, laid the blame squarely at the door of the 'Munich School' of climbers. He saw it as no coincidence that disturbing political stirrings were emanating from the same quarter. The *Bergfilme*, once he became aware of them, were deemed to carry all the taint of their geography along with a suspicion of fakery and a threat to the old order.[5] They were (as he repeatedly warned readers) a revolting epidemic. He had identified Arnold Fanck early on as the perpetrator of the 'malignant' genre, and mistakenly held him responsible for a controversial retelling of a mountain classic, *Struggle for the Matterhorn*, which had preceded *Piz Palü* to British cinemas.

According to Strutt, the story of this was 'absurd' and the acting 'grotesque'. But he did have fun – with his exhaustive knowledge of the Alps – in identifying for his readers the different mountain locations employed in the film. With triumphal flourish he declared that 'for the final and ridiculous tragedy, no better setting could be found than the frozen water conduit leading to the Silvaplana electric-light turbine!'

Fanck had based his script for *The Struggle for the Matterhorn* on a novel by Carl Haensel. The directors were the Italians Mario Bonnard and Nuntio Malasomma, and the film was produced by Homfilm of Berlin, with Luis Trenker as the star and chief advisor. Riefenstahl was not involved, although many other of Fanck's regulars were, including his nephew Ernst Peterson, Hannes Schneider and Fanck's trusted first cameraman Sepp Allgeier. The story was a controversial retelling of the events leading up to Edward Whymper's dramatic ascent of the Matterhorn, taking as its hero not Whymper but Anton Carrel, the Italian guide who was his rival through the years of vain attempts running up to the 1865 tragedy. Flagrant liberties were taken with facts, including cooking up a romance between Whymper and Carrel's wife. After the fateful first ascent (from the Swiss side of the mountain), Whymper is accused of having cut the rope in order to save himself – thus causing the deaths of his four friends – and it is Carrel, by repeating the climb, who manages to prove that the rope broke because it was too light for the job, and that Whymper is innocent.

Meddling with revered events like this was naturally offensive to Swiss and British mountaineers, who sought to have the film outlawed in their own countries. Even if the long-dead protagonists were not libelled technically, the Alpine Club had been quick to draw the attention of the British Board of Film Censors to its objectionable nature. A tart note in the *Alpine Journal* subsequently drew satisfaction from having the 'revolting travesty' banned throughout the United Kingdom.[6] By the time *Piz Palü* came to be released in Britain in 1930, Strutt's pen was ready charged with sarcasm:

The inevitable accident, or accidents, take place: a party of Swiss Academicals – the one kind of guideless caravan likely to be immune – is overwhelmed by an avalanche of sugar or flour. The first party then falls off and a member breaks his leg. Having accomplished this feat, he performs a more difficult one: he snaps an ice axe across his shin and secures the shaft to his leg for a crutch. His movements, hitherto a cause of anxiety to us, now become far safer – in fact he climbs well, although hampered by affectionate motions of the lady. The other member meanwhile has gone mad. The Swiss are found, mutilated in the depths of a bergschrund, by a rescue party provided with inexhaustible Roman candles. The bodies are brought down on tea-trays by skiers, coupled two and two, moving at magical speed down the icy slopes of the N. arêtes . . . An aeroplane starts to rescue the man with the crutch, together with his affectionate and insane companions . . .[7]

'The story, lasting some hours,' Strutt concluded, was, 'of course, slush', and none of the purported mountaineers looked as if they had any business on a mountain except possibly the 'lightly clad lady' with 'a true sex-appeal squint'. The one small mercy, he said, was that the 'talkie' had not invaded the Alps, and the audience was spared the sorrow of hearing Swiss guides speaking American. Though not for long, as it turned out.[8]

★

The prompt commercial success of *Piz Palü*, and in particular the praise for its acting performances, made Harry Sokal more sanguine about tackling Arnold Fanck's *Black Cat* project, especially when Homfilm agreed to making it a co-production. Leni was overjoyed: the *Black Cat* role was still hers and it could not have come at a more opportune moment. With or without Pabst, she needed a substantial follow-up part to reinforce her reputation as an actress if she was ever to break free from the niche of mountain films and be taken seriously by the rest of the industry. Never mind the terms, she was happy to sign her contract.

Preparations progressed smoothly until Fanck picked up alarming news on the grapevine that Luis Trenker had embarked on a similar venture. His *Berge in Flammen* (*Mountains in Flames*) centred around the same Castaletto tragedy but without the Black Cat element. What was worse, he appeared to be farther advanced, if the announcement of his plans in *Film-Kurier* was anything to go by.

Fanck telephoned Riefenstahl in great consternation. He was certain that Trenker had stolen the film script, certain too that one of his own cameramen must have passed it to him. Albert Benitz, who for years had been his Second Assistant was the chief suspect. He had not been required on *Piz Palü* and was known to have done some camerawork with Trenker during 1929 and 1930, when Trenker was said to have first begun developing his script. Trenker himself always maintained the idea had come to him much earlier, back in 1923 when he revisited the old trenches and emplacements of his Dolomite war-days.

Harry Sokal was furious. He sued Trenker for plagiarism, and won. But Trenker appealed against the verdict, and his appeal was ultimately upheld. Within two weeks, early in 1931, Trenker had begun shooting his ski shots in the Arlberg. *The Black Cat*, as Leni would graphically remark, had to be put to sleep. With bitterness, she declared, 'Here was another excellent screenplay by Fanck, which could not be filmed; and in both cases it was Trenker's fault.'[9]

Had Trenker stolen Fanck's script? He had known Schneeberger far longer than Fanck had done and would have been well aware of the Castaletto story. In any case, this was South Tyrolean folk history: it was not necessary to have been involved for it to be a potent source of national pride. It is hard to believe that the idea of turning it into a film had not occurred to Trenker – nor indeed that it was not discussed at some time on the set of one of Fanck's movies. Ideas passed around, and were gleaned from multiple sources: *Piz Palü* had been inspired by a newspaper cutting. You could say ideas hang from the sky and drop like fruit when they are ripe. Benitz would have no need to hand over a script – as he testified he did not. Word would easily get to Trenker, one way or another, that Fanck was writing such a screenplay, and so provoke him to action.

Once they were in contention, Trenker boxed more cleverly than Fanck. The magazine *Die Filmwoche* gave them each space to put their cases prior to the final judgement. Honest Fanck felt obliged to admit that, as Trenker now told it, his manuscript was not a 'direct' plagiarism of his own. Trenker used his right of reply to emphasise his own war experiences, subtly indicating how well qualified he was to make such a film. The part played by Schneeberger in all this, whose story it was after all, is not clear. Nor indeed, is that of Homfilm who, though in partnership with Sokal during the dispute, had shot two films with Trenker in the same period.

What it did represent was an irrevocable change in the dynamics between those in the *Bergfilme* world. Trenker had learned all he could from Fanck and gone it alone; his star was in the ascendant. Benitz left the fold. All the experienced cameramen would now be courted and used by both factions. Leni Riefenstahl had lost what she long believed to be her greatest acting opportunity. Even worse, she had lost Schneeberger. He never returned to her after the *Piz Palü* shoot, and wrote to say he loved someone else.

It took her months to believe it, bleak, bleak months when the pain, as she said, crept into every cell of her body. 'I wanted to jump out of every window, throw myself in front of every train. Why didn't I do it? I suppose I hoped Snowflea would come back, but I was deluding myself . . .'[10]

Looking back over a long and ultimately tragic life, Leni Riefenstahl still sees this as the worst betrayal of all. She would never let herself feel as much for anyone again.

VI

The Blue Light

As a child Leni Riefenstahl's favourite reading had always been fairy stories. Though boisterous and strong-willed, and the undisputed ringleader for all sorts of neighbourhood mischief, she yet had a dreamy side, and throughout her teenage years would frequently float off into worlds of her own fancy. She enjoyed dressing up and acting, and steam-rollered her little brother Heinz into playing out her games of make-believe: he was a gentle, sensitive child, easily moulded to her will. Her love of theatre and music she shared with her mother. Life was comfortable. The family lived in Berlin, where her father ran his own heating and plumbing business, and they had a weekend cottage in the lake country south-east of the city, where the young Leni could indulge her love of the outdoors, and her over-active imagination.

Political affairs barely touched her consciousness. She remained remarkably naive throughout her adolescence, so that the war came and went with little effect upon her cocooned and largely internal existence. In the year of the armistice, her sixteenth summer, she was still spending her pocket money on the weekly magazine, *Fairy Tale World*, and weaving her romantic fantasies of love and magic. Perhaps to modern eyes, this obsession with whimsy seems odd, if not perverse, but it is easy to forget the strong hold folk tales and magic have always exerted over the Teutonic soul, and in the early days of cinema what a rich source these provided for artistic reinterpretation. The works of Fritz Lang and Wendhausen's *Stone Rider* come particularly to mind. Leni's fondness for such stories provided the inspiration for her dance routines. After her diversion into mountain films they would come to preoccupy her again.

Following *Piz Palü*, she worked on a couple more mountain films

59

for Arnold Fanck, but with little heart. She had survived the rift with Schneeberger well enough to face him every day on set, but the acting itself no longer satisfied her. Not only did she regret losing her role as the *Black Cat* but, while still living in hope of winning back the Flea's affection, she turned down what was perhaps her greatest opportunity – of going to Hollywood to be groomed for stardom by her friend Joseph von Sternberg. Instead, the young Marlene Dietrich, who had secured the star role over her in *The Blue Angel*, followed Sternberg to America – and immortality.

Riefenstahl's part in *Stürme über dem Mont Blanc* (*Storms over Mont Blanc*)[1] – another high action melodrama, centred this time on the lonely weather observatory on top of the highest Alpine peak – carried the usual brushes with danger of all Fanck's enterprises. But it did not stretch her dramatically, even with the added challenge of dialogue. Talkies, by now, had begun their inexorable takeover, although the early sound cameras were too heavy for vigourous mountain work. *Mont Blanc,* conceived as a talking picture, had to be dubbed in the studio afterwards. Leni employed an elocution coach, but in fact her pleasant, well-modulated speaking voice needed little work upon it. She survived the transition into talking pictures with no problems.

Mont Blanc was another box office success – or another 'faked atrocity' if you listen to Strutt. The film historian Siegfried Kracauer, chief proponent of the proto-Nazi allegations which would be levelled at all the mountain films after the Second World War, felt compelled to allow that this latest was:

> . . . one of those half-monumental, half sentimental concoctions of which he was master. The film again pictures the horrors and beauties of the high mountains, this time with particular emphasis on majestic cloud displays . . . Impressive sound effects supplement the magnificent photography: fragments of Bach and Beethoven from an abandoned radio on Mont Blanc intermittently penetrate the roaring storm, making the dark altitudes seem more aloof and inhuman.[2]

After this, however, he once more adopted his characteristic stance of censure, drawing attention to re-hashed themes like Udet's stunt flights and what he called 'diverse elemental catastrophes', as well as the inevitable rescue party. Picking up with some glee an American criticism that the plot was 'woefully inadequate', he added, 'it follows a typically German pattern, its main character being the perpetual adolescent well-known from many previous films. The psychological consquences of such retrogressive behaviour need no further elaboration.'

Riefenstahl was dismissed as 'mountain-possessed as ever' – which indeed she was, even if somewhat jaundiced with the characters she was required to portray. In compensation, she had developed an interest in every aspect of film making. *Mont Blanc*, more than any other, had brought home to her the power of the camera. She became fascinated by lenses and filters, and above all in editing possibilities. Fanck was grateful for her help in the cutting room; and for her part she could not stay away, hungry to see the effects a master could achieve with intelligent montage. It became a 'magic workshop' to her, and before long she caught herself looking at everything around her with a filmmaker's eye, just as long ago she had experienced the world through the senses of a dancer.

She could absorb technicalities like a sponge, but she could not be relied upon to keep her mouth shut. Never one to accept anyone else's views or directions on trust, and with an unswerving conviction in her own intuitive sense, she always tried to influence events. Before *Mont Blanc* went into production, there had been the usual dilemma over who should play her leading man. In many ways, Luis Trenker was still sorely missed. A story told in her early volume of film reminiscence, but which does not make it through to her later memoirs, well illustrates her developing cinematographic awareness – and her tenacity.

For weeks, she says, director Fanck has been looking for an actor-alpinist to fit the image in his mind and is at his wit's end. Despite an almost pathological aversion to 'professionals', there seems no option this time but to hire a 'real' actor through a Berlin agency. Riefenstahl suddenly remembers a chance remark of Sepp Allgeier's a year or so earlier about a magnificent skier he had met in Obergurgl. The man was a police radio operator from Nuremberg. She remembers a photograph being flashed around. Such a striking face . . . whatever *was* the man's name. And then it comes flooding back – Rist, that was it! Sepp Rist. Immediately, she knows he is the one they're after, and tells Fanck excitedly, 'Your troubles are over!'

'Leni, what can a photograph prove?' The director smiles indulgently but he is not taking her seriously. 'It's a big part we're talking about here. The man's a public official, a functionary. What makes you imagine he'll be able to act?'

Employing what she calls 'all her old tactics', she seeks to change his mind by persuasion, but Fanck remains unmoved. He has already started negotiations for a big stage name. In a way, she can understand his attitude, but it rankles not to be taken seriously. Sepp Rist is becoming something of an obsession with her. Without any authority to do so, she sends a telegram to the Nuremberg Police Department, asking for Rist's address. When it arrives a few hours later, there is no holding her:

> I telegraph him, invititing him to come at once to Arosa for filming. And I sign Fanck's name! Next morning I lie in wait and intercept the answering cable: 'AS LUCK HAS IT HAVE TEN DAYS LEAVE (stop) WIRE IF TIME ENOUGH (stop)' Without turning a hair, I wire back: 'COME AT ONCE FANCK'. A load falls from my heart. Let Fanck just see, I think, he will sign him up.[3]

Needless to say, the director is dumbfounded at her impudence. But that is all. Rist arrives, and Leni greets him in the hall. Fanck merely walks around the young man, staring, unable for the life of him to see what all the fuss is about. The rest of the film team eye the newcomer with unconcealed hostility. Leni alone, and now more than ever, believes they have found the right man.

Fanck's only concession is to give him a screen test. Out of politeness, nothing more. But, it slightly changes the complexion of matters. The director is struck by the police radio operator's fluid movements. Leni herself takes still photographs, snapping him from every angle, and putting the prints beside Fanck's supper plate that evening. He is warming to the idea, but has yet to work on the opposition of the production manager. Unsure the Doctor's conviction is that strong, Riefenstahl is on hot bricks, despairing of Fanck's stiff-necked attitude:

> I keep arguing for Rist, and before we know it his ten days' vacation has evaporated. Something has to be decided, one way or another. And at last, Fanck agrees to apply for five months' leave of absence for the Nuremberg policeman. The contract is signed on the understanding that further screen tests are successful.[4]

The rest, as she says, 'measured in film time, happens like lightning.' Rist flies to Berlin. The tests prove magnificent, and Leni is assigned the task of transforming him for the role. A shopping spree in Innsbruck sorts that out: 'With some sporty clothes and a new hairdo our police official becomes the perfect high alpine man.'

For the first time, Fanck really understood what Leni Riefenstahl saw in Rist, the special quality the rest of them had missed: his pupil was learning fast. On location, no longer the blind acolyte, she was to find herself frequently at odds with Fanck's filmic ideas. Although, like him, she had been drawn to cinema through her love of Nature and beautiful imagery, she grew increasingly exasperated – her personal sense of art 'violated', as she said once in interview – when he did things which did not accord with how she envisaged them. 'This is when I came to ask myself how I could give outlet to this artistic sense of mine':

> I set myself to look for a thread, a theme, a style, in the realms of legend and fantasy, something which would enable me to give free rein to my youthful sense of the beautiful image and of romanticism.[5]

Where she felt herself most at variance with Fanck was in the juxtaposition of reality and magic. Fanck's filming was magic, no question about that: he produced glittering, unearthly, fantastical images, yet he would persist in trying to marry these to such obstinately prosaic plots. Everyday realism, in Leni's opinion, called for realistic, rather than fairy tale visuals. To make the most of his beautiful shots, he ought to be realising plots from fable or fantasy, the sort of stories, in other words, which so strongly appealed to her. This overriding feeling that form and content should coincide reinforced in her the desire to write her own ballad or legend for such a film, in very much the same way as she had for dance. She began constructing situations and scenes in her own mind, not at first with any intention of directing the film herself, for she still saw herself primarily as an actress. That was her chosen career, after all, the career in dedication to which she had given up her beloved dancing. And she had talent for it – perhaps not a great one, but one she did not care to fritter away. Yet there remained this growing need to encompass more. She was being impelled into film making by her very nature and by the knowledge she was soaking up so readily. She had had her fill of icy cold, of tempests and glaciers. Though mountains still held her in thrall, it was those sunwashed Dolomitic pinnacles that she hankered after, the dream mountains she had first fallen in love with:

> Mountains, trees, people's faces, I was seeing them quite differently, in their particular moods and movements. The urge to create something of my own grew ever stronger. Whether I found myself on a lonely hill path or a train to Berlin, or in the bustle of the city,

always images kept rising within me . . . A waterfall, crystals, the menacing branches of a stark, solitary tree, sunbeams breaking through mist, twinkling dew on grass, flowers . . .[6]

Gradually, the damburst of images and scenes flooding her imagination began coalescing into the single stream she had been seeking.

She saw a young girl, living in the mountains, a creature of nature, ragged, outcast . . . She saw the harsh, lean heads of mountain peasants . . . saw these peasants hunt the girl through narrow village streets, hurling stones . . . She saw a bridge, heard the echo of vengeful cries off the mountain wall . . . And high above, beyond everything, the rock face gleamed with a strange blue light . . .

The tragedy of *Das Blaue Licht* (*The Blue Light*) was taking shape. It was not an old Dolomite legend, as many supposed, though its roots were in the true tradition of folk and fairy tales. Riefenstahl was often asked where the idea came from, and she would say only that one of her early successful dances had been *The Blue Flower:* she supposed she must have drawn inspiration from that.[7]

From the beginning, 'Junta', the young girl of the story, was conceived as an embodiment of herself – or at least she only ever saw herself playing the role. It was the summation of all the parts she had ever wanted to play. The name Junta came to her from nowhere, she said; she had never consciously heard it before. In her story, this strange faerie-creature, sleepwalking, climbs towards the blue light, which is only visible on nights of full moon. It is the glow emitted by rock crystals in a secret grotto when lunar rays catch it from a particular angle. It is symbolic, too, of the light or ideal that young people should always be seeking. Junta is the only one who can reach it because she is pure of heart. Village lads, when they try, fall to their destruction, and the light has therefore come to be seen as a curse on the little community. Parents seek to keep their children at home behind closed shutters.

One day, a Viennese artist, 'Vigo', arrives in the village. He learns of the mysterious light that lures young men to their doom, and of a strange wild girl who lives high on the mountainside. He sees how the villagers shun her, drive her away with stones if she ventures into the valley. After witnessing one such scene, Vigo follows the girl back to her mountain retreat. Soon he is hopelessly bewitched by her and when, at the next full moon, the blue light gleams once more and Junta slips out to climb her Monte Cristallo, a bewildered Vigo is only a few steps behind her. As he follows higher, he suddenly realises she has known the mountain's secret all along, the secret which so fatefully eluded the villagers. She leads him up a hidden gully towards the summit, completely unaware of his presence. Soon, he too is party to the mystery: never has he seen anything so wondrous as this cavern of glimmering crystals in the moonlight.

Excitedly, Vigo returns to the valley to tell all, convinced that by sharing the discovery he will dispel the superstitious dread of the mountain and, with it, all antagonism towards Junta. Soon he is leading the villagers back to the cave, from where they remove all the crystals.

Junta finds a dropped crystal on the track and knows at once that some dreadful violation has taken place. Immediately, she begins clambering the rocky cliffs to see for herself. But without the blue light to guide her steps, she slips and plunges to her death. Vigo, on finding her body the next day, comes to realise, too late, that in his attempt to do right by the village and Junta, he has been responsible for this tragedy. The realist had killed the dream.

Shyly, Leni shows her outline script to a few friends. They seem to like it, but she cannot raise any enthusiasm among film producers. Everyone tells her it would be practically impossible to film (in black and white, as it still was then). She is devastated. How can they say that? To her, it is blindingly obvious how it could be done. She even has a good idea how the night scenes might be brought to life. Far from losing heart or faith in the whole idea, she sees that to make it come true is up to her alone.

Could she direct it herself? It was not something she felt completely happy about, though if she played the lead as well, that would be two fat salaries dispensed with . . . and everything could be shot out of doors; there was no need of elaborate sets – apart from the crystal grotto . . . She still needed money. What would be the smallest crew she could get away with – eight? It might just be possible. If only they could be persuaded to work without wages until after the film was completed, all she would have to fund initially would be the film stock – and subsistence in the mountain huts. It was no good, she couldn't make the sums add up, even so. She tried Sokal, who was quite a mogul these days, having made a killing out of *Piz Palü,* but though he professed faith in her talents, he was not ready to sink his own money into such a flimsy venture.

Fanck was let in on the secret, but he was far from encouraging, quite unable to share her vision. To his mind, legendary subjects needed the monumental treatment Fritz Lang had bestowed upon *Die Nibelungen* in 1924, when all landscape had been stylised, involving the construction of elaborately decorated forests and mountains. The climate was different now: where would she find anyone willing to entertain such an enormously costly 'art' film? Her ideas for using lighting and, in particular, special filters to achieve an ethereal stylisation went completely over Fanck's head. She could take it from him, he told her, mountains had to be filmed in bright natural light. He should know. Rock would always look like rock. Solid and real, that's what it was. No, her ideas were quite simply nonsense. She was crazy to believe otherwise, he told her.

The shocking narrowness of Fanck's preconceptions irritated Riefenstahl beyond words, but at the same time provided the goad she needed to resolve outstanding problems of artistic effect. Of course rock could be softened and made mysterious, and easily too, merely by employing wisps and veils of fog. How was it a master of light and shade could not understand that? Still, in the end, it was Fanck who indirectly provided the solution to all her problems.

His own next film was to be another uninhibited ski spectacular, *Der Weisse Rausch* (*The White Frenzy*, once described as 'perhaps the happiest movie ever to come out of Germany').[8] There was a part in it for her, if she wanted it, as a novice skier so well coached by 'headmaster' Hannes Schneider as to be able to compete against him in a magnificent swooping 'fox hunt' by the end of the film – an exhilarating paperchase over the snows in which some fifty crack international skiers take part.[9] In the old days she would have jumped at the prospect of a few months in the mountains with some of the best ski stars of the day, but this time her heart was not in it. She was fed up with all these empty-headed, decorous roles Fanck kept dreaming up for her. This one seemed more vacuous than usual, requiring her as a city-brat of a heroine to keep uttering 'Oh, super! Jolly super!' at every opportunity. None the less, she signed up – as a means to an end. All her salary could go into *The Blue Light* kitty. She just had to grit her teeth and get on with it. Every day would bring her own film that much closer.

The one consolation on set was to be visited by the respected Hungarian screenwriter and theorist Béla Balàzs, a noted Marxist. She had never met him before, but had sent him a copy of her treatment for comment. Balàzs had gone out of his way in the past to defend Fanck's mountain films against noted detractors, and Leni felt sure he could be relied upon for sympathetic and sound advice. In the event, he gave far more than that. *The Blue Light* was a charming piece, he told her, with enormous cinema potential. So enthusiastic was he that he offered to help develop the screenplay – for no immediate fee, nor prospect of one. The two put their heads together, working day and night whenever Riefenstahl was not required in front of the cameras, and in five weeks, with some help also from Carl Mayer, the final shooting script was ready. 'It was an ideal collaboration, and we had a wonderful and good relationship,' Riefenstahl would recall afterwards.

Balàzs agreed to come back and assist in the film's direction. Schneeberger – who, after working on *The Blue Angel* with Sternberg, was now regarded as one of the best film cameramen operating out of Germany – was to have overall charge of the camerawork. Riefenstahl set up her own production company, L.R. Studio Films, and began engaging the other members of the crew, mostly from among old friends. She needed people tried and tested for the rigours of mountain work, not necessarily for their film-making skills. Once away from valley comforts, being willing and cheerful and good company were by far the greatest assets. She and Schneeberger could supervise the technical side of things, along with Karl Buchholz who was to be second cameraman and production manager.

For the Flea's assistant Leni settled upon Heinz von Javorsky, who for some months had been working as her secretary. As a schoolboy, this young man had read an article about the making of Fanck's *Mont Blanc* film, and pedalled out to the French Alps on his bicycle. It took him nine days to reach Chamonix, and several more wandering the snows and glaciers of Mont Blanc in search of the crew. Penniless and half-starved, he had just about given up hope when he was invited to join a group in a café who were intrigued to know if he really had been to all the places written on the placard on his bicycle. Javorsky pulled out his newspaper cutting and explained how he had come to look for these film people, but they must have finished their movie and gone home. Now he had to earn some money and do the same. To his surprise, everybody started laughing.

'What's so damned funny?' he wanted to know.

The bearded man of the group put him out of his misery. 'My name's Fanck,' he said, 'and this is Fraulein Riefenstahl. And these are Allgeier, and Schneeberger, and Angst . . .'

Then Fanck told him, 'If you are so crazy about filmmaking, why don't you get yourself to the cable car at 7 o'clock tomorrow morning, and I'm sure we can find you something to do.'

Thus, Javorsky had been able to earn himself a few francs and a new pair of shoes by working as a porter. And when the filming was over, the 'Tramp of Mont Blanc' remounted his pushbike and pedalled home. Six months later a well-dressed young man presented himself on Riefenstahl's doorstep with a homemade book about his adventures, a book so engagingly written and so full of enthusiasm that she was immediately intrigued, and offered him a job. Now, the star-struck youth's cup was filled to overflowing at the prospect of being apprenticed to a sorcerer of Schneeberger's calibre – if only for a salary of fifty marks a month. (Later, as Henry Jaworsky, he would enjoy considerable acclaim himself as a Hollywood cameraman.)

Walter Riml, the lanky Hamburger from the comedic ski-duo in Fanck's *White Frenzy* was entrusted with the stills photography (though he had never done any such work before), and another of the Arlberg ski-stars, Rudi Matt, agreed to look after the silver sheet reflectors which would redirect the sun's rays to provide some of the special lighting effects. Walter (Waldi) Traut, a promising young student (later also to go on to greater things) was put in charge of finances, modest as these were.

When it came to casting, Leni's instinctive choice for leading man was Mathias Wieman, a professional actor whose brooding blond good-looks had taken her fancy. He projected just the blend of sensitivity and ruggedness she was after for her artist, Vigo. His experience was limited almost entirely to the stage, but although she saw that as no problem she hesitated to offer him the part until she was absolutely certain the film would go ahead. The first task was to scout out suitable locations and identify peasant extras. She was after those earthy, elemental faces of her original fantasy, traditional faces untouched by modern preoccupations and inspired, she would say later, by the paintings of Segantini or engravings by Dürer. In June of 1931, she and Schneeberger set off to look for what she wanted.

Many studies and analyses have been written on the subject of *The Blue Light* over the years. Its structure and implications are dissected and reconstrued with varying degrees of imagination and constructive hindsight by successive critics, cinema historians and film students. Yet, for the actual making of the film and the interpretations and inferences laid into it intentionally by its creators, the only substantive accounts are, sadly, Riefenstahl's own, to be found in her 1933 book *Kampf in Schnee und Eis* and in *The Sieve of Time*, memoirs published in old age. The former (even if produced with the assistance of a ghostwriter) can be regarded as the purer source for being written

68

when events were fresher, and especially in having appeared before any suspicion of Nazi taint attached to the film-maker – before, that is, a need existed to doctor recollection with justification or apology. In this, as in other matters, it is of interest to note where changes occur from one account to the next.

For four weeks Riefenstahl and Schneeberger scoured the Alps, traversing the Italian Dolomites and the Tessin (Ticino) in Switzerland. The Flea took her to a half-deserted hamlet he remembered, tucked beside a waterfall. Delighted, Leni had to agree it would make a perfect 'Santa Maria', the village of her legend. For 'Monte Cristallo', they settled upon the soaring Crozzon di Brenta to the west of the Dolomites in Trentino. As to the villagers, did those peasant faces exist anywhere beyond Riefenstahl's imagination? After the pair had wandered the highest and loneliest alpine valleys for some time, they began to fear not, for though there were plenty of spartan communities and faces etched with character, none gave that sense of introversion, of a sealed society complete within itself. They were almost resigned to disappointment when a chance meeting in Bolzano pointed them towards the Sarntal, one of the alpine valleys radiating from this South Tyrolean town. Follow it up for eighteen miles or so, their artist friend assured them, and they would find exactly what they were looking for.

They arrived in the picturesque village of Sarentino on a Sunday morning, just as its inhabitants were emerging from church and beginning to cluster in small groups in the square, passing the time of day. With a thrill of recognition, Leni knew the long quest was over. Here were strong, black-clothed, stern-featured figures, proud and forbidding . . . men and women, who would let nothing get at them. 'Direct descendents of the western Goths,' their friend had said.

All overtures to engage them in conversation were rebuffed. The villagers simply turned their backs on Leni Riefenstahl and her camera, and with long strides left the square. It was not going to be easy. The best would be to take a room at the local inn, she decided, and stay for as long as it took to get herself recognised and accepted. Confiding her plans to the innkeeper, he shook his head uncertainly, telling her, 'You have to understand, these people hardly know what photographs are, let alone a film. Few of them have been out of their valley, fewer still have ventured beyond Bolzano. You'll never persuade them in a hundred years to become players in your drama.'

She refused to be intimidated. They had come too far along the road for that. All day she would be out on the streets and hillsides of the scattered hamlet, greeting everyone she met and making a special point of speaking with the women and children. By the following weekend, the atmosphere was already less chilly, and as she began passing around some of her photographs, it was not long before everyone was laughing and pointing, struggling to take a look. One man accepted her invitation to a glass of wine and soon she was ordering carafes all round. In time, she won the agreement of the whole community to assist with the film, but not until September, they told her, when the last harvest was in. Reflecting ruefully that the players did not yet know exactly what was expected of them, Leni knew she was not home and dry, and had to confess that the prospect of staging some of the difficult scenes scared her half to death.[10] What would they make of hounding Junta through the streets? Or the wild carousing of a near-pagan festival? From a film-maker's point of view, some of the dramatic moonlight scenes would be no picnic either.

Still, this was not the time to worry about that. At least Wieman could be approached for the part of Vigo – which, praise be, he accepted. Now to cast the lesser characters. In that way she had of never forgetting a face, Leni trawled her memory, retrieving from aeons ago the image of her first tennis coach, Max Holzboer. One can imagine his surprise on hearing out of the blue that he was wanted as a tavern keeper in her new production; yet he was intrigued, or flattered enough to fall in with her plans. Beni Führer, the young guide who had pulled her from a collapsing snowbridge on Mont Blanc, was brought in to play 'Tonio', a newly-wed, and a local lad, Franz Maldacea, agreed to be Junta's little goatherd brother. The only role left to sort out was that of Tonio's bride, 'Lucia'.

Here Leni was seeking a simple country girl, instinctive and untarnished, through whose eyes the fate of Junta would be revealed. For this was to be a story within a story (a device with resonant echoes of *Piz Palü*). As the title and introductory words fade, the film would open with a shot of the arrival at a village inn of a young honeymoon couple who are instantly mobbed by children trying to sell them crystals, for which this village is famous. One little fist holds out a small oval portrait of a gypsy girl with mysterious eyes, and Lucia, her curiosity aroused, enquires later of the innkeeper if such a person ever existed. This is his cue to bring out an old, leather-bound volume, '*The story of Junta, 1866*', and as a hand turns the pages, the picture of Junta dissolves to moving film leading the audience into the story proper. The married couple appear again at the end of the film, thoughtfully closing the book and gazing out of the window at the

70

luminous bow of the waterfall, which is understood to be a living symbol of the mysterious mountain girl.

This rather contrived framing story was omitted when Riefenstahl re-edited the film in the 1950s, but originally she saw Lucia as of supreme importance – essential to have exactly right. She and Schneeberger tramped further up the Sarntal to Pennes, which in those days comprised no more than two or three primitive chalets and a small chapel. Here they found a young woman returning from her devotions. She was dressed entirely in black, and the eyes beneath her dark kerchief were indescribably large and expressive. It was the face of a Madonna. Experiencing another of her electrifying flashes, Riefenstahl darted after the girl, following her into her cottage: 'She responds only hesitantly to my advances. I cannot take my eyes off her. All her movements have a wonderful grace . . . I know I must have her for the part at any cost, but I am going to have to tread warily.'[11]

The woman's name was Martha Mair. Her parents were dead. When Leni enquired if she would be prepared to leave her village for a few days to be photographed, Martha shook her head firmly. She had never been out of the village. Leni was permitted to take a few snaps, and later, as she and the Flea retraced their long way home, they comforted each other with the thought that when they returned to the valley that autumn they would be coming as friends, and by that time all the Sarntalers, men and women, should have warmed to the film idea. Even Martha, so they hoped.

In July, with an advance team of six, Leni began filming in the other locations, going first to the waterfall village of Foroglia in the Tessin, a two hour walk beyond the road head. Here was no inn nor mountain hut where they could stay: most of the houses had lain empty since their inhabitants departed for an easier life in America earlier in the century. Only nine adults and a few children remained now. Each of the film crew was able to select a house for himself, the simple luxury of a plank bed and a water-basin being all that was required in those midsummer days.

First, they wanted to secure the waterfall scenes; and for the rest of her life Leni would remember the ecstatic release she felt at last to be doing what she most wanted, with the friends she loved best in the world. No one to breathe down their necks, no studio hacks spying on them; cut off from telephones, newspapers and all the trappings of the outside world, it seemed the ideal atmosphere in which to be creative, to achieve the 'stylistic unity' of which she dreamed. Some days, she said, they could shoot for only a few minutes, anxious to catch just the right quality of light and sparkle off the water. Test rolls of film would be developed each night, when all would gather around a log fire in one of the old houses to discuss whether they were achieving the mood they wanted. Everyone had a say, no one hiding behind any particular speciality. They mucked in together for whatever was required, and as the work progressed, so it grew more intense.

The cameramen were experimenting with 'R-material', a new infra-red film stock under development at the Agfa laboratories, with which Leni had been collaborating for some time. Its low blue and high green and red sensitivity produced a heightened, romantic effect, and when used in conjunction with coloured filters yielded even more surreal images. A heavy red filter, for instance, excluded the blue altogether for a dramatic darkened effect which would be particularly useful for the night shots – a technique later to be widely adopted throughout the cinema industry.

Thrilled with the results, Leni egged Schneeberger to push the distortion further: 'Try green *and* red filters together,' she urged for the forest scenes, refusing to listen when, with some impatience, he protested that the image would be lost entirely. Why couldn't she stick to what she was good at and not tell him what could or couldn't be done? But she could not, of course. Stubborn as always, she kept on at him, until finally, for a quiet life, he did as she wished. And her instincts were proved right: the result was a highly-stylised ethereal image, all the green leaves turning to white, an absolutely magical effect.

By the end of four weeks they had exposed ten thousand feet of film, which was sent back to Berlin for processing. Would it be all right? This was the great moment of truth; so much depended on the outcome that when, a few days later, a telegram arrived for her, Leni could barely bring herself to open it.

'CONGRATULATIONS ON THE RUSHES! WONDERFUL, BEYOND WORDS – NEVER HAVE I SEEN SUCH IMAGES. ARNOLD.' His earlier discouragement forgotten, Fanck was generous and quick to give credit where it was due. Leni was jubilant. The more so when a second telegram swiftly followed – from Sokal, offering a partnership. He would pick up all outstanding post production costs; Agfa had already promised an editing suite and assistant. The film's future was assured! The whole team jigged for joy in the street outside the post office, and that night celebrated with a huge bowl of mulled wine round their fire.

Now they worked with more passion and resolution than ever. Jaworsky, the Tramp of Mont Blanc, years afterwards remembered the heady intensity of making films with Riefenstahl:

> She had a source of energy that is incredible . . . I've never seen that woman sleep. Her mind is always winding. What do you call that thing a horse has? She has blinders [sic]. She looks only in one direction and that's the project she is on . . . People are dead tired, she doesn't care . . . She reminds me of Nero, like a Roman emperor. I have great respect for her, but it was hard working with her . . . And boy, eight hours climbing up the mountain before we did a shot, with everything on our backs – no cable cars and that nonsense. We carried the equipment on our backs. You had to be an 'idealist' to work like this, you had to love it . . .[12]

To Riefenstahl, looking back after her career became complicated, this period took on a special quality, her last carefree adventure. Maybe there was more tension than she remembered through the misty eyes of nostalgia, but the fact that everyone worked so harmoniously together, and to such great effect, was as much thanks to her instinctive selection of the right individuals, as to her power to infuse them with her vision:

> Throughout the three months of this shoot, there was never any bad temper between us, no petty jealousies, nor even dissatisfaction. Perfect togetherness we had. All eight of us were a family. Everything was paid for out of a common kitty, and everyone did his best to make do on as little as possible, to spin out the money for as long as we could. If someone needed their shoes mending or anything else vital, we paid it out of the kitty. For myself, I did not buy anything personal for fourteen months – and it didn't upset me that much.[13]

At the beginning of August, Wieman joined the others as they moved to the Brenta Dolomites for the climbing sequences and the shots outside Junta's mountain refuge with their 'Monte Cristallo' soaring in the background. 'Malga-Brenta-Alta is the name of our new location,' Riefenstahl wrote, and: 'Of all the idyllic and splendid places we have found for this work, this is the most beautiful. Wildly romantic, as if it had been spirited here just for us.'[14] The sense of special enchantment was heightened one morning when a handsome snow-white chamois appeared on a ledge high above them, leading

73

forty others in his wake. A rare and fabulous creature, like a unicorn: it had to be a good luck sign.

Two more hard-working weeks flashed by, each morning up into the mountains, every evening back to the hut for bread and cheese, their daily fare. But even here, because of the experimental nature of their filming, they needed to develop daily rushes. Two of them would be dispatched down to the valley each evening after sunset to process the footage in Madonna di Campaglio, often not arriving back until after midnight: then it would be up at five to view the material.

Balàzs joined them to supervise some of Riefenstahl's dramatic scenes. And soon it was time for the shooting in Sarentino, as had been arranged with the villagers. On the appointed day two post buses were to arrive in the square at 7 a.m. to whisk everyone off to some castle ruins ten miles away. But would people show up?

After a restless night, Leni peers out of the window at around 4 o'clock to discover it raining heavily, Surely, no one will turn out in such filthy weather, particularly those with a two or three hour walk to get here? By dawn it is still coming down in torrents, and there is not a soul to be seen. This is serious, for Wieman has soon to return to Berlin for a theatre engagement; every hour is precious now. They cannot afford the loss of a single day's shooting.

Then, just before seven, people begin drifting into the square:

They stand about patiently, under enormous umbrellas. Two ancient grandmothers and an old lame man, all wearing their Sunday best, the women in big shiny satin aprons. My spirits begin to lift. Another group approaches, a complete family by the look of it, with grandpapa and children. And still they come. Gradually the square fills. My heart leaps for joy – I want to hug them all, my darling peasants, for turning out so bravely despite this torrential rain. I rush downstairs and shake hands with each and every one.[15]

The two charabancs roll up and everyone is packed inside, far more people than had been expected. A few of the older folk need coaxing aboard these strange monsters, but at last 'stuffed in like herrings in a barrel, the Sarntalers drive away to the wonders of filming.'[16]

For authenticity, Leni wanted to show the villagers in all aspects of their daily routine: at work, at home in their cottages and farmhouses, at their devotions and seasonal celebrations. In those days it was customary for all filmed interiors to be reconstructed in the studio, but Leni hired a special lighting van from Vienna in order to be able to wire up natural settings. In this, too, she was conscious of stepping

into experimental areas, beyond even the experience of Schneeberger, but fortunately the lighting engineer knew his craft, and the
Flea's telling close-ups of peasant faces were afterwards likened to
work of the great master, Eisenstein.

At the Schloss Runkelstein, long tables have been set under the
trees, and as Leni's Sarntalers arrive they are greeted with as much
wine as they can drink and shown the film equipment. Reserve and
inhibitions melt away, and even on that first day, it proves possible to
get important scenes in the can. Late in the evening, the peasants are
driven home. Another week like this and the worst would be over.
Every day the villagers are bussed back to the castle, where from
before dawn the crew have been laying cables and lugging heavy
spotlights up into the ruins. 'What my people achieve during this
period is unbelievable. With every last pfennig budgeted for, we
cannot employ extra helpers. Normally, one would have used three
times as many.'

On the final day in the castle, the last day the villagers are available
all together, they are still there at midnight despite an early start. And
they have not yet begun filming the climactic revels. They've blown
it, surely? All the film crew are dog-tired and Leni herself can barely
stand for backache. She sinks weepily on to a barrel, script in hand,
unable to concentrate. For days now she hasn't slept a wink and she
has lost count of all the meals she has missed:

> Snoring peasants are slumped in every corner, and with these I
> should now celebrate a roistering festival! Like ants carrying their
> eggs, my people lug around the floodlights, collect tables, benches,
> barrels, everything necessary for rustic merrymaking. The musi-
> cians are rounded up and awaken the whole company with a
> deafening polka. Fresh wine and beer are brought in and we work
> ourselves up into the mood once more.[17]

Leni leads the dance, whirling around with the village boys, first
one then another, encouraging everyone to their feet. Soon, amid
laughter and flowing glasses, the party is in full swing. Her crew tuck
themselves into corners and behind tables, filming furiously. The
gangling Riml clambers on to a barrel to get shots looking down on
the scene. And by two in the morning, the whole nightmare is over.
'As the peasants are driven out of the castle yard back to their homes,
and my brave lads are reeling in the cables, I collapse on my beer barrel
again, striking out whole pages of script with a red pencil.'[18]

Next morning they allow themselves the luxury of sleeping in.

Wieman is already on his way back to Berlin, where he will shortly be followed by a hastily nailed-up crate containing a further 8,000 metres of film for processing. Back in the Sarntal, it remains only to wrap up the kitchen interiors and hearthsides. As the villagers welcome them into their homes, it is hard to remember how remote and mistrustful they seemed when Riefenstahl and Schneeberger had first arrived. Now they are all dear friends, full of humour and concern. Even the vicar permits filming inside the church during divine service. In her wildest dreams, Leni could not have hoped for better. All too soon it is time to take their leave, a sad wrench, as much for the villagers as themselves. On the morning of departure, the Sarntalers are once more up early, to serenade them on their way. One little old mother presses into Leni's hands a spray of wax flowers she has made, flowers which will never wither, while others of the little village accompany the film crew as far as Bolzano, a film crew shrunk once more to the six who started out together at the beginning. Summer is almost over and a sprinkling of snow already transforms the higher peaks. Before the landscape slithers too far into winter, the last scenes of a barefoot Junta climbing her Monte Cristallo must be safely in the can. Fortunately, the Brenta continues to bless them with warm days sufficient to finish filming, and they return to Berlin three months to the day from setting out.

VII

SOS Eisberg!

Leni Riefenstahl had very little experience of film editing when
she sat down to construct *The Blue Light* from her mountain of
celluloid, but she soon came to think of those days of learning as 'the
most beautiful part' of what in truth had been an exciting project from
start to finish. 'I cannot bear to leave my cutting room,' she wrote.
'Best of all would be to sleep there.' The rushes were more powerful
than she had dared to hope, and she experimented, this way and that,
with long and short versions, searching for the most fluent juxtaposi-
tions. Perversely, the air of suspense she wanted to introduce proved
elusive, and with some diffidence she turned at last to Arnold Fanck
for his opinion.

'Bring it round,' he said, when she called him. 'Let me take a look
first, and then we can run through it together.' But he did not wait,
and by the next afternoon when she called round, he announced with
brutal lightness, 'See what you think now. I had to alter almost every
scene. It kept me up most of the night, but really it was quite
impossible the way you had it.'

'But you promised we'd look at it together.' She was stunned,
protesting, 'You were not supposed to touch anything without
me . . .'

'I thought you wanted my help.' Fanck's air of injury was too much
to stomach and she burst into a fury of tears. Her mentor beat a tactical
retreat.

Once she had cried herself out, Leni carefully gathered up the
cutting copy and the hundreds of film snippets, and bore them home.
It was days before she could bring herself to look at Fanck's
handiwork. Meanwhile she tried to persuade herself it would not be as
bad as she feared. In fact it was far worse than she ever imagined.

77

'What I saw was a mutilation.' (Years did not diminish the sting. This she wrote in 1987, more than half a century later.) At least now she knew what she must do: 'Of the myriad tiny pieces, which I splice back together, a real film gradually emerges, more visible week by week, until finally the legend of *The Blue Light*, my dream story of just a year ago lies finished before me.'[1]

The film was premièred at UFA Palast am Zoo on 24th March 1932, an ambitious venue for what was immediately seen as an 'arty' film. The first reviews were mixed, though nobody could fault the photography: 'beautiful in the extreme' – 'film effects approaching fine paintings,' *Variety* told its readers, while considering Riefenstahl weak as both director and actress, and concluding with some pomposity, 'The production company should realise the business failure of this picture.' The *Film-Kurier*, on the other hand, was rapturous, telling how when the lights went up, the spectators came back from a different world, 'A courageous woman, faithful to her work and to her obsession, has turned the film world upside down.' As Riefenstahl toured Germany and Europe for the film's opening in other cities, it became increasingly clear that she had succeeded beyond anyone's expectations. At the first Venice Biennale that year *The Blue Light* picked up the Silver Medal.

When it arrived in New York the film was hailed as 'flawless' and 'a highly fascinating fantasy'. In London even the stony heart of Colonel Strutt melted. At last, he enthused, we have a really beautiful mountaineering film. The attractive Fraulein Riefenstahl (whose work he considered 'spoilt hitherto under the direction of the notorious Fanck in the grotesque *Piz Palü*, *Stürme über dem Mont Blanc* and other faked atrocities'), under self-direction 'now came deservedly into her own'. She rock–climbed in beautiful style despite her 'extremely inadequate *Kletterschuhe*'. That the story was 'a slight if pretty legend' was of no consequence.[2]

Leni Riefenstahl revelled in the adulation. While still seeing herself primarily as an actress, she welcomed the new independence her film brought her, and expected now to continue making pictures of her own choosing. Certainly there was no shortage of ideas buzzing around in her head, so that when Universal Studios cabled to offer her the female lead in Arnold Fanck's latest production, which would be shot in German and American versions, she felt few qualms in turning it down.

Riefenstahl was reckoning without Hollywood. Hers was the name the studio wanted, and at any price. (What other actress would or could film in such rugged conditions?) Higher fees were dangled – unbelievably high, so it seemed to her – yet when she eventually capitulated, it was not the money which tipped the balance. In the end, she said, she had been unable to pass up the chance of sharing one more, perhaps final, adventure with cherished colleagues.

The plot of *SOS Eisberg* was typical Fanck: raw passions set amid raw nature, only this time with Arctic ice replacing the Alpine backdrop. Riefenstahl would play a woman pilot, 'Hella', whose famous scientist husband was missing in the Greenland wastes. In its timing, the theme was in poor taste, coming hard on the heels of the disappearance on the Greenland Ice Cap of the celebrated real-life German scientist, Alfred Wegener. Indeed, Wegener's body had been discovered only that spring in a carefully prepared grave on the ice, though no trace was ever found of his Eskimo companion, who must have perished soon after burying him with full honours.

Fanck's story shies away from unpalatable tragedy. Hella locates her husband, only to crash-land on an iceberg and become stranded herself. No matter. She, her husband, and the leader of the search expedition are all dramatically whisked to safety by the barnstorming Ernst Udet, once more playing himself. A full-blown expedition had to be put together to make the film – the Universal Dr Fanck Greenland Expedition, no less – financed by Carl Laemmle, President of Universal Pictures and supported by the Danish Government. This was Arnold Fanck bridging his two worlds of geography and film making. To add legitimacy to the venture (and one could cynically add, to deflect any accusations of insensitivity), four scientists from Wegener's last expedition were incorporated into the team. They would advise on suitable locations and continue their studies of Greenland's fjords and glaciers. Knud Rasmussen, a polar explorer of half-Eskimo descent and sometimes known as King of the Eskimos, agreed to be the expedition's 'Protector', a role halfway between liaison officer and a 'Mr Fixit'; he would oversee all arrangements in the field.

Those of the old gang, with whom Leni had been unable to resist working again, included Sepp Rist, her leading man from *Mont Blanc*, the lanky skier Walter Riml and his diminutive partner Guzzi Lantschner. There was her old chum Ernst Udet, cameramen Schneeberger, Buchholz and Angst, and Waldi Traut as production assistant. Yet despite so many familiar faces, it was going to be a far cry from those days when Leni had been the sole female distraction on set, flirting outrageously with whomsoever she chose. Snowflea

79

was now married, and his young wife, Gisela, was coming as a photographer in her own right, one of seven women on the trip. Udet's girlfriend would be there (a glamorous redhead who went by the curious nickname of 'Louse'). Fanck was bringing his secretary, later to become his wife, and several of the scientists were to have their partners along. If Leni's nose was put out of joint by so much competition, she did not show it. Her attention was anyway quickly taken by one of three big-name mountaineers employed as safety advisers and stuntmen to the expedition.

Hans Ertl had the green eyes of a cat. He was lively and impetuous, always ready for fun, and he was supremely fit. Little wonder then that Leni found him 'without a doubt the most attractive male member of the expedition.' He had shot to fame the year before with a daring first ascent of the Ortler North Face together with Franz Schmid of Matterhorn fame. The two other climbers on the team were Swiss guides Fritz Steuri and David Zogg. There was a doctor, a cook, an animal handler, a second airman, various mechanics and operators, the stills photographer and a sound-man: Fanck had put together his usual cosmopolitan group, which he was proud to introduce at the going-away press reception.

Leni was in his bad books because she failed to catch the train taking everyone to the boat. She only showed up on deck the following morning, glowing with excitement but refusing (as she says in her memoirs) to tell anyone where she had been. In all, thirty-eight members sailed aboard the *Borodino*, a British tramp-steamer which left Hamburg for Umanak towards the end of May 1932.

Trenker liked to put around the story of Leni missing the train rather differently, though we have to remember he was not of the party – and, where Riefenstahl was concerned, was never above spicing up his version of events. He had her 'missing for days', leaving Udet and Fanck beside themselves with worry, convinced everyone would have to miss the boat. 'At last,' he said, 'there came a telephone message. Hitler's private plane had just landed. Leni had been the Führer's guest in a place near Nuremberg. She walked into the hotel lobby with a tremendous bouquet of flowers; her eyes seemed to gaze into the distance, her whole being was transformed. She wanted everyone to know that she had just passed through a wonderful experience.'[3]

★

Wrapped up in her film work, Leni Riefenstahl had been paying scant attention to politics, although no one could have failed to notice Germany's foundering economy and widespread unemployment. Her own father, whom she had always considered comfortably off, had been obliged to scale down his business and sack two-thirds of the workforce, moving with her mother into a small rented apartment. For years the Communists and the National Socialists had been at each other's throats, with gangs of violent young men stalking the streets and public order breaking down. This was the Berlin of Isherwood and Spender, the 'Weimardämmerung', when the catchphrase 'It's all the fault of the Jews' was becoming increasingly heard, and not only from Nazi mouths. Touring with *The Blue Light* brought it home to Leni how the name of Adolf Hitler was on everyone's lips, at home and abroad, and she was surprised how many of her countrymen believed he alone held the answer to all the nation's ills. His private army of stormtroopers, the Sturmabteilung (SA), strutted openly, dispensing retribution on all whose faces did not fit their distorted vision of a new order.

Returning to Berlin in that spring of 1932, Riefenstahl found the streets peppered with posters announcing an appearance by Hitler at a public rally in the city. She ought to hear what he had to say, her friend Ernst Jaeger told her, wake up to what was happening, as the Nazis were urging Germany to do. Jaeger, a journalist, was strongly anti-Nazi; and Leni had to agree that, so far, she did not care for the image the newspapers were presenting of this man Hitler. Nevertheless, she was curious to see the phenomenon for herself. What made him so charismatic?

The meeting in the packed *Sportpalast* was a revelation. Though she does not mention it, this must have been the occasion when Goebbels announced publicly that Hitler was to run for President against Hindenburg. Leni was too far back, she tells us,[4] to see Hitler's face when he arrived late to address the throng, and instinctively distrusted the hysteria being whipped up with the incessant '*Heil! Heil! Heil!*' Yet when the Führer began to speak, his voice and rhetoric had an almost apocalyptic effect, upon her as everyone else:

> It seemed as if the earth's surface were spreading out in front of me, like a hemisphere that suddenly splits apart in the middle, spewing out an enormous jet of water, so powerful that it touched the sky and shook the earth. I felt quite paralysed.[5]

Without following much of his argument, she was fascinated by the man himself and the way he held his audience in bondage. Although

81

by now thoroughly immersed in preparations for Greenland, she was so disturbed by the experience that she could think of little else. Over the next few days she took every opportunity to discuss her confusion with friends. Socialism – with a small 's' – held considerable appeal for her, but National Socialism? Was one to take all Hitler's inflammatory cant at face value? What could be put down to campaign fervour and what was intrinsic Party policy? For without doubt, much of what this man declaimed with such passion was deeply abhorrent. How then to explain his attraction?

As always, Leni took her concerns to those in the know, speaking first to her friend Manfred George, the Jewish editor of *Tempo*, a Berlin evening newspaper. How did he rate the Hitler phenomenon? In common with masses of Germans – Jews and non-Jews alike – who regarded National Socialism as merely a fad, and Hitler a hothead, George seems not yet to have fully appreciated the potential for horror if the Nazis were to sweep to power. 'Brilliant but dangerous,' was his conservative assessment. Leni went next to the horse's mouth. Shortly before leaving for Greenland she addressed a letter to Nazi headquarters, to Hitler himself, requesting a meeting. It seems less of an extraordinary thing to have done when you consider the pattern she established early in life. Whenever anyone made an impression on her, she had to meet him: in this way she had introduced herself to Froitzheim and Trenker – to Fanck, Sternberg, and Pabst, too, in all probability. She knew that, once she started chattering, she could captivate. It had always worked for her, giving her an ability to create opportunities for herself, to fashion her own destiny.

What she could not have known at the time she wrote was that Hitler was already an admirer of hers, having been won over by her dance of fluttering veils in her very first movie. The romanticism, the remote yet sensuous gyrations, the sun setting over the North Sea – all struck special chords for him. From then on, he had followed her career with interest, *The Blue Light* in particular catching his imagination.

The only account we have of Leni Riefenstahl's first meeting with Adolf Hitler is her own. On the day before she was to catch the train for Hamburg on her way to Greenland she received a telephone call from the Führer's adjutant, Wilhelm Brückner. Hitler would like her to meet him the following day, near Wilhelmshaven, Brückner said, and brushing aside her surprised protestations, assured her she would be delivered safely to her boat in time. She need have no worries on that score. Fanck, on the other hand, was expecting the star of his film to be present at his important press conference on the ship-bound train, and Universal, she knew, also set great store by her being there. How could she let them down? None the less, next day found her aboard a different train from that of her colleagues, rattling towards the Baltic coast. A few hours later an official black Mercedes picked her up from the station and whisked her to the little resort of Horumersiel where Hitler was waiting. They walked along the beach, his aides trailing at a respectful distance, and Riefenstahl was surprised to find the Führer 'natural and uninhibited, like a completely normal person' and 'unexpectedly modest'. He talked about her films, and she was charmed. More than ever, the man seemed separate from his public image.

She told him (so her memoirs inform us) that she could never be a member of his Party; and he, in turn, informed her that when he came to power she was to make films especially for him.

That evening they walked again on the strand, warmly arm in arm, Hitler telling her of his tastes in music and architecture, and sharing with her what he saw as his mission to save Germany. But when he moved to embrace her, Riefenstahl, startled and unready, shrank from his grasp, and she knew at once that she had failed him. Their conversation over breakfast next morning was distant and formal, and no sooner was the meal over than Hitler kissed her hand and took his leave, telling her to be in touch when she returned from Greenland. His private plane delivered her to Hamburg.

★

The storyline of *SOS Eisberg!* demanded a wide fjord, with icebergs and blocks of ice floating in it. Apart from a few scenes with Eskimos, almost all the action was to take place on crumbling ice floes. Though there were icebergs in plenty around their base at Umanak, they were more than usually mobile and unsteady, melting fast, and certainly not inclined to hang about for the days at a stretch required to shoot critical scenes. Udet was dispatched northwards on a reconnaissance mission and eventually found what seemed a more suitable location at Nuliarfik, a hundred miles away. Here, at the mouth of the Kangerdluk Fjord, two glaciers, the Rink and the Umiamako, came down to the water's edge where they calved off colossal icebergs. Fanck set off at once with an advance party to get activities under way and, while the cat was away, it became playtime for those of the crew left behind.

Leni was enraptured by the Greenland spring, with its silk-soft air and warm sunshine. She would spend days drifting among the fluted bergs in the bay in her inflatable boat, beyond reach of the midges and mosquitoes which plagued the shoreline. One day she took along a rubber Lilo and 'boarded' a particularly attractive ice structure to sunbathe on its glittering surface. Melting ice had collected into a small pool on top, which nestled invitingly in the ice 'like an emerald'. She treated herself to a dip before settling down to doze. Seldom, she said, had she felt so refreshed and carefree as on that berg, drifting slowly through the fjord: 'All of a sudden an ear-splitting crash tore me from my reverie. My iceberg juddered, the lake washed over me. I slid down the slope on my belly and grabbed hold of my paddleboat, which I dared not lose at any price. Luckily the berg didn't roll over, merely heaved and pitched to and fro before gradually calming down.'[6]

Only then did she understand the cause of the disturbance. A nearby iceberg had shattered, shedding huge blocks of ice and yawing wildly in the narrow channel like a stricken sea monster. Its fierce wash pursued her as she paddled urgently away. 'It was the first and last time that I visited an iceberg for my own pleasure,' her memoirs record piously – though this is not quite true, if Ertl is to be believed.

From the outset Hans Ertl was warned to give Riefenstahl a wide berth. With all the bitterness of a yesterday's man, his friend Walter Riml had urged, 'Don't let that little tramp bamboozle you with her wiles. She can't keep her hands off young studs like us. But we are only candies to her . . . to be nibbled for just so long as it is fun!'[7]

Far from being dissuaded, Ertl regarded her notoriety as intriguing. Finding himself waylaid by Leni on his way up the beach one evening, he was more than happy to play along with the famous film star's plans. After all, she was a a director of note now, too – apart from consciously oozing sensuality and fun.

'I have been watching you in your kayak,' she told him. 'I love the way you grip the paddle, low down almost to the blade. It makes your whole torso twist, like a dancer's. So elegant! Will you teach me how to do that?'

He mumbled clumsily that it was the way they paddled on his native Isar, and, yes, he'd be happy to show her any time. 'Always glad to be of service,' he smiled.

'*Al-ways?*' She fixed him with her startling eyes. 'Like, now, for instance?'

A long day on the water had left Ertl ravenous for his supper, but he clenched in his stomach to stifle its rumbling and replied, with what he hoped was just the right hint of diffidence, 'Sure. Why not?'

Linking her arm affectionately in his, Leni steered him towards her tent, which stood apart from the rest among some rocks, and produced from inside a plateful of sandwiches and a thermos of drink, saved from afternoon tea. 'There you go – tuck in,' she told him, 'I'll just get myself ready. Won't be a moment.'

When she re-emerged a few mintues later, the sight of her kayaking garb almost took Ertl's breath away. Prinking before him with a radiant smile, she showed off a sleeveless poplin shirt and the briefest of khaki shorts. Her dark hair was caught back becomingly with a leather bootlace. 'Will I do?'

Ertl laughed. 'You'll need something a bit warmer when we get round the icebergs!'

Grinning back at him, she pulled from behind her a duffle bag with extra clothing and what she called emergency rations. 'In case we get shipwrecked,' she breathed coyly.

The last thing Ertl wanted was to be spotted disappearing with her just before bedtime. He scuttled warily to the water's edge, carrying the sack while Leni leaped light-footedly ahead of him from rock to rock. She had good legs, Ertl noticed, 'slim and gazelle-like.' Quickly the few belongings were stowed into the bow of the boat and Leni clambered aboard to squat in front of her tutor.

'Best hold up your paddle, out of the way,' Ertl told her, 'while I get us clear of the bay. We'll be out of sight once we're round the icebergs.' Riml's gaze in particular he sought to avoid, although his friend's heartfelt warning was quickly fading into oblivion as he and Leni slipped between the Umanak floes.

'In order to demonstrate to my pupil and the more easily correct her mistakes, we dispensed with the backrest of the front seat,' Ertl related in his frank memoirs. 'Leni now slid back towards me, sitting as it were on a sledge between my legs, which were operating the steering stirrups. I don't think I have to take sole responsibility for the fact that, on this magical night of Arctic midnight sun, the kayak lesson had to be postponed indefinitely.'[8]

After that, whenever their programme allowed, the pair would slip away in their canoe on private excursions in the surrounding white world, picnicking on icebergs. Sometimes, Leni, in the front of the boat, would manage to bag a duck which they would joint and cook over their primus stove, adding smoked bacon pieces and cream filched from the stores, to enjoy a tasty 'Leipzig mixed grill' on their crystal roof-garden. 'Wearing only climbing boots, we two, like naughty children, romped around a blue-green lake, which the hot July sun had provided on top of the ice, inviting us to splash each other with fresh water to cool down,' Ertl wrote. 'What hours we enjoyed in our dream paradise, freely detached from all worldly cares.'[9]

Sometimes, he said, Leni would suddenly run down to the boat, which for safety's sake they had beached on the ice, to return a few moments later dragging, by its corner, the large awning from their tent. This she spread out carefully beside the sparkling lake, smoothing out all the creases. Then Ertl would take his place on the opposite side of the emerald green water, 'in the proscenium box, that is to say on my rubber mattress' while the erstwhile prima-ballerina, who until her tragic accident eight years before had thrilled the public of the whole of Europe, 'took off her clumsy climbing boots and – for me alone – began slowly to dance.'

Just as well, as he remarked, Ernst Udet did not choose that moment to fly over the spot with his messages and supplies.

Their midsummer nights' dream lasted a week. The two hunted and fished together, inseparable, until Ertl was summoned north to join Fanck's party. Leni, who had sworn after her break-up with Schneeberger never to fall in love again, allows herself to be swallowed by location fever once more, and without a single regret. 'We were both visual creatures who loved nature,' she wrote years afterwards, explaining how 'a casual flirtation turned suddenly into passion.'[10]

The shoot, meanwhile, was not without its difficulties. Some scenes demanded polar bear action, for which Fanck had bought along three fully grown animals from Hamburg Zoo, as well as a couple of Hagenbeck seals. It wasn't that Greenland was deficient in either creature, but the prospect of days spent trailing wild animals across the pack-ice for uncertain results did not appeal to the film-maker. Instead, he pinned his hopes on institutionalised bears, with their keeper in tow. After several weeks cramped in crates, however, the bears were fractious and in no mind to be co-operative. Dr Sorge, one of the scientists, recalled how Leni would try to sweeten their tempers with sugar lumps, only to be caught off guard one day when the biggest animal took a swipe at her with his paw through the bars. Her leggings were ripped to shreds, and only nimble recoil saved her legs from the same fate.[11] The team tried building a bear pit, but 'Tommy', the large bear, was quick to escape and struck out into the open ocean in a desperate bid for freedom. He was recaptured by the boldest of the Eskimo bear-hunters who were working on set, but later he would not be so lucky. A bullet ended Tommy's promising film career when it proved impossible to recage him after his location work was over. The Greenland authorities had been adamant that no alien bears were to be released into the environment for fear of spreading *trichina*, a parasitic worm which could be passed on to humans through imperfectly-cooked meat.

With Fanck installed at Nuliarfik, and the base twenty minutes outside Umanak, Udet was kept busy, when not filming, ferrying messages between the two camps. At neither place could he land, nor any longer touch his sea planes down among the melting floes, so he was obliged to operate from a third base at Ingloswid. (It was becoming a very spread out expedition.) Tossing messages and supplies from one of his planes was easy enough, but picking up letters involved some nifty aerobatics as Udet, with a line and hook, endeavoured to fish up mailbags which ground-based members would suspend from long poles.

The news was not encouraging: neither of the large glacier-mouths was as safe as had been hoped. Huge calvings took place every few days, agitating the fjord and grinding the icebergs against one another, making navigation impossible. The best way for a boat coming in was to risk the lull between these titan birth pangs. Even so, there were twenty-five miles of water to cross.

Back in Umanak, Leni finally got her orders to sail north and join the film team. One of the expedition's two little motor boats was sent to pick her up, along with two of the bears. Gerda Sorge, the scientist's wife, was missing her husband and decided to hitch a ride. The two women knew to expect a more primitive existence from now on. Everyone in the film camp had been crammed into two tents, with fresh water obtainable only by melting snow or chunks of ice, an endless chore given that they had no more than a single cooking stove between them. For some while now, as they waited for more rations to be sailed in, this advance party had been living off an Eskimo diet of gulls and seals.

Leni Riefenstahl and Frau Sorge took refuge in the ship's tiny cabin, an unsavoury hole smelling of sodden wood, rancid oil and bears. The only place to stretch out was clasped together on a plank-bed no wider than an ironing board. One of them had only to loosen her grip a fraction, and both would tumble amid the sardine boxes and petrol drums. Broken pack ice rumbled against the sides of the boat, and it was bitterly cold. When hunger overcame them they raided tins of liver sausage from the stores and brewed tea over a spirit stove. After twenty-four hours at sea they clambered on deck for air, to be entranced by the beauty of the strange fjordland that greeted them, enveloped in a soft blue mist. Oblivious of the cold, they squatted on coils of rope to gaze in wonder.

The pack ice was becoming denser. They could be no more than an hour from Fanck's camp, yet it could have been a continent away, for the boat very soon stuck fast in the ice, where it would have to wait until the currents or conditions forced a fresh channel through. Were that to take more than a few days, they ran the risk of hitting another calving of the glacier. 'That's Greenland for you!' Kraus, the helmsman, remarked with resignation. He had over-wintered with the Wegener expedition and knew all there was to know about biding his time. Leni was more impatient. The shore looked close enough: would the intervening ice bear her weight, she wondered? Supposing she and Gerda were to make a dash for it, could they reach Fanck overland? Gerda was game to give it a try. If they made it, a party could be sent back to help Kraus and Buchholz unload the boat. Goodness knows what could be done about the bears.

The two women scampered across the floes, then hiked for an hour over hills and rocks till they saw the mushroom dome of what could only be Fanck's tent below them. Yodelling a greeting, they charged down the slope into the arms of their surprised colleagues. A subtle change in the weather next day loosened the grip of the pack ice, enabling their little motorboat to sail round and join them. Now the camp boasted fifteen inhabitants and three tents; and the weather, fortunately, held fair.

Leni's first thoughts on reaching the film camp were of seeing her lover once more. Ertl was away on a climbing trip, but with the satisfaction of two first ascents behind him, it would not be long before he came paddling the three hours back in his canoe. Approaching the anchorage, near where his tent stood, his eyes took in the motorboat, the new mess tent, and a great pile of luggage. Clearly, the rearguard had arrived, even though the place seemed deserted. With some irritation, he noticed someone had been to his tent in his absence. The door fastenings were still untied.

Flinging back the flap, Ertl was surprised by a familiar giggle from the interior, and his rancour dissolved in a flash. There sat Leni, lightly clothed and smiling on the bed, inviting him into his own tent. 'In one dive I was beside her, and it was a good thing that I'd stopped for a siesta before paddling over from the other side of the fjord.'

Filming *The White Hell of Piz Palü* on location in the Upper Engaline,
Switzerland, in 1928

Young Leni passes her screen test and appears for the first time in front of
the camera for Arnold Fanck's *The Holy Mountain*, 1925

Fanck (left) with cameraman Hans Schneeberger, the 'Snowflea'

Leni and Snowflea (centre top)
on location for *The Blue Light*, Leni's first attempt at directing a
feature film in the summer of 1931

Leni's lover and
professional rival,
mischief-maker Luis
Trenker, 'The Rebel',
1932

First World War ace
and stunt pilot
Ernst Udet

One for the pot.
Leni bags a duck in
Greenland, 1932

Drama in the fjords –
Arnold Fanck's film
SOS Eisberg, released
in 1933

Going over the plans for the 1934 Nuremberg Rally. Leni Riefenstahl has just failed to persuade Hitler to release her from making a film of the event – the notorious *Triumph of the Will*

Waiting for the Führer to arrive at the Rally from the skies

Leni with lads from the Hitler Youth

While attempting to turn military display into film art at the Nuremberg Rally,
Leni has time for a comforting word for the young.

Leni shares with the Führer a warm reception from the citizens of Nuremberg

Later, in order to create a sense of propriety, he erected her tent close to his and stowed her luggage inside it.

Camerawork on the floes was proving fraught in the warmer air. Ice was collapsing faster than usual, while the water remained bitterly cold. The crew fell in frequently, but the trick was to keep the camera equipment dry. Fanck could see what dangers they were running, and agonised over them, but with almost every scene calling for dramatic iceberg action, there seemed no escape. Either they took chances, or the film was stillborn. For one of his scenes Sepp Rist had to leap from floe to floe in the treacherous water. He has told how, when they arrived in the Rinksfjord, they were astonished by the monstrous size of the bergs detaching themselves from the glacier. These came in a variety of shapes and were soon identified by such names as 'Matterhorn', 'Zeppelin hall', 'the Chalice, 'the Pope' and so forth. Could anyone climb on to one of these colossi, and how dangerous would that be? That was the big question.

From a high moraine overlooking the fjord, Fanck's attention was caught by one very high iceberg, floating far out in the water. He turned to his leading man. 'What do you reckon, Sepp? How does a first ascent on that grab you?'

'Don't get excited,' Rist replied. 'Let's see if I can get to it first.'

A barrier of ice blocks floated offshore, which could be reached by rowing boat. From these Rist began his stepping-stone routine, jumping nimbly from block to block, before any had a chance to roll over. It still left some sixty or more yards of open water between him and his goal. Suddenly, he noticed how, upstream, every so often a block would break free of the barrier and begin floating swiftly towards the iceberg. That was it! He would hitch a ride. The water around the wallowing berg was quite turbulent from the effects of suction, but Rist was a man of iron nerve, and as his floe passed closely under the massive ice walls, he made a gigantic leap and clung to the 50 degree face. Then, slowly, with the aid of ice pegs, he worked his way upwards, to the constant accompaniment of cracking sounds from the immense tensions within the ice:

> Finally I reached the sharp summit. I cast a look over towards the moraine where the cameras stood, then ran along the crest of the berg and began climbing down again. This was much more difficult than coming up. My hands went chalky white and hard with the cold, but my only worry was whether I would make the waterline connection again without falling into the 'stream', as we

optimistically called it. And it did work, exactly according to plan. Fortune again sent a cluster of ice blocks just where I wanted them. I had only to jump and my floes delivered me back to a barrier downstream where these things were collecting.[12]

The row-boat, in turn, delivered him back to shore. 'Good God, Sepp,' Fanck greeted him. 'We were afraid you were going to jump all the way to the North Pole.'

Now it had been proved that man could scale these monsters, the next step was to get cameras on to them. A berg was selected of flattish profile, capable of being mounted straight from the boats. Ignoring the reservations of their Eskimo friends – who Riefenstahl tells us could not be induced to paddle close to any iceberg, even for a score of whales – they anchored their motor boat as close as possible alongside 'the Rasmussen', and everyone began scrambling on to the ice. Film equipment was hauled up with the aid of an ice piton, and steps cut to assist in getting it as high as possible. Rist and Fanck had already reached the top when a series of cracks whipped through the ice, sounding for all the world like a battery of gunfire, and the whole side of the berg nearest the boat sheered off into the fjord. Tremendous water spouts were thrown vertically into the air, and the little craft was tossed wildly backwards between the dancing blocks of ice. Three of its crew – Zogg, Schneeberger and Ertl – were tipped into the freezing foam, along with Angst who had been scrambling ashore at the time and was still belayed by a rope from above. Riefenstahl was one of those stranded on the see-sawing iceberg, and watched appalled and helpless as first one, then another head broke surface only to be swamped again. The four were fighting for dear life, threatened by the lunging blocks, some of which were as big as whole rooms.

Horrified, Leni watched as her 'dear Snowflea' disappeared under the ice. Every time his head emerged from the seething water, the blocks pressed in on him again. He tried bracing himself against them in an effort to hold them apart with his hands, but his strength was visibly failing in the ice-cold water.

There was little the boat could do to bring help, almost submerged as it was, and with the bear cages sliding around wildly on deck. Traut and Rist on the iceberg still had hold of the rope to which Angst was hanging, and it was Angst who proved himself the hero of the hour. Aware that Schneeberger could not swim, Angst threw him the end of the rope, at the same time casting a nervous glance up at the overhanging ice above. If that were to give, both of them would be lost. He yelled for those on the ice to pay out more rope. Then he grabbed hold of Schneeberger, yanking him clear of the blocks. Those in the tossing nutshell boat meanwhile flung planks and ropes to their comrades in the water and were able at length to haul all four aboard. Riefenstahl was in no doubt that Snowflea owed his life to his friend's presence of mind.

Once all were safe, it was a relief to learn that the camera equipment too had come to no harm, having been successfully hauled on to the ice before the incident, well clear of the section which fell away. Only a few ice axes were lost, but the whole crew felt shocked for days afterwards, with little desire to see another iceberg, let alone try to clamber aboard one. Still they had not shot a single foot of iceberg action and the polar summer was already drawing to a close. Soon it would grow too cold to do much. Nights would become nights again, and a dull grey twilight would settle over land and sea. There was no time to lose. A frantic new spirit of determination pervaded the team, compounded with resignation and a justifiable apprehension.

Ernst Sorge has told how, seduced by Greenland's evanescent displays of light, each appearing more magical than the last, Fanck would have his leading man repeat the great leaping sequence time after time in search of the ultimate shot, though everyone else felt it could hardly be surpassed.[13]

'Sepp, what you've got to do,' he would shout, 'is just leap over these first six pans until there are no more, and then take to the water. Swim to the nearest iceberg. It's only about fifty metres.'

If he couldn't make it on to the iceberg, Fanck would instruct poor Rist to slip back into the icy pulp and strike out for the nearest floe to the right. True, it looked dicey, Fanck might concede, could even roll over once he set foot on it. Still, if he did manage to clamber on to it, he could grab a short breather before the next take. 'Then swim back to land in a wide curve to the right.'

To Sorge's mind, the most marvellous aspect of it all was Rist's patience. 'He was never put out or lost his good humour even if the feats had to be repeated ten or twenty times. The only thing he asked for after his icy immersion was something to warm him up inside.' A flask of rum was an indispensable necessity when making these films.

Nor did 'our daring Leni' have any mind to lag behind the men. According to Sorge, someone had only to remark, 'I fancy that the water hereabouts is too cold to bathe,' for her to spring in courageously whether or not the film required it of her. Her constitution could not keep pace with the hardihood to which she subjected herself.

Fascinated as he was by the intricacies of filming, Sorge was becoming fretful about finishing his scientific exploration before they all had to pull out for the winter. He had already ventured north with one of the Eskimo hunters to take measurements on the mighty Umiamako glacier, which could be seen from camp, gleaming in the distance in the midnight sun. Now his 'dearest desire' was to visit the more remote Rink glacier, unexplored unknown ground, the approach to which by water was 'debarred by a fleet of icebergs, and by the walls of the pack-ice', and by land by 'high, wild alpine ranges, with precipitous rocks and deep valleys filled with glaciers.' It was a job for his collapsible *Klepper* kayak. Three attempts to force the ice-choked fjord brought him no nearer than ten miles from the end of the glacier. At the end of July he tried again, this time without an Eskimo escort. He warned Gerda not to worry if she didn't see him for a week, but if there was still no sign on the eighth day to conclude something had gone amiss.

This time he hacked at the ice with his boathook and, when no water could be discovered anywhere, hauled his canoe over the intervening plates of ice, till at last he stood on some yellow rocks beside the snout of his glacier. It was, he was quick to discover, a particularly 'active' glacier. Giant fountains 500 yards or so behind the front were indications that enormous *tranches* of ice-slab were breaking away at a time. This was a dangerous place. As the slab compressed and crumbled in the fjord, the rocks on which Sorge stood quaked with the concussion of ice mass on ice mass.

The scientist in him stood transfixed by the spectacle of such stupendous power. He watched broken masses of glacier ice careen over backwards, slowly somersaulting until that portion of the former front which had been under water, came uppermost, as smooth and polished as if it had been planed. The reverse side reappeared 700 yards down the fjord, much farther from the front than he expected. The movement of these gigantic ice masses threw the fjord water into the wildest turmoil. Bit by bit, with booming and cracking, each ice block broke down into smaller chunks, and twenty vast icebergs would float away from the new glacier wall, driving before them all the ice lying in their way. Enormous tidal waves rushed ahead, scouring the gorge throughout its entire length.

Marvelling at this demonstration of glaciology in action, Sorge forgot his little boat on the beach. When its perilous position suddenly dawned upon him, he hurled himself down the rocky slope to the water's edge. Not only the boat, but the beach itself had gone.

Now was the time for some hard thinking. The nearest settlement was on an island off the coast; nothing could be gained by trying to get out overland. Yet a whole week had still to pass before his wife would raise the alarm. Could he hold out that long? With care, his rations could be stretched for ten days. He thought at first to augment them with fish, only to discover there were none this far up the fjord. 'The only edibles Nature supplied to me were plants,' and only such berries as the grouse and other birds had passed up on.

He was very hungry, and his wife very worried, when Udet and Schneeberger finally spotted his beacon from the air during the second week. But he'd had plenty of time to make his measurements. The front of the Rink glacier, he told his wife excitedly when she and some of the others picked him up by motorboat, rose at least 360 feet above sea level, was the highest such ice cliff in the world, and the fjord was almost 3,500 feet deep. Did she realise the glacier was moving at sixty, sometimes nearly a hundred feet a day? That was 23,000 feet a year, very likely the fastest in the world. In nine years it could reach Nugatsiak. And he related the elemental calving, declaring 'Such a stupendous phenomenon is worth ten collapsibles! We've absolutely got to get it on film.'

'You're never thinking of going back again?' His wife was aghast.

It was up to Fanck, of course, and the Doctor first read Sorge the riot act for going off alone in the first place. Next they held a great party with the Greenlanders from Nugatsiak to celebrate his safe return – and to provide a good scene for the film:

Men, women, children, granfers, all who could mumble their jaws at all, even the blind and the lame took part in the glorious guzzle. The men and women ate separately from each other, but at the long table in the Blockhouse, and all who could find no further room crowded round with their coffee-pots in their hands. We had all our work cut out to provide enough coffee, milk, sugar, knackerbrot, butter and jam; everything disappeared in a twinkling.[14]

With dancing afterwards, the celebrations went on well into the early hours of the next morning, Sepp Rist proving the star of the show, delighting the locals with a spirited clog-dance.

Fanck was greatly tempted at the prospect of capturing the Rink glacier calvings on sound film, but with August upon them, he could put off no longer the work with the polar bears. That had to be safely in the can first. Once more a suitable iceberg was selected, this time in the open sea off Nugatsiak. A lump of seal meat was laid out on the ice and the bear coaxed and poked from his cage. Sepp Rist was landed on the far side of the berg and the photographers took up their positions. It was clear to the bear that no more seal meat was forthcoming, and once Rist began tossing chunks of ice in his direction to provoke a reaction, the animal decided enough was enough and slid off into the sea. He swam for all he was worth back towards Nugatsiak, two motor boats, two rowing boats, ten kayaks and Udet in his plane in hot pursuit. The film operators kept their cameras rolling, to be rewarded when the bear briefly mounted another iceberg with just the shot Fanck had been after: a polar bear atop a shapely crystalline ice-peak and seas dashing against the berg. Indeed, his greatest expectations were exceeded as the berg itself began slowly to waltz in front of the cameras, complete with bear.

At length the bear fell once more into the sea and struck out again for shore. This gave the best of the Eskimo bear hunters the opportunity of paddling up close and roping him in, like a steer. The poor creature was trussed and hoisted into the motorboat, but refused to return to his cage. He was ultimately put on to another iceberg while everyone debated what to do next. Here was his chance: as a sudden squall blew up, the bear made his getaway and disappeared among the white-capped billows.

For poor Tommy there was no real escape. He was spotted next morning on a rocky islet not far offshore, where another short sequence was filmed. Then, there being no further advantage in keeping him once all his scenes were shot, the weary bear was shot in his turn. 'After this mournful execution the motor boat returned to harbour with its flag at half-mast,' Sorge tells us.

Towards the end of August, Sorge, his wife, Fritz Steuri and some Greenlandic helpers were landed with the soundman Zoltan Kegl and thirty hundredweight of gear near the Rink glacier to film and record the cataclysmic calvings. Three weeks later they were picked up again, having successfully completed the mission. Meanwhile, an oppressive air was falling over the expedition. They were so behind with the dramatic shooting that the reluctant decision had already been taken that some of these scenes would be collected in the Alps the following spring. That released them to film only such material as could not be mocked up elsewhere, including some of Riefenstahl's flying sequences in which icebergs featured.

The script called for pilot Hella (Leni) to search for survivors of the missing expedition. She discovers four people on a large table-shaped iceberg and attempts a forced landing upon it, only to crash in the process. Later, she has to abseil from the 'table-top' to be rescued by Eskimos, who have made a raft of kayaks. A suitable tabular berg was earmarked in the Kangerdluk fjord, not six miles from camp. It had steep, broken cliffs, some two hundred feet high, rising vertically out of the water. Zogg and Ertl hacked steps to make it easier for the team to reach the top. An armada of kayaks, some eighty strong belonging to West Greenland's best seal hunters, assembled around the berg for the big scene and Udet, with a cameraman aboard, passed repeatedly overhead collecting unrepeatable aerials. Then, without warning, a sinister booming indicated the berg had been hit below the waterline by another. Soon it was oscillating wildly, creating panic among its passengers, several of whom skidded down the steep slopes into the water, to be fished out later.

Fanck, the fanatic, insisted on trying the sequence again with another iceberg. This one disintegrated, nearly drowning Ertl who was weighed down by his heavy climbing gear. Leni, exhausted and soaked to the skin, had to be scooped up, with others, from a ledge just above the troubled waters.

These icy immersions were taking their toll. Soon she was complaining of serious pains in the kidney area and running an alarming fever. She could not stop shivering. It was so unlike her to be sick. Their Danish doctor was at his wit's end, having nothing to give her that helped at all. Udet was still needed for filming, but his young assistant pilot, Franz Schriek, volunteered to fly Leni to Umanak, where a small children's hospital might be persuaded to care for her.

She would remember a beautiful moss-green sky, which turned in quick succession to yellow, then violet. It presaged a storm, and by the time they came in to land, or rather to touch down in the bay, conditions were so bad and the threat of damage to the plane's floats in the sea-swell so real, that they were obliged to fly back to Nugatsiak.

The patient remained in near-delirium. There was nothing for it but to wrap her in blankets and try again – this time by motor boat. Her pain grew worse by the hour, and there was little comfort in a wildly swinging ship's hammock. Somehow the twenty-four hours were endured and, after nearly three months of living under canvas, Leni spent her first night in a bed with a roof over her head.

Everyone was very kind, but her cystitis failed to respond to treatment. The lady doctor explained – as best she could without a shared language – that Leni ought to leave Greenland when the next ship called in two weeks' time. It was imperative to get treatment from a larger hospital: her illness could only get worse here in this climate.

Two weeks! No time at all. 'What will become of me, and what of the film if I must return to Europe?' Leni agonised. 'The picture is ruined if I cannot do any more filming.'[15]

Her mind went back a couple of years to when director Fanck had forced himself up Mont Blanc while suffering from a bad bout of 'flu, so as not to endanger the film, and it became clear that she should do likewise. Allowing herself to be muffled in blankets, she once more sailed back up the fjord to rejoin the others.

For her last fortnight in Greenland Leni moved from the tent Ertl had set up for her to a room in the Overseer's house. Now, sick or not, she would attempt her aerial shots. Ertl, still her willing slave, collected poppy seeds and camomile to brew herbal teas for her, and with grim doggedness Leni dragged herself out day after day for the shooting. Ertl would write afterwards that it was heartbreaking 'suddenly to see such a life-loving, merry person, who one had taken to one's heart, suffer in this way, without really being able to help.'[16]

For the flying sequences where Hella is scouring the floes for her husband, it was decided that Udet should crouch behind her at the dual controls, doing the necessary and ducking out of camera shot. In this manner they swooped through narrow gaps, banking steeply to accommodate the wing-span – like 'crazy lightning', Riefenstahl would describe it – weaving in and out and over skyscraping towers of ice so that her heart and breath almost failed her. Finally, the crowning, most crucial shot of all, demanded the aircraft smash into an ice wall and she jump clear just as it bursts into flames. Even Udet was nervous at the prospect of this stunt. And reasonably so, since he had to stay with the blazing craft until the cameras had tracked Leni's plunge into the water, by which time he should be well out of shot.

This scene, too, was secured without damage to anything but Udet's famous little Tiger Moth, which ended its days in charred pieces in the deep fjord water. Or so Riefenstahl tells us. Her interpretation is echoed by Ertl's, and the film too bears this out, although the manner of obtaining the component shots is rather differently accounted for in Sorge's book. Explaining that all the Moth shots had to be obtained in a single flight since the plane could take off, but not land on the rocky Greenland terrain, Sorge goes on to describe how Udet brought the plane down in the middle of floating ice-pack. 'Beyond hope of salving, the machine drifted on the current out to the open sea and slowly sank, together with her pilot.'

That makes it sound as if Udet drowned. Which he didn't, happily, though he contracted a terrible cold from his dunking. Sorge's book includes photographs of the plane drowning amid the ice fragments, Udet clinging first to its wings, then the fuselage in his efforts to stay clear of the icy water.

Schriek then disposed of the 'last water plane' in a fine bit of stunting, Sorge tells us. Making for a towering iceberg, he grazed its walls as he came down on the sea. 'The machine burst into flames and Schriek only managed to save himself by springing overboard and swimming off.'

Sorge proves a confusing witness. Having, in one chapter, thus written off the last seaplane – Udet had brought two float aircraft, a BFW and a Klemm – in the next one Sorge tells of a further risky flight with another 'last plane' (presumably the one flying machine not at the bottom of the fjord was subsequently repaired). Udet was in the water with the two motorboats and thirty kayaks when a two million ton berg split in two, throwing up massive waves. He took off at once amid the welter of shattered ice, only to be caught by the great 'foot' of the iceberg as it turned turtle. Fortunately, the plane skidded back into the water without damage and was able to take off once more and circle over the oscillating mass. Marvellous pictures were once more obtained by sheer chance.

On her last day with the crew, Leni was again required to board an iceberg, but the shot could not be finished before they were rammed by a larger berg. 'In our flight,' she writes, 'Snowflea trips and quite unnecessarily breaks his foot.'[17]

Once back on dry land she packed her belongings in great haste, for there was less than an hour before their boat had to leave to get her to the freighter on time.

> I am scarcely conscious. Only as my iron box is put aboard the little motor boat and I sit on a mountain of empty petrol drums, wrapped in thick blankets, does it sink in that this is goodbye. Each person squeezes my hand and passes on greetings for me to take back to Germany. They all stand on the shore. In the grey twilight I can still make out the faces of my comrades. What am I doing squatting here alone on these barrels? Why are the others waving? Truly, truly I have not grasped it, but when Angst gives a solemn three-gun salute with the hunting rifle, I begin to weep – to weep

as I have not done for years, unable to stop. Swimming in a haze of tears, the shore recedes ever further . . .[18]

Sitting on the wobbling drums, freezing in spite of her blankets and suit of dogskin, she watched the first stars come out. After months of midnight sun, this was the first real night. Only a blood-red streak lit the horizon as, like spectres, the icebergs floated by, holding out arms towards her as if beckoning her back. Would she ever see Greenland again?

VIII

Burning Questions

'The magic of Greenland is like an unending veil,' Riefenstahl had written soon after location filming came to an end, 'binding us with thousands of invisible silk threads.' In Greenland's pure wastes the trappings of modern life had seemed superfluous ballast, incapable of making anyone happier. There, too, in a land of different values, gentler pace, the besetting problems of Europe appeared so remote as to be almost incomprehensible. Back in Berlin, everyday time and reality were rudely restored – and with interest.

In the July Reichstag elections, in that troubled year of 1932, the Nazis polled almost fourteen million votes (37 per cent) and won 230 out of 608 seats in the Reichstag, almost a hundred more than their nearest rivals, the Social Democrats. It was still not an overall majority. The Nazi leader, Adolf Hitler, found himself the most powerful man in German politics yet unable to negotiate his way into the chancellorship, an appointment constitutionally made by the German President, and not requiring Reichstag approval. The President, Field Marshal von Hindenburg, chose Franz von Papen, nominally a member of the Catholic Central Party, an aristocrat of some charm but little political experience, with whom Hitler steadfastly refused to co-operate. In the ensuing squabbles, Hitler lost some ground and earned a humiliating and well-publicised censure from the President for his intemperate threat to mow down the Marxists.[1] His storm-troopers, the SA, were almost beyond control, pillaging, intimidating and murdering at will, mostly in skirmishes with the Communists. (Earlier in the year the force had been temporarily banned.) In August Hitler faced the dilemma whether or not to intervene on behalf of five SA Nazis, who were sentenced to death for brutally beating to death a Communist miner. He could not risk antagonising his militia

99

– there were already rifts developing between him and some of its factions – yet he was well aware that by its continued excesses he risked losing the support of industrialists and businessmen, to say nothing of a wider electorate and the more moderate among his own Party members.

That autumn Riefenstahl returned to a strife-torn nation with perhaps as many as eight million people out of work and the prospect of a bleak winter ahead.[2] Little wonder that Greenland seemed such an enviable, if distant paradise. But, from here on, her continued protestations of a disinterest in politics ring hollow. By her own admission, she was fascinated by the person and presence of Hitler. A well-thumbed copy of *Mein Kampf* had accompanied her throughout the Arctic trip to be peppered with marginal comments. It was 'never out of her hands,' Sorge had commented, declaring her openly in agreement with most of its conclusions – though she has another tale to tell about the remarks she had written in Hitler's book. 'She found a visible means of expressing her great admiration for Hitler by hanging up his picture, framed in sealskin', both in her tent and then in her new quarters in the Overseer's house.[3]

Being dazzled by the man led naturally enough to a curiosity about his beliefs. It is impossible to imagine it not extending also to the Machiavellian political powerplay in which he was now enmeshed. Certainly, almost as soon as she set foot on native soil, Leni contacted Hitler's aides by telephone and arranged to take tea with the Führer that afternoon to apprise him of her Greenland experiences. It is no coincidence that this happened also to be the day he was to address another of his Berlin Sports Palace rallies. In due course she found herself whisked along in the official party to hear him speak.

Her memoirs recall little of the performance itself beyond the Führer's 'demonic' appearance as he swore to create a new Germany and put an end to unemployment and poverty. Otherwise, the effect was similar to the earlier rally she attended, his words seeming 'to lash the spectators.' She felt scourged herself by his injunction that collective good must take precedence over individual good. 'You are nothing. Your *Volk* is everything!' he reiterated. Riefenstahl's whole life had been spent in perfecting the art of bending events to her own will. Besides a strong sense of self, she had an enviable independence; and, for the first time, Hitler's words stirred in her a sense of shame at such personal egocentricity.

The Führer's wilful ability to stir the emotions of a crowd in the manner of a super-evangelist could produce instant conversions

– as at revival meetings – but with what permanence? For Leni, the magic hold relaxed as the words faded. Her only thought at the end of the tirade was to get home as fast as possible. She was not cut out for collectivism. Not yet, at least.

In hindsight, she supposed this to have been an almost instinctive flight from danger, as well it may have been, but her instincts were confused. When the next day brought an invitation to the home of Joseph and Magda Goebbels, all her misgivings seem to have evaporated. The opportunity of mixing in such influential company was too attractive to pass up. It turned out to be quite a party, one of the regular gatherings Frau Goebbels hosted when Hitler needed to relax. He was among the forty or so guests, chatting animatedly with a young musical comedy actress, Gretl Slezak – as too was Hermann Goering. The future Reichmarshal had been a colleague of Udet's in the First World War[4] and was eager to hear from Riefenstahl all about her flying adventures with him in Greenland.

As she was about to leave, Hitler suggested bringing his long-time friend and personal photographer to Leni's apartment the following day. According to her memoirs, he specially wanted Heinrich Hoffmann to see *The Blue Light* stills. They arrived accompanied by Dr Goebbels and 'Putzi' Hanfstaengl, a well-connected cosmopolitan playboy and early benefactor of the Party, who had become one of Hitler's closest cronies. Hanfstaengl, a giant of a man with what has been described as a 'curiously-shaped head',[5] had been educated at Harvard and was known more for his sardonic humour than his sagacity. He was also a virtuoso on the piano. Later, when the National Socialists came to power, he would be appointed first foreign press secretary until he fell from favour and fled the Fatherland in 1937. Hanfstaengl, who died in 1975, has left an amusing account of the visit:

> Riefenstahl was a very vital and attractive woman and had little difficulty in persuading the Goebbels and Hitler to go to her studio after dinner. I was carried along and found it full of mirrors and trick interior decorator effects, but what one would expect, not bad. There was a piano there, so that got rid of me, and the Goebbels, who wanted to leave the field free, leant on it, chatting. This isolated Hitler, who got into a panic. Out of the corner of my eye I could see Hitler ostentatiously studying the titles in the bookcases. Riefenstahl was certainly giving him the works. Every time he straightened up or looked round, there she was dancing to

101

my music at his elbow, a real summer sale of feminine advance. I had to grin myself. I caught the Goebbels' eyes, as if to say, 'If the Riefenstahl can't manage this, no one can and we might as well leave.' So we made our excuses, leaving them alone.[6]

Photographer Hoffmann, one notices, has vanished from Hanfstaengl's account, but he does record that a few days later a raised eyebrow in Riefenstahl's direction elicited merely a hopeless shrug. Her summer sale had failed to tempt the customer.

Riefenstahl's account of the evening in her apartment speaks of discomfort at seeing Hitler glancing through her copy of *Mein Kampf*, which he found lying on her desk:

I had jotted such comments in the margins as 'Untrue ... Wrong ... Mistaken', though sometimes I'd put 'Good'. I didn't like Hitler reading these marginalia, but he seemed amused. He took hold of the book, sat down, and kept leafing through it. 'This is interesting,' he said. 'You're a sharp critic, but then we're dealing with an artist.'[7]

Years later, shortly before the outbreak of war, Riefenstahl says that Hitler embarrassed her by recalling the incident in public among a large group of artists, musicians and stage and screen performers at a function in the Reich Chancellery. She arrived rather late, she says, and was alarmed to hear him telling a cluster of people around him of the critical comments he had found in her copy of *Mein Kampf*:

I wanted the ground to swallow me up, especially when he described our first meeting on the coast of the North Sea, where I had told him I could never join the Nazi Party. He recited it all as if he were on stage, imitating our dialogue like an actor; yet when my presence was noticed, I was swamped in embraces from my colleagues.

★

Hitler and Reifenstahl met twice more in 1932, first in November, two days after another election had lost Hitler more than two million votes, along with 34 seats. Though Riefenstahl would not have known this, it was also only a week to the day since his mistress, Eva Braun, made her first suicide attempt, jealous of the attention Hitler was devoting to politics and the company of other attractive women. Goebbels escorted Leni to a Munich restaurant, where Hitler already sat at table with a group of his closest supporters. Expecting to find him downcast, she was amazed by his confidence and optimism as she watched him injecting new courage into his flagging companions. Others have written of this period as one of deep despair for Hitler, how more than once he threatened to take his own life, but Riefenstahl came away with the impression that he resolutely refused to see his set-back as anything but temporary.

The coming month, however, brought deep divisions within the Nazi movement, in particular a stand-off between Hitler and Gregor Strasser, the leader of a radical anti-capitalist wing and probably the next strongest and most popular man in the Party after the Führer. Strasser was advocating a coalition with General von Schleicher, who had become the latest (and last) Chancellor of the Weimar Republic; and if not that, a 'toleration' of the Schleicher Cabinet. Schleicher, sensing the opportunity to divide the Nazis, made Strasser an offer of the posts of Vice Chancellor of Germany and Minister-President of Prussia, with a portfolio to deal with unemployment. This, although attractive, Strasser declined, but he let it be known in the Party that he intended putting up his own list in a future election. Whipped to white heat by the strenuous antagonism of Goebbels and Goering towards Strasser, Hitler finally provoked a showdown on 7th December. In one of his famous frenzied rages he accused Strasser of stabbing him in the back and trying to destroy the Nazi movement. His ears were deaf to Strasser's protestations that, as always, he had only the Party's best interests at heart.

With some dignity, Strasser picked up his briefcase and left, returning to his quarters in the Hotel Excelsior long enough only to write an impassioned letter of resignation to his Führer. Out spilled grievances old and new as he prophesied that Hitler's persistently wayward management of events could bring only catastrophe. Strasser then left Berlin, rounded up his family from Munich and disappeared to Italy on vacation.

The bombshell of a letter reached Hitler on the 8th, and by that evening the story was front-page news. Leni, returning from a concert, saw the screaming headlines – GREGOR STRASSER LEAVES HITLER, HITLER'S STAR FALLS, NAZI PARTY FINISHED. She bought copies of all the newspapers, and (it is hard to believe by chance) stepped into the lobby of the Hotel Kaiserhof to read them. This was Hitler's Berlin headquarters, and it is small wonder she was soon discovered there by Brückner, the leader's adjutant. Within minutes, though it was past midnight, she was being ushered into Hitler's suite where, in some agitation, the Führer was pacing backwards and forwards.

He shook hands abstractedly, muttering more to himself than to her that, if the Party crumbled, there would be no alternative but to put an end to his life.[8]

Here Riefenstahl's recollections mirror – or, one is tempted to say, maybe were prompted by – those of Joseph Goebbels, whose published diary entry for that day reads:

> Treason! Treason! Treason! . . . For hours the Führer paces up and down in the hotel room. He is embittered and deeply wounded by this treachery. Finally he stops and says: 'If the party should fall to pieces, I'll put an end to things in three minutes with a pistol.'[9]

In old age, Riefenstahl professed to remain baffled why Hitler had 'sent' for her that day. She had been required to do no more than listen while he soliloquised in an effort to calm his inner turmoil. Then, catching sight of her as if for the first time, he merely pressed her hand and thanked her politely for coming. She had barely uttered a word. Maybe Hitler did send for her, on learning of her proximity, though it is more likely that his distraught aide was clutching at straws when he spotted the film-maker in the lobby, hoping against hope that she could divert the Führer from his self-destructive passion.

The day following her visit, Hitler mustered his Party leaders and Gauleiters for an emotional denunciation of Strasser and his treachery. The break in his voice and his theatrical sobs had the desired effect on those assembled, who, in Goebbels' words, 'burst into a spontaneous ovation for the leader. All shake hands with him, promising to carry on until the very end and not to renounce the Great Idea, come what may.'[10] With chilling finality this man, who was indubitably one of the chief conspirators in the whole affair, added, 'Strasser is a dead man.'

Strasser, too, knew he was marked by death, telling a friend as much that same evening, and warning, 'Germany is in the hands of an Austrian, who is a congenital liar; a former officer, who is a pervert; and a club-foot. And, I tell you this for nothing, the last is the worst of them all. He is Satan in human form.'[11]

Strasser's club-footed devil incarnate – Doctor Goebbels – had his hands full. In those days he was responsible for trying to hold together Party morale and finances, managing its campaign, underpinning a despondent leader, as well as fulfilling his new role as Chief of People's Education. To this was added the worry of his wife being taken seriously ill. Yet in the ensuing weeks he found time to chance his arm with Leni Riefenstahl.

For six whole years he had worshipped her, he told her. He had been there in the crowds outside the UFA Palast for the première of her first film, *Der Heilige Berg*, straining to catch a glimpse of her. Now she must be his mistress; he needed her, had earned her indeed, earned solace in these days of travail. In vain, she protested disinterest as he besieged her with visits and phone calls. Riefenstahl has given a colourful account of one thwarted overture just before Christmas, when Goebbels begged her yet again to have an affair with him.[12]

'Without you my life is torment!' the bantam Doctor tells her, sinking to his knees and beginning to sob. But when he grabs her ankles, it is too much for Riefenstahl and she orders him to leave, demanding, what kind of a man was he – with a wonderful wife, and a darling child. What in the world was he playing at?

Oh, of course he loves his wife, her grovelling suitor chirrups, and his child. It is just that he loves her too, madly, passionately, and will do anything to gain her affection.

'Get out! Get out!' Leni claims to have screamed at him, opening the apartment door and pressing the bell for the lift. 'You are quite mad!'

With hanging head and averted eyes, the future Minister of Propaganda slinks away, never, she adds, to forget or forgive her for the humiliation.

There is something in her telling of this story which recalls Riefenstahl's version of the Fanck-Trenker confrontation at the start of her film career, and it is not hard to see parallels in most of her descriptions of emotional encounters in her memoirs, *The Sieve of Time*. Riefenstahl makes a point of highlighting her ability to recall conversations verbatim, with particular reference to Hitler and the important members of his entourage. Actually, she relates them as scenes from a silent movie – with over-exaggerated actions to convey emotion and the dialogue between characters. People beat their chests and heads with fists, fling wide their arms, are shaken by sobs. It is not surprising that her memory codifies material in this way. This was the medium of her brilliance, after all, and even when in her career she progressed to making sound films, sound was very much part of the overall composition, rather than a means of dynamic communication.

The remaining days before Christmas were spent completing a book about her location adventures, *Kampf in Schnee und Eis*.[13] This was the first time she had written for publication, although Arnold Fanck regularly produced illustrated books of their film shoots, as he intended also for *SOS Eisberg!*. Sorge, too, was compiling his personal account of the Greenland trip, though it is not clear whether Riefenstahl would have known as much at the time. The suggestion that she should pen her own side of the film-making story came from her friend Manfred George at the Berlin evening newspaper ·*Tempo*. He wanted to serialise the story in his paper; and this must have been one of the last editorial decisions of his reign; by the time the book was published, the Nazis were in power and George had fled to Prague.

The *Eisberg* shoot was of course as yet unfinished. Besides realising those scenes which had to be postponed through her hasty departure from the ice-cap, work was required on the American version of the film, for which – in close up and talking sequences – she had a different 'husband', Rod La Roque. Elaborate ice sets were being prepared in the Bernina, where filming was expected to resume within a few weeks and continue until late spring or early summer. Leni intended to fill in the time until she was required on location with winter sports holidays in St Anton and Davos, glad of the opportunity to escape from Berlin for a while with all its dangerous liaisons. Before long, the sun and snow and a carefree atmosphere reclaimed her. She formed an amorous attachment with a handsome Swiss ski champion, Walter Prager, whom she had first met on the set of *White Frenzy* in the Arlberg, and who was a climbing partner of Ertl's. She and Prager remained together for a couple of years, she tells us, and in her memoirs idly wonders why all the romances which meant anything to her in life were with modest, easygoing and fun-loving men, rather than those who were 'socially, politically or artistically prominent.' Men of dangerous ambition in other words. Her poor mother felt that Leni's talents should have landed her anyone she fancied, any intelligent man of standing to shower her with gifts, and could never understand her daughter's simple tastes.

In Davos, on the last but one day of January 1933, news came through that Hitler had finally realised his ambition to become Chancellor of Germany. The first day of his promised Thousand-year Reich had begun.

★

It was June before, with her filming commitments finished, Riefenstahl tells us she was free to return to Berlin, a very different city from the one she had left. After the Reichstag fire at the end of February (blamed on the Communists, but quite possibly orchestrated by the

Nazis), new elections on 5th March had given Hitler an increased number of seats in government; coalition with the Conservative Nationalists brought a slight majority, though not the two-thirds necessary to amend the constitution. Notwithstanding, on 23rd March he forced through an Enabling Act which freed him from the restraints of both Reichstag and the presidency. Now, he could write his own laws. As the historian Alan Bullock remarked in his splendid *Hitler, a Study in Tyranny*, 'The street gangs had seized control of the resources of a great modern State, the gutter had come to power.'[14] Democracy was dead.

Up in the Bernina, and later the Bernese Alps, only sporadic news from Germany had reached Riefenstahl. She has claimed no contemporary knowledge of the May book burnings in Unter den Linden opposite the University of Berlin, nor of the first Jewish purges, and the shock on arriving home to find the execrable Dr Goebbels installed as Reichsminister of Popular Enlightenment and Propaganda, with a brief to ram German culture into the Nazi straightjacket, was bitter indeed. Art, literature, films even – no! films especially – were to be strictly controlled in what the Führer described as 'a systematic campaign to restore the nation's moral health.' Riefenstahl was horrified to learn how many artists, from theatre and films as well as writers, musicians and painters, had fled the country; Jewish talent in particular, but not exclusively. Besides Manfred George, other friends to vanish, she now learned, included Béla Balàzs and Harry Sokal (the latter without handing over her share of *The Blue Light* profits) and the master film and theatre producer of Berlin's Golden Era, Max Reinhardt, who had launched so many performing careers (including Riefenstahl's own). They were joined by stars of the calibre of Lotte Lehman, Conrad Veidt, Oscar Homolka, Richard Tauber, Lilli Palmer and many more. Writers who fled included Thomas and Heinrich Mann, Stephan and Arnold Zweig, Berthold Brecht, Franz Werfel, Erich Maria Remarque, and Vicki Baum.

Here was a draining of the life blood of popular culture, not a moral resuscitation. She could not help but broach the subject a few weeks later, she says, when she was summoned to the Reich Chancellery, once more to take tea with Hitler. The Führer checked her flow of words, telling her sharply that he had no intention of discussing the Jewish question with her, now or ever. On no account was she to raise it again. His manner then softened as he began outlining why he had sent for her. He had exciting news; truly, it was the most brilliant idea: she should assist Dr Goebbels in his supervision of the cinema industry. 'He has no experience in the area of films, and I immediately thought of you. You could be in charge of the artistic aspect.'[15]

Riefenstahl was appalled. Of course she and 'the Goebbels' could never work together . . . but she could not tell the Führer that. Nor why. Any more than she dared bring up again her absolute opposition to the whole concept of creative control, with its attendant hounding out of Jewish and Communist artists. At last she managed to stammer her apologies, 'Really, my Führer, forgive me, I do not have the ability for such a task . . . I don't think I could make a success of something I do not have a feel for . . .'

She expected him to be angry, or at least to seek to change her mind. But he seemed calm, proposing instead that she should make films for him. A film about Horst Wessel, perhaps, or something else illustrating the movement? Wessel, a rather unsavoury Brownshirt thug, had supposedly been killed for the cause (though it may have been an underworld score-settling), and subsequently was elevated to martyr status as an inspiration to the Hitler Youth. To make a film of him seemed scarcely any better than working in concert with the devilish Propaganda Minister.

'I can't, I can't . . .' Riefenstahl tells us she protested weakly, to be dismissed in short order. Hitler was clearly disappointed by her lack of enthusiasm.

★

Riefenstahl supplies no dates for her first meetings with Hitler and Goebbels after they came to power. By disclaiming knowledge of the book burnings in May and saying she had been away from Berlin for six months, the impression is given that these encounters could not have taken place before June at the earliest. Such an interpretation is challenged, however, by references in Goebbels' source material emerging now that access has been gained to East German and Russian archives. The Institute for Contemporary History in Munich has been bringing out Collected Fragments from Goebbels' Diaries since 1987,[16] in which he refers to several meetings with that 'clever thing', Leni Riefenstahl, during the time she was supposed to be tucked away in the Swiss Alps, besides pointing to a much later disintegration of the working relationship between them than she has always inferred. Only one week after the book burning, on 17th May, Goebbels mentions meeting Riefenstahl to hear of her film plans. 'I put the proposal to her that she should make a film about Hitler,' he says, adding, 'she is very enthusiastic about the idea.' That evening Riefenstahl accompanies Goebbels and his wife Magda on a trip to the Berlin theatre. By 12th June, the Propaganda Minister was noting – 'She alone of all the stars understands us.'

IX

Into the Whirlpool

Despite the overriding air of despondency which followed
Germany's defeat in the First World War and resentment over
the swingeing reparations demanded by the Allies, it is inconceivable
that Hitler could have risen to power without his symbiotic
attachment to Joseph Goebbels. Of Hitler and his dark muddled
fancies, Goebbels fashioned the myth of a brooding, omniscient
saviour in whom not only the German *Volk* but Hitler, and even
Goebbels himself, came to believe. Without such a definition of
purpose, Goebbels would probably never have risen beyond a bright
career in journalism, films or political oratory. As it was, 'two highly
schizophrenic individuals', as historians have observed, secured
'unlimited power over a nation which, under pressure of catastrophic
events, had itself become schizophrenic.'[1]

Goebbels held a doctorate in Philosophy and, like Hitler, was
burdened with a ragbag of complexes and grievances. From Rheydt
on the Rhine, he was the loved youngest son of pleasant, well-
meaning *petit bourgeois* parents, though his childhood was marred by a
disfigured limb which left him with a permanent limp and frail
appearance. More than that, it created in him the sense of being an
outsider. His frustration at being unable to join in normal boisterous
activities of boyhood was translated into cynicism and a contempt for
his fellow man. He was physically weedy, with an adult height of little
over five feet, but he had a good voice, large expressive eyes and
considerable personal magnetism. By all accounts he knew when to
turn on the charm and was attractive to women. He was highly
intelligent – and easily suggestible. At university in Munich, he had
been acolyte to the Marxist nihilist, Richard Flisges, and having once
transferred his allegiance to the NSDAP worked closely with Gregor

Strasser's Bavarian social radicals against central party organisation before contracting his final and fatal alliance with Hitler in 1926. They completed one another's dreams. Goebbels worshipped the Führer he largely created, yet despite Nazi doctrine and his own propaganda, he never completely shook off grudging admiration for the teachings and person of Christ.

When Hitler secured power at the end of January 1933, he wasted no time implementing his *Gleichschaltung,* or unification of the Reich, in which every aspect of life was meant to conform to the Nazi perspective. (The word itself means bringing into the same gear.) The appointment of Dr Goebbels as Reichsminister for Public Enlightenment and Propaganda on 13th March represented the first stage in ensuring that the public was fed only that material the Party felt safe for its consumption. It gave the Doctor effective jurisdiction over all forms of public expression – all news services, press and radio, film and theatre, literature, music, cabaret, light entertainment (the circus, even), the graphic arts, as well as exhibitions, advertising and sporting contacts abroad – everything, in fact, by which Nazi influence might conceivably be spread. However, Hitler never granted power, without at the same time diffusing it. The boundaries between Goebbels' empire and those of the Reich press supremos Amman and Dietrich, and the ideologue Alfred Rosenberg, were never well defined.

Neither Hitler nor Goebbels were under any illusions about the formidable power of film when it came to influencing public opinion. Both indeed were cinema lovers – they had gone together to see the First World War submarine movie *Morgenrot* two days after Hitler became Reich Chancellor. Hitler viewed films for relaxation; it is said his personal projectionist screened at least one for him most evenings in the Reich Chancellery, and these often included films banned from general release. He liked Marlene Dietrich – but his preference was for musicals and such fantasies as *King Kong* and *Mickey Mouse.* Goebbels leant more towards 'art films' and epics. He was well read, with cultivated tastes, and for years had almost obsessively followed the latest trends in cinema and theatre. He, too, had a private screening room in all his residences. Garbo was one of his favourites. As a young man his dreams revolved around becoming a playwright himself, and his continuing wide circle of friends in the performing arts reflected a psychological need to maintain contact with this particular branch of cultural creativity. It is said he nurtured the hope of one day writing a treatise on films, a standard work which would have the same importance for the film as Friedrich Lessing's book has for the theatre.[2]

Two weeks after his appointment as Minister, Goebbels called representatives of the German film industry together for a meeting at the Hotel Kaiserhof to outline the new role of cinema in a National Socialist state. He knew he must tread eggshells, for nothing short of a complete metamorphosis was planned, and he was going to need co-operation from within to effect it. The Nazis had been quick to recognise this as a Jewish-dominated industry – in Germany, as in Hollywood – a truth which of course had not escaped a jittery industry either. Official estimates (doubtless exaggerated) suggested that some 90 per cent of all German films were distributed by Jews, as many as 86 per cent turned out by Jewish producers, and 70 per cent of scriptwriters were also believed to be Jewish. Everyone knew such a state of affairs would not be tolerated for long.[3]

At the Kaiserhof, Goebbels was at his most charming, taking pains to emphasise his own passionate devotion to cinematic art, and his belief that German films were on the brink of a new and great era. Those assembled were told that the cinema had a special cultural mission within the new order; and in an endeavour to allay understandable fears over restrictions this might bring to artistic freedom, Goebbels singled out four films of recent years as glowing examples of their particular genres.

The first, in a somewhat surprising selection, was Eisenstein's revolutionary *Battleship Potemkin* (1925), a film celebrating a historic Marxist revolt, and one which Goebbels now informed his bemused audience was 'marvellously well made,' revealing 'incomparable cinematic artistry':

> This is a film which could turn anyone with no firm ideological convictions into a Bolshevik. Which means that a work of art can very well accommodate a political alignment, and that even the most obnoxious attitude can be communicated if it is expressed through the medium of an outstanding work of art.[4]

Film-makers were to infer that the Nazi struggle could be glorified in similar fashion. In praising this, and Greta Garbo's performance as Anna Karenina in *Love* (1927), and to a certain extent also Fritz Lang's *Die Nibelungen* (1924) – 'an epic film, not of our time, and yet so modern, so contemporary, so topical' – Goebbels was not only indicating the broad divergence of films which the Reich were prepared to accommodate, but cannily underpinning his assertion that he understood what serious cinema was all about. He wanted the company lulled into the belief that he was one of them, on their side in all this.

Paying tribute to Fritz Lang, the Propaganda Minister made no mention of Lang's recently-completed film *The Testament of Dr Mabuse* (late 1932), with its chilling portrayal of a mad scientist who plans to conquer the world, and whose hypnotic powers extend even beyond death. The story carried allusions to the terror tactics of the Brownshirts, but critics have doubted whether the German public would have grasped the parallel. Dr Goebbels had no such difficulty, for he banned the film before it could be released in Germany.

His final commendation, Luis Trenker's *Das Rebell* (*The Rebel*, 1932) was perhaps the most predictable of the four, since it was known to be a favourite of the Führer's. The allegory offered in this film was acceptable, relating as it did a Tyrolean peasant uprising against the Napoleonic army of occupation in 1809. Trenker himself played the patriot leader 'Severin Anderian' (with echoes of Andreas Hofer), who although captured and killed, rises in spirit in a visionary concluding sequence to lead his marching forces in their continuing struggle. This image, so guaranteed to stir, was purloined a number of times in later films of the Nazi epoch.[5]

Hitler and Goebbels had seen *The Rebel* together on 18th January, the day after its Berlin opening at the UFA Palast am Zoo and only a fortnight before the Nazis came to power. Both were strongly impressed. Hitler later told Trenker that he had watched the film four times 'and each time with new enthusiasm.' Goebbels praised its 'grand mass-scenes, composed with enormous vital energy.'

Trenker affected surprise at the reception given to the film in Germany. 'The public became wilder with each new stone avalanche,' he said, 'clapping and stomping without inhibitions. I sat rigidly and helplessly next to Paul Kohner and could not understand – and yet I understood.' Only then, he claimed, did it dawn on him 'how clearly Hitler had fanaticised the masses.'[6]

Originally, when he proposed the film as a co-production with Deutsche-Universal's parent company in Hollywood as one of a sixteen-film deal, he had to work hard to persuade Carl Laemmle, Universal's president, that this was not so much an obscure chapter of Tyrolean history as a universal cry for freedom. The largely enthusiastic reception given to the American version upon its release in July that year, proved his point. With a cause and a good script,

Trenker had pushed the *Bergfilme* into new dimensions. The film critic of the *New York Times* was captivated:

> Action and physical movement, troops defiling down long winding roads, midnight alarums in sleepy mountain towns, the thrill of the manhunt along broken ridges and up past the snow line, the excitement of bodies tumbling into space or rolling over and over down rocky slopes – these are the materials in which it deals.

'Kauf', writing for *Variety*, agreed the photography and scenery were beautiful, and Trenker's performance stood out, but the dialogue 'hurt', falling short of the standard of American 'talkies' – too much of it and too many accents – and with anti-Hitler feeling running high in the United States, as indeed elsewhere in Europe, he doubted the film would reap financial reward. France would surely not take it without radical changes.

Goebbels came away from his Kaiserhof meeting, pleased with the way things had gone.[7] In his diary that evening, he noted, 'I gain the impression that all present are honestly willing to co-operate.' He was quick to follow this up with overtures to both Lang and Trenker. Lang pointed out to the Propaganda Minister that with Jewish ancestry on his mother's side he had reasonably assumed there was no place for him in the reborn German film industry. Oh, that could be overlooked, Goebbels reassured him, in light of his service during the Great War. But *Gleichschaltung* held no attractions for the independently-minded director and, ignoring the barracuda smile, Lang quickly left Germany for France and later Hollywood. It was a decision he never regretted, he said in a 1945 interview: 'I give up my fortune, my fine collection of books and paintings. I must begin over again. It is not easy. But, yes, it was good. I was arrivé – fat in my soul, fat around my heart. Darling, too much success . . . Oh, it is not good for the man.'[8]

Trenker's relationship with the Third Reich was always equivocal. He was clearly flattered by the Führer's extravagent praise but had little time for side-kick Goebbels. As a South Tyrolean, he was technically neither German nor Austrian, since this German-speaking region south of the Brenner had been ceded to Italy following the Versailles Treaty. Still, he was ethnically 'German', and a fierce patriot, even allowing that he felt distanced from Hitler's 'fanaticised masses'. Never one to button his lip, from his eccentric position he felt emboldened to warn Goebbels against interference with Deutsche-Universal, or imposing racial restrictions within the industry. Not a wise move politically – and compounded later when he spilled the story to *Film-Kurier*. The hapless journalist to write up the interview was sacked; and the magazine found itself one of the first to be assigned a new editor in sweeping governmental measures to effect 'co-ordination' of the many cinema periodicals.

His film *The Rebel* was perceived as anti-Nazi in America, pro-Nazi at home. His book of the story, which appeared in April 1933, carried a dedication couched to curry favour, but which in effect was equally ambiguous:

> Sacred is the belief in our Fatherland, for the love of Heimat and Volk be as our soul's trust in God! Blessed and unimpeachable is the remembrance of the men who struggled and died for home and Fatherland! Their spirit lives among us, imbues us with strength and hope. In memory of the heroes of 1809, I dedicate this book to the youth of Germany. *Luis Trenker.*

His good connections with Laemmle and Universal Studios assured him of being able to join the exodus to Hollywood any time he wanted – yet the pull of Heimat was strong. It is no coincidence that Trenker's next film dealt with just such an emotional tug of war. *Der verlorene Sohn* (*The Prodigal Son*), which he worked on during 1933–4, was the rags-to-breeches story of a young mountain guide who expects to find love and fortune in the New World, but ends up in the soup queues of the Great Depression. When he returns at last to his native Tyrol, he joyfully discovers that his childhood sweetheart has waited for him. The film was bi-lingual, employing subtitles as necessary (you have to hand it to him, the man learned fast), and it won the Grand Prize at the Venice Festival in 1935. Today it is regarded as one of Trenker's finest works and 'close to being a masterpiece'[9] – but it was not one to win the support of the Minister of Propaganda, and probably only got off the ground at all by Trenker finding himself able to flourish the 'Hitler-card', as Riefenstahl also learned to do.

Trenker continued playing the game by his own rules until he finally fell out of favour with both Hitler and Goebbels. There is some suggestion that he was incautious enough even to flirt with Eva Braun. Certainly after the War he tried to sell what purported to be Eva's 'diary', but it was ultimately exposed as a fake. He was slow to opt for German citizenship when the choice was put to South Tyroleans in 1939 – and then only under pressure from Goebbels. By

1942 Hitler was regarding him as a spent force, only kept in business by Catholic finances.[10]

When, on April Fool's day, 1933, a boycott of Jewish shops throughout Germany launched the Nazi's official anti-Semitic campaign, letters were sent to six American film companies with branch offices in Berlin, calling upon them to dismiss all 'representatives, rental agents and branch managers of Jewish extraction.'[11]

A full ban on Jews in any part of the film industry was announced on 30th June under the so-called *Arierparagraph*, or Aryan Clause. The prohibition also applied to American moving picture concerns producing in Germany. It was presumably soon after this that Riefenstahl, just home from the Bernina, paid her visit to the Reich Chancellery to be offered a key role in the 'new' industry. It is safe to assume that, if Goebbels knew anything of Hitler's offer to her, he was less than happy about it. He had been carefully consolidating his position as propaganda supremo, commissioning Hitler's architect Albert Speer to refurbish his impressive offices opposite the Chancellery in grandiose style so that no one should be under any doubt of his importance and power.[12] The last thing he wanted was to have to share this power, particularly with someone who was at once a popular idol and had a direct conduit to the Führer. To suggest, as Hitler had to Riefenstahl, that Goebbels had 'no experience in the area of films' was mischievous since Goebbels had been responsible for the Nazi Party film section and produced a number of short campaign films, including *Hitler Over Germany,* but it was a recurring tactic of Hitler's to chip at the standing of his subordinates. He liked to foster an air of aggrieved competition between them.

A minor incident which features in the autobiographies of both Riefenstahl and Ertl, though differing in detail, could suggest that Goebbels did not know in advance of Hitler's plans for Riefenstahl, and that he learned only a day or two afterwards of her meeting with the Führer.

When work finished on *SOS Eisberg!* Ertl, with Leni's new love Walter Prager, stayed on in Switzerland for a climbing holiday. On returning to Berlin all three were preparing a meal in Leni's apartment when the telephone rang. The Propaganda Minister was demanding to see Riefenstahl urgently. Her guests agreed she should not fall out with the Doctor any more than was necessary and accordingly, although it was already late, she soon found herself driving him towards Grunewald in her sporty little Mercedes. It was raining heavily. Goebbels was incognito in a raincoat with the collar up and his broad-brimmed hat pulled well down over his face. He took a pistol from his pocket and snapped it into the glove compartment – whether to impress her or be ready in case of an attack is not clear. Goebbels' official chauffeur-driven limousine trailed them for a while but vanished soon after they entered the Grunewald forest.

Riefenstahl makes no mention of a meal, but Ertl, with some degree of clairvoyance, has them dining discreetly *à deux* in the corner of a quiet tavern, even going so far as to describe the menu (lobster, caviare and pheasant on *Weinkraut*) and their mood ('Goebbels, known as an amusing raconteur, leased off a brilliant firework display of witty topics'). Whichever version you choose – Riefenstahl's or that of Ertl – shortly after midnight the two are rattling along forest tracks towards Roseneck, where both storytellers agree Goebbels (or 'Jupp-the-heartbreaker', as Ertl says he was known amongst themselves) tried to lure Leni off the straight and narrow. As she weaves in and out among the trees the amorous doctor makes his lunge, and the little silver-grey sports car tips over an embankment before stalling to a halt and rocking gently with its back wheels in the air (if you take the Ertl version), or buried to the left running board in soft mud (according to Riefenstahl) and tilted dangerously with its front wheels dangling over space. Ertl:

> Furiously the 'Cavalier' jumped out of the car, pulled his overcoat collar up high on both sides, like blinkers, for camouflage, and disappeared into the night. . . . How long 'Jupp, the Unlucky Bird' hobbled through the darkness remains his secret. Leni was picked up by late guests from the Jagdhaus where she went back to raise the alarm.[13]

Leni has it that she gets herself to the tavern after wandering around for a long time. The inn-keeper lends her some warm clothes and she rings Ertl and Prager for help. Ertl says he was woken by telephone and a giggling Leni some time after midnight. 'Hannes,' she said, 'you have to come and help me right away!' He rounded up Guzzi Lantschner and Waldi Traut and took a taxi to Roseneck at two in the morning. Not that there was anything they could do that night. 'Balancing over the embankment like a helpless cockchafer', the little Mercedes had to wait for morning and more muscle power.

Neither Riefenstahl nor Ertl read any more into Goebbels' overtures than that the incorrigible womaniser was still trying his luck with Leni. Even so, to judge from his near paranoid behaviour on other occasions when he suspected Hitler's interference in film

117

matters, it is not beyond possibility that Goebbels engineered the Grunewald meeting to find out for himself what, if anything, he had to fear from this quarter. Still, if he had been hoping to raise the question of Riefenstahl's film plans, it would appear he let himself be sidetracked. A few days after this escapade, Riefenstahl was called to the ministerial office.

Unfortunately, Riefenstahl's published memoirs put no exact date on these events beyond summer 1933. She was working on the treatment for a new film, a spy story set in Germany and France during the First World War, based on Fanck's experiences in German espionage. Leni still regretted the lost *Black Cat* role, and sought through this new *Mademoiselle Docteur* idea to procure a similarly demanding part for herself. UFA were interested, and had set one of their best scriptwriters on to the story. With no ambitions to direct this herself, Leni was looking for a talent capable of extracting from her a performance to surpass anything she had achieved before, even with Pabst. Her preference, and one agreed by UFA, was for Frank Wisbar. Shooting was all set to begin in mid-September.

To have advanced the project so far suggests that if she returned to Berlin some time in the middle of June, as she says, it could have been well into July, or even August, when she attended on the Goebbels. But there is a major discrepancy between the Riefenstahl and Ertl accounts of the Grunewald incident. Riefenstahl is adamant it took place in the summer 1933, before filming that year's Nuremberg Rally; Ertl, on the other hand, suggests 1935, before filming the Wehrmacht film. Were he right, it could affect the interpretation of her relations with Goebbels during this whole period.

Goebbels' Chamber of Film (the *Reichsfilmkammer*, or RFK), was officially established on 14th July in advance of his full Chamber of Culture (*Reichskulturkammer* – RKK), of which it formed a part. It supervised every aspect of film-making and distribution.[14] Soon, all workers employed anywhere in the industry were required to present proof that not only both their parents, but all grandparents were 'Aryans'. Leni Riefenstahl was no exception to this. Persistent rumours (at the time and since) have suggested she had Jewish blood on her mother's side. This was never proved and in due course she received her occupational identity card.

Her visit, then, to the Propaganda Minister came at a critical time in his programme of usurping complete control over the industry. He had read in the press of her collaboration with UFA on *Mademoiselle*

Docteur and wanted to hear from her lips how that idea had come about. This, she told him.

'And what are your plans after that?' was the the next question.

She confided a long-standing desire to play Penthesilea, the last Amazon queen, in the tragedy by Heinrich von Kleist. Goebbels cut her short – and here we come to the real purpose of the summons. What, he enquired, had been the subject of her discussions with Hitler?

The Minister was surely expecting her to reveal some hint of Hitler's wish that she make that year's Nuremberg Rally film, for he – Goebbels – would already have been apprised of the Führer's wishes in this respect. That is not to say he would have been happy, regarding the granting of such 'honours' very much his personal preserve. To his surprise Riefenstahl made no mention of the matter. And neither, therefore, did he.

Instead, he launched into great detail about a pet idea of his own; something in which he would welcome her collaboration. Why not a film illustrating the power of the press? It could be called *The Seventh Great Power*. He would write treatment and script, and she might help with the direction? Riefenstahl demurred. As she had with Hitler, she put forward the name of Walter Ruttman instead, telling Goebbels that a documentary master like Ruttman would be far more sympathetic to what he had in mind.[15] It is interesting that at this time Riefenstahl did not see herself as a documentary-maker, although many scenes in *The Blue Light*, particularly of the villagers, were pure document, as was much in Fanck's *Bergfilme*.

Towards the end of August, Riefenstahl was called back to the Reich Chancellery; Hitler wanted to know how plans for the Rally film were progressing. Riefenstahl claims absolute astonishment. We cannot know exactly what passed between her and the Führer on the earlier occasion. She may well have misunderstood his intent, but whether or not she formally accepted any official executive role in the Nazi film industry, it seems certain Hitler never wavered from his declaration to her at Horumersiel that she was to make films for him. And there was no question in his mind but that she would comply. One can be reasonably certain, too, that Goebbels had dragged his feet in passing on the necessary messages and authorisations, although his diaries recall an afternoon meeting with Riefenstahl on 17th May, 1933, when she assures us she was tucked away in the Swiss Alps, filming.

Furious to discover his plans had been flouted, Hitler immediately had the Propaganda Minister instructed to support Riefenstahl in every manner possible. Any room there may have been for manoeuvre was thus slashed from beneath her feet. With only a week or two before the event, the time for demur was past. Soon after returning home from this audience with Hitler, Riefenstahl learned from Goebbels' ministry that her spy film project had been cancelled.

X

Nuremberg Rallies

Hitler's grasp of the power of mass persuasion was largely intuitive. Experiences at the front in the First World War had convinced him that propaganda was a weapon like any other, to be used as a means to a desired end – an end which, as he saw it, was nothing less than 'a struggle for the life of the German nation'. The more skilful its operator, the more effective a weapon it became. What had so disheartened him during the war was that Germany's opponents seemed very much more proficient in this martial skill than his own side.

Propaganda, as a refined and consciously applied art – or more properly, perhaps, as a science – is essentially a phenomenon of the twentieth century, or in other words post-Freudian. The suffragettes are often given credit for being among the first to develop specific techniques of mass persuasion, particularly in their use of newsworthy stunts and dedicated lobbying. Few have doubted their passionate belief in their cause, or would go so far as to imply that this monstrous regiment of women resorted to deliberate falsehood (initially at least), although among their own followers they would whip up excitement, make emotional appeals for sacrifice and employ neo-Fascist tactics for arousing irrational hostility. Amber Blanco White, a left-wing observer writing in 1939, certainly looked back on the women's suffrage movement in its final period as 'an organisation run on Fascist lines and characterised by an authentically Fascist violence and emotionalism and exaggeration'.[1]

There is no indication that Hitler followed the activities of these distant suffragist women, nor yet of Christian Science's founder Mary Baker Eddy, another with whose tactics his are sometimes compared, but a preoccupation with propaganda and its application can

121

be seen running as a leitmotif through *Mein Kampf*. Time and again through its pages he examines the necessary techniques, barely if ever questioning the moral issues involved.

From the outset he knew it was the masses he had to win over, rather than the intelligensia (for whom he had little time), and in his orations he would pitch his message unerringly at the emotions and imagination of his audience, touching that spring which released its 'hidden forces', simply, directly – and cynically:

> The receptive ability of the masses is very limited, their intelligence small. On the other hand, their power of forgetting is enormous. This being so, all effective propaganda must be confined to a very few points, which must be harped upon in the form of slogans, until every last member of the public comprehends what you want him to understand by your slogan. As soon as you sacrifice this principle in the desire to be many-sided, the effect piddles away.[2]

The enormous power of forgetting, which Hitler assumed, and his choice of oratory as a preferred medium, freed him from the need of consistency of argument. His propaganda was repeatedly tried and tested, trimmed and embellished, tailored to fit. It evolved from his raw street-fighting days to the measured performances of the later Nuremberg rallies, by which time every breath, every gesture had a calculated effect. Rhetorical stances could be altered, slogans slotted in to suit the occasion, and still the fundamental fervour be induced. Nothing was left to chance. Even the time of day had its importance, for he had been quick to recognise that an audience's powers of resistance waned in direct proportion to its tiredness. Evening was when you overcame prejudices and won hearts and minds.

Reason held no place in Hitler's arguments, any more than he felt bound by truth. The greater the lie, the greater the chance of having it believed, he had written in *Mein Kampf*. Philosophies were offered, which were at the same time elaborate and inchoate; they need not be understood beyond insistent keywords and reductionist slogans. 'Blood and soil', 'Strength through Joy', 'our national myth', '*Lebensraum*', 'our indomitable wills', 'culture and race', 'the Aryan race', 'our destiny', 'Volk' . . . Allegiance was the object; so long as the people cottoned on to the immutable *Führerprinzip* – leadership principle – little else mattered.

Goebbels' importance to Hitler rested in his equal appreciation of mass control through propaganda and the spoken word. He, too, could whip a crowd to frenzy, indeed with even more artfulness and belligerence than his Führer. He masterminded Hitler's campaigns through half a decade of struggle, and he had long known that when the Nazis eventually came to power he would be given that Ministry which they both considered of utmost consequence.

By this time practice had perfected the orchestration and pageantry of the Nazis' greatest showcase, the ambitious *Partei-Tage* (Party Days), which had become an integral part of the National Socialist calendar. Every trick and contrivance was brought into play at these showy displays of power, with the object of implanting awe and fellowship among their followers. Much had been learned from the cinema – this was state-of-the-art special effects, with every year some new device of lighting or illusion incorporated – and it was important to the Party that any filmed record of the events should be as strictly stage-managed and controlled as the spectacles themselves. Only in this way could the rallies' propaganda value be extended reliably beyond the masses in attendance. Thus, although spectators could take a limited number of stills photographs during the proceedings, the use of cine-cameras was forbidden to all but accredited newsreel cameramen.

Nuremberg had not always been home to such rallies. In the early days minor 'German Days' were staged around the country. The first officially to bear the title 'Party Day' was a relatively small affair held in Munich in January 1923. Later that same year a second took place in Nuremberg, but in 1926, when the Party had to be 're-founded' after the failed *Putsch* and Hitler's imprisonment, Weimar was chosen as the most appropriate venue for a third rally. The following year the Nazis returned to Nuremberg and thereafter this ancient city remained the dramatic setting of all further rallies until the last (and greatest) in 1938. Certain rituals became enshrined in the programme, none more hallowed than the emotive 'Blood Banner' ceremony, in which new Party standards were introduced to the stained and bullet-riddled flag hoisted aloft by a dying Nazi loyalist during the doomed *Putsch*. Hitler would pass among the ranks of standard bearers, holding one corner of this tattered relic, consecrating each flag with its touch. The Blood Banner had become, in short, as one observer remarked, 'the Host of National Socialism, the source of all holiness.'[3]

In 1933, the plan was to make the Party Day the biggest ever in celebration of the National Socialists' accession to power. Hitler would perform the blood-blessing rite over 316 banners, take the salute of a million men of his militia and address 60,000 Hitler Youth. From the doctrinal point of view, this would be the congress at which the campaign for racial purity would be openly launched, Hitler himself speaking on the subject with two addresses *Kultur und Rasse* and *Volk und Rasse*, reflecting the influence of Darré and Rosenberg. At the suggestion of Hess, the rally would be known as the Party Day of Victory. *Victory of Faith* was the title the Führer decreed for the documentary film he ordered Leni Riefenstahl to make for him.

She arrived in Nuremberg with only a few days for her preparations. Despite Hitler's intervention, there had been no confirmation of a contract from the Ministry of Propaganda, nor was anyone in the government cinema department empowered to make cameramen or film stock available to her. It was clear she was going to receive no official co-operation, and the easiest course would have been to throw in the sponge there and then and go home. That did not square with her innate stubbornness, nor the obligation she felt to her Führer; even so it is doubtful she could have proceeded further had she not at this juncture made the acquaintance of Hitler's architect, Albert Speer. This young man was commissioned to produce the necessary decorations in the stadium and had come up with a dynamic outspread eagle device, over a hundred feet in wing-span, to crown the Zeppelin Field. In his book *Inside the Third Reich*, he tells how he spiked it to a timber framework 'like a butterfly in a collection.' He also relates his meeting with Leni Riefenstahl, whom he recognized immediately from her famous mountain and skiing films. She had been a pin-up of his in his student days, and impressed him still as she battled against hostile Party officials. He was astonished to discover that this woman was aware also of his existence. With mischievous flourish, she pulled out a yellowing newspaper clipping she had saved from three years back when he reconstructed the Gau headquarters in Berlin. Why on earth should she want to hang on to his photograph, he asked, bemused. She said it was for his fine head. Rather in the way she had stored in her mind images of Sepp Rist and of her first tennis coach, she had pigeon-holed Speer as a possible player in some as yet undreamed-of movie.

Speer's advice to Riefenstahl in her present predicament was that she should ride the hostility and not allow herself to be edged out. He found one cameraman for her, Walter Frentz, a promising young man with whom she would choose to work again several times; and she managed to round up two more – Sepp Allgeier, the most experienced 'graduate' from Fanck's 'Freiburg School', and Franz Weimayr. Riefenstahl's brother was dragooned into being her personal assistant for six days, and her father lent money to tide her over. Fortunately, her relationship with Karl Geyer of the Agfa studios had remained good after *The Blue Light*, and the company supplied all the necessary film stock. She was ready to roll.

Nothing, it seems, is easy. Repeatedly, crew members found themselves harassed or thwarted by SA and SS-men, who could always fall back on the excuse that the crew had not the permits to go wherever they wanted to be. Rudolf Hess took it upon himself to upbraid Riefenstahl for allegedly speaking disparagingly of the Führer. Riefehstahl was outraged, and suspected the hand of Goebbels behind all the provocation. However one looks at it, someone meant her ill. Speer's account confirms there was a definite campaign against her. The Nazis, he said, by tradition anti-feminist, 'could hardly brook this self-assured woman, the more so since she knew how to bend this men's world to her purposes.' Later, Udet, too, would warn her that she had enemies within the SS. She was, he said, too close to Hitler for her own good. Among the Party faithful were those so jealous of her position they would stop at nothing to see her out of the way. His grim words seemed to be borne out when during the editing period, Riefenstahl found herself assigned protective surveillance, apparently on Reich Minister Goering's orders. Rumours were thick at this time . . . that she was Hitler's mistress . . . was half-Jewish.

Despite all, an hour-long film was eventually premièred at the UFA Palast before Hitler and the whole German Cabinet on 1st December that year, though it is believed never to have gone on general release. Riefenstahl was of the impression that Hitler and his party bigwigs were well enough satisfied with the result, but for her part she remembered it as an imperfect fragment, without real plot or script. 'I could only try to collate the images in such a way as to create visual rhythm and variety,' she said, which of course is exactly what she did to such stunning effect in her later documentaries. In a sense, therefore, this has been a useful dummy run, particularly as it also brought her together with the composer Herbert Windt, who would go on to score most of her other films.

The *Observer* newspaper in London carried the following report on the film on 3rd December, 1933:

The film is one long apotheosis of the Caesar spirit, in which Herr Hitler plays the role of Caesar while the troops play the role of the Roman slaves. It is certainly to be hoped that this film will be shown in all cinemas outside Germany, if one wishes to understand the intoxicating spirit which is moving Germany these days. Herr Hitler handed Leni Riefenstahl a bouquet at the end of the performance.

More than that it has been impossible for film historians to say until recently, for the original negative of the film was lost during the final days of the Second World War – as was that of her later *Triumph of the Will*. Riefenstahl was sure that duplicates and the 'lavender prints' survived in bunkers in Kitzbühel and Berlin after hostilities ceased, only later to be confiscated by the Allies. But whereas *Triumph* resurfaced in America, for almost half a century the earlier work might as well have vanished from the face of the earth. Many doubted it had existed at all beyond a few reels of unedited footage. Or, if it had, that it must have been suppressed for portraying Ernst Röhm, Chief of Staff of the SA, and later a victim of the Night of the Long Knives, as a constant figure at Hitler's side.

Only recently was a copy rediscovered, in time for extracts to be included in the award-winning television documentary *The Wonderful, Horrible Life of Leni Riefenstahl*, directed by Ray Müller of Omega Film in Munich. Although there are scenes that demonstrate Riefenstahl's distinctive feel for handling large-scale spectacle, her dismissal of the whole as fragmentary was evidently fair. Not only does the film-making include amateurish footage, flaws are thrown up in the staging of the rally. As Müller's commentary points out, the Nazis had not yet learned to march like Nazis.

Frequently during the editing of her film, a stressed Riefenstahl had longed to exchange all the hassle this commission was bringing her for the peace of the mountains. As soon as possible after the first showing, she disappeared to her beloved Davos.

★

Leni Riefenstahl knew that Hitler was expecting her to make a bigger and better film of the next Party Day in 1934, knew too that she could do a far superior job, given more favourable circumstances. But she was still unable to see herself as a documentary film-maker, and hoped, rather against hope, that before the time came she would be able wriggle out of the assignment.

Early in the New Year, Terra Film of Berlin invited her to direct and play the lead in a movie based on Eugen d'Albert's opera *Tiefland* (*Lowlands*), a simple tale set in Spain in the time of Goya and telling of the conflict between a highlander and a lowlander, both in love with the same Gypsy dancer. With echoes of *The Blue Light,* the mountains were to embody all that was good, while the lowland influence was unadulterated evil. The girl – like Junta – was a free spirit.

This was far more to Riefenstahl's taste than another Party rally film, but that project, too, was progressing inexorably. Since she could clearly not be in two places at once, some scheming was necessary to make it all possible. UFA, who at that time was not yet completely subordinate to the Propaganda Ministry,[4] was prepared to sign a distribution contract for the Nuremberg film to the handsome tune of 300,000 marks. This gave Riefenstahl freedom to sub-contract some of the direction work, and, once again, her thoughts turned to the progressive cinéaste, Walter Ruttmann, whose praises she had sung earlier to Goebbels. He was delighted to get involved and immediately came up with the idea of prefacing all the rally glitz with a historical look at the National Socialists' rise to power. There should be enough newsreel footage, he believed, to make this section a substantial part of the film. Beyond allocating him the services of Sepp Allgeier, whom she trusted implicitly, Riefenstahl appears to have given Ruttmann a free hand while she disappeared to London on a lecture tour and then with her old friends Guzzi Lantschner and Walter Riml to Spain to supervise location seeking and casting for *Tiefland.*

At this stage in her career Riefenstahl was enjoying the supreme confidence of success. Everything she had ever set her sights on, she had achieved – often against great odds. She was obsessively per-fectionist in all she did, and no shirker when it came to pulling out one last squeeze of effort after another. Apart from clashes with Dr Goebbels, which so far she had always survived, she could bend most people to her will. All who knew her described her as formidable, forthright, and highly intelligent – but her intelligence had been directed almost exclusively into the mastery of whatever sphere she was operating in at the time. There were gaping holes in it when it came to the understanding of interpersonal – and political – dynamics. Whatever else might be said, she was being supremely optimistic, not to say naïve, in supposing her plans for the rally film could press on unchallenged.

Hitler may have promised there would be no interference or pressure from Goebbels or his Ministry in the making of this film, but she completely underestimated what the Führer was actually after. By entrusting her with this commission, he wanted that spark of mysticism he had seen in *The Blue Light.* In flirtatious conversation,

Riefenstahl's fearless candour may have amused the Führer; and doubtless he drew enjoyment from her tussles with Goebbels; but when it came to clashes with his will, he brooked no argument: he was always supposed to triumph.

There was the matter, too, of Ruttmann. Riefenstahl admired the swift and rhythmic cutting he achieved in his abstract and documentary films, building strong emotional impact from shots that were not always obviously related nor necessarily of individual interest. It seems not to have occurred to her that Ruttmann's well known Communist sympathies would raise problems in the prevailing climate. Ruttmann's motives, too, give rise to curiosity here, given that he was no friend of the Nazis. Of course, any work was welcome in difficult days; or he may simply have recognised this as a unique opportunity for chronicling extraordinary affairs, for creating a commentary that could outlive even a thousand-year-Reich.

★

Riefenstahl still regarded the Führer as in some way apart from the vicious excesses of his Party – excesses of which by then she could hardly fail to be aware. She had never joined the Party, nor had any intention of doing so, being unable to reconcile herself to its policy of Jewish persecution. Why – having read *Mein Kampf*, which few others could claim to have done, despite the vast numbers printed, and having been in Nuremberg when Hitler was underscoring his racial policies – why, then, should she still resolutely believe he would learn moderation in power is hard to fathom. Yet, this was a trap many fell into at the time, particularly the young, who in their years of idealism were being given hope, brotherhood and causes to die for. 'The young people are happy,' one German Frau tried to put it into words for an English traveller in 1934. 'Everything is done for them. They think it's a wonderful world! They adore the Führer. They love marching about with flags. They love their sports and games. Yes, the young people are happy!'[5]

There was some unease in the population at large about so much overtly militaristic display, but few within Germany believed they were actually heading towards war. Hitler continually harped on about the desirability of peace, while at the same time promising more *Lebensraum* (living space), and the incompatability between these two states went largely unremarked. In days before there was any whiff of Final Solution in the air, people were as exercised about governmental attitude towards Catholicism as the plight of the Jews. Some may have had qualms over lost liberties, but for most to see an alleviation of mass unemployment and some sense of discipline returning after the years of chaos, the price seemed not excessive.

Albert Speer has described how he detected 'rough spots' in the Party doctrines, but assumed, like Riefenstahl, these would be polished in time. In retrospect, given his education, he admits he should have seen through the 'whole apparatus of mystification', and that not to have done so was 'already criminal.' Had Hitler announced, before 1933, that a few years later 'he would burn down Jewish synagogues, involve Germany in a war, and kill Jews and his political opponents,' he said, 'he would at one blow have lost me and probably most of the adherents he won after 1930.'[6] Goebbels, who feared infiltration of the party by bourgeois intellectuals, made it his business that Speer and other 'Septemberlings'[7] did not see through this calculated gauze of mystification. Putzi Hanfstaengl flirted assiduously with Hitler and his cohorts for twelve years, apparently under the delusion that his influence could civilise their radical rough spots (and intolerable manners), yet he did not put sufficient pieces of the jigsaw together to see its sinister pattern until the 1933 Nuremberg Rally. And even then, as foreign press chief in Berlin, he found himself inextricably part of the mystifying process – until the frighteners were put upon him and he fled the Fatherland in 1937.

Perhaps, then, with her sketchy conception of politics, we should not be surprised that Riefenstahl allowed herself to be carried along on the surging foam of *Zeitgeist*.

★

Meanwhile things were not running smoothly with *Tiefland*. In Spain, Leni was rapturous about the landscape and itching to get started, but the money only dribbled through from Berlin, and no film stock arrived at all. Nor did the rest of the production crew, as promised. It was impossible to get any sense out of the studios. On hearing that everything was being put on hold for a further two weeks, Leni suffered some form of collapse and remembered nothing more until she woke up in a hospital in Madrid. This proved all the excuse the studio needed to cancel the project altogether – and clean up on the insurance money.

Thank goodness, Leni thought, that she had left Ruttman in charge of the Party film, although she was beginning to admit a certain disquiet on that score after he visited her during her convalescence in Barcelona. Airily assuring her that all was under control, he nonetheless remained vague over details and finances. It was August before she felt fit enough to return to Berlin, and she did so in gloomy apprehension. Once again, a Nuremberg deadline was bearing down upon her, and once again, she would seek to have the mission aborted.

Matters, she soon discovered, were far worse than she feared. Ruttman's footage, to her eyes at least, was scrappy and incomprehensible, comprising nothing but a jumble of shots of newspapers blowing along a street, their headlines charting the rise of the Nazi Party. Quite unusable for what she envisaged, yet he had worked through a third of the film's total budget. Moreover, an ominous letter awaited her, from Hess, expressing surprise that she had delegated to Ruttman at all when the Führer had been most adamant it was her alone he wanted. She was summoned to explain her actions.

What a nightmare! She could hide from it no longer, and in one last effort to be relieved of the whole unwanted obligation, she departed immediately for Nuremberg where the Führer was inspecting the rally preparations.

She found him in one of the arenas with Speer, Brückner and Hoffmann (architect, adjutant and photographer, respectively), going over plans for the intricate set-piece parades. He was in good spirits and brushed aside her protestations. 'All I want, Fraulein Riefenstahl,' he told her, 'is six days of your time. You are young. Is that too much to ask?'

Of course that would not be all, not by any means. Six days at the rally would be followed by the long, lonely days of editing, but she was given to understand very clearly that this was his last word on the subject. She had better buckle to and make the best of it. Sensing her capitulation, Hitler seized both her hands in a firm clasp and promised never again to make such demands upon her. She was assured of all the co-operation and artistic freedom she required.

And that was that. Photographs, taken in the rally ground, presumably just after this tussle of wills, show a thin-lipped Leni Riefenstahl visibly shaken and quite lacking in her normal animation.

One of the reasons she had dragged her feet so long (even after *Tiefland* folded) was clearly apprehension in the face of so sensitive and grandiose a project. There had been excuses for failure the year before, but there would be none this time. It was a monstrous responsibility, and she doubted her suitability to undertake it, green as she still was in all matters political.

'Why, I can't even tell the SA from the SS,' she protested to Hitler.

'That way, you will only see the essentials,' he reassured her. 'I am not looking for a newsreel, but an artistic document.'

In the circumstances, Riefenstahl has to be given credit for not succumbing to panic. As it turned out, Hitler's belief in her was justified, even if Goebbels and others had her marked down as a hysteric. In fact, once the decision was taken, there is every evidence that Riefenstahl enjoyed the challenge. All later photographs show her confident and in control of the situation. Time was short and, by her account, finance tight after the Ruttman episode, yet the organisation and effort that went into securing coverage of this rally was almost incredible. One can assume that Allgeier, as director of photography, had already set in train some ideas of his own, but when Riefenstahl claims that she had only two weeks in which to make all her preparations, this would appear broadly true. It brings new meaning to the notion of Teutonic zeal.

The problem with the previous rally film had been insufficient material when it came to editing. That would not happen this time. In the commemorative Party Day book, produced after the event and telling the behind-the-scenes story of making this film,[8] are listed eighteen movie-cameramen with nineteen assistants (many of them colleagues from mountain film days). Aerial photographers in light aeroplanes and the dirigible T/PN 30, as well as almost thirty newsreel cameramen from Tobis and elsewhere provided back up. Altogether, 400,000 feet of film were shot. Expense would not appear to have been any object, but it is unclear what Leni's company paid for and what was made available in the name of goodwill. Her team included technical staff, soundmen and lighting assistants. With production helpers, office personnel, and chauffeurs for the cars put at the disposal of herself and each of her camera teams, some 170 people worked under Riefenstahl during the week of the rally. An all-important production assistant kept tabs on where they all were and what everyone was doing. Security guards from the SA and SS watched over them. A house in the city was put at their disposal, where every morning and evening Riefenstahl viewed rushes and held the production conferences so essential to her manner of working.[9]

The 1933 rally was required to be a grand affair in celebration of the Nazis' assumption of power, but it was the job of that of 1934 to surpass it conclusively. By now the Party leaders had mastered the art of strutting around like Nazis. The really important message to project was of solidarity after the Röhm purge. Together with the unifying control brought about by increased employment and sense of purpose, this should reinforce Hitler as leader-father-God of his Volk.

Nor was that all. Another major political development had to be reflected: the death of Hindenburg in early August and Hitler's aquisition of the mantle of presidency alongside that of Chancellor. At a stroke, as the recently-arrived American correspondent William Shirer observed in his *Berlin Diary*, any doubts about the loyalty of the army were done away with before the old Field Marshal's body was cold in its grave. The army was forced into swearing an oath of unconditional obedience to Hiter personally. Shirer added laconically, 'the man is resourceful.'

Some military display, therefore, would take place for the first time at this year's Party Day. Speer's refurbishment of the Zeppelin Field had begun, most notably the construction of a monumental platform and flight of stairs worthy of Cecil B. de Mille.

The book about making the rally film has a picture caption declaring that preparations for the Party Day went hand in hand with preparations for Riefenstahl's film. This has been seized upon as evidence that Riefenstahl played a crucial role in staging the actual pageant – as opposed to merely recording a spectacle in progress, a spectacle which would have taken place whether she was there or not. As it would have been filmed whether she was there or not. The picture to which this caption refers is that of the crestfallen film-maker being shown the marching plans by Hitler, who is quite obviously playing to an audience of uniformed subordinates.

Putting aside for the moment Riefenstahl's role as a propagandist in what is universally considered a propaganda film, this particular illustration and caption raise other points of their own. First, the rally book itself is a propaganda offering – put out by the Central Publishing House of the NSDAP – and it should be seen as such. The pictures will have been chosen and captions couched (not necessarily by Riefenstahl, as the given author) to reflect an air of total control and efficiency.[10]

Secondly – and it doesn't matter whether or not one believes Riefenstahl when she says she was seeking release from her assignment on the day this picture was taken – what it depicts is her being shown blueprints of an *already-orchestrated* tattoo. So, the caption does not tally with the picture. This is demonstration that her film preparations – of necessity – had to come *after* the marching plans. It is hard to see how otherwise her film could have been made.

The point is worth making since analysts chew over it endlessly.

Many people seem to imagine that Riefenstahl was responsible for the rallies in Nuremberg, forgetting they began before she arrived on the scene to film them, and continued afterwards. To the question 'Which came first, the rally or the film?', the answer of course has to be the rally. It was important to the Nazis for the *Parteitag* to be filmed – in this year of 1934, more perhaps than any other. Riefenstahl enjoyed unprecedented co-operation in her work, but the pageantry cannot be said to have been staged for her cameras.

Whether we believe the propaganda vehicle was the rally, or the film, or both – and whether Riefenstahl was being used, with or without her appreciation of the fact, as a propaganda tool – her contention is that she was objectively recording a historical event. She was fulfilling a documentary commission, and the event itself was immaterial. It could as easily have been of a convention of fruit and vegetable merchants (her own metaphor). As Jaworsky once remarked, there was a conflict in Germany in 1932 between the Communists and the Nazis, and the Nazis won. Had the Communists won, then Riefenstahl would have made films for the other side.

Newsreel coverage of the various congresses took place before she made her Nuremberg trilogy: *Victory of Faith*, the accomplished *Triumph of the Will* and a shorter Wehrmacht film, *Day of Freedom*. Hers were the only 'features' dedicated exclusively to these artfully staged Nazi Party conventions, or indeed to the person of Hitler in power. Goebbels preferred not to overexpose the Führer and favoured short newsreels.

How did Leni approach her task? What were the particular problems, and how original the solutions she came up with?

The sheer number of people – players and spectators – who thronged into the city was impressive (an estimated 700,000 for the 1934 rally), and could not fail to appear so on film. Yet the events themselves were repetitive. For the most part, they were also static, contained within city halls, or narrow streets, or in the specially-constructed arenas. Speeches and marches were followed by march-pasts and tableaux, more speeches, more marches . . . To introduce the variety and 'movement' required in a motion picture was where Riefenstahl and Allgeier displayed special talent, drawing on the deep wells of improvisation that were a legacy of their *Bergfilme* days. If the subject didn't move, the camera had to be mobile. Tracks and dollies were employed, commonplace for feature film production but barely if ever used in documentaries. For Hitler's address to his League of

Youth, Riefenstahl had a circular track installed around the podium, which would provide one of the most memorable sequences in her film as the low angle camera crept slowly around the demagogue in full flood. Speer came up trumps by affixing a tiny lift to the tall flagpoles in the Luitpold Arena. In town, cameramen were placed on roofs and specially-extended balconies, in cars (including Hitler's own limousine), up fireman's ladders and, most notably, in the air, in the dirigible or the low-flying *Klemm* aircraft. Allgeier even practised shooting on roller skates. Everything he and Leni, the Lantschner brothers, and Prager and Riml had ever learned between them, whether skiing, climbing, aerial filming on Mont Blanc and in Greenland, played a part in their thinking, besides giving them the head for heights and sheer stamina which enabled their creativity to work.

This is not say there were no problems. Lights and full sound facilities were lacking in the Congress Hall, and some of the film towers were not completed until part way through the rally week. One cameramen Leni sought to engage refused to work under a woman and the newsreel cameramen, to whom she looked for backup material, were similarly disinclined to be bossed around by her. SS-men shoved a sound van into a ditch, and a bitter row blew up with UFA when it became known she intended printing her film, not at their studios but at the Geyer, where she had been provided with up-to-the-minute editing facilities.

Once she had her team together, Riefenstahl managed her special trick of keeping them motivated throughout the days of intense activity. Everyone worked around the clock, the cameramen being dispatched each day with instructions to avoid unneccessary detail but on no account to miss anything. Once away, there was no easy means of contacting them – no walkie-talkies. Riefenstahl was dependent on their intuitive skill, and they rose to the occasion, even if (as she afterwards estimated) roughly half the footage that found its way in to the finished film came from the camera of Allgeier, the master.

The Rally itself appears to have gone like clockwork, and though not the biggest ever in Nuremberg – that came in 1938 – it had found its form. Albert Speer recalls it as the event at which he introduced the spectacular features he calls his 'Cathedral of Light'. This may be a confusion with the Olympic Games of 1936, but he tells an entertaining story of how Riefenstahl's earlier film highlighted the ragged presentation of the *Amtswalter*, the middle and minor party functionaries who rallied every year in the Zeppelin Field. Yet the event could not be dropped; it was essential for maintaining goodwill and a sense of unity, even if – as Speer remarked in his memoirs – 'for the most part these men had converted their small prebends into sizable paunches; they simply could not be expected to line up in orderly ranks.' It was a matter serious enough to provoke concerned high level conferences and sarcastic comment from the Führer. Speer's inspired pragmatism saved the day. 'Let's have them march up in darkness,' he said:

> The thousands of flags belonging to all the local groups in Germany were to be held in readiness behind the high fences surrounding the field. The flagbearers were to divide into ten columns, forming lanes in which the Amtswalter would march up ... bright spotlights would be cast on these banners, and the great eagle crowing them all. That alone would have a dramatic effect. But even this did not seem sufficient to me. I had occasionally seen our new anti-aircraft searchlights blazing miles into the sky. I asked Hitler to let me have 130 of these.[11]

No matter that this represented the greater part of the strategic reserve, it was a grandiose enough notion to win over Hitler, who instructed Goering to comply. Relaying Speer's argument, Hitler told his Reich Marshal, 'If we use them in such large numbers for a thing like this, other countries will think we're swimming in searchlights.'

The effect surpassed even Speer's expectations. The 130 sharply defined beams shot some 25,000 feet into the air before merging into a diffuse dome of radiance. 'The feeling was of a vast room, with the beams serving as mighty pillars of infinitely high outer walls. Now and then a cloud moved through this wreath of lights, bringing an element of surrealistic surprise to the mirage. It was, Speer supposed, the first 'luminescent architecture' of its type, and throughout his life would believe it his most 'beautiful architectural concept', adding wryly that after its fashion, it was moreover the only one to survive the passage of time.[12]

One of the fullest and most memorable written accounts of the 1934 Nuremberg Rally is that provided by William L. Shirer in his *Berlin Diary* (first published in 1941). A young, ambitious foreign correspondent, Shirer had just left a poorly paid position in Paris for one with Universal Service in the German capital ('going from bad to Hearst,' he amused himself by saying), arriving in Hitler's Third Reich only a week before the Nuremberg festivities. At this, his first assignment, he was not altogether surprised when Putzi Hanfstaengl, in his role as foreign press chief, 'had the crust to ask us to "report on affairs in Germany without attempting to interpret them". "History alone," Putzi shouted, "can evaluate the events now taking place under Hitler." ' Putzi's words fell on 'deaf, if good-humoured', ears among the American and British correspondents, Shirer said, for he was popular with them despite his 'clownish stupidity'.

Shirer caught his first view of Hitler riding into the mediaeval town at sundown 'like a Roman emperor'. He watched the Führer fumble his cap with his left hand as he stood in his car acknowledging the delirious welcome with 'somewhat feeble Nazi salutes from his right arm. He was clad in a rather worn gabardine trench coat, his face had no particular expression at all – I expected it to be stronger – and for the life of me I could not quite comprehend what hidden springs he undoubtedly unloosed which was in the hysterical mob greeting him so wildly.' The expressions of ecstasy, transfiguring the women's faces particularly, called to mind the crazed expressions of Holy Rollers, he said, but as the week wore on he began to comprehend some of the reasons for this idolatry. Hitler was restoring pageantry, colour and mysticism to drab modern lives. Even the undignified and 'outlandish' goose-step struck an inner chord in the 'strange soul of the German people'. Most of all, he was surprised that no one made attempts on the lives of Hitler or other Nazi leaders during the week, when there must have been plenty of relatives of those purged who would dearly have wanted to have a go. Even when Hitler faced the SA storm troopers for the first time since the Night of the Long Knives, though the tension in the stadium was palpable and Hitler's SS-bodyguard was drawn up protectively in front of him, not one of the 50,000 Brownshirts made a move.

After seven days of 'almost ceaseless goose-stepping, speech-making, and pageantry', Shirer had to admit that, dead tired as he was and 'rapidly developing a bad case of crowd-phobia', he was glad he had come. He understood a little better Hitler's hold on the people, and could 'feel the dynamic in the movement he's unleashed and the sheer disciplined strength the Germans possess.' Half a million men would now 'go back to their towns and villages and preach the new gospel with new fanaticism.'[13]

Riefenstahl returned to Berlin, oppressed by the knowledge that she had only five months to organise the sixty-one hours of film they had collected into a documentary film of around two hours. The manner in which she worked to her private vision, rejecting any semblance of received newsreel format, prohibited her from accepting creative editorial assistance. She tried it once in desperation, calling in Herr Schaad, considered one of the top editors of the day, but his material was no more acceptable to her than Ruttman's had been. There was no option but for her, her cutting-room assistant Erna Peters (who helped her sort and splice) and a schoolboy volunteer to slave alone every day and half of every night, rarely seeing the world outside. Post synchronisation was a nightmare, matching Herbert Windt's fine original score to the variable speed of the filmed action and the rapid cuts Riefenstahl had introduced. She recalled: 'Despite hours of practice, neither the conductor nor Herr Windt was able to synchronize the music correctly; and Herr Windt even suggested that I simply leave out the entire parade. So I myself took over the task of conducting the eighty-man orchestra. I had every frame down pat, and I knew exactly when the music should be conducted faster and when slower.'[14]

The final tinkering was completed with only hours to spare before the film's opening night at the UFA Palast on 28th March 1935. Leni changed into her evening gown in the printing laboratory to arrive at the theatre, in some dishevelment and nervousness, within minutes of the curtain going up.

XI

Triumph of the Will

With the possible exception of D. W. Griffith's inflammatory *The Birth of a Nation*, no film in the history of cinema has aroused such lasting controversy as *Triumph of the Will*. It is almost impossible to approach unemotionally; we cannot divorce it from the horrors we know happened afterwards. And the fact it is intrinsically an emotional production, engineered to work on the feelings and senses, makes it almost as hard to argue for a rational assessment as to obtain one. So, whether taking the view of Keith Reader when he says the film 'deifies a human being with more pernicious skill than any shot before or since',[1] or that of the French historians Bardèche and Brasillach who maintain that it is a simple yet miraculous record of witness to the huge festivals of Nuremberg,[2] few can doubt its artistry. Yet critics long withheld any expression of praise, sensitive to the risk of appearing more fascinated by Fascism than by film.

For years after the war the film was considered too dangerous to be viewed, though today its significance, artistically and politically, is openly discussed in film schools and university courses, with discursive learned papers available from (mainly) American professors of cinematography. Richard Meran Barsam (late of the City University of New York) produced in 1975 a student's *Filmguide to Triumph of the Will*, analysing the work in some detail and providing what his publishers described as 'the first full and accurate English translation of the many German speeches' included within it. A more extensive shot-by-shot examination by Steve Neale appeared four years later. He felt the film had not been accorded the painstaking study it deserved.[3] This has proved a perennial cry, although nowadays it is possible to obtain full videocopies of *Triumph of the Will* with English subtitles for historical research.

138

Riefenstahl was often asked how she came to put her films together, to stamp such an individual mark upon her editing. Well, she would say, she had never collaborated: if overall harmony and voice were to be achieved, she could not stress enough the importance of a single editor, any more that she herself could envisage that editor being other than the person who had conceived the film. Perhaps nowhere has she given better account of how she transformed ideas into reality than in an interview granted to Michel Delahaye for the French publication *Cahiers du Cinéma* in September 1965:

> If you ask me today what is most important in a documentary film, what makes one see and feel, I believe I can say that there are two things. The first is the skeleton, the construction, briefly: the architecture. The architecture should have a very exact form, for the montage will only make sense and produce its effect when it is wedded, in some fashion to the principle of this architecture . . . The second is the sense of rhythm.[4]

To achieve the harmony and rhythm she was after, she would make innumerable tests, putting together and taking apart sequences till the ensemble worked as she wanted, with 'silent . . . dramatic efficacity'. It was all very hard to explain, she said, but not unlike building a house:

> . . . first of all, the plan (which is somehow the abstract, the précis of the construction); the rest is the melody. There are valleys, there are heights. Some things have to be sunk down, some have to soar. And now, I am going to be specific about another thing; this is that as soon as the montage takes form, I think of the sound. I always have a representation inside of me and take every precaution that the sound and image together never total more than a hundred percent. Is the image strong? The sound must stay in the background. Is it the sound that is strong? Then the image must take second place to it. This is one of the fundamental rules I have always observed.[5]

The most abiding after-images for anyone viewing the film are its opening shots of Hitler descending on the city of Nuremberg from storm-clouded skies like some promised saviour; abstract patterns of massed humanity, banners jostling like a field of sunflowers; the interaction between Führer and delirious Volk; the high level shot of Hitler, Himmler and Lutze walking the length of the Luitpoldhain through the cloven masses to pay homage to the dead; the lava flow of torchlit parades down narrow Nuremberg streets, and in all – as the title reinforces – the sheer subjugation of will as untold thousands relinquish minds and individuality to a single, mesmerising fanatic.

The film's programme, put out by the party-controlled *Illustrierte Film-Kurier*, describes six main elements in the film: Introduction, Happy Morning, Festive Day, Joyful Evening, Parade of the Nation and The Führer. In fact the composition divides naturally into twelve or thirteen sequences, depending on how the fine association between some of the scenes is interpreted.

The only contribution that Riefenstahl retained from Ruttman's involvement was his opening captions, which followed a slow fade-in of the German eagle, wings outspread, talons clamped around a swastika device, and the film's title in monolithic gothic *Triumph des Willens*. In retrospect, for all the trouble these gave her, Riefenstahl may have done well to discard these as well, but with the strains of Windt's Wagnerian score, at first mournful and then welling in triumph, they effectively set the mood for what follows. In translation, the title captions read:

Triumph of the Will

Documentary record of the Reich Party Congress 1934

Produced by order of the Führer

Directed by Leni Riefenstahl

On September 5, 1934,
**20 years after the outbreak of world war,
16 years after Germany's woe and travail began,
19 months after the start of Germany's rebirth,
Adolf Hitler flew once more to Nuremberg to muster his faithful followers . . .**

1934, the Party Congress

As the last title rolls away, the tempo becomes more restrained for the Führer's famous approach from the skies, his plane butting through streamers of cloud, cloud-billows banking up artistically around the cockpit. We do not see Hitler, but we feel his presence. The music is reflective. Suddenly the cloud wafts apart and there below are the roofs and gables of Nuremberg. Now the orchestra

140

strikes up gently with the *Horst Wessel Lied* and, in a most remarkable shot, the plane's shadow passes over marching columns in the streets below.

In 1947 Siegfried Kracauer, attempting a psychological history of German film in the touchy immediate postwar period, was quick to point out echoes of the *Bergfilme* in the surging cloudbanks, using this in development of his argument that the mountain cult and the Hitler cult were but facets of the same coin. For him, Hitler, flying through the 'marvellous clouds' spelled 'a reincarnation of All-Father Odin, whom the ancient Aryans heard raging with his hosts over the virgin forests.'[6] For years, subsequent critics of German cinema touched caps to Kracauer, his views on *Triumph* becoming established dogma, as also the notion that the *Bergfilme* were proto-Nazi. In 1969 Richard Corliss of the Museum of Modern Art was bold enough to challenge such 'outrageous' conclusions, to be echoed nine years later by David Hinton, who felt Kracauer was attributing to this opening sequence far more symbolism than it deserved. Hinton pointed out, rightly, that welling clouds were among Riefenstahl's stock compositional devices by the time she made *Triumph*, and would be used again when she came to put *Olympia* together a couple of years later, when the prologue once more featured a 'traveling-through-the-air device' before the viewer was brought to earth in the Berlin Stadium.

Once the Führer touches down, he is whisked off by car through cheering crowds. Throughout this fast-paced sequence, Hinton is again a good guide, drawing attention to the 'measured, rhythmical alternation of object-spectator, object-spectator':

> . . . a one-to-one rhythm that flows throughout the sequence. The object is either the plane or Hitler, and the spectator either a close-up of one particular member of the crowd, or the crowd itself . . . Throughout the scene of the plane landing, the camera viewpoint is objective third person . . . but with the beginning of the parade scene, the viewpoint suddenly shifts to that of Hitler; the car passes under a bridge and the view looking up at the bridge is Hitler's. The parade route is seen through Hitler's eyes, particularly when viewing non-human or inanimate objects, such as the tracking shots of a statue, a fountain, and a cat perched on a window ledge. They are the fleeting glimpses of an object a person catches as he passes by.[7]

Hitler's 'viewpoint' is actually a spot just behind his back – with him in frame – and is achieved by Walter Frentz with a hand-held camera riding in the limousine with him. At such close quarters the Führer can be seen to be relaxed, exuding a benevolent paternal air. A feature we notice in all the crowd scenes, as indeed in the coverage of Hitler, is Riefenstahl's deft use of the telling intimacies – a child proferring a bunch of flowers, gap-toothed tots smiling in wonder, teenagers thrilling to the excitement. The long telephoto lenses provided unconscious reactions which she well knew how to exploit. She makes use of a technique Hinton calls 'dissection of detail', which immediately lifts the coverage above the everyday:

> Following a shot of uniformed SS men standing in a row, there is a tracking close-up down the row with the SS men interlocking their hands on each other's belts to form a human chain. The close-up is of the hands gripping the belts. This attention to the details of an object, rather than to the object as a whole, is a Riefenstahl trademark.[8]

As night falls over the city, a band serenades Hitler's hotel, outside which crowds gather for a glimpse of their Führer – a 'mob of ten thousand hysterics', according to Shirer, wearing crazed 'inhuman' expressions. In the film it seems an ordered vigil in the flaming torchlit darkness; this is the Joyful Evening sequence of the programme:

> The army marches up. Torches and searchlights break through the evening darkness. In large, beaming lights a welcome shines from the hotel: 'Heil Hitler!' The army band groups in a ceremonious circle, the grey of the steel helmets gleam in the dazzling light. The conductor raises his baton. On up to the starry sky there rise the festive melodies of the tattoo. Again and again the Führer appears at his window, again and again he is cheered by the cheerful and exalted people on this festive, happy evening.[9]

Next comes a lyrical dawn as the soft early light catches the rooftops of the wakening city. Casements open and the party banners inflate limply in the light summer breeze. The music is dreamy as the camera takes in the baroque skyline and church spires in sleepy, seamless fashion which owes much to the influence of Ruttmann's *Berlin: Symphony of a Great City*. While floating over idyllic countryside we hear bells before descending upon a vast and ordered camp, a tent city, where with *Reveille* the mood changes. Youngsters, roused by drums and bugles, wash at a hewn trough, spray each other with hoses, help one another to spruce up. They give the cooks a hand to stoke fires under huge cauldrons of porridge, retrieve boiled puddings and vast bunches of frankfurters from scalding pots, and line up for breakfast with their billycans. It is very jolly, like a Scout jamboree, with laughter and brisk businesslike music. Horsing around, they wrestle on piggyback, hold mock chariot races, toss one of their number sky high from a blanket. Comradeship is the message here; and they are clearly having a lot of fun. A five-minute folk parade follows – all lederhosen, dirndls and concertina music – then the Horst Wessel anthem breaks through again as Hitler arrives to review a troop of flag bearers before being swept on. Once more we see the crowds, and never far away the children, straining for a glimpse of Hitler, the young girls, all good honest folk. The air is one of hope.

Action cuts to the opening session of the Congress in the Luitpold Hall, 'more than a glorious show'. To Shirer it had 'the mysticism and religious fervour of an Easter or Christmas Mass in a great Gothic cathedral':

> The hall was a sea of brightly coloured flags. Even Hitler's arrival was made dramatic. The band stopped playing. There was a hush over the thirty thousand people packed in the hall. Then the band struck up the *Badenweiler March*, a very catchy tune, and used only, I'm told, when Hitler makes his big entries. Hitler appeared in the back of the auditorium, and followed by his aides, Goering, Goebbels, Hess, Himmler, and the others, he strode slowly down the long centre aisle while thirty thousand hands were raised in salute.[10]

As Beethoven's *Egmont* Overture dies away, an impassioned Hess, in storm trooper dress, greets the delegates, pays tribute to Field Marshal Hindenberg and to fallen comrades. He welcomes the revival of the Wehrmacht under the Führer. And to the Führer ('My Führer') he pledges loyalty and gratitude, asserting: '*You* are Germany! When you act, the nation acts; when you judge, the people judge!' He continues:

> Our gratitude is our promise – in good times and in bad – to stand by you, come what may. Thanks to your leadership, Germany will attain her aim to be the homeland of all the Germans of the world. You have guaranteed our victory, as you are now guaranteeing our peace. *Heil Hitler! Sieg Heil! Sieg Heil! Sieg Heil!*

He glistens with sweat, wears a watchful, sly smile. Short excerpts follow from the speeches of twelve other Party leaders. Adolf

Wagner, Gauleiter of Bavaria, reads Hitler's proclamation, sparing the Führer's voice for more critical solo performances:

> No revolution could last forever without leading to total anarchy. Just as the world cannot exist on wars, nations cannot exist on revolutions. There is nothing great on this earth that has ruled the world for millennia and was created in decades. The highest tree has had the longest period of growth. What has withstood centuries will also need centuries to become strong.

Then we have Rosenberg (entrusting the young to carry on the fight), Dietrich (calling for truth), Todt (promising autobahns and work), Reinhardt ('Wherever your eyes focus, new buildings rise, values are improved and new values created'), Darré, Streicher (this renowned Jew-baiter making his plea for racial purity), Ley, Frank, and Goebbels:

> May the shining flame of our enthusiasm never be extinguished. It alone lends life and warmth to the creative art of modern political propaganda. Springing from the hearts of our people, that is to where it must return for its power. We need guns and bayonets, but better by far to win and hold the hearts of a nation.

Finally, Hierl speaks for the Reich's Labour force. Film analysts have been quick to point out that this substantial scene comprises excerpts from various sessions at the conference, not just the welcoming ceremony. Barsam goes so far as to suggest that, by selecting unfaithful representations of what was said, reality is further distorted. He believes the way they are edited together falsely unites the speeches 'with motifs of hope, progress and unity, bending the actual substance of each speaker's remarks to the general purpose of the film's propaganda.'[11] Critics of course can never agree: Hinton finds the snatches so short as to be meaningless. The line between art and tedium is a fine one, he admits, yet recognises the real purpose here is to introduce the nation's new leaders to the Volk.[12] Riefenstahl herself has written of the difficulty of selecting clips from the many and long orations throughout the Rally, giving as her criteria the simple need for each to have a beginning, an end and a strong self-sufficient statement.

The scene shifts to the Zeppelin field for a vast outdoor rally at which Konstantin Hierl introduces his frighteningly well-drilled *Arbeitsdienst* to the public. This Labour Service is Germany's solution to unemployment and hope for national recovery. Although mandatory for unskilled school-leavers, membership is peddled as a privilege and honour. Each man carries a spade. 'My Führer!' Hierl addresses Hitler, 'Fifty-two thousand men await your order.'

'Heil, worker volunteers!' Hitler greets the company and triggers a chanted tableau.

'Heil, mein Führer,' chorus the fifty-two thousand.

Their corps-leader tells them, 'Take up arms!' And to drumrolls the men present their shovels like rifles.

'At ease.' The spades are lowered.

As the recitation is tossed backwards and forwards, the camera captures each speaker in close-up, meanwhile cutting to Hitler, Hierl, and the relentless masses.

The entire *Sprechchor.* 'Here we stand. We are ready to carry Germany into a new era. Germany!'

'Comrade, where are you from?'

A young worker comes into frame. 'From Friesia,' he says.

'And you, comrade?'

'From Bavaria.'

'And you?'

'From the Kaiserstuhl.'

'And you?'

'From Pomerania', 'From Konigsberg', 'From Silesia', 'From the coastlands', 'From the Black Forest', 'From Dresden', 'From the Danube', 'From the Rhine', 'And from the Saar.' The camera flits between eager faces.

'*One Volk, one Führer, one Reich!* Today we work together on the marshes, in the quarries, in the dunes. We dyke the North Sea, we plant trees (murmuring trees), we build roads, we prepare new acreage for the farmers. From village to village and town to town. For Germany!' They break into merry peasant song, binding blood to soil.

Flags are solemnly dipped in commemoration of the dead of famous First War battles to the strains of 'I had a comrade.' Rebirth is promised as the young men pledge with their hammers, axes, shovels and hoes to be the new soldiers of the Reich. Hitler, who has been watching sombrely now promises the ardent assembly that no longer will the idea of manual toil be regarded less highly than any other form of work. Earth and labour shall unite everyone. 'In time everyone will have to go through the same training as you. Germany is deeply proud to see its sons marching in your ranks.' A premonitory glimpse of marchers is here superimposed on the dissolve of a fluttering flag, which later returns as the final motif in the film.

The flowing pattern of half-profile faces as they march away with their songs and their *Sieg Heils* is impressive. Other events in the rally programme employ a similar *Sprechchor* format, but none is seen in the film as completely as this. Its artificiality appears awkward to modern eyes, and it is not easy to resist comparison with Hollywood's Seven Dwarfs as the young men shoulder their shovels and march off to work, singing.

Another night scene follows, up-tempo this time: a torchlit rally of storm troopers, with fireworks and bonfires, drums, music and singing. Viktor Lutze, who inherited the leadership of the SA after the bloody purge of Röhm and his followers, identifies with his men, promotes calm. Nevertheless, there is a pagan air to the vulgarity, which Riefenstahl heightens with her mastery of half light and shadow, and not least by the effects of firesmoke and magnesium flares. For Barsam, 'the dark, smoky mystique of the SA rally reinforces the men's blood brotherhood and suggests their mythic origins in fire.' It is in striking contrast to the next sunlit scene of massed Hitler Youth:

> The boys are fresh and unititiated; they know nothing of smoke, fire, or purges of disloyal members from their ranks. Here, as in many places in the film, Riefenstahl juxtaposes light with dark, leaders with troops, boys with men, peace with war, and the kinetic with the static.[13]

Again, the emphasis in this emotional sequence is on disciplined formality, counterpointed with regular reference to the lonely, superior Führer or some humanising anchor figures in the crowd. Winsome, fresh-faced and suitably Aryan youngsters defuse the relentless symmetry of bodies and banners. But there is no relief from the hypnotic order: tents come in ranks, tin hats, hoisted colours. No wayward element distorts the pattern, and we are never allowed to forget Hitler remains the focus. This is where the clockwork camera on its low-level track begins circumnavigating the Führer as, outlined against stadium or sky, he inspires the boys to obedience and courage, urging them to harden themselves against weakness and collapse. 'We shall pass away,' he tells them, 'but in you, Germany will live on . . . You are flesh of our flesh, blood of our blood. Your young minds are fired with the same spirit that fires us. As the great columns of our movement march victoriously through Germany today, I know you are among them. And we know that Germany is before us, within us, and Germany follows us.' (Cue: the official Hitler Youth song, as Hitler departs by car to continue his mission.)

There follows a brief scene of Hitler, Goering and other military officials reviewing a mock battle in the Zeppelin meadow. This militaristic display, openly challenging the Versailles treaty, takes place in the rain, and the footage, shot by one of the newsreel companies, is visibly inferior to that achieved elsewhere by Riefenstahl's own cameramen. It adds little to the film. Riefenstahl would have rejected it happily, but for Hitler's direct intervention.

Though she has always maintained that neither Hitler nor Goebbels saw any of the film before it was finished, she was paid a visit in the cutting room during December by two eminent generals. They sought reassurance that the military's role was being given sufficient prominence in her film. Remembering how part of the function of the 1934 Parteitag was to demonstrate that the army stood united in its loyalty to the Führer, it is easy to imagine their fury at being told bluntly that the material fell below the overall standard of the film and was all being omitted. Some weeks later Leni found herself summoned to Hitler to explain her decision.

Once more she explained her regret that there was simply no footage suitable. With utter consternation, she received Hitler's idea of a compromise. Why not muster the generals for the camera, he said. She could pan along their ranks, and it would provide a useful sequence for the opening credits. Her own introductory assembly of clouds and aeroplane was already completed in rough cut, and she knew it was good. No way would she tolerate replacing it with an idea that to her seemed so banal and, with tearful vehemence, burst out that she *could* not, *would* not do such a thing!

Hitler was furious. It was, Riefenstahl says, the only time he ever lost his temper with her as with menace he snapped, 'Don't forget who you are talking to.' Then, with more resignation than heat, he added, 'You can be a real mule. Whatever makes you so stubborn?' He was only trying to help, and was well aware he had promised not to interfere. If she wouldn't entertain it, she wouldn't, and that was that – whereupon he shrugged off the whole affair. She realised she was dismissed. Realised too, belatedly, the political significance of the Wehrmacht appearing in this film. In this indifferent sequence, we see that Riefenstahl has clearly salvaged what she could from the maimed footage. Seeking to mend fences with the generals, she promised to produce a short film dedicated entirely to the Wehrmacht at the next rally in 1935, even though she had vowed never to make another Party rally film.

Triumph continues with the evening muster of the Amtswalter, for which Speer claimed he prepared his 'Cathedral of Light'. It has to be said, it is not obvious in the footage.[14] A vast gathering of up to 200,000 (with another 250,000 spectating) advances through the dusk with banners upraised, surging towards the podium and its spotlit eagle, where the Führer waits. Barsam found the juxtaposition of faceless masses and an elevated Führer distorted through the telephoto lens highly reminiscent of Fritz Lang's *Metropolis* (reputedly one of Hitler's favourite films).

Riefenstahl develops the theme of Hitler as God. As words spill from his mouth, he stands alone on his podium, washed by the beams of searchlights. 'Our movement is alive,' he tells his faceless Party workers and, acknowledging their privation and effort, exhorts them 'to think only of Germany every hour of every day, the nation, the Reich, and our German people.'

Now comes that incredible, indelible scene in the vast Luitpold Arena, which Riefenstahl filmed from her little lift attached to one of the 140-foot oriflamme poles, high above the throng. Speer's monolithic eagle, perched on its carved bay wreath containing the swastika, dissolves to a long shot, from behind, of three tiny figures – Hitler, flanked by Himmler and Lutze – making their long, lonely walk the length of the stadium through the parted ranks of fifty thousand SS-men. Only at the last moment does the camera switch to an opposite viewpoint as the trio reaches the war memorial to pay solemn respects before turning to walk back along the broad swath. These are moments of extraordinary power. Analysts agree that they exhibit the consummate skill Riefenstahl has by now achieved in direction, camerawork, and of course, in her editing. The dignity and restraint perfectly matches the solemnity and simplicity of the occasion. Even as the figures approach the memorial, Riefenstahl's dramatic use of the slow moving shot emphasises the stillness and contained emotion.

'There are no close-ups here, for it is the tribute – not those evoking it – that is important,' Barsam points out.[15] And Hinton remarks upon Riefenstahl's uncanny ability for selecting the ideal camera location to give the most graphic coverage possible. Building the elevator, he says, reflected her film background, which could be seen also in her 'striking composition within the frame.' The little lift is visible in some of the shots.

148

In the parade of flags, which follows the tribute scene, again one is struck by Leni's absorption with pattern. Hinton particularly admired one continuous shot in which the frame is filled completely with flags, moving up, down, and forward 'as if they had lives of their own'. Although something of the beauty of this composition could be gleaned from a still, he said, its true impact lay in the animation of the flags within the frame.'[16]

Again the tension builds as Hitler addresses his storm-troopers. 'Men of the SA and SS', Hitler reminds them, 'a few months ago, a black shadow spread over the movement . . .' This is that moment of uncertain confrontation after the bloody purge to which William Shirer refers in his *Berlin Diary* when Hitler 'absolves' the men from all blame for the Röhm 'revolt' and Shirer half expects one of the fifty thousand to go for his gun. The crackle of tension in the stadium is maintained in Riefenstahl's film.

'Nobody but a madman or a liar could think that I, or anybody, would ever seek to dissolve what we have built up by our own efforts over so many long and difficult years.' Hitler is making a desperate bid to bind raw wounds. He urges his 'comrades' to stand firmly together for the Fatherland. 'I give you the new flags, convinced that I am handing them over to the most faithful hands in all Germany. You have proved your loyalty to me a thousandfold in the past; it cannot and will not be different in the future. Thus, I greet you, my old faithful men of the SA and SS. *Sieg Heil!*'

Viktor Lutze, Röhm's successor as chief of the SA, acknowledges the Führer's gesture. 'He has a shrill, unpleasant voice, and the SA boys received him coolly, I thought,' remarks Shirer.[17]

As the Führer moves along the ranks of banners for the blood flag ceremony, he takes care to look each standard bearer intimately in the eye. His face is seen by the camera, but rarely those of the men hidden in the foliage of banners. Among the endless flags and massed heads, Hitler almost always stands proud in the frame, not buried among his aides, the lonely leader.

With some suddenness and a complete change of mood comes the penultimate episode: the long parade before the Führer. Riefenstahl compresses this five-hour event to around eighteen minutes. Endeavouring to make sense of the relentless march pasts and adulation in the streets of the old city, she employs her most imaginative camera angles, freely indulging those dissection-of-detail shots and impressionistic patterns that have become her trademark. Caravans of official cars, jackboots goose-stepping on the cobbles, sleek jodphurs, helmeted warriors march into evening light once more. *Oompah-pah!* It is Roman pageantry. They pour over the bridge in the old town, banners reflected in the water. Echoing gargoyles, people crane from the rooftops to catch a view. Outstretched arms thrust like cilia from window embrasures. Then come aerial shots of the marchers, ground level views, stolen glimpses through archways – even more *Oompah-pah* – and the overall sensation is to be bowled over at such sheer numbers of people gathered together. Some have remarked on the fact that most of the faces picked out of the crowd are of women, underlining the message it is for men to march, women to cheer them on.

You wonder at the stamina of Hitler as he stands on staunchly, hour after hour, with his wayward quiff, acknowledging the tributes. Riefenstahl allows the occasional glimpse of fatigue as he flicks a wrist to relieve the cramp from so much saluting and stiff-standing. She hovers on his lurking smile.

No other scene demonstrates so clearly the excitement and anticipation Riefenstahl can build with rhythmic montage. This is the longest passage in the film, could easily have been its most boring, yet it holds. To Barsam, it invites comparison with her later, famous diving sequence in *Olympia*, when she 'transcends the finite limitations of time and space, and explores the infinite suggestiveness of cinematic space and form.'

The party standards are in evidence again at the Closing of the Rally in the thronged Luitpold Hall, when Hitler enters to his favourite *Badenweiler March* to give his most measured and animated performance of the entire rally. All the studied histrionics – 'waving arms, to pounding fists, to visionary stares and enraptured ranting' (Barsam) – are there. William Everson particularly appreciated one brief, almost imperceptible vignette of Hitler, lasting less than a second – 'The mob roars approval . . . even he is a bit surprised at the enthusiasm. There is . . . a suggestion of a smile which says, more clearly than reels of film, "Boy, I've got them just where I want them!' Of such moments is the real truth of history, and some of the most valuable moments of film documentary, composed.'[18]

The content is little different from earlier exhortations – a politician's speech, more rhetoric than substance – although buried within it is the unlovely assertion that the leadership of the party now comprises the 'nation's best blood'. The delivery is all – and quite the reverse of the image of an aloof, restrained Führer promulgated earlier in the film. Here we have the Hitler we have all learned to know (and hate) from stereotype. His purpose is clear: to send home his followers recharged with fanaticism, that they may diligently continue obeying his inflexible will. As he closes, Deputy Hess leaps to his feet, eyes ablaze: 'The party is Hitler,' he shouts. 'Just as Germany is Hitler! Hitler! *Sieg Heil! Sieg Heil! Sieg Heil!*'

Rapture is unrestrained as arms shoot upwards in a tidal wave, and the answering shout comes back like thunder, '*Sieg Heil!*'

The hall is a sea of upraised arms. Up strikes the Horst Wessel theme once more, and in a sequence of dissolves from hall, through swastika, we reach the final ethereal passage of silhouetted figures marching heavenwards into the clouds, the shot which carries such strong echoes of Luis Trenker's concluding frames in *The Rebel*.

★

The most characteristic element in Riefenstahl's films, discernible first in her performances and later more convincingly under her direction, is fantasy. She offers a stylised world, not anchored in everyday cares or ordinary mechanics. Most of her acting roles found her set apart from other humans: if not a superwoman exactly, then certainly endowed with supernormal athleticism and inexplicable powers of communion with the natural and spirit worlds. She is seen thus as unworldly, or otherworldly; and though patently sensual, is at the same time almost asexual. Knowing everything, but as it were unconsciously, she embodies the innocent fixed in permanent adolescence, unwilling or unable to embrace the ordinary, the adult.

She achieves the same fantastical disorientation in her film direction by not tying real images to accepted reality. Buildings and people are as often seen in relation to the sky as the earth. They do not stand on lowly clay. They soar, they swoop, they inhabit an altogether higher plane. This transfiguration was her vision, already fixed by the early 1930s, and already publicly known. It might be thought to have rendered her the very last person to be entrusted with a documentary – if, that is, the documentary is seen merely as a conventionally factual form.

To the layman, the word 'documentary' is almost a synonym for any informative non-fictional film, whether a newsreel or a *Panorama* investigation, the coverage of a climbing expedition, a pop festival, or a televised study of some faraway community. Within cinema terminology, however, it appears The Documentary is but one of several forms of non-fiction film, the word itself having been coined in 1926 by the film historian and theorist John Grierson (after seeing

Robert Flaherty's *Moana*) to describe a 'creative treatment of actuality'.[19] Some degree of dramatised 'reconstruction' has become tolerated in achieving this, where it assists the understanding of the subject, although the cine-pundits squabble endlessly over where the line of acceptable licence should be drawn. And especially whether or not actors can be allowed to reconstruct the activities of real people.

Since the essence of creative expression is to push hard against accepted boundaries, and this is what gives art its freshness and vigour, it can be argued that to attempt a too precise definition of any particular art form is a nonsense, and an invitation to immediate redefinition. It takes little logic or appreciation to acknowledge that a non-fiction film is the more compulsive for being 'dramatic'; that a fictional drama has to persuade its audience with the reality – or realism – of its main characters at least; and that the line between document and fiction is extraordinarily fine, if indeed it exists at all. And because every film (like every recorded experience, every memory) is edited – distilled through the vision of those responsible for it (as also through the eyes of the beholder) – a strong case can be put for there being no such thing as a non-fiction film at all, or a non-fiction any-other-work-of-art, come to that. Still, as arresting a concept as that is, it is hardly the point here. Going back to accepted generalisations, a documentary film is said to be distinguishable from a merely factual film by having encoded within it some message or socio-political enquiry.[20] From here, to seeing it as a work of propaganda – a concerted effort to promulgate a particular message (through information or deliberate misinformation) – is a short enough step, in all truth.

'Propaganda is hardly less true than any traditional art which seeks to achieve certain specific emotional effects, to manifest a vision of the world compellingly' – so wrote Ken Kelman in 1973 in a thoughtful study of *Triumph of the Will*. He added that its poor reputation rested largely on the fact that propaganda so seldom succeeded in its aims. *Triumph of the Will*, by contrast, is successful in almost every context one seeks to judge it – artistically, cinematographically, documentarily – and as a potent piece of Nazi promotion. Riefenstahl herself has always denied that it can be interpreted as propaganda. Such was never her intention, she says. It is *cinema-vérité*. 'How can it be propaganda,' she demands in Ray Müller's 1993 film of her, in that curious, querulous manner she adopts, of coy imperiousness, 'when there is no *commentary*?' Yet the message is clear – commentary or no. And one feels almost bound to ask, what is the matter with this woman that she can overlook so obvious a truth? Can anyone be so ingenuous, or is she dissembling? After all, she chose not to put in a commentary presumably because her pictures spoke for themselves. She may not have set out to glorify Hitler in any conscious or devious way, but her feelings for him at that time were so worshipful that she could portray him only through the shining eyes of admiration. Not until much later would she accept that she had been hoodwinked. For Riefenstahl, in 1934, as for millions of her countrymen and women, the Führer represented the saviour who would restore Germany to some (imagined) former glory. This is what she filmed.

Everyone in Europe in those days was aware of living through momentous times. Perhaps in the thick of them in Germany, and drunk on a surfeit of event, it may not have been so clear just how historically crucial the 1934 Party Day was. There were good reasons for Hitler wanting this to be the year Riefenstahl made her film. It is not so obvious that Riefenstahl appreciated the urgency. For him, it was crucial to demonstrate his Party's solidarity after the bloody upsets of the past six months; and, in those days before television performed the task ad nauseum, he sought to impress the image of the Party's leaders on the public consciousness. Abroad he wanted to be seen as in control of a willing populace, and it would not hurt (as David Stewart Hull points out in his study *Film in the Third Reich*) if the film scared the hell out of foreign audiences.

Hitler may have commanded the rally be dedicated to the memory of the late President, Field Marshal Hindenburg, but it was in truth a celebration of the old gentleman's death, marking the completion of the Nazi revolution. Hitler acknowledged as much in his Proclamation to the crowds on 5th September, though back-dating the struggle through history to emphasise the prophetic nature of his Coming: 'The age of nerves of the nineteenth century has found its close with us. In the next thousand years there will be no other revolution in Germany.'[21]

Why was it so important to Hitler that the task of committing the Party Day to celluloid should be entrusted to Riefenstahl, and no one else? There was more to it, surely, than that he admired the atmospheric quality of *The Blue Light*, and fancied her imagery chimed neatly with his own ideas on myth and idealism? In recognising the power of film to create and maintain superstars, he wanted to be similarly immortalised on that liveliest and most telling of media, and he had faith in her to do that with sensitivity. Equally, it is plain he had no wish for the rally film to be produced under

Goebbels' supervision by Ministry of Propaganda hacks, for the truth was he did not see eye to eye with Goebbels on film propaganda. True, they shared an appreciation for such films as *Morgenrot*, and Trenker's *The Rebel*, as they shared the hope that something of the quality of *Battleship Potemkin* would one day emerge to glorify the Nazi cause. But it was Goebbels contention (initially, at least) that propaganda should permeate every film made, especially feature films, whereas Hitler famously said, 'let it be either art or politics.' He could see the popular appeal of Riefenstahl's art, whereas Goebbels' acedemic 'artiness' left him cold.

If we remember how reactionary and generally banal was Hitler's taste in art — his favouring of kitsch, not to put too fine a point on it — his artistic approval could be considered no recommendation at all. But his faith in Riefenstahl was not misplaced. She may have imagined at the outset that there was a possibility of persuading the Führer to allow her to be relieved of her task, that it was sheer chance she came to film this particular rally rather than any other, it was merely a commission which could as well have been a fruit and vegetable show; but, if that is so, it is clear now she was deluded.

However, if a knowledge of subsequent historical events colours the way *we* see the film, it cannot have affected the manner in which Riefenstahl approached her subject. It may stretch our insight to ask, rhetorically, what difference it would have made if Leni Riefenstahl had not agreed to film the Sixth Nuremberg Rally, yet surely it is important to resist the overwhelming force of hindsight when judging her role? She may now concede she made a pact with the devil,[22] but at the time she claims to have believed she was promoting peace and industry. The main cause of her reluctance then had nothing to do with politics; she just wanted to resume her acting. She had no spontaneous wish to film the rallies and afterwards deeply regretted having done so. Then she resented it getting in the way of her career. She couldn't know the disruption would prove permanent. Once committed, she says, she performed the job to the best of her ability.

As it was, her total immersion in the cutting room paid off. It was clear on that opening night in the Ufa-Palast that Riefenstahl had triumphed. From what might be imagined as unpromising material, such hackneyed icons, she had conjured a masterpiece, although she herself dared not believe as much until the film was over. So tense was she during the performance, she had her eyes screwed shut for much of the time. Afterwards, when the prolongued applause at last died down and a delighted Führer presented her with a bouquet of lilacs, the exhausted film-maker swooned away.

Despite his orchestrated attempts to sabotage the film, Goebbels too was completely won over by the result, recommending that *Triumph of the Will* be awarded the National Film Prize for 1935. A month after the film's première, he made the presentation personally, praising a very great and topical achievement:

> It is a magnificent cinematic vision of the Führer, seen here for the first time with a power that has not been revealed before. The pitfall of being merely a politically slanted film is deftly avoided. The powerful rhythm of this great epoch has been translated into something outstandingly artistic; it is an epic, forging the tempo of marching formations, steel-like in its conviction and fired by a passionate artistry.

The film also picked up a gold medal at the Venice Biennale later that year and a Grand Prix from the French Government at the Paris Exposition of 1937. It went on general release throughout the Reich, although its performance was patchy elsewhere, authorities wary of its power to disturb. The *Observer* newspaper regretted that British diplomats Anthony Eden and John Simon – in Germany that week for talks with Hitler – had not accepted the proffered invitation to stay for the film's opening in Berlin. The statesmen, it said, 'would have received from the film document convincing proof that the passionate, dynamic, explosive energy displayed by Chancellor Hitler this week in the diplomatic talks is the concentrated personal expression of a national energy equally passionate and dynamic.'[23]

Riefenstahl has been accused by postwar critics of seducing people with this film, to which she retorts that at the time it was made 90 per cent[24] of Germans were in favour of Hitler. It presents a rosy view in that it contains relatively little Party dogma, and nothing to suggest the Nazi's virulent racist doctrines or political persecution. But that is down to the rally, not to Riefenstahl. She offers hypnotic ceremonial, brilliantly crafted and sustained, brilliantly orchestrated by Herbert Windt's largely original score to capture just the right mood for each moment. Others have found it difficult to fault cinematically, beyond identifying the inspiration of earlier masters. Though it stuck in his gullet to say so, Paul Rotha – in his monumental *The Film Till Now* – felt bound to admit:

> The triumph here was due to the fact that the mixture 'of a show

simulating German reality and of a German reality manoeuvred into a show'[25] really was inextricable, except to the eye of the experienced analyst, and that it had been cast into the melting pot by a talent which we must, however reluctantly, recognise as one of the most brilliant ever to be concerned with films . . . Let it suffice to say that this woman's knowledge of the power of editing images was profound, nearly as profound as Pabst's or Eisenstein's.[26]

Echoes, too, have been claimed with Ruttmann's work or that of Murnau. Others see Fritz Lang's *Nibelungen* as the inspiration, with Hitler its new Siegfried. Yet the most readily recognisable influence has to be the *Bergfilme* – the earlier output of Riefenstahl, of her mentor Arnold Fanck, and to a lesser extent Luis Trenker. This particular way of looking at things, this vision, she shared with her chief cameraman Sepp Allgeier. Certainly, Riefenstahl had always demonstrated an extraordinary capacity for learning from others; it was not just from Fanck that she sopped up ideas and skills, as it were osmotically. It is of course possible to claim glibly that all art is 'borrowed', that the Almighty was the last great original and everyone else plagiarists; and of course all leaps into new territory are made from stepping stones provided by those who have gone before, but it is churlish to suggest this is a derivative work. The artist's eye was her own, and it had been evident from well before she choreographed her own dances, in her juvenile preoccupations with drama and the stage, a talent encouraged during her brief attendance at art college.

Felicitous incidence, or coincidence, played its part, too. As it does in most art. Much is made of Riefenstahl's 'trick' of isolating Hitler, of shooting him from below waist height to make him tower over other mortals. The fact is that in the stadia, apart from the flagpole set-up, it was difficult to shoot him from any other vantage point. Cameras had to be as discreet as possible, in pits in the ground, running around on little rail-carts, while Hitler did all his addressing from rostra and podia.

Apart from the patently false assertion that the 1934 *Parteitag* was staged for the camera like some colossal Hollywood production – these Nazi soap operas grew in scale annually thereafter till 1938, with no Riefenstahl to film them – a recurrent criticism of *Triumph of the Will* has been Riefenstahl's tinkering with the chronology of some events. In fact, this is slight, the transposition of a mere handful of sequences and always within the logic of the structure, the particular threads Riefenstahl was developing at the time. Were it any other film, or any other film-maker, it would be hard to imagine offence being taken. Ken Kelman remarks that, despite its devices and its expressionism, and even in its most extravagantly romantic passage – that of Hitler dipping from the skies – 'the technical bounds of "documentary" are never strained beyond the breaking point':

> The Führer's ministry on earth which follows – complete with speeches or sermons or prophecies, and vast throngs, titanic structures or miracles – never exceeds 'correct' reportage. Thus Riefenstahl ultimately succeeds by virtue of her objective genre and material, combined with her intensely but subtly subjective vision, in creating perhaps the definitive cinematic obliteration of the division between fantasy and 'reality'.[27]

Riefenstahl fuses truth with propaganda, he posits, compromising neither. Traditionally, the documentary turns its back on the cinematic magic available to fiction, being considered 'the spinach or castor oil of cinema fare, the occasional dose of fact that can be sugar-coated or spiced, but never can have magic or even much imagination without becoming something other.' This documentary tradition, he says, is the formal point of Riefenstahl's departure, and subtle play with its convention her basic alchemical technique.

XII

Goebbels' Dream Factory

Riefenstahl did not forget her promise to the generals. She returned to Nuremberg in the autumn of 1935 to film the Wehrmacht, taking with her five cameramen. Three had worked with her on *Triumph* – Frentz, Lantschner and Kling – to whom she added the great documentarist Willy Zielke (shortly to assist with the prologue for *Olympia*) and her erstwhile lover, the green-eyed Hans Ertl. By this time she was committed to covering the Berlin Games in the coming summer and, with all the preparations required for that, was unwilling to spare much time 'on manoeuvres' with the army. A couple of days took care of the shooting, and the film was quickly edited. Its title, *Day of Freedom – Our Armed Forces*, echoed the ironic theme decreed for a rally at which the infamous anti-Semitic Nuremberg Laws were introduced. It ran for twenty-five minutes and trailed a few experimental techniques which would become Riefenstahl trademarks after *Olympia*, but in the main it fell into the mould of her previous masterpiece. The generals were delighted. When the lights went up after the film's première in Berlin, it was to hugs and handshakes all round. 'Leni here – Leni there – there was tremendous enthusiasm and I could tell by Goebbels' expression how deeply he resented my success,' she said.[1] According to Ertl, the film went on general release 'at home and abroad' in tandem with an official propaganda production, Gerhard Lamprecht's *Der Hohere Befehl* (*The Higher Order*), a period piece paying homage to Britain's alliance with Prussia in the fight against Napoleon.

The re-emergence of Ertl is interesting. Leni had not seen him two years or more, during which time he had diligently converted himself into a cine-cameraman. In Greenland his role had been stunt climber and general dogsbody, and no special aptitude impressed itself on his colleagues. He even mislaid his precious Leica for over a fortnight while distracted by his midsummer flirtation with Leni. When it came to light again, by chance, behind some rocks a hundred yards or so from his tent, it was battered and pock-marked with dog-bites, its leather case completely gnawed away. What Ertl could not fail to notice on location in the Arctic was the glamorous lifestyle his colleagues enjoyed through their peripatetic camerawork. Even if no one was making a fortune, it was exactly the life of adventure for which he hankered. No sooner was he home, than he read everything he could on camera technique. In 1934 he worked again with Arnold Fanck on a film about the early alpinist Jacques Balmat, this time as a cameraman, and then it was off to the Karakoram with Günther Oskar Dyhrenfurth's International Himalaya Expedition, which climbed several peaks between twenty-three and twenty-five thousand feet and produced the controversial motion picture, *Dämon Himalaya*.[2]

By the time he and Leni renewed their acquaintance sometime in 1935, the careers of both had moved on from the days of their Greenland idyll, and they delightedly caught up on each other's news and successes. 'Leni looked radiant and was full of plans for our collaboration,' Ertl recalled. What she perhaps did not recognise immediately was that Ertl was less ready to play her slave than before. Hungrily ambitious to get on in his new vocation, he had high-flying plans of his own. They were rivals now.

Goebbels, meanwhile, had spared no effort in bringing the German cinema industry under the jackboot heel. Through its various bureaucratic divisions, the State Chamber of Film (RFK) exerted critical influence over all aspects of film-making, and this control was systematically tightened by a series of decrees to parallel the *Gleichschaltung* measures being taken in other walks of life. On 19th January 1934, when the purge of non-Aryans from the industry was well under way, the *Völkischer Beobachter* (Hitler's State newspaper) carried a prohibition on the production of films ('either professionally or for the common good, under public or private management') except by members of the Chamber. Within twenty days, all producers and moving picture enterprises were required to affiliate themselves to the appropriate branch of the Chamber. Draconian censorship was introduced in the Reich Film Law soon afterwards and films were to be classified according to political, artistic and educational merit. Productions scoring the highest aggregate of points were to receive maximum co-operation. All scripts and scenarios had to be vetted to ensure the suppression of topics running counter to 'the spirit of the time' – for which of course, should be read: 'the constrained moral and artistic concepts of National Socialism.' Goebbels served notice on the expressionism which had been the strength of Weimar cinema, when he announced 'We do not want art in any milieu that does not exist in life, we do not want characters who cannot be discovered in reality.'

Once completed, no film could be passed for distribution until image, dialogue, and even the music satisfied the thirty-three articles contained within the new censorship bill. So German cinema became subject to the most comprehensive restrictions of anywhere outside Soviet Russia. In his book *Film in the Third Reich*, the film historian David Stewart Hull recalled a laconic press release of the day: 'Hitherto film censorship has been negative. Hereafter, the new State will assume entire responsibility for the creation of films. Only by intensive advice and supervision can films running contrary to the spirit of the times be kept off the screen.'[3]

Another scholar, economic historian Julian Petley, took issue with Hull over his interpretation of these developments in a little booklet prepared for the British Film Institute in 1979. Petley argued that you could not infer (as Hull had) that Goebbels 'subverted' the film industry. The new regime's measures to extend 'a degree of control' were *overt*, and not resisted by all factions within the industry, who on the contrary were busily pressing the government to help solve their problems. The advent of talkies had resulted in not just the German but all European films losing ground to Hollywood even before the haemorrhage of Jewish talent across the Atlantic. In an ailing industry, there were many, Petley contended, more than happy to relinquish a degree of 'freedom' in return for financial resuscitation. And while he agreed that 'much film censorship during the Third Reich was of an extremely paranoid and trivial nature, very few films had to be banned outright. They were usually re-cut and passed as they could in no way be described as "anti-fascist" in the first place.'[4]

Doctor Goebbels even entertained the vision of Nazi cinema enlightening the world; of Berlin overtaking Hollywood, Scandinavia and everywhere else as the cultural centre of excellence. It was a schizophrenic dream when at the same time he was killing creativity with his personal brand of political correctness, and insisting on the missionary role of German films in reshaping morale and moral thinking at home. The rest of the world had little interest in the warped morality plays coming out of the Third Reich, and German film exports fell disastrously.

160

Viewers in the Fatherland also found these patently propagandist movies tedious. The first, *Hitlerjunge Quex*, adapted from a best-selling novel, enjoyed limited popularity but, after the box office failure of such didactic follow-ups as *S.A.-Mann Brand* and *Hans Westmar*, the genre was quietly suppressed. Goebbels now changed tack completely. Entertainment was the priority. Any message he wanted to get over had to be gently insinuated into more palatable vehicles – the everyday comedies, musicals, costume dramas so beloved by Hollywood, but in this instance designed almost exclusively for the domestic market. As he was simultaneously banning from German release an increasing number of foreign pictures (new and old) – for their unsuitable ideas or the Jewish talent employed in their making – there was theoretically a growing market for home-produced wares.[5]

However, in the disturbed year of 1934, caution and uncertainty actually resulted in a twenty-five per cent drop in production, leaving cinemas with very little to show. Goebbels' Film Chamber initiated 'working sessions' to train new talent, but by the end of November he was forced to admit that Nazi efforts to improve films had been largely fruitless. The Reich film industry did not appear to recognise the honour that had come to it. He complained that he had personally felt bound to suppress two films passed by the censor, despite the film shortage, not because they contained any matter injurious to the State's policy but because they simply did not match up to his ideas of artistic accomplishment. He served warning on the industry to pull up its socks and heed the suggestions he and his subordinates offered,[6] but in truth the industry was so confused by this time, it was frightened to do anything.

To spark things up, in April 1936 Goebbels held an International Film Conference in Berlin, where two thousand delegates from forty nations were treated to his views on Creative Film. The British delegation, which was to have been forty-strong, took a last-minute decision to boycott the event – an arresting stand in the year of the Olympics, when British authorities and sportsmen vacillated endlessly but never seriously looked like withdrawing from the Berlin Games.

Hard on the heels of the conference, at the now-annual May Day awards for cultural excellence, Leni Riefenstahl was honoured with the top film prize for *Triumph of the Will*. Later that year Goebbels gagged the film critics. 'The reporting of art should not be concerned with values,' he said. Beyond simple description, only brief, positive comments on a film's artistry were to be allowed. Critics had been making the mistake of judging aesthetics without appreciating the political implication of what they were seeing. This was 'an overall perversion of the concept of criticism dating from the time of Jewish domination of the arts,' he said.[7] Nor was he just concerned with curbing dissent; above all, nothing must be said which might induce cinema-goers to stay away and so jeopardise a film's profitability. Goebbels needed more from the film industry than it be self-supporting; it should be a major contributor to Nazi funds.

If creative excellence was taking time, the purging of 'non-Aryans' progressed smoothly. On the 1st October 1935 Goebbels had been able to pronounce his whole Culture Chamber, the film section included, '*Judenrein*', free of all Jews. Audiences were steadily increasing, partly as a result of the modest affluence brought by widespread employment, but even more from an understandable desire for escapism. In the Chamber's first nine years, we are told, cinema-going within the Third Reich quadrupled to a thousand million a year by 1942.[8] Propaganda was restricted mainly to the newsreels. Feature films were the bait to draw people in to see them.

Goebbels' economic control was strengthened by the relentless purchase of stocks and shares. Such acquisitions, which began in 1936 and continued into the early years of the war, were made 'surreptitiously' until his stranglehold on the industry was complete. Thus, UFA was anonymously acquired in March 1937, with its extensive studio complexes at Neubabelsberg and Templehof. Tobis followed in December 1937. 'By 1942 all the remaining studios had become subordinate to the State.'[9]

Yet for all the complicated machinery Goebbels set in place to monitor and control German film-making, he could not keep his own fingers out of the pie. He insisted on personal control at all stages of production and in having the ultimate veto on finished films. He banned the first fictionalised life and death of Horst Wessel, which he had worked so hard to get filmed, declaring, National Socialism must not be licence for artistic failure. 'The greater the idea to be expressed, the higher the demands made on the artist,' he said.[10] The film, which had already been premiered, was hastily re-edited and re-released as *Hans Westmar*.

Most evenings found the cultural dictator scrutinising scripts. The green scribbles of his notorious 'Minister's pencil' were the bane of directors who had little choice but to take aboard suggested revisions. He liked to drop in unannounced at the studios to meet stars on the set or to check rushes; and he made it his business to keep tabs on all up-

and-coming talent. Actors and film-makers were obliged to pander to him if they had any career aspirations, and he in turn wooed them. By promoting the star cult, he 'made these people pliable for the purposes of a regime whose leading functionaries liked to be seen in public with the stars,' commented his biographer, Ralf Georg Reuth, adding, 'Amid royal splendour Hermann Goering led "state actress" Emmy Sonnemann to the altar in the Berlin Cathedral' (in 1935).[11] The opportunity his position afforded Goebbels for indulging his own appetite for sexual conquest was a matter of some notoriety, although his affair with the Czech actress Lida Baarova proved more serious. Press reports claimed the Propaganda Minister was soundly beaten up by Lida's film star boyfriend. In 1938, the romance threatened both his marriage and political position, so that Hitler, fearing further scandal, ordered it to be broken off immediately. Goebbels toyed with the idea of 'giving up everything' – told Lida he would 'sell ties' if he had to – but in the event he was quick to heed His Master's Voice, though never reconciled.[12]

What was Hollywood's reaction to the sinister developments in Germany's film industry? Certainly able refugees, whose careers had been blocked by the *Arierparagraph*, were easily absorbed into the Californian film scene, where most of the studio directors were themselves Jewish. In fact Hollywood has often been seen as an Empire invented by the Jews, and the Hollywood League Against Nazism (later the Anti-Nazi League) saw to it that the national and film press maintained relentless coverage of what was going on in Germany.

The foundation of a German Film Academy in 1938 took care of training directors, scriptwriters, technicians, actor, costumiers and all creative, management and distributive personnel to a high standard, so that by the time war came in September 1939, German cinema had attained the technical polish to regain its position in Europe and take on America on equal terms. Where then were these great films to conquer the world? Too often they were cold and heavy and wearisome. This was the heyday of *Blubo*, as the blood-and-soil peasant genre has come to be known, extolling *völkisch* virtues. In the eyes of many, the *Bergfilme* are considered among the Blubo films and Riefenstahl's *The Blue Light* one of the most important of them all.

Luis Trenker made his greatest films between 1933 and 1938, but he was always a maverick and they have been hard to categorise. He flirted with the Nazis and, as has been seen, contributed many of the images which later became clichés of both Blubo and Nazi cinema (waving corn, waving flags and the ethereal ghost-marchers in the sky), but he fought shy of Goebbels' control and as far as possible found alternative sources of finance. Two of his films were set and partly shot in America, including his greatest work, the bi-lingual *The Prodigal Son* (1934), with its haunting and authentic images of New York in the Depression which were filmed with a hidden camera. His *Der Kaiser von Kalifornien* (*The Emperor of California*, 1936) challenged and easily surpassed a rival and more expensive Hollywood production (*Sutter's Gold*), and although sometimes described as 'a Nazi Western', its story[13] carried a warning on the perils for self-made dictators. It is said to reflect 'both the mountain film and the Nazis' message of German anti-modernist rebellion. But with its lush cinematography and cold-blooded violence, this story of the California gold rush is also a Western ahead of its time.'[14] Trenker's later films contained even stronger criticisms against national aggression, so that his work was banned within Germany during the war years – 'except for showing to the armed forces, amongst whom it could do no harm.'[15]

The massive Babelsberg film factory worked at full stretch throughout the war and was an exciting place of talent and co-operation. 'So glamorous and alive, so important and overwhelming' one actress remembered. Two grossly noxious anti-Semitic films were made (*The Eternal Jew* and *Jud Süss*) and the Propaganda Ministry put out a few of what have become known as 'killing films' advocating euthanasia,[16] but the vast majority of movies were made to boost spirits and encourage patriotism. Louis Marcorelles, reviewing the Nazi-period output a decade later had to admit that even 'the plastic genius of Pabst' (who returned from Hollywood to work in the Barrandov studios in Prague during the war) had difficulty transcending all the 'nationalistic claptrap'. In his view: 'Perhaps only the two famous Leni Riefenstahl films, *Triumph* and *Olympia*, with their pagan exaltation of athletic prowess, their percussive rhythm, really succeeded in conveying something of the new *mystique* that Nazism claimed to introduce into all spheres of cultural life.'[17] He could detect her influence in the high standard of German newsreels and campaign film produced during the war, even if as a whole these documentary works lacked the passion to constitute a 'national school'.

He concluded that, Riefenstahl apart, 'genius, real excitement, and a flair for improvisation' were the most difficult qualities to discern in the German cinema of the Nazi period.

XIII

Olympiad, 1936

The student generation of the mid-1930s, outside the German Reich, showed a remarkable literacy in international affairs. With the rise of the fascist dictators in Europe there was much with which to keep abreast, and during the summer of 1936 the country offering the cheapest travel was Nazi Germany, where railways were giving sixty per cent reductions in fares and advertising it as International Festive Year throughout the Reich. The young flocked there, curious to see for themselves the great social revolution that had been taking place. The XIth Olympiad was just the icing on the cake.

A first impression of order, cleanliness and modest prosperity lulled many from the firm anti-Nazi convictions they had brought with them. It was swiftly followed by the shock of just how many people were by then already in uniform. One American youth, the writer and journalist Howard Smith, said it took his breath away. Back home in his native New Orleans he could sum up in 'a figure of two integers' all the uniforms he had ever seen. He had read of Nazi rearmament, to be sure, but it was only a word to him, not what he called a 'sense-idea' until he saw the 'milling hive' of sailors of Germany's war navy, soldiers in full war kit with rifles, and small towns 'like garrisons' with every third or fourth man in uniform. Smith noticed long 'caravans of camouflaged tanks, cannon and war-trucks lashed to railway flat cars' and freight depots 'lined with more of these monsters hooded in brown canvas.'[1] As a pacifist, Martha Gellhorn, who had already had unpleasant encounters with young Nazis in 'clean blond khaki-clad formation' and lacking 'one parrot brain among the lot', tried to excuse her instinctive dislike with sympathy for the swingeing retributions exacted after the First War. However, by 1936, she said, no amount of clinging to principles helped her: 'I saw what these bullying Nazi louts were like and were up to.' The novel she had been writing she shoved 'forever into a desk drawer', and instead took up her pen against fascism, her pacifist days behind her.[2]

Berlin was to have played host to the Olympic Games in 1916, had Europe not been in the throes of the Great War. Unlike the ancient Greeks who stopped wars for their Games, modern man puts the Olympics on hold when he goes to battle. The event was recommenced in 1920, hastily staged by an impoverished Belgium, when feelings still ran too deep for the Germans and Austrians to be allowed to participate. Russians, too, found themselves excluded for their Bolshevism. Paris provided the setting in 1924, Amsterdam four years later when the Germans were readmitted, and Los Angeles – despite the effects of the Wall Street crash – in 1932 for the most lavish and festive Games ever. By this time, Berlin was back in the picture, designated as the venue for 1936 – a decision taken by the Olympic Congress in Barcelona in 1931. In other words, the honour (which in any case is granted to a city and not a government) was made during the period of the Weimar Republic. Talk of retracting it after the Nazis rose to power came to nothing, although many countries had strong misgivings.

It was already clear by that time what the National Socialists thought of the inter-racial nature of top sporting competition. Deploring the number of medals won by negro contestants in Los Angeles, the *Völkischer Beobachter* had asserted that when the next Olympics were held in Berlin, 'The blacks must be excluded'.[3] The ancient Greeks must be turning in their graves at what modern man had made of their holy games, the newspaper said.

By 1936, Jewish athletes and gymnasts within Germany had been all but purged from national sport. The *Gleichschaltung* process, instigated within months of the Nazi takeover, required all sporting clubs to be subsumed into the Reich Federal Sports Association and Jews found themselves systematically banned from swimming pools, running tracks and all other facilites. They were forbidden to train and compete with 'Aryan' athletes, even where national teams suffered as a result. As early as April 1933 Germany's best tennis player, Dr Danny Prenn, was dropped from the Davis Cup side. A network of Jewish sporting associations managed to maintain an apartheid existence for as long as possible, organising independent championships. Teams were even sent abroad to join others from Czechoslovakia, Poland, America and other countries for a kind of international Jewish mini-

Olympics – the *Maccabiah* – held every four years in Tel Aviv.[4] Yet however good they were, these German athletes could not look forward to representing their country when it came to the real thing.

Ironically, the president of the German Olympic Committee, Dr Theodor Lewald,[5] was himself a *Mischling* (a person with some Jewish ancestry): one of his grandmothers had been Jewish. Although he, along with Dr Carl Diem, had been largely responsible for Berlin securing the XIth Olympiad, the Nazis wasted no time in removing him from his post – to the outrage of the International Olympic Committee. Prompted by its American members, it threatened immediate withdrawal of the Games from Berlin unless Lewald was reinstated. Furthermore, Germany must guarantee that all discrimination against Jewish athletes would cease. In the event, Lewald was moved sideways to a position of 'adviser' and authorised by his Nazi masters to reassure the IOC that the Olympic spirit would be upheld. On his way home from attending the IOC meeting in Vienna in June 1933, Brigadier General Charles E. Sherrill, who had led the protest, wrote to Rabbi Stephen Wise in New York that it had been 'a trying fight':

> . . . even my English colleagues thought we ought not to interfere in the internal arrangements of the German team. The Germans yielded slowly – very slowly. First they conceded that other nations could bring Jews . . . Then I went at them hard, insisting that as they had expressly excluded Jews, now they must expressly declare that Jews would not even be excluded from German teams. All sorts of influence was exerted to change my American stand. Finally they yielded because they found that I had lined up the necessary votes.[6]

When Réich Sports Leader Hans von Tschammer und Osten took over the presidency of the German Olympic Committee, a token number of Jews was selected to train with German athletes. Few abroad were taken in by the smokescreen, however, and dissent continued. There was a serious threat that America would boycott the Games, as indeed Jewish sportsmen of all countries were being urged to do by the Maccabi World Union. Sherrill went to see Hitler and, on 24th August 1935, secured permission for the fencer Helene Mayer (a *Mischling* who had been living in California since winning the gold medal at Los Angeles in 1932) to represent the country of her birth. A few days later the Nuremberg Racial Laws were announced.

★

Leni Riefenstahl has always taken pains to insist that her *Olympia* films were not financed by the Nazi Party, nor undertaken at its instigation. They were not influenced by it in any way. Her commission, she asserts, came from Dr Diem and the International Olympic Committee and, to fulfil it, she engineered a distribution contract worth one and a half million Reichsmarks with Friedrich Mainz, production head of the Tobis organisation. This arrangement is elaborated upon in her book, *The Sieve of Time*, where she adds that it found no favour with Dr Goebbels. Even so, the matter remains confusing.

Nominally, the State-owned Film Credit Bank (FKB) was the main funding agency for film-making in Nazi Germany. In practice, the conventional banks remained the ultimate source of loans which were now simply channelled through the FKB[7]. In the case of *Olympia*, it may be that Tobis put in a loan application to the FKB, only to learn that documentaries, such as Riefenstahl proposed, fell outside its remit.[8] Protracted negotiations with Goebbels' Ministry seem to have secured the loan from Reich funds, independent of the Film Credit Bank.[9] Shortly afterwards, in what Riefenstahl describes as a form of tax dodge, the stockholding of her new company *Olympiade-Film GmbH* was temporarily transferred to the Ministry of Propaganda until such time as the loan, together with the interest it had accrued, was repaid. Negotiations were handled on her behalf by Waldi Traut and her lawyers, leaving Riefenstahl free to concentrate on filming preparations. Her only regret concerning the outcome was that the Ministry of Propaganda still had leverage over her, which is exactly what she had hoped to avoid.

Quite where this left Tobis contractually is not clear, although Riefenstahl gives the impression that the company was still involved, and this is borne out by the fact that Friedrich Mainz was sacked from his position in the spring of 1937, specifically because of the extravagant contract he had negotiated with the film-maker for *Olympia*.

A number of scholars have trawled through old Propaganda Ministry documents in the Bundesarchiv of Koblenz and other libraries, not always reaching the same conclusion. The suspicion has to be that everyone involved in securing the financing for this expensive and controversial project took care to cover his tracks with obfuscating documentation. Cooper C. Graham, preparing his Ph.D dissertation in Cinema Studies for New York University, with *Leni Riefenstahl and Olympia* as his subject, spent six months investigating the film's origins in German archives during the early 1980s.[10] He takes issue with Leni on a number of points. In the first place, he feels convinced she secured this filming commission primarily at Hitler's insistence. The Führer wanted a showcase film for the air of peace and hope he was promulgating, and he wanted her to film it as he did not trust Party functionaries to handle the task artistically. She had already demonstrated her trustworthiness on this score with the acclaimed Nuremberg films. Diem and the Olympic organising committee may have believed that Leni Riefenstahl was their choice – and that the choice was theirs to make, having been given responsibility for reporting and publicising the Games. Perhaps they even thought they had made it without the intervention of the Propaganda Ministry, or anyone else – this is what Diem later testified. On the other hand, the Reich clearly held that all efforts in advertising and reporting (which included filming) devolved upon Herr Funk, State Secretary of the Propaganda Ministry. To Graham's thinking, the most likely scenario is that Leni was the choice both of Carl Diem and Adolf Hitler, with the Führer obviously having final say in the matter. He draws attention, and attaches some weight to an alternative version of events the film-maker gave once in interview. Diem wanted her to make the film (so she said then), but she turned him down, pleading other work (her long-standing pet project, *Penthesilea*). After that Diem approached Hitler, and Hitler asked Riefenstahl, who in the circumstances could no longer refuse. At the same time, she demanded the same full artistic control as she had enjoyed with *Triumph*.

This would have been in August 1935, and there is mention in Goebbels' diaries to corroborate discussions on the subject with both Leni and with the Führer at this time. Indeed, it appears it was the Führer who introduced the figure of 1.5 million Reichsmarks as a sensible budget for the production – the director's share of this to be a quarter of a million. 'She is a clever thing!' commented Goebbels on 17th August. And on the 5th October he again 'discussed thoroughly her Olympic film with Leni Riefenstahl. A woman who knows what she wants!' On 13th October he reported that a contract had been worked out and approved, and that Funk was 'happy'.[11]

Cooper Graham found a memorandum of this latter date, indicating that while the Reich Finance Ministry would have preferred private funding, for example through the Film Credit Bank, Herr Minister Goebbels specifically 'wished the financing through Reich funds'.[12]

There is indication that a contract between the Propaganda

Ministry and The Olympia-Film Gmbh (though not with Leni Riefenstahl by name) was signed on 7th November of that year. Graham was unable to unearth a signed copy, but earlier drafts on file, which may or may not be substantially the same, appeared to him 'remarkably casual' for such a major undertaking. 'The property rights to the film were not spelled out – a factor which would cause Dr Goebbels considerable headaches in the future'.

Was *Olympia*, Graham wondered, the property of the Reich or Olympia-Film? Were the 1.5 million Reichmarks to be paid back? And if so, how and when?

Graham holds that Goebbels' insistence on Reich finance was on a par with Hitler's similar demand for the building work incurred by holding the Games in Berlin: it guaranteed the project would be finished satisfactorily, whatever contingencies were thrown up. There was always the possibility that the event could be cancelled, and besides, however generous, private finance would impart some power to the releaser of the purse-strings. There is evidence that the *Reichs Kredit Anstalt*, though happy to put up the money for the Olympic film, wanted Riefenstahl to give a firm undertaking to deliver the finished film before 1937. Funk had accordingly turned them down and picked up the tab, Graham says.

Riefenstahl's memoirs maintain that she advised Hitler of 'her' decision at Christmas-time, 1935, when he looked at her in some surprise before remarking, 'That's an interesting challenge for you. But I thought you didn't want to make any more documentaries?'[13]

In fact, the *Völkischer Beobachter* had announced more than a fortnight earlier, on 10th December, that Fraulein Riefenstahl had been entrusted 'by Dr Goebbels' with the task of making the Olympics film. 'The new Germany must be made visible,' it explained. The film maker had turned down a similar assignment for the Winter Games, since that would impede her summer preparations. Acordingly, Hans Weidemann, vice president of the Reich Film Chamber, would be in charge of the winter film.[14]

Graham ends the 'financing' chapter of the book which grew out of his dissertation by quoting the entry in Dr Goebbels' diary for 7th November: 'Fraulein Riefenstahl has her contract . . . A 1.5 million transaction. She is entirely happy.' Graham could not resist adding, 'She should have been.'

Whether you take Graham or Riefenstahl as your guide, you are still left with the sense that the matter was a foregone conclusion. Leni had met no competition when it came to securing what must have

170

been seen as (and ultimately was) a highly lucrative assignment – quite apart from being an altogether exciting proposition. Graham picked up a reference that the Italians had wanted to make a similar film. It is hard to imagine how such a thing would have been allowed, yet he suggests that Riefenstahl was 'dispatched' to Rome to meet Mussolini and deflect him from his purpose. Her memoirs, published later, reveal this to have been a misreading of events. She was invited to meet Il Duce in the spring of 1936 after he had been bowled over by her *Triumph* film; he was evidently hoping to persuade her to make a propaganda film for him about draining the malarial Pontine marshes. With *Olympia* on her mind, she politely refused. In her account, she could not resist casting herself as a special ambassadress, carrying messages of good intent between the two fascist leaders. She even claims to have brought up with Mussolini the vexed matter of annexed South Tyrol.

If Italy had no designs for an Olympic film, Luis Trenker was often to remark afterwards that he had been first choice for the project. He claimed to have been solicited by the president of the Reich Film Board before anyone broached Riefenstahl. Only when he declined in order to make his movie *The Emperor of California* was it that 'Riefenstahl hurried to Hitler'.[15]

Goebbels, on the other hand, can be assumed to have wanted to keep the whole production 'in house' under the artistic direction of Hans Weidemann, and that could well be why Riefenstahl found him unenthusiastic at the start. Hans Ertl – something of a wild card in all this? – was one of six 'mountain' cameramen working for Weidemann at the Garmisch Winter Olympics.[16] In his book *Meine wilden dreissiger Jahre*, he could find few kind words for his erstwhile boss. Weidemann, he said, a reformed abstract artist, was out of his depth and only in his position at all from taking credit for the efforts of others. He was particularly disgusted at the 'dilettante' way Weidemann had chopped up one of his own long shots of the winning ski jump. Ertl had perfected a technique he called the *Drehschwenk*, a swivelling hand-held pan-shot which kept 'human projectiles' in frame throughout their jump, making it seem as if they were flying like eagles. Indeed, in his view, the entire editing of Weidemann's offering was whimsical to the point of absurdity. It diminished the Olympic ideal and scotched any hopes Ertl and his colleagues nurtured about changing the shape of winter sports coverage using the experience gained in Dr Fanck's 'Freiburg School'.

From this can be seen that Ertl, now in his early thirties, had come a long way in his film-making. He clearly saw himself at the whetted edge of a highly specialised form of sport-filming, to which he brought considerable ingenuity and vision. Coupled with his well-developed sense of ambition, it is fair to speculate whether Hans Ertl was hoping to secure the *Olympia* commission for himself? Or in alliance with Trenker? Although he ended up as one of Leni's most trusted right-hand men in the summer film crew, he was one of the last to be recruited. She very nearly lost him to Fanck's next (and final) project, *Daughter of the Samurai*, which was being filmed concurrently in Japan.

Besides Ertl and the excitable Willy Zielke, Leni's inner circle of helpers on *Olympia* included Walter Frentz, the cameraman Speer had recommended to her and who had worked on all three of her Nuremberg films. This time he would have special responsibility for the yachting events. Guzzi Lantschner was to film the high diving and gymnastics, as well as horse-riding. His association with Leni went back even further – to the Fanck ski films, when (besides camera work) he played the diminutive half of a brilliant and lopsided slapstick duo with Walter Riml. Guzzi was a Bavarian, a keen sportsman, and something of a hero, having just won a Silver Medal for the Combined Slalom at the Garmisch Games. His brother, Otto, would be joining the team to shoot a documentary about the making of *Olympia*. Heinz Javorsky, the Tramp of Mont Blanc, still young but already a competent camera operator, was one of the group to travel to Greece by car to join Leni (who had flown out by plane) for the torch-lighting ceremony. Afterwards, he accompanied the torch-bearers on their seven-country run to the Berlin stadium until Leni pulled him out at the Czech-German border to get a shot of the opening ceremony from the airship *Hindenberg*. Kurt Neubert, a slow-motion specialist who had worked with Fanck, and Hans Scheib, master of the long-distance lens completed the nucleus of her team which began work several months ahead of the Games.

Other cameramen were added nearer the time for their special skills in sea photography, aerial work, or operating from cranes. Altogether more than forty are listed by name in the credits for *Olympia*, which reads like a roll call of the most celebrated camera artists of the day. H. O. Schulze, who had been first cameraman on Weidemann's winter film, was hired as an expert of the 'transfocator', an early form of zoom lens. Leo de Laforgue was solely to photograph Hitler's reactions at the Games. In contrast to the godlike image the Führer had been given in *Triumph*, the intention this time, whenever he appeared, was to portray the leader's homeliness, show him as a man of the Volk. De Laforgue was ecstatic on one damp day to capture Hitler being passed a raincoat by one of his aides and wrapping it round himself absent-mindedly without taking his eyes off the playing field; then cast into the depths on another occasion when his camera spring broke. 'I am lost, kaputt, destroyed!' he wailed, and it was not a good moment for a radio interviewer to have invited him to tell listeners what it was like working on Leni Riefenstahl's film. His camera joined the queue for repairs in the cellar of Haus Ruhwald, the film team's castle head-quarters in parkland near the stadium, where camera engineers were working overtime to keep everyone in business.

Leni's contract entitled her to the pick of all footage shot by German newsreel cameramen. She had leave to allocate camera positions and to influence what was shot, and the 'reel companies' were supposed to send representatives along to her regular direction conferences in the Haus Ruwald. Their material could only be used for one bulletin, to be compiled within four days; after that it became hers. Understandably the national reel companies baulked at the conditions forced upon them, and it is not clear if these were spelt out in formal contracts. Foreign reel companies were obliged to comply with even stricter provisos, including the edict that all cameramen should wear prescribed 'Nazi Olympic uniforms'. Incensed, the American *Motion Picture Herald* told its readers:

> The American newsreel managements cannot even be certain that their staffs will not be conscripted by the Hitlerites, for a clause buried midway in the contract provides that the newsreel companies, if so requested, have to put at the disposal of the G.m.b.H. . . . any of their cameramen who are not busy.[17]

Resentments soon focused upon Riefenstahl, especially when her orders seemed high-handed. Grudges harboured then would be remembered later. She demanded of her whole camera army that they be intimately familiar with the sporting facilities. Her own detailed reconnaissance had revealed the best camera placements, and she specified which angles she wanted and even the camera lenses required for the job. The constant search for novelty was necessary to identify one sport from another. Where an element of repetition was inevitable, such as in portraying winners on the podiums, inventive-ness was deemed even more important. Ernst Jaeger remembered the 'frightening tempo' at which she worked and the 'chaos of notes' that

173

only she could comprehend in what became known as her 'Manuscript'. He describes a stopover in Belgrade during her flight to Greece, where she was fêted like visiting royalty. Having met the press, distributed leaflets about her film preparations, taken tea with dignitaries and toured the city in 95-degree heat, instead of collapsing when she had the chance, she seized the opportunity of a lull to work on her manuscript with Walter Frentz:

> After an hour she has transferred her memos with many critical comments into her manuscript, has dictated letters – what Kebelmann, what Neubert should shoot in Berlin – has selected photos that have been collected from German and foreign newspapers in order to preserve original sports shots, pictures of the Reich Sport Field, of the Olympic training; has had more and more revelatory ideas, notions, perceptions, all of which are transferred into the manuscript.[18]

From the outset, Riefenstahl had earmarked certain events for special treatment: the marathon and the decathlon for their epic qualities; the men's high diving for its visual potential. Always it was the individual human effort she found most fascinating. She wanted to see physical strain depicted through pulsing temples, bow-tight muscles. Breaking records was by the way. As Sports commentators later observed, she concentrated on people performing greatly, rather than on people giving great performances. Even so, she produced a film that works as well for the sports fan as for the cinema enthusiast. With so little filmed sports coverage before, and nothing to speak of on the Olympic Games, a virgin world spread at her feet. There were few clichés to avoid. She could – and did – satisfy unjaded curiosity with intelligence and gusto. According different disciplines different treatment, she gave each its own pace and style, and in the editing deftly blended them to an overall rhythm.

Without distracting the athletes, her lenses needed to be brought in as closely as possible if drama was to be brought to the screen. Ertl's imagination, in particular, was invaluable here. He had been fired by the work of the American oceanographer William Beebe, whose bathysphere explorations in 1934 offered a submarine world to view for the first time. When it came to his own filming of Olympic swimmers, he wanted to add underwater immediacy by doing away with the window and having the camera in the same dimension as its subject. He designed a watertight housing for his Sinclair, with which he could sit in the pool and, in a single take, follow a diver from the moment he left the springboard until he resurfaced after completing his bubbly underwater arc. With practice, he soon worked out the adjustments required at different stages in a dive, switching to slow motion as bodies hit the water, changing focus and keeping the camera on them. An extension of his *Drehschwenk* technique, which he saw as transposing the yearning to fly into visual terms, it provided the raw material for Riefenstahl's celebrated impressionistic high diving sequences.

For the swimming races, Ertl contrived a sort of camera platform in the water using a weighted, long-legged stool. Filming above the waterline, he tucked his feet into two loops on the 'seat'; to go underwater, he had simply to crouch down. Faces of swimmers in close-up were shot from a little rubber dinghy, pushed about gently by poles so as not to rock in the water. Other swimming shots made use of a travelling crane or the diving boards. At Grünau a tracked platform was built over the water so that camera 'dollies' could follow the rowers' movement, and a tethered hydrogen balloon gave a unique perspective for 'establishing shots' in days before helicopters were available. There was panic when they used it at Kiel too close to a naval minesweeper; it was feared that sparks and hot gasses from the stack would trigger an explosion. At Grünau, the balloon had to be brought down swiftly in the face of thunderstorm. Then it deflated so fast that poor Frentz, in the dangling basket beneath, was pitched into the water. Smaller unmanned balloons with cameras attached were released each day, in the romantic hope of securing bird's eye views of the stadium. Attached labels, backed up by advertisements in the press, requested finders of the cameras to return them with their film to Leni Riefenstahl. A catchy publicity gimmick, it failed to produce any usable pictures.

The most outlandish of Ertl's inventions was an automatic catapult camera, designed to run on a green cast-iron rail alongside the hundred metre track. Sadly, the device was held to be too distracting and banned by the athletic authorities. These days it is not at all unusual to see a similar gadget whirring round at athletic events.

Cameras went into rowing sculls and under the saddles of horses. As her cameramen made exhaustive tests, the Geyer laboratories got into their stride. During the two weeks of the Games themselves a non-stop, two-car special shuttle service was achieved, exchanging exposed and developed film. So much was shot, it was soon impossible to keep up with the viewing, and this led to duplication as cameramen could not be sure what had or had not been satisfactorily captured. By day thirteen, almost a million feet of film had been exposed, and two experienced judges were detailed to conduct a random check through the material.

By the end of July, frenetic preparations reached their peak. All the cameramen and reel photographers had arrived and been given their orders. They lived mostly in dormitories in the Haus Ruhwald. Leni had a model of the entire sports field set up, which she used to demonstrate required camera locations. Sunken passageways allowed the technicians to get to their various pits and stations unobtrusively. Everything and everyone was in place and as ready as they ever would be. The weather, which had been fine throughout July, began clouding over. Berlin, in the grip of Olympic Fever, swarmed with visitors. Red velvet bunting and swastika banners decked boulevards and government buildings. Albert Speer had designed garlanded festoons, linking tree to tree in gold ribbon along the six-mile parade route from the Brandenburg Gate to the Olympia complex. On the eve of the Games, Leni made a last check of the stadium with Frentz and Ertl. She would have sixty-five cameramen deployed during the opening ceremonies. Things were ready to roll. She could do little now other than offer up a prayer and keep her fingers crossed.

Although she had power and resources unprecedented in sports reporting, the filming was by no means plain sailing. Shortly before Hitler entered the Olympic Stadium on the first day of the Games, a posse of blackshirts attempted to throw out Leni's two sound cameras. They had been lashed to the rostrum through lack of space and were restricting the view of a couple of (as yet empty) front-row seats. Riefenstahl rushed protectively to the aid of her cameramen whose protests were falling on deaf SS-ears. The equipment had to be removed under Goebbels' instructions, she was told brusquely. On the contrary, Leni retorted, it was staying by special order of the Führer! In the face of her tirade the men shrugged their shoulders and retreated, but for how long? Leni forsook other duties to mount guard over the cameras, provoking the first of several public rows with Reich Minister Goebbels. As he screamed at her, the appearance of Goering in his sky-blue air-force uniform signalled that the affected seats belonged to the portly Field Marshal's party. There was no love lost between this ill-matched pair of Hitler's henchmen, who rarely missed an opportunity to score off one another. Observing Goebbels' discomposure, Goering, all oozy charm, smiled at Riefenstahl and told her to wipe those tears. 'There's still room here for a little one!' he said, squeezing good-naturedly into the narrow gap.

Later in the week, Goebbels got his own back. At the hammer-throwing event Riefenstahl had become involved in another shouting match when a referee demanded the ejection of Guzzi Lantschner from the stadium. A circular track had been constructed for Guzzi's camera around the protective throwing-cage. This was to provide close-up shots and had been agreed in advance with the authorities, provided only qualifying rounds were filmed. The row erupted during a thrilling duel of record-breaking throws between the two German contestants, Karl Hein and Erwin Blask. The film makers clearly felt this fell within what they were allowed, but officials disagreed and Guzzi was manhandled from the field. When pleading failed, Riefenstahl once more vehemently invoked the Führer's displeasure. Jaeger, reporting the incident three years later – by which time he had fallen out with Leni Riefenstahl and was in Hollywood – has her yelling at the judge, 'If you dare to order my cameraman off the field, I will drag you by your ears to the Führer's box, you swine!'[19] She herself admits to calling the fellow 'a bastard' in her fury. Whatever the words uttered, the abused umpire, who pulled some weight, lodged a formal complaint which passed, via Hans von Tschammer und Osten, up to Goebbels a couple of days later. Leni Riefenstahl was promptly forbidden to enter the stadium in any circumstances.

There is reason to believe that, with the Reich Sports Leader's backing, Goebbels was already looking for excuses to ease Riefenstahl out of her filming contract, and her outburst played into his hands. Still, the last thing he needed was a scandal in public. This was not the moment at which to topple the darling of the world's press. Let her shoot everything first and then bring in someone else for the editing. He demanded that Leni make a grovelling apology to the judge before permitting filming to continue. She was among the celebrities with the Führer in his box for the hammer-throwing finals,[20] and her cameraman caught the leader's gasp of excitement as Hein beat Blask by half a metre. The important close-up shots she had wanted, however, were lost forever.

Goebbels wrote in his diary on the evening of 6th August, 'Afternoon stadium. Running and jumping. We are not winning much. I give Riefenstahl a dressing down, she has behaved herself indescribably badly' – 'a hysterical woman. Not like a man at all!'[21]

Mainz, the Tobis executive who lost his job through support of Riefenstahl, would later testify to 'a witch-hunt without bounds' having been instigated against Leni during the Olympics, principally at the hands of the Propaganda Ministry, but also the SA and the SS leadership. Tobis' own press chief (a senior civil servant put into position by the Propaganda Ministry) had told him Frau[22] Riefenstahl had a reputation for being 'unendurable', and was universally discredited 'by the controlling functionaries of the Party'. The allegation that she was half-Jewish resurfaced at this time, and that she was politically undependable because of her known traffic with Jews. Mainz heard it prophesied that she would never finish her Olympic film, and his sworn statement supports Riefenstahl's assertion of complete independence in her work, and that she was not a member of the NSDAP and its organisations. Despite this ugly campaign, she worked on with 'demonic energy', Mainz said, throwing herself wholeheartedly into her task.

The battles with referees and police continued. Guzzi Lantschner was thrown off the field six times in three days and was in despair. He told Jaeger, 'I've hardly been allowed to make any of the special shots or camera movements I had prepared.' Kurt Neubert had been instructed to 'Get that thing out of here at once!' when his 180-pound slow-motion camera was ready mounted in position. One camera assistant was forbidden to work anywhere in the vicinity of the stadium – for no other reason than that she was a woman! Frustrations were not helped by the continuing poor weather and growing exhaustion. Even so, towards the end of the first week, Leni was euphoric. The footage had style, and exactly the style she was after. She told Ernst Jaeger, for one of his daily reports in *Film-Kurier*, 'I do not like doing things by halves . . . I hate halves . . .'[23]

Jaeger's bulletin that day revealed also that a use had been found for the catapult camera. There had been no second thoughts on the matter – its motor attachment was still banned – but the crew was permitted to set up the track alongside the 5,000-metre course. A young mountain-climbing friend of Ertl's, Albert Höcht, selected by Leni for his fleetness, ran pushing the automatic camera manually along its rail. As the runners completed each circuit, he flew ahead of them, filming. He deserved a gold medal of his own.

The emphasis during this first week had been on track and field events in the main stadium complex, close to the Haus Ruhwald; even so, Leni's drivers had clocked up mileages of up to several thousand kilometres per car. This was bound to increase in the days ahead as more events took place out of town. Riefenstahl had become a familiar figure in the stadium, in her flannel slacks and peaked jockey cap. As she darted between one cameraman and the next, or thrust herself forward to congratulate the winners, the crowd would set up a chant, 'Give 'im a kiss, Leni!' She was a good sport and played to the gallery, though her conspicuousness was not to everyone's taste. Society reporter Bella Fromm declared Leni's air of exhaustive efficiency was a sham. 'On and off she sits down beside her Führer, a magazine-cover grin on her face and a halo of importance fixed firmly above her head.'

The *New York Times* complained that Leni's word was law, and any cameraman who received from her two dreaded admonitory pink slips in a single day knew that it spelt 'permanent removal of the offender, forcibly if necessary'.[24] She liked to keep the most important cameramen under her personal supervision – no pink slips for them. Jaworsky has told how she would rush among them 'like a maniac, shouting, "How are you doing, how are you doing?" – Screaming and hollering . . . oh, she was an absolute maniac, she was wild!' But, he added, then of course so were they all, 'Either you are crazy in this business or you don't get anything done.'[25] Ertl agreed that her flights of ego could be infuriating. She was always getting up the noses of officials and sometimes the public – and, if he were honest, up those of some of her co-workers as well. She had a habit of materialising at their elbows during the tensest of moments to play the big director with exaggerated gestures, and always with her was her personal photographer like a shadow in her wake, shooting publicity pictures. She pestered Ertl only once. His unequivocal 'Don't bother me now!' even got a cheer from a referee who was standing nearby.[26] Still, if Leni's demonic directing was superfluous when things were going well, her team knew she would fight for them like a tigress when the occasion demanded. She was one of them. And, when it came to the editing, they could rely on her not to chop their hard-won long shots wantonly into little pieces, like Weidemann.

The overwhelming sensation of that first week had been Jesse Owens romping away with four gold medals. He was electrifying. During the fourteen times he appeared in the stadium for his heats and finals, this 22-year-old American all-rounder, a student from Ohio University – described variously as the black panther, the black arrow, and the black bullet – broke Olympic records eleven times. The crowd loved the beaming, modest hero, egging him on with a chant of 'O-vens, O-vens . . .' If he presented an open challenge to Nazi ideas of racial supremacy, it counted for nothing in the popular mind, even if the Führer could not bring himself to shake hands or be photographed with him.[27] Leni has revealed that the world was nearly robbed of Owens' phenomenal performances. One of her photo-graphic pits lurked like a tiger trap some seventy yards beyond the finishing line of the 100-metre track, and it was only a very quick reaction on his part which saved Owens from plunging headlong into it as he slowed down after one of his early heats.[28]

These first runs left no one in doubt that Owens was the man to watch. When it came to the sprint finals a tense hush settled over the arena. Owens is on the inside track. Leni has cameramen within a few feet of him, including Arthur Grimm, whom Jaeger has described as their 'artist-photographer'. He captures Owens' profile full-frame, brow crinkled, jaw taut, swallowing nervously but perfectly under control as he crouches at the start. Ertl is 'high above on the broadcasting roof' with a huge telescopic lens and Hans Scheib, too, has his longest lens trained like a canon on the line-up. Frenz, Leni and Guzzi are in the pits at the finish, Siegert manning one of the towers, Neubert and Dieze poised with the slow motion cameras. Even Jaeger finds a Leica thrust into his hand. The light is not good. Inky clouds conceal the sun. '*Fertig!*' shouts the referee and the starting pistol fires . . . 'One blink later and Owens is nearing the finish line,' wrote Jaeger. '10.03 seconds. Exactly the time it takes to gulp in amaze-ment.'

That was gold medal number one. Next day it was the long jump – a win for Owens with a leap of 8.06 metres. The restrictions placed on Riefenstahl by the International Amateur Athletic Federation forbad her from filming finals of jumping or throwing events at anything approaching close quarters. Owens obligingly repeated the feat for her cameras, except that this time, he pulled out of the bag an astonishing unofficial 8.08 metres! His other gold medals were for the 200 metres and the men's 400 metre-relay.

Re-enactment out of hours became a feature. On Sunday morn-ing, no events being scheduled until the afternoon, Leni went early to the Olympic village and rounded up several of the previous week's finalists for retakes and close-ups in the stadium. They may have been looking forward to a well-earned rest, but warmed to the challenge. 'The Japanese, the Finns, the Americans – they sensed what the cameramen had in mind. A dozen cameras stood ready . . . Ertl, Lantschner – it was their moment of glory. De Laforgue got close-ups – Morris, Parker and Clark threw on untiringly. While the others had long since stifled their enthusiasm with lunch, they continued until two o'clock.'[29]

That evening, after the marathon, Leni was back in the stadium to

180

restage the men's pole vaulting. This had provided a dramatic struggle a few days before, lasting twelve hours, which by late afternoon had whittled down to a contest between three very strong Americans and two 'short, almost delicate' Japanese. When Earle Meadows produced his award-winning, record-breaking vault of 4.35 metres, it was 10.30 at night, dark and cold, and the 30,000 spectators were almost as exhausted and hungry as the finalists. Lacking enough good shots of the tournament, Leni lured the athletes back to vault again under spotlights.[30] The Americans, who had been out on the town cele-brating, needed some persuasion, but gradually even they began to enjoy it, until at last the contest was as nail-biting as the original. All her best cameramen were there, at fever pitch by this time, and Leni, laughing wildly, cheered the jumpers on. The men vaulted as high in the almost empty stadium as they had for the roaring crowds, and it all provided a memorable finale for Part One of the finished film.

By the second week, the pace was getting to everyone. Camera-men were tired and tempers apt to flare with little warning. As events in the stadium tailed off and many of the athletes left for other com-petitions, a sense of anti-climax was inevitable. There was no let-up in the workload, however, even if Leni found time for a short fling with Glenn Morris, the American gold-medal decathlete, who went on to become (briefly) a Hollywood Tarzan, and to attend some of the ostentatious functions by which the Party glitterati sought to outdo each other. Ribbentrop roasted an ox in his garden, but was easily outshone by Goering and Goebbels. At the Reichmarshal's gala in the park of his palace on the Leipziger Platz hundreds of tables of food were provided, but the wind was cold and damp. Despite electric heaters dotted around the grass, Ambassador Dodd of America was not alone in sitting around in his hat and overcoat, waiting for a chance to escape the chilly vapours. Actors and actresses, dressed in eighteenth-century costume, danced quadrilles on the lawn, and Goering's old chum Udet put on a spectacular show of stunt-flying. A few nights later it was the turn of Goebbels. Between two and three thousand guests were invited to his island home near Dahlem, fifteen miles outside the city. A specially-installed pontoon bridge, lined with ranks of young female dancers bearing blazing torches, led them to the lantern-bedecked islet. Three orchestras kept dancers tripping till dawn and the champagne flowed freely.

The Games ended on Sunday, 16th August. After the last medals and honours had been awarded, Speer's cathedral of light mounted into the night sky. 'The great stadium field was lit by electric machines from the top rows of the seats all around and by curious electric streams of lights meeting some two or three hundred feet above the performances,' wrote Ambassador Dodd, adding that he had never seen such an elaborate show. The display of extravagance throughout the Olympian fortnight was quite flabbergasting, and he continually tried to imagine what it had cost. 'The propaganda of it all may have pleased the Germans,' he said. 'It had a bad influence on foreigners, as reported to me, in spite of the fine entertainment of all concerned.'[31]

Leni retained her best cameramen until the end of the month, while a few athletes still remained in Berlin. In September, seeing an opportunity to collect the hammer throwing close-ups lost when her cameras were ejected from the Olympic stadium, she dispatched Ertl and Höcht to Nuremberg. The German finalists were to appear at a sports festival in connection with that year's Party rally. On arrival, Reich Film Chief Weidemann ordered the pair to film for him. When Ertl protested they were in Riefenstahl's employ, Weidemann retorted that was of no consequence: whatever they had been asked to get, they could do it for him. When they refused, the pair had the terrifying experience next morning of being dragged from their beds by SS-men and held in custody. Riefenstahl complained later to Goebbels about the incident, but got nowhere. He dismissed her as 'hysterical', further proof women could not be trusted to handle assignments of this nature.

Meanwhile, there were still sections of the prologue to complete. Willy Zielke disappeared with a bevy of hand-picked dancing maidens to the Baltic coast near the border with Latvia, where he set up a tented camp in a nature reserve. Two weeks among the pristine dunes and the sensuous temple-dancing was in the can. Next, he began work on the dissolve Leni wanted between a life-size cast of Myron's Discobolus and a living discus thrower – in this case the German decathlete Erwin Huber. Leni arrived with more cameramen and sportsmen, and plenty of vaseline, to bring more ancient Greek bronzes to life. Her cameras caress the shiny sleek, classic contours of javelin throwers and shot-putters under a high mackerel sky. Though Zielke would complain afterwards that her editing had ruined his artistic footage,[32] the Prologue is nevertheless wonderfully atmospheric, and a high quality introduction to the Olympia films.[33]

★

It was late September before Leni could hide away in her editing room to embark on the initial review of all the material. Now was the time for Goebbels to strike. From his point of view the propaganda value of the Olympics had been realised. Newsreels had been seen around the world, and he saw no sense in Riefenstahl squandering time and more money on an ambitious production which would have no topicality – if indeed she ever finished it. It also stuck in his craw how much publicity she had drawn to herself, not just during the Games, but before and after as well. She had flouted every regulation, had been wildly extravagant, and had undermined his authority on all fronts. He recalled the umpire incident and the business of Anatol Dobriansky, who he considered had been virtually kidnapped from Greece – and an unsavoury character to boot, who got involved in a brawl at the Haus Ruhwald. All this was useful as evidence that she was unsuitable to be entrusted with cutting her film,

Von Tschammer und Osten would be a handy ally. He had been miffed by the way Riefenstahl seemed to pay more attention to the Americans than German athletes; Goebbels felt confident of his backing when it came to supplanting her with Weidemann. As a first move, he would see to it that Riefenstahl's activities were no longer reported so avidly in the press. At the same time, he gave instructions for a team of auditors to go through the Olympia-Film accounts with a fine tooth comb. Its report was damning. She had, Goebbels confided to his diary, 'turned the company into a complete pigsty' requiring immediate 'intervention'.[34] No further credit should be given to Fraulein Riefenstahl, who had almost run through the one and a half million marks secured for the project and was looking for a further loan.

As Goebbels confidently mustered his ammunition, he issued orders that she should sack Ernst Jaeger, her press chief, whose wife was 'non-Aryan'. Also, another and long-standing employee, Walter Grosskopf, should be dismissed. The auditors had told him that Riefenstahl's company owned no safe or strong box; Grosskopf, as the financial head, had been walking round with between 14,000 and 15,000 Reichsmarks in his pocket, doling out money to people when asked to do so.[35] Any film about the Olympics should be completed quickly and devote little screen time to the exploits of Jesse Owens and other black athletes.

Riefenstahl ignored the Reich Minister's demands, but her position was precarious. She desperately needed money to continue. Company assets, which could have been sold to eke out funds, had been distributed among her favoured workers after the Games. Guzzi appears to have come out with a second-hand Daimler at less than half price, payable by instalments over a year. By November, Leni had seen enough of the footage to know that her plans for two films could be realised, but she would require another half a million marks to finish.[36] 'Out of the question,' scrawled Goebbels over the official application passed to him by Dr Ott of his Propaganda Ministry. When Leni appealed in person on 6th November, the Reich Minister steeled himself against her impassioned sobs. 'Pulling hysterical fits on me . . . does not work any more'.

There was no way left to Leni but to play her trump card. The following week she secured an interview with Hitler.[37] Receiving her, she says, with his usual warmth, the Führer appeared nonplussed when she blurted out that she would have to emigrate. As conditions were, she explained tearfully, it was impossible for her to work within her homeland. 'Why should Dr Goebbels want a vendetta against you?' Hitler asked, giving the impression he knew nothing of what had been going on. She told him about the SS picking up Ertl and Höcht, how she was convinced that Weidemann wanted to scuttle her Olympics efforts and surpass *Triumph* with a rally film of his own. Then there was the press ban and the withholding of funds. In her book, Riefenstahl tells us that the Führer grew very quiet at the news and his face 'paled'. He told her tersely to leave it to him. Cynically, one might say, Hitler saw a way of exerting his power over both her and Goebbels. A few days later, adjutant Brückner telephoned Leni to say she could continue her work undisturbed. Goebbels' ministry would no longer be involved beyond servicing the loans and carrying out audits. She would be responsible directly to Rudolf Hess and the Brown House. As a result, the film was completed without further harassment. Indeed, Leni managed to remain clear of the Propaganda Ministry until war broke out.

*

It had taken ten weeks just to view her 250 miles of film. Someone without Leni's legendary sense of order would have been swamped by so much. As it was, she worked out a system of coloured boxes that enabled her to keep tabs on what she had seen, what had been worked on and what in all probability would be rejected. Material was sorted into subjects and moods. Transluscent walls in the newly-furbished editing suite, which Weidemann had attempted to usurp, aided quick identification of film strips.

Settling on the need for two films was partly in response to the

Production Manager Waldi Traut (left) discusses with the director of the Olympic film, Leni Riefenstahl, where cameramen Neubert and Kebelmann are to be posted

Inspecting the Olympic Stadium with Guzzi Lantschner before the 1936 Berlin Games. Guzzi himself had won a silver medal a few months earlier at the Winter Games

Leni with Walter Frentz in one of the camera pits which caused such an outcry

Young Anatol Dobriansky lights the Olympic torch in Greece

Leni with Frentz aboard a camera truck specially designed for moving shots

Jesse Owens, four times gold medallist, and Glenn Morris, American winner of the Decathlon, at the 1936 Olympics

Below left: Hitler and Reich Sports Minister
Hans von Tschammer und Osten at the Olympic Games

Below right: Leni berates Propaganda Minister Goebbels for obstructing her Olympic filming

Filming the high diving for what was to be called by some critics
'the greatest documentary ever made'

Leni with Hans Ertl as he takes close-ups from the rubber boat

Closeted away for the editing of her two-part, four-hour Olympic film

The Scream. After witnessing a massacre at Kronskie on her first day at the Polish front, Leni abandoned war reporting

With her husband, Peter Jacobs, who was decorated in France and wounded on the Russian front

Leni filming in Africa in her mid-seventies

Leni with her Nuba friends in the Sudan

wealth of material, but mainly for the structure. There were two distinct themes, she found, and each sequence automatically suggested where it should go in relation to these and to the all-important 'intensification'. For instance, once having decided to put the most important track and field sports together in Part One, since these in most people's minds formed the heart of the Olympics, then it followed that the decathlon ought to go into Part Two to avoid repetition. Yet, it couldn't go at the beginning or the end – since she wanted to use the Olympic village to introduce the second film, and the closing ceremony had to be near the end – so it positioned itself naturally somewhere in the middle. As swimming and diving produced another high point, that could come just before the closing ceremony. And so it went . . . When she came to look at the three-day riding, she could see that the audience would laugh when the riders fell with their horses in the water:

> And I thought this would have the most effect if preceded by something that was somewhat gripping. And of all the events what was the most gripping? The rowing, because of the strain of the rowers. It was very dramatic. Only the riding could come after that, because it was a relaxation, and this was supported through the music, a convalescence for the ears since the drama of rowing was built through a background of noise intensity.[38]

The marathon, while one of the most emotive events, posed a considerable challenge. How could she shape a 26-mile race into a few short minutes? She has often explained that it was the 'inside feeling of the marathon runner' she wanted to convey: how tired he was and how he longed for the race to come to an end. His leaden legs would be almost sticking to the ashphalt. Willpower alone drove him on. Sometimes you do not see the runner, just hear the sounds he hears, see the grass ruffle at the side of the road, the dappling shadows spilling from the trees overhead. At other times his shadow runs for him. You know that he hears the cheers and that these, and the insistent music, give him the will to pound on. At last, the stadium looms back into view. Nazi-helmeted trumpeters welcome the exhausted men back with a mediaeval blare as stewards rush to wrap them tenderly in blankets. The stragglers come in unco-ordinated and disjointed to collapse into the arms of first aid men. It is infinitely touching and heroic.

Part One, is brought to an end with a parade of nations, flags in rolling motion and the Olympic bell tolling. The Olympic flames lick the sky, fluttering flags dissolve (like the banners at the end of *Triumph*) over the stadium in moonlight.

The sequence most people call to mind when they think of the *Olympia* films is the exquisite diving collage in Part Two. Riefenstahl reported the women's diving realistically; the contestants were given names, but when it came to the men's event, she wanted to emphasise the kinetic beauty and produce a crescendo of intensity. To achieve this she edited highlights, using shots of different *tempi* – first in real time, then slightly slower, and then slower still until finally slow motion is reached. She wanted the divers to resemble birds swooping. It was an extraordinary compilation and, as Müller's biographical film of Leni Riefenstahl has shown, it should be seen on an editing table to be appreciated fully. Running the film through slowly, shot by shot, reveals her brilliant handiwork, how some shots have been spliced in back to front, so that the diver is flying upwards through the air back towards the springboard, to enhance the sense of movement.

Some weeks into the editing Hans Ertl, on a visit from Munich, dropped into the cutting room. 'Little Peters', Leni's master-cutter-cum-girl Friday, Erna Peters, rushed up to tell him the 'Boss' was in the middle of a very difficult montage and she did not like to disturb her. But Leni must have heard Ertl's loud 'Greetings, my dears, how's it all going, then?' for she emerged at the door of her cutting room, all wan and dressed in white – 'like a ghostly nun,' Ertl said, 'who, after the thousand-and-one nights, has decided, finally, to forswear the joys of the world.' She offered him a cup of tea, 'perhaps in memory of past sins.'

Truly, he said, she was not to be envied. Alone with her celluloid snakes she had untold days and nights to sacrifice before the final versions of *Festival of the People* and *Festival of Beauty* were 'flawlessly and artistically complete'.

186

XIV

The Door Begins to Close

If the editing of *Triumph* had seemed interminable, that of *Olympia* was like one of those dreams where you never arrive at your destination. For eighteen months Leni Riefenstahl and her little band of assistants toiled in the cutting room at the Geyer laboratory, rarely working less than a ten-hour day, and often fourteen hours for the two months of sound mixing. It had become something of a joke in the film world that long after the Games were all but forgotten, this documentary about them appeared no nearer to completion.

After the first year, when one of the two two-hour films was finally assembled (*Festival of the People*), Leni allowed herself a short holiday. Desperate to blow fresh air in to her lungs, she headed for the mountains. For a long time she had wanted to climb the Guglia di Brenta. That spectacular, jabbing Dolomitic needle which featured in the first mountain film she ever saw, setting her on the path to her own film career, had lost nothing of its allure over the years. To her, it truly was the prophetic *Mountain of Destiny* invoked by Fanck. She arranged for the celebrated South Tyrolean climber Hans Steger to guide her up one of its easier routes.

Her hopes were dashed on arriving in Bolzano, when a waiting telegram told her that Steger had been called away to conduct King Leopold of the Belgians on a climbing excursion.[1] He suggested that she might team up with the Bavarian mountaineer Anderl Heckmair, who would be waiting for her at Wolkenstein.

This was the summer before Heckmair's triumph on the Eiger-wand, and that grim north wall was already filling his horizons. He had just spent six weeks sniffing around the foot of the face, incognito among that year's Eiger-hopefuls. The Swiss authorities had imposed a ban on all climbing there after the deaths of Toni Kurz and his companions in 1936, not that it would have stopped Heckmair if conditions had favoured an attempt. An earthy individual, without pretence but with all the youthful confidence of knowing he was one of the toughest of contemporary hard men, Heckmair was comfortably at home in the Alps. He was a product of what has become known as 'the Munich School' – the 'dangle-and-whack merchants' so resented by E. L. Strutt and the British traditionalists. With the aid of new techniques and developments in climbing hardware, they were revolutionising alpine climbing. A resourceful group of impecunious mountaineers, mainly from Bavaria, saw out the workless days of the early-1930s in the mountains, living off air, passion and the occasional hunk of bread or sausage scrounged from a kindly farmer's wife. They slept in haylofts or earned communal bunk places in the mountain huts from chopping wood and other chores. In between, they picked off most of the unclaimed prizes of the day on the great walls of the Eastern and Western Alps.

Leni took to Heckmair from the moment they shook hands. Rough diamond that he was, with something of a reputation as a daredevil, he was responsible for her most thrilling mountain adventures, and she would always be grateful to him for that. Before taking on the engagement, Heckmair had been primed by his brother on the grapevine gossip surrounding the glamorous film director. He recognised the name, of course, but he was not much of a cinema buff and had not seen *The Blue Light*, which was shot largely in the Brenta area, where they were now headed.

She belonged to Hitler's intimate circle, his brother told him. Word was she was the Führer's mistress. He had better watch out! 'Whatever you do, don't let on you've never seen any of her movies,' his brother had said, reminding him that the Nuremberg Rally picture was one of hers, and she had been filming at the Olympics, too.

Heckmair admitted later to some misgivings over the Hitler connection, but he could not fail to be impressed by all the attentive bowing and scraping that came his way from the moment he asked for Fraulein Riefenstahl at the hotel. The lady herself made a deep impression, too – she was 'radiant and more beautiful' than he had imagined. 'Her feminine charms and untroubled naturalness soon dissolved my inner reservations,' he said. 'Whatever her relations with Hitler might be, she was obviously a fabulous woman, and her years spent in the company of Arnold Fanck's casts of outstanding climbers and skiers seemed to have taught her not to play . . . the capricious diva.'[2]

Clearly, one or two practice climbs were called for before committing themselves to the Guglia, and at Heckmair's suggestion they kicked off with the west ridge of the first Sella Tower. There was a tricky pitch near the top which he knew would soon sort out what kind of a climber this young woman was. If she had trouble with that, she could find herself another guide and he would shove off home. In those days, by his own admission, he was cocky, 'interested in nothing but the difficult stuff.''

To his astonishment, she danced up it. Knowing little about women, he would never have believed it of 'such a delicate-looking creature', he said, and promptly dragged her up a series of harder and harder climbs. After a quick ascent of the Schleierkante, he felt satisfied she was ready for the big one. Success had made him presumptuous, as he admitted in his book, *My Life as a Mountaineer*, for instead of the Guglia's ordinary route, he elected to go for the more difficult Preuss line up the pinnacle's east face.

They climbed as a rope of three, one of Leni's skiing chums, Xavier Kraisy, making up the party. This was all right with Heckmair, who knew Kraisy to be a good climber, though not a guide. After oversleeping at the Brentai hut, the three started out rather late and stopped for lunch at the Tosa hut, so that by the time they stood at the foot of their climb it was already two in the afternoon. Even so, there should be plenty of daylight left. Heckmair was reckoning on three hours up and one down, but he soon realised this was to 'add up the bill without the tip'. Another mistake was to plump for a direct start when a likely-looking corner promised to short-cut the zig-zagging system of ledges normally adopted. It soon proved less likely than it looked, and he and Leni squabbled over the best way to proceed before wasting effort on a diversion which got them nowhere. Cross with himself for listening to her, Heckmair took some tension on the rope and stormed straight up into the corner, unprotected. When he called for the others to follow, one look around the edge at the corner's smooth wall and overhangs was enough to rivet Leni to her spot. She refused to take another step.

That was it, then. Stalemate. Heckmair started hammering in a ring piton so they could abseil off and call it a day. Leni could always hire another guide to take her up an easier way, he told her. At once, a violent tug came on the belay rope as his client flung herself into the corner, like a pendulum, from where with all his strength he was able to haul her, tearful, on to the ledge beside him. Kraisy followed her up, grinning with embarrassment. By now it was already five in the afternoon and, though on route at last, the bulk of the Preuss climb still lay ahead of them. Prudence dictated they should turn back, but Leni was adamant. More than ever, she was determined to complete the climb.

When they finally hauled out on top of the slender pinnacle it was almost dark and a sinister bank of black cloud was bearing down on them from the west, lit by flickers of blue lightning. Any moment now, a gigantic storm would break, and it mustn't find them on the summit or any of the exposed edges. Heckmair took a quick look round and spotted a small niche a short way down the north face.

'Tuck yourselves in there,' he ordered. 'Let's just see if we can survive this.'

'But we can't possibly stay out in the open all night!'

Horrified, Leni was haunted by the fear that if she got thoroughly soaked and chilled, it could bring on a recurrence of her old Greenland trouble. Her protestations were lost in a terrifying clap of thunder as the storm burst over them, battering them with hailstones. She had a point, though, as Heckmair quickly realised: they would not be able to hold out up here till morning, and he set off once more to scout out some place from which they could abseil. It was pitch dark now, except when the lightning flared.

'We waited and waited . . .' Leni recalled how she and Kraisy kept shouting into the storm, only to have their voices swallowed up immediately. It was like a hurricane. Heckmair was gone so long that they feared he must have met with an accident. They were going to have to descend on their own – even if they could move only in the intermittent flashes of light.

Then, suddenly, he reappeared, illuminated by the lightning like 'a glowing ghost', to shepherd them down.

It was one long nightmare. A heart-stopping moment that lingered in Leni's memory years afterwards was when Heckmair lost his footing and pulled all three of them off the mountain. Had he not managed to grab a rock and check their fall, they must surely all have perished. The incident is missing from Heckmair's account: his most vivid recollection was of the endless hammering in of pegs by the lightning's glare. Kraisy had to descend unbelayed on the two 130-foot ropes in utter blackness, and Leni could only be secured on a thin cord for the first eighty feet of each abseil. 'We abseiled all night, arriving exactly where we had left the sacks at the bottom of the climb.

It was either pure chance or sixth sense, as most of the time I had no idea where we were.'[3]

With the worst behind them, it was still too dark to find their way back along the trail to the Tosa hut without torches. Just below, an ice-filled gully gave off a faint shimmer in the gloom. Anxious to keep the party moving, Heckmair cut a zigzag of steps down its steep slope. The hail was easing off now, but a wet fog rolled up from the valley to blanket everything. Once off the ice, he instructed them to sit down and shunt themselves further downhill on their bottoms. They would be perfectly safe, he promised; it was a technique he often used. Well it might be, but they couldn't say they cared for it much. Still less did they wish to bivouac at this late stage and bumped on down in the darkness. Between them, they managed to miss the little track which led out of the gully at the bottom and instead found themselves in a vast boulder field, 'a wilderness of blocks the size of tables or even houses.' After tumbling over one rock, Heckmair found his readiness for self-sacrifice evaporating fast. 'I stretched out and announced that I was going to sleep until it got light,' he said. And, 'In a moment I was snoring.'[4]

It was raining now, and the other two had no choice but to huddle under boulders themselves. Soon, they too had fallen asleep, exhausted. When they awoke some hours later it was to brilliant sunshine and the realisation that they had bivouacked within a few yards of the hut.

The holiday was over. Leni records that she returned to Berlin with a new lease of life – even if her hands were so grazed and bruised she could not 'hold a comb' for a week afterwards. Looking back, in old age, she never remembered feeling so healthy and vital as after that vacation.

In his book, Heckmair tells how, after a banquet in Bolzano and before going home, Leni took him on to Nuremberg, where she had been invited by the Führer as a guest of honour at the Party rally. They stayed in the Gauleiter's house, where Heckmair's recollection is of everything 'costly and hyper-refined except the Gauleiter himself.' (He refers, of course, to the monstrous Julius Streicher, rabid anti-Semite and sadist, who was ultimately hanged as a war criminal after the Nuremberg trials.) At Leni's side, Heckmair found the phalanxes of bodyguards parted as if by magic to sweep them into Hitler's presence in the Deutscher Hof Hotel, where the Führer greeted the film maker with outstretched arms and compliments on her appearance. The two were invited to share his table for afternoon tea, which gave Heckmair the opportunity of studying Hitler at leisure as Leni told of their recent climbing escapades. Making no claim to be a profound observer of men, Heckmair could find 'absolutely nothing so extraordinary' about this man. When eventually drawn into the conversation, he was struck by the Führer's pertinent questions, even though it was clear that Hitler understood little about mountaineering. Why one should want to do it interested him, and what it actually felt like to be isolated on a big and serious climb. His own experience stopped at gentle mountain walking.

As they sipped their tea it grew dark outside and was time for a torchlight march-past. Heckmair recalls how, as he rose to take leave, Hitler put another question to him which called for a lengthy response. Nobody dared to interrupt:

> . . . and so it was that I accompanied him out on to the balcony, still talking, there to find myself in my grey suit amid all the uniformed Party dignitaries. Below us the crowd clamoured its unceasing cry of 'Heil'. The torchlight procession came to a halt. Hitler saluted it with stiffly outstretched arm, something rigid in his gaze as though staring into the distance. For the first time in my life I raised my hand in the Hitler salute.[5]

Even as he did so, his position as an anonymous, apolitical unbeliever, an ordinary climber, standing shoulder-to-shoulder alongside this 'fanatically acclaimed leader', struck him as so grotesque that he felt like laughing out loud. For the two hours the procession lasted, Heckmair remained at Hitler's elbow, pondering on the loneliness of the mountains and the inexplicable masses below. There was little he felt able to conclude from it all, but he was profoundly disturbed; and this feeling persisted throughout the following day when he and Leni stood together in the special enclosure watching more parades and ceremonies. You had to admire the organisation, he admitted, but how could people allow themselves to be herded in this way? It gave him what he called a 'kind of shudder' in his soul, and he could only speculate what great power this was that swept everything before it? Where on earth was it taking them?

Though her own memoirs make no mention of the fact, it would appear that Leni took Heckmair with her when she returned to Berlin. She had been pulling strings on his behalf to further his mountaineering career. Now, with a pass into the national stadium, he embarked on serious training for his forthcoming Eiger attempt and was soon running up to thirty miles twice a week. He did not return to Bavaria until that winter, to take up a position as ski instructor in the 'Strength through Joy' movement. Introducing simple, mainly working class young people to the beauties of the winter mountains was far more to his taste than pandering to ski-tourists in the fashionable Swiss resorts, as he had been obliged to do in earlier seasons. His Eiger aspirations saved him from any temptation to become involved in politics – that, and a native pragmatism. Reflecting on it afterwards, he supposed he was 'unwilling to give way to this suggestive urge which could not be rationally explained.'

★

The mountain-climbing Schmid brothers of Munich were awarded Olympic medals for achievement after making their outstanding ascent of the Matterhorn's North Face in 1931. The race was then on among European climbers to claim the other great north faces of the Alps, in particular that of the Grandes Jorasses and – more especially still – the Eiger, which loomed above Grindelwald in Switzerland. As the 1936 Olympics approached, it was popularly believed that Hitler had offered gold medals to any German mountaineering party who could forge a route up the virgin face on which six men had perished in the preceding twelve months, all Germans or Austrians. It had not taken the popular press long to transform 'North Face' (*Nordwand*) into 'Killer Wall' (*Mördwand*), and outside Germany the myth was soon swallowed that young men – blinded by their devotion to the Führer – were pitting themselves against impossible mountain precipices in death-or-glory bids for State recognition.

Certainly when Heckmair and his three companions finally climbed the Eigerwand in 1938 it provided a gift to Nazi propagandists. Not only was it a stupendous feat, it had been neatly accomplished by two Germans and two Austrians within months of the *Anschluss* between their nations. Nothing could have more aptly symbolised the supposed invincibility of the new union. Hitler was quick to congratulate the frostbitten victors, and in the official book of the climb, brought out by Nazi publishers, the portrait of the four men taken with the Führer bore the caption: 'The greatest reward of all.'

In all truth, it can have been no more than chronological accident that the fight for the Alpine north walls and some of the greatest achievements by German and Italian mountaineers coincided with the rise of fascism in Europe. But in the eyes of many the 'cult' of mountaineering came to be subsumed (along with the cult of the Superman) into the confused ideology that characterised the cult of

National Socialism. Even today, in some respectable publications, the dominance of German achievement in the Alps during the 1930s is glibly referred to as fascist mountaineering and the mountaineers themselves portrayed as programmed robots daring and dying for the Fatherland. Yet, advances in mountaineering, as in other fields of human endeavour, are incremental and dependent on all the achievement that has gone before.[6]

Supposing the struggle for the Alpine walls had been delayed by some twenty years, these sweeping precipices would still have been surmounted, but by climbers of a different epoch, by 'new Europeans', let us say. It is interesting to speculate whether the protagonists then would have been accused of nurturing an unhealthy death wish, of being 'dervishes' of any 'new dogma'.[7] The chances are, on the contrary, that over and above any national pride taken in their success, they would have enjoyed international acclaim for their courage and laudable spirit of enterprise – in the same way as did Hillary and Tenzing when they climbed Everest in 1953. Hillary's knighthood and Tenzing's regrettably inferior British Empire Medal are not regarded as inappropriate baubles, in the way German Eiger-medals would have been if presented by the Führer.

All the same, for a variety of reasons – which included his weakness for *Bergfilme* – Adolf Hitler is perceived to have endorsed the sport of mountaineering enthusiastically, when in reality his love of mountains was far more Nietzschean. They provided an allegory for the heroic effort and suffering demanded in the furtherance of a cause. As slopes steepen, weaklings are winnowed away, but he who endures earns the lonely summit. 'Ever fewer climb with me up ever higher mountains,' Nietzsche wrote in *Thus Spake Zarathustra*. His own mountain retreat, the Berghof in Obersalzberg, was Hitler's personal reward for years of struggle; it gave him a solitude from which to contemplate the lower orders, a space to be shared only with chosen disciples. He enjoyed tramping in the surrounding Bavarian forests but had absolutely no time for climbing or skiing, which he would have banned if he could. Riefenstahl was chided for risking her neck in the mountains, when she had important work to do. Albert Speer's recollection is that the only purpose for such sports in Hitler's view was that the mountain troops drew their recruits from 'such fools'.

Heckmair and his companions had hoped their Eiger success would secure them places on a prestigious national expedition to Nanga Parbat in the Himalaya, but Hitler had other plans. They were whisked off to the Sonthofen Ordensburg, one of the SS 'castle schools' for training an elite youth cadre, there to be enrolled as mountain sports guides; and although this did not necessitate joining the Party, they were in the employ of the State. Only Heinrich Harrer was granted dispensation to accompany a reconnaissance trip to Nanga Parbat, where he found himself when war broke out and was interned in British India. Heckmair, after active service on the Eastern front, was eventually able to see out the rest of the war in a mountain training unit near Innsbruck.

★

After her Alpine intermission, Leni Riefenstahl returned to her editing with vigour, and the two parts of *Olympia* were at last completed by the end of February 1938. Long, intimate sessions in the dubbing studio with her sound engineer Hermann Storr, a gentle wizard who rescued the complicated multi-track post-synchronisation from disaster, cemented a close personal bond between them which would endure beyond the film. 'We decided to stay together,' Leni remarks coyly in her memoirs, though fails to record the subsequent break-up two years later. In an interview with Gitta Sereny in 1986, Riefenstahl revealed that this most tender of her romances finally foundered – as had so many others – on the altar of her art. 'He wanted to sleep with me the nights before the biggest takes,' she said (referring to the protracted shooting of *Tiefland*.) 'It was impossible.'[8]

The gala première of *Olympia*, scheduled for mid-March, had to be postponed at the last minute on account of the *Anschluss*. Devastated, Riefenstahl feared this could mean the autumn before her film was seen, if at all. One of the most astonishing episodes in her testimony reveals that, without a second thought, she dashed off to Austria to waylay the Führer during his triumphal tour following the 'bloodless' annexation of his native land with no other intention but to implore him to intercede on behalf of her film. It was madness, of course, and she recognised it as such as soon as she saw the delirious crowds stretching 'their arms and hands towards Hitler in almost religious ecstasy'. How could she expect Hitler to be bothered with her problems at a time like this? None the less, instead of scuttling home, she pushed through the crowds, the blockade, the cordons and bodyguards to reach her euphoric leader. And instead of congratulating him on what he, and she, and apparently the majority of his Austrian compatriots at that time saw as a great victory, she whinged on about what a laughing stock it would make her if her film was not screened in the very near future.

Why not launch it on his birthday, she suggested impulsively, 20th April? Wouldn't that be a suitable date? Hitler – whom the moment had made magnanimous – first protested too many engagements; then, with sudden change of heart, he told her not to worry. His schedule would be rearranged. Leave it to him; Goebbels could make the necessary arrangements, and he personally would attend. She could rely on it.

The temptation is to suspect Riefenstahl of some revisionism here, to concur with Gitta Sereny's suggestion that Riefenstahl's memoirs are full of events and 'quotes' she would like to have taken place, rather than actually did and that her memory for dates – as with that of so many of her contemporaries – was in any case extremely shaky.[9] The fact is, however, that *Olympia* was premièred on Hitler's forty-ninth birthday in 1938, with the Führer himself as guest of honour.

There was just enough time before the big night for Leni to take a quick vacation in Davos to top up her tan. The prestigious and now-familiar Ufa Palast am Zoo was 'gift-wrapped' for the occasion in gold ribbons and giant Olympic banners and the glittering, invited audience included representatives of the International Olympic Committee, German and Austrian Olympic medallists, Nazi and film notables and many foreign dignitories. Nervous with apprehension, particularly over the length of the film, which in its two parts ran for almost four hours, she arrived at the theatre with her parents and her brother. At the end of Part One – the Nazi press reported later – Hitler, 'still clapping, rose and congratulated the artist on her success'. Führer and film-maker chatted animatedly in the foyer during the half-hour intermission, and when Part Two drew to a close around midnight, he once more publicly praised the work.

★

After its sensational first night, it came as no great surprise to anyone, Leni included, that *Olympia* should run away with the Reich Film Prize of 1938. Later it would also pick up the international grand prize at the Venice Biennale as 'the world's best feature film of the year', besides earning high praise and recognition from other festivals and governments. Jubilant that her vision and fanatic attention to detail had been vindicated – even the film's extravagant length proving no discernable drawback – she needed little coercion to fall in with the distributor's wishes and accompany the work on its première tour of major European cities. It was seen first in Vienna, and Graz, then Paris and Brussels. The French had been apprehensive about the number of scenes featuring Hitler and other Nazi leaders watching the Games, requesting Riefenstahl to consider cutting them. Under protest she made two minor snips, where fascist salutes and swastika flags featured, but was adamant about the rest, and she was proved right. In France, as elsewhere, the film was screened almost intact with no trouble at all.

Anyone seeing it now, as an historical document, will find the telling glimpses it gives of leaders who don't know they are being watched more fascinating than offensive. We want to know how Hitler reacts when Ilse Dörffeldt diasastrously drops the baton in the last leg of the 400-metre relay, robbing Germany of a certain gold medal. We need to see him straighten and sniff as the magnificent young Jesse Owens storms yet again across the finishing line. And Goering jigging like a little boy at a German win. These vignettes in any case are only cutaways to the action, although – as in her editing of *Triumph of the Will* – Riefenstahl deliberately sets up a contrapuntal rhythm between players and observers to heighten the electricity between them. The animated responses are almost as memorable as the sporting exploits, but she does vary them between cheerleaders and compatriot supporters, ordinary men and women crammed into the stands and the bigwigs in their special enclosures. Nazi salutes are in evidence in the team march-pasts at the start of the Games; but again, it is of interest to know which nations raised their arms to Hitler and which kept them tightly pressed to their sides, like the British and American contingents.[10]

Gala performances of *Olympia* followed in Copenhagen, Stockholm, Helsinki, Oslo, everywhere to be met with the same rapturous enthusiasm. Leni's mother accompanied her on this Scandinavian tour and was thrilled to meet prime ministers and crowned heads and to see how warmly her famous daughter was received. When she had been a fellow conspirator all those years ago in Leni's secret dancing lessons, she could never have guessed where her precocious offspring's talents would lead. Culture, it seemed, could still cross international boundaries no matter how uneasy the political situation. After the tour, Leni and Hermann Storr grabbed a short holiday on the Venetian coast before the Biennale festivities at the end of August. Despite British and American delegates protesting that a documentary film had no place in the feature film category of an international festival, *Olympia* was awarded the Mussolini Cup, the event's top

197

prize, edging Walt Disney's *Snow White and the Seven Dwarfs* into second place, though with a special jury mention. Harold Smith and Neville Kerney, the American and British representatives were unplaced and resigned from the adjudicating panel.

Later, Riefenstahl went to Rome with the intention of screening the film before the Duce himself, but developments in the Sudetenland dragged the Italian leader off for consultation in Berlin, and he missed it. During November, it was arranged for the film-maker to accompany *Olympia* on an extended tour of the United States of America. With Ernst Jaeger and Werner Klingenberg, secretary to the German Olympic Committee, she sailed for New York on the luxury liner *Europa,* which proved something of a voyage into fantasy. The idea was to travel incognito, and on the passenger list she was 'Lotte Richter' – so that the initials on her expensive luggage would raise no eyebrows. Her cover was soon blown, however, and she rather enjoyed being a shipboard celebrity. She and Jaeger were not above making notes about which of their rich fellow travellers were likely to prove useful as contacts later. While she abandoned herself to the cocktails and entertainment or, wrapped in blankets, sipped beef tea and braved the winter sunshine on deck, anti-Semitic violence was simmering like a volcano back home.

The explosion came with the infamous *Kristallnacht* of 9th–10th November (Night of Broken Glass), when rampaging young Nazis of the Hitler Youth, disguised as civilians, smashed thousands of Jewish store-windows, homes and synagogues throughout Germany, killing Jews at random and looting indiscriminately. Ninety-one Jews were murdered that night and an estimated 20,000 carried off into concentration camps, though the full extent of this would not emerge for some time. Riefenstahl's memory has telescoped days here. Her recollection is of stepping, smiling, down the gangplank at the start of her much-publicised tour, to be instantly surrounded by a pack of journalists, demanding to know how she accounted for these vicious outrages. In reality, she docked in New York a few days earlier, on 4th November, when she was certainly besieged by the press, wanting more than anything to know if she was 'Hitler's honey'.[11] She made a favourable enough first impression,[12] though the mood of course changed instantly in the wake of the pogrom. Anti-German feeling had never run so high. As the German Ambassador in Washington reported to his bosses in Berlin just before he and his opposite number in the German capital were recalled, 'A hurricane is raging here'.[13] Leni was advised by the German Consul and the American representative of the Propaganda Ministry to leave America at once, but she decided against it.

Had she more experience of press interrogation, or not been so resolutely blinkered in her admiration of Hitler and all his works, she might have found the good grace to be discomfited when confronted with the Kristallnacht reports. She could have said, in all truth, that she knew nothing of these dreadful things. She hadn't read the reports and couldn't possibly comment at this time. And, stretching the speculation further, she might thereby perhaps have affected the course of her life. Instead, she blurted out vehemently that it couldn't be true. No! No! It had to be lies – all wicked lies put about by the American newspapers. Inevitably, the headlines soon trumpeted that Leni Riefenstahl denied all truth in the reported stories of Nazi horrors.

Cut off on the high seas from press and radio reports, she had little whiff of the way things were building up at home. She has strenuously maintained that, while at the same time admitting that 'old' American newspapers lying around on board seemed filled with what she took to be heavy-handed anti-Nazi propaganda. Muddling the dates of her arrival inevitably raises suspicions, for it is hard to believe that someone so dependent on favourable press coverage would not be eagerly scanning the American newspapers once in New York. She would have seen the *Kristallnacht* reports as early as anyone. Perhaps we should not forget that Germans had been force-fed propaganda for so long by then, they were ill-equipped to judge what news they should or shouldn't question. Despite Hitler's occupation of the Sudetenland within weeks of signing the Munich Agreement, Riefenstahl still clung to the belief that the Nazis wanted nothing but peace. The Jewish question was not so clarified in her mind – and she would have done well before her visit to research the attitudes she was likely to bump up against in the New World, particularly among film people.

Or maybe she did? In choosing Ernst Jaeger as her business and press manager, perhaps she thought she was taking out an insurance policy against trouble. He had been her friend for almost fifteen years, and she knew well he was no admirer of Hitler. It was Jaeger who had packed her off to listen to the Austrian hothead at the Sportpalast all those years ago, as part of her education, never for a moment expecting her to swallow the man's preposterous message quite so gullibly. In those days he had been editor-in-chief of the *Film-Kurier*, Berlin's important motion-picture magazine, but after marrying a Jew, was relieved of this position by Dr Goebbels and told that unless he renounced his wife through the divorce courts, the possibility of following any kind of profession within Germany would be denied to him. This he refused to do, and, to her credit, Riefenstahl flouted the embargo, employing him whenever possible in some capacity or other. It was Jaeger who ghost-wrote her behind-the-scenes book on the 1934 Party rally,[14] and he also worked intermittently as her press secretary. Obtaining permission for him to come on this trip had not been easy. Leni had to lobby the Propaganda Ministry vigorously on his behalf before Goebbels could be persuaded to relent. Her persistence stemmed from an obvious affection for the gagged reporter, who had helped her early career. She must also have believed that his good relations in the capital of the film industry would smooth her own passage there. If the thought ever occurred to her that he might 'jump ship' and seek asylum once safely across the Atlantic, or indeed if she was consciously affording him such a possibility with her invitation, that is not how she portrays it now.

In Hollywood, the tirelessly energetic Anti-Nazi League carried enormous influence through weekly radio programmes and its bi-weekly tabloid, *Hollywood Now*.[15] It had every intention of picketing Leni Riefenstahl's tour even before her injudicious dismissal of *Kristallnacht*, seeing her as a travelling representative of the desired Reich, a 'Ribbentrop in skirts'. Telegrams had been sent to all leading firm distributors warning that *Olympia* was part of a Nazi propaganda attack. Now the demonstrations were stepped up, at first with patchy results. In New York, and Chicago where Avery Brundage welcomed her, Riefenstahl was well received and the film successful. Once in California, however, it was a different picture. Newspaper advertisements urged a boycott against her – 'Post this on your bulletin board!' they said, 'There is no room in Hollywood for Leni Riefenstahl . . . in this moment when hundreds of thousands of our brethren await certain death. Close your doors to all Nazi Agents.' Demonstrations protested her presence, and invitations that had been proffered were speedily withdrawn. Only Hal Roach and Walt Disney greeted her publicly, the latter showing her around his studios where his great work *Fantasia* was in production. Yet even he drew the line at screening her film during the visit, afraid of the strength of the boycott.

On the few occasions *Olympia* was seen – largely at private showings, and in a version with the scenes of Hitler deleted[16] – its reception was as enthusiastic as elsewhere. Some correspondents openly challenged allegations that it was a work of propaganda for the Germans. 'The finest motion picture that I have ever seen,' said Henry McLemore of the United Press, and an anonymous editorial writer for the *Los Angeles Times* declared it 'a triumph of the camera and an epic of the screen.' All the same, anti-Nazi feeling was understandably so great at this time that the content and sentiment of the film were irrelevent; its Germanic origin was enough to damn it. Distributors all across the country took fright. They could see the film's promise as a money-spinner, but one after another, deals would be set up only to fall apart before signature. It was almost as if a bush telegraph were at work, one bunch of lawyers sending warning messages ahead to the next. At last it was clear that *Olympia* was unlikely ever to be seen commercially in the United States. Sadly, Leni Riefenstahl boarded the train to take her back to New York and the voyage home.

As she left Hollywood, she was warned by a friend not to expect Ernst Jaeger to be sailing with her. He was in cahoots with the Anti-Nazi League, this woman told her, and had been selling stories about her to interested parties. His plans were to remain, and have his wife and child join him in California. All along, he had used the trip to set up contacts to his own advantage, and he planned to launch a Hollywood gossip paper. When he failed to appear on the boat, Leni recognised this assessment of affairs bore some truth and she saw it as a personal betrayal.[17] She had acted as his guarantor: how was she going to explain the defection to Goebbels? Even worse – and this gave her real trepidation – what beans could Jaeger spill? He knew more about her and her indiscretions than perhaps anyone; he had seen her correspondence and diaries and well knew how Leni and her colleagues joked about Goebbels behind his back. In his efforts to ingratiate himself in Hollywood, Jaeger would have no qualms in sensationalising stories for maximum effect, she could bank on that. Not that Hollywood concerned her – already her name was blackened there – as much as the deep, deep trouble she would be in if injudicious stories were to get back to the Ministry of Propaganda.

She was right to worry. Throughout the Spring of 1939, *The Hollywood Tribune*, a staunch anti-Nazi weekly, carried a series of eleven articles by Jaeger entitled HOW LENI RIEFENSTAHL BECAME HITLER'S GIRLFRIEND. Her friend mailed her copies, showing how fact was blended seamlessly and shamelessly with fabrication. Riefenstahl was at once Hitler's mistress, Goebbels' mistress, even a plaything of

Goering's. 'Highflown romanticism and unscrupulous intrigues, both masked behind a brilliantly-maintained camouflage, surround the rise of Riefenstahl to the position of the most enviable woman in Hitler's domain,' Jaeger had written. Through all the embellishment, it would be clear to any of those named – Fanck, Sokal, Hitler, Goebbels – from where these stories had emanated. That Riefenstahl did not keep her mouth shut, however sensitive the matter, was revealed for all to see. Jaeger told how Hitler had been enraptured by Leni's dance of the fluttering veils, and of her tryst with him on the Baltic coast ('a Valkyrie Flies to Valhalla', ran the sub-head): 'That night Herr Hitler became her Hitler' (his prose had clearly gone through the Hollywood processing-machine). Most damaging of all was the account in one of the early articles of a train journey to Munich when Leni discovered Goebbels in the next compartment. His warning to her to stay away from the Führer, who belonged to the Party and the people and would never belong to any woman; and the rider, added in a persuasive voice, 'One shouldn't aim for the head man; it's *so* much safer with the second,' was probably a fair representation of what had taken place. It sent Leni into utter panic.

What should she do? Keep quiet and hope Goebbels never saw this periodical? Some hope. Pre-empt matters and tell him? Tell him what? Her memoirs reveal that an opportunity presented itself in July at the 1939 Day of German Art in Munich, when she found herself sitting next to the Doctor at a state banquet. In a flash of inspiration, she whispered to him that he had been right all along about Ernst Jaeger. She should have taken his advice.

It did not seem as if Goebbels had been forewarned on the matter, and she was able to continue, 'Something awful has happened.'

Goebbels listened with ill-temper, but no particular interest, merely snapping at last that he had told her so. 'I knew you couldn't trust that slimy hack,' he said.[18] He had troubles of his own. His health and nerves had been playing him up since Hitler ordered an end to his romance with the Czech actress Lida Baarova the previous autumn. The required reconciliation with his wife, Magda, was not proving easy to engineer since she had formed a consolatory attachment with his own under-secretary. At the same time, his career rival Rosenberg was conducting a smear campaign against him; and over all lurked the fast-approaching inevitability of war. Goebbels could no longer believe Hitler merely wanted to expand into Poland; England and France were also being worked up into enemies. In such a bad and lunatic time, he was in no mind to get worked up over what sounded like salacious gossip about Riefenstahl in some distant broadsheet. Serve her right, he probably thought; he had been right in marking her down as an hysteric.

She breathed a sigh of relief, convinced she had just experienced a very lucky escape.

XV

Leni's War

Leni spent a year promoting *Olympia*. In all, this film had consumed four years of her life. She was relieved when the excitement at last died away, giving her the chance to develop an idea which had been tantalising her for a long time, and with which she hoped to sever herself from documentaries and *Bergfilme* once and for all. She planned an historical epic about the Amazonian queen, Penthesilea, who fought the Trojans and the Greeks in the post-Homeric legends. Her ideas were based on a verse-play by Heinrich von Kleist which had enjoyed great popularity in Germany in the mid-1920s and focused on Penthesilea's great and ultimately tragic love for Achilles. From the moment she first encountered it, Leni had found the story deeply affecting. She said in interview that she loved Kleist as she loved no other poet or dramatist.[1] His every word struck resonances for her, and Penthesilea's strong character uncannily mirrored her own. Max Reinhardt had agreed that the part could have been tailor-made for her, and Henry Jaworsky remembered the project as a pet theme when they were filming *The Blue Light*. The crew used to pull her leg about it whenever she got too domineering, saying, 'You know what it means, don't you? You'll have to burn off your right breast. All the Amazons did that to be able to draw their bows properly.'

From the start, she had realised this was not something to rush into, but should be saved until she had reached the pinnacle of her artistic development. It could be her masterwork, her *Ring of the Niebelungs*, but at the same time, she wanted it to be an expression of the full potential of cinematic art. With the experience of *Olympia* behind her, she felt the time had at last come and withdrew to a cottage on the Friesian island of Sylt to write the screenplay and begin her Amazon training. Penthesilea needed the horseback agility of a circus rider, so

Leni's beloved white mare, 'Fairytale', went with her. Writing in the mornings, riding or practising other sports in the afternoons turned out to be as near perfect an existence as she could wish. It was one of the most creative periods of her life. The structure of the film and all the individual scenes sprang complete into her imagination, like sprouted dragons' teeth. She had only to write them down.

She held it as essential to keep true to the spirit of Kleist's poetry, even if sometimes this were rendered into visual lyricism wherever images could replace words 'with at least equal force'.[2] She saw poetry and cinema as similar expressions, in any case, each progressing in a sort of wave motion, 'like an alternating current of electricity'. An audience should not be overloaded with beauty and splendour, in her belief, but brought to a peak by the expressiveness of a sequence and then allowed to subside before rising again. 'The thing to do is to chart these two wave motions,' she explained, 'and see that they work in an inverse ratio one to another. This is one of the things that the sound film in the full sense of the term should be about; rhythm is at the basis of everything.'[3] To her mind, this kind of balance, honouring poetry and film equally, had never been fully explored. Picking up the theme again in an interview after the war, she supposed that Laurence Olivier's *Henry V* came the closest, but was disappointing, to her mind, because Olivier 'vacillates, sacrificing first one, then the other – now a bit of cinema, now a bit of Shakespeare again.' And Orson Welles, too, drew 'marvellous pictures in the margin of Shakespeare,' but his films were not Shakespeare himself.

She conceived a prologue for her film which owed nothing to Kleist. With no dialogue at all, it would simply set the temper of the film by filling in the background to the Greek wars and suspending everyday sensibilities. By the time her players spoke in verse, she wanted this to seem perfectly natural to the viewer. By the end of that summer, everything was ready. The production had been approved by the Propaganda Ministry, she had engaged a top theatre director to assist with the dramatic scenes, and a hundred young women were training in Libya in preparation for the mounted battle sequences. Libya was chosen for the conflicts between Amazons and Greeks for its flawless Mediterranean skies, which she would film in colour, but using filters to impart a subdued, classical cast. She wanted the image to appear like an ancient bas-relief:

Some of the visuals would be very detailed – exquisitely formal . . . and brooded over by a giant, coldly beautiful moon or a vast burning sun, five times larger than life. But as the poetic intensity of the text increased, so the visual intensity would diminish until everything was reduced to perhaps just two pure profiles outlined in silver as the greatest lines were spoken.[4]

The final duel between Penthesilea and Achilles she intended to shoot on Sylt, where dramatic clouds could supply a moody backdrop, similar to those achieved so successfully in the introductory set pieces to *Olympia*.

Before joining her fellow Amazons in Libya, Leni decided to seize a few days' climbing and took off for the Dolomites. With Hans Steger, she enjoyed one glorious day in the hills above the Sella Hut, only to be met that evening by Steger's companion Paula Wiesinger with terrible news.

'Leni, you've got to get back to Berlin right away!' Paula told her. 'They have started mobilising. War is expected at any minute! Hermann has been on the phone to say he's already in barracks, and so, too, are Guzzi and Otto and most of the others.'

'I'll come with you,' Steger offered, and together he and Leni hurtled back through the night in her open sports car along an almost empty autobahn. She went straight to the military quarters, where her boyfriend Hermann Storr and the others were expecting to be sent to Poland within days. A million and a quarter men had just stormed Danzig.

'We ought to be an official camera unit,' her friends told her. 'See what you can do. Try to set up a newsreel company and get us to the front line.'

In the crowds at the Reichstag later that day, Leni heard Hitler announce that the Germans had been exchanging fire in Poland since 5.45 that morning. This was rather a euphemistic turn of phrase for an act of aggression on the part of Germany; by 6 am Hitler's aeroplanes were bombing Warsaw. Frantic weeks of diplomatic message-carrying between capitals had failed to avert disaster. Hitler was implementing his long-threatened seizure not only of 'Free' Danzig but of coveted Lebensraum further east. Two days later, as his lightning strike scorched on towards Warsaw, on the 3rd September, Britain and France declared war on Germany.

★

Naturally there could be no more thought of *Penthesilea*. Even without the war, it is hard to imagine the film would have been allowed to reach fruition. Its setting in classical antiquity may have suggested escapism – which is what the film industry was after by this time – but Riefenstahl's Amazon warriors and their Queen could be seen as a direct challenge to the Gretchen-image of 'three-K' womanhood so vigorously peddled by the Third Reich.

Her friends were right – the only way to continue filming now was as war correspondents. She submitted a proposal to the Wehrmacht, which was promptly sanctioned, and within days Riefenstahl and her cameramen, who included Sepp Allgeier and the Lantschner brothers, along with Waldi Traut and Hermann Storr as sound-man, were issued with the field-grey uniforms of the press corps and given a crash course in the use of gas masks and handguns. Just a week after the outbreak of war, her mobile documentary unit was on its way to the Polish front.

She arrived at the small town of Konskie, an outpost in chaos, where a short while before resistance fighters had killed some Germans. Leni reported to the General in charge, surprised to see it was Walther von Reichenau, one of those to have visited her studio when she was making the Wehrmacht documentary. The last thing he wanted was film people getting in the way and he directed them away from the firing line. On their first morning, before they had a chance to start any filming, Leni and her companions fought through an excited crowd to discover the army taking rough revenge on a group of civilians. Some Poles were being made to dig a pit, which she took to be a grave for the murdered soldiers. The terrified hostages clearly thought they were digging their own grave – which in the event turned out to be nearer the truth. As one German police officer ordered the men to be released and a few soldiers tried to haul them from the pit, others began viciously kicking and stamping on them, pushing them back in. Outraged and incredulous, Leni screeched for them to stop. 'What sort of soldiers are you? Didn't you hear what the officer said?'

'Shut the bitch up!' one of them yelled, raising his rifle ominously, and Leni's friends quickly pulled her clear. As she went in search of von Reichenau to lodge a complaint, a shot suddenly rang out from somewhere in the crowd.

Everyone scattered in panic. In a matter of moments more than thirty Poles lay dead, mown down in senseless carnage. As Leni tells it, neither she nor any of her camera crew saw the victims fall but, thoroughly sickened by the incident, she left immediately for Berlin, abandoning all ideas of becoming a war reporter. She visited a combat area only once more,[5] a couple of weeks later when, after the occupation of Warsaw, Ernst Udet – by then technical chief of the Luftwaffe – secured her a return seat on a military plane to the Polish capital to check on the welfare of her film crew. They were fine and expected to be home shortly.

As the Germans had pushed eastwards into Poland, Soviet forces began a matching advance from the opposite direction. By the end of September the two aggressive powers had carved up the Polish nation between them, and in the process demonstrated the superior effectiveness of a *blitzkrieg* over the demoralising attrition of trench warfare.

Leni's active war service may have spanned no more than three weeks, but its repercussions would dog her for decades. She had been caught on camera at the time of the massacre by a German soldier in the crowd, his shutter clicking at the very moment her face warped into a scream of revulsion. When, after the war, she refused a blackmail demand to buy this picture, it was used to imply her involvement in recording Nazi atrocities against the Jews. Accusations were made in a Munich periodical,[6] and more damaging still on television as late as the 1980s, where the screaming picture and scenes from *Triumph* were intercut with material showing executions of blindfold prisoners, deportations, the *Kristallnacht* pogrom and other images of the Holocaust. Anyone viewing the compilation would quite naturally assume that Leni Riefenstahl had been present at these atrocities. The Denazification Tribunal of Berlin studied the Konskie photograph closely when accusations were first made, and could find nothing incriminating about it. On the contrary, the look of stricken horror on her face bore out Leni's testimony of events better than that of her accusers.

Anxious to avoid being drawn into making war or propaganda films,[7] Riefenstahl decided instead to busy herself with something as neutral as possible. Expensive epics like *Penthesilea* clearly stood no chance, but how about revitalising *Tiefland*, the opera-inspired project which had foundered in Spain five years before? She no longer felt as close to the subject as once she did but it would be the perfect antidote to war and all its obscenities. She tried to be philosophical about it – with luck the film could be finished in a few months, by which time normal conditions might have returned. She was wide of the mark on both counts.

At the beginning, the war had made no great impact on film production. Cinema audiences were still growing and clamouring for stories, and Tobis — who in the end had done well out of *Olympia* — was happy to go along with Riefenstahl's new plans. She installed herself in a rented chalet on the Austrian ski slopes near Kitzbühel to work on the script and, remembering the blissful productivity of her days on Sylt, she interspersed her writing with snow sports. The trick worked, but in a rather different manner than she planned. When inspiration was slow in coming and the sun beckoned outside, it was hard to stay indoors.

One day, on the ski slopes, Riefenstahl ran into a lawyer friend, Harald Reinl, who had worked with Fanck and as Guzzi's camera assistant on *Olympia*. He hankered to get back into the business, and showed her a film script he was working on. She could see he had talent as well as enthusiasm, and on the spur of the moment Leni invited him to be her assistant director. Bouncing ideas between them, they knocked out the dialogue for *Tiefland* in just six weeks, at the same time greatly improving the original story by the added tension of a peasants' uprising against their greedy landowner.

The snowy slopes yielded the male lead as well. An army ski instructor at St Anton impressed Riefenstahl with his air of un-worldliness and inner goodness — just the qualities she was seeking, for in this film *The Blue Light* plot was reversed in as much as the leading man was the child of nature and the woman the well-meaning realist. Unfortunately, her 'Pedro' had never acted before, and no one else, the studio included, could fathom what she saw in him. She had not thought to star in the film herself — as was her intention five years before — but when no other suitable gypsy dancer could be found, she agreed to take on the lead if an experienced director supervised her scenes. Pabst, who had recently returned from Hollywood, was her first choice, but when Goebbels earmarked him for work in Prague, Mathias Wieman was called in.

There was no problem in obtaining foreign currency so early in the war, and an advance crew began location shooting in Spain with some of the lowland scenes. They planned to move to the Pyrenees for the pastoral uplands, but as fighting in Europe extended southwards, the entire production had to be pulled back to Bavaria, where all film work was being concentrated on the war effort. With no special priority, Riefenstahl was obliged repeatedly to interrupt operations, on one occasion for as long as two years when — after she had just taken possession of some very expensive sets — her studio was comman-deered by Goebbels, and none other could be found. She had no choice then but to start letting her workers go, one by one, though not before she had managed to secure most of the outdoor scenes. The mountain material gathered in the Rosengarten area of the Dolomites was startling in its atmosphere, and completely justified her decision to go for black and white rather than colour. This – what she calls her 'painterly' effect – was achieved in the first place by careful composition within each frame, but more especially by pushing her use of coloured filters to new limits.[8]

For crowd scenes she called first upon her old friends, the Sarntalers, who in features could be mistaken for farmers from northern Spain as the plot required. When more 'peasantry' was needed, Harald Reinl was sent in search of gypsies, and sixty Romanys – men, women and children – were hired from a camp near Salzburg. Though not a concentration camp at this time (1940–41), the centre seems to have become a holding camp for Auschwitz later in the war, and the slur that Riefenstahl knowingly employed 'slave labourers' in her production has been the most politically damaging accusation ever levelled against her. It has also proved impossible to argue away. Two court cases and at least two appeals after the war found that she could not have foreseen the Auschwitz connection, but she failed to convince lawyers that she had not personally selected those 'extras'. Some of the gypsies were prepared to speak up for her, saying they had been treated well, but the fact that so many of the group perished in the gas-chambers of the Third Reich, has made this a morally suicidal issue to challenge.[9]

In no respect did *Tiefland* satisfy Riefenstahl's hopes for an easy and politically neutral time-filler. Hardly anything went as planned. Sets were constructed wrongly and had to be rebuilt; location work would be abruptly cut short by winter snowfalls; a specially trained wolf, which the hero was to wrestle, died of overeating; and one borrowed from the zoo escaped and had to be shot. As the difficulties and delays mounted, so too did the bills. She has said she put up a lot of the money for *Tiefland* herself from the profits of *Olympia*. Goebbels noted in his diary on 16th December 1942 that 'Already more than five million marks have been wasted on this film and it will take another whole year before it is finished. Frau Riefenstahl has become very ill from overwork and worry, and I urged her earnestly to go on leave before taking up further work.'[10] He was glad, he said, to 'have nothing to do with the unfortunate case', and hence bore no responsibility. This somewhat curious washing-of-hands from the overseer of *all* films made within the Reich, indicates that Riefenstahl still enjoyed special status, and presumably was still answerable only to the Führer.

In fits and starts the film lurched forward throughout the war.[11] Ill health dogged Riefenstahl, who fell victim once more to the chronic bladder condition that had struck her down in Greenland. No manner of treatment worked and she was told that an operation would be useless. At its worst, acting was out of the question but bundled with hot-water bottles in blankets, she directed what she could. There are stories of her in 1941 overseeing some of the scenes from a stretcher.

It is sometimes suggested that Leni Riefenstahl deliberately spun out this movie to see her through the war. It was Henry Jaworsky's impression she was so appalled by what she had seen in Poland, and so unwilling to be involved in Goebbels' propaganda machine, that her only thought was to survive. With amused incredulity he told Gordon Hitchens of *Film Culture*, 'Seven years she managed to work on an opera film!'[12] Whether there were indeed any spinning or no, she could not have wished all the delays upon herself. Certainly, towards the end of the war, expecting defeat and unsure what abyss awaited after, she pulled out all stops to get the film finished.

★

In August 1939, Albert Speer had approached Riefenstahl about recording the radical reconstruction plans for Berlin, which were being carried out under Hitler's personal supervision. He and his team of architects had produced a gigantic model of this monstrous new 'Germania' – could she film it for him? At the time, Leni was utterly wrapped up in her *Penthesilea* preparations, and suggested Arnold Fanck for the task. Her mentor's career had collapsed under Goebbels, presumably because he was known to have worked happily with Jews and Jewish money. Fanck took on Speer's commission under the umbrella of Riefenstahl's company, and was answerable directly to the architect without reference to the Film Chamber. It led to other short government-funded 'culture films' which enabled him – and her production company – to survive the war.[13]

Quite apart from the work on *Tiefland*, Leni was able to offer employment to many of her cameramen and assistants throughout the hostilities. In the same way that Arnold Fanck had brought on apprentice film makers, Riefenstahl trained protégés, both personally and by giving them the opportunity to experiment. Several short films were put together by her assistants from the out-takes of *Olympia*. A Tyrolean skiing film was produced also, while Guzzi Lantschner made his co-directorial debut alongside Harald Reinl with a highly praised white-water kayaking documentary for which Leni's favourite composer, Herbert Windt, wrote the musical score. Both would go on to do more in this field. Albert Benitz she kept as her chief cameraman for most of the *Tiefland* shooting, and Waldi Traut, too, worked with her closely throughout this period. After the war he enjoyed a successful career, mainly with Gloria Films.

Henry Jaworsky, who had refused to work on *Triumph of the Will* on political grounds (but had no such qualms about *Olympia*), remained on good terms with Leni for most of his life. He would have nothing said to her detriment. His training with Schneeberger had given him a reputation for aerial work and, with the Flea, in 1934–35 he worked for Udet on a 90-minute feature, *The Wonders of Flying*.[14] Jaworksy had to swallow his political principles after war broke out and contributed to on a number of propaganda and feature films including *Baptism of Fire* and *Campaign in Poland*.[15] When it was discovered that he had a Jewish grandmother, he was demoted from his technical rank of army lieutenant to private, second class. Alarmed at what this might imply, he sought Leni's advice. She asked Frentz to put in a word for him with Bormann – Frentz was by now official Luftwaffe cameraman at Hitler's headquarters – but all Frentz got from Bormann was the chilling advice to mind his own business, or so much the worse for him. Udet stepped in, pulling out Jaworsky to work on two features to do with flying. After Udet's suicide in 1941, Jaworsky found himself once more back in the ranks.

'Keep your head down,' Leni told him. 'Do what they tell you, no more, no less. Just try to survive.' It was of course exactly what she was doing; Jaworsky formed the opinion that by then she already believed that the Germans would be defeated. 'Hitler is surrounded by gangsters,' she explained.

Jaworsky was on good enough terms with Fritz Hippler of the Nazi Film Chamber to be allowed to continue serving as a cameraman within the army and, in the interview he gave to *Film Culture* in 1973, he claimed to have worked with the French resistance later in the war, passing over copies of certain film material in Tunisia. Later he emigrated to America.

Writing of his experiences as a war cameraman,[16] Hans Ertl described frying eggs on Rommel's tank in Libya, and standing with Bavarian troops on the summit of Mt Elbrus in the Caucasus. Willy Zielke passed most of the war years in hospital after the breakdown brought on by *Olympia*.[17] Jaworsky has told of the fate of other film chums of Leni's who worked on *Olympia*: Hans Gottschalk went down with the battleship *Bismarck*, while Eberhard van den Heyden was killed filming a parachute raid to blow up a bridge. Ernst Sorge, the Greenland scientist who went on to work for Riefenstahl, became an important spy for the Soviets. Guzzi Lantschner, like Ertl, went to South America after the war.

The death of Ernst Udet, in circumstances which were not immediately made known, shocked his many friends, including Leni Riefenstahl, who claimed to have received an early-morning telephone call from the Colonel-General on the day he took his own life. Though she never completely forgave Udet for seducing the Snowflea away from her to his fun-loving lifestyle, she could not bring herself to dislike the old rake. He drank too much, he womanised, but the wisecracking charmer was always the best of company.

With warmth, she remembered all those times he had picked her up in his light plane and whisked her about the Alps or Greenland, and how he liked to scare her half to death with his stunt flying. You could never tell with Udet where the fantasy began or ended. In Fanck's films, he always played himself: whatever the drama, it was Udet to the rescue! In real life, when the first climbers went missing on the Eigerwand, who but Udet flew in dangerously close to the lethal rock wall to spot a frozen body at 'Death Bivouac'? In the same way it was Udet who was called in to drop supplies to the teenage Frey cousins, marooned on the East Face of the Watzmann. His popularity, prowess in the air and a comradeship with Goering which went back to their Richthofen days, assured him a high-ranking position in the new Luftwaffe, even if at first he resisted Goering's overtures. He was not interested in politics, nor had any wish to get back into uniform. The life he had then was the life he wanted. He revelled in his fame and freedom, seeing himself as a merry Bohemian, wanting nothing but to continue flying.

Goering assured him that it was just his 'hands-on' expertise that the country needed, and sent him immediately to America to study the development of military aviation there. By the time Udet joined the Aviation Ministry in 1934, he had drawn up plans for a new kind of dive-bomber, which he – but few others – believed represented a vital attack weapon. Two prototypes were produced by Junkers. The first Udet crashed when he failed to pull it from its first dive but, stepping unscathed from the wreck, he immediately took off in the other. A dazzling display had him screaming down on the field to drop his dummy bombs, this time pulling out safely in the nick of time. He won over his Air Force colleagues, even if the 'Stuka' would clearly require very delicate handling. In 1935 Udet was put in charge of all production for the Luftwaffe. It was not so many years since he had been bumming around America, almost penniless, a barnstormer with the personal gimmick of performing in top hat and full dress suit.

Udet was not well suited to the strains of administration, nor to the intrigue or malicious infighting which goes with high office. He loathed red tape. Some of his decisions proved disastrous, and aircraft production fell seriously behind. He covered up. After the Battle of Britain, it would have taken two years to make up losses to the strength that everyone, including the Führer, thought existed. By the following year things were worse: half the precious Junkers 52 fleet was lost in the conquest of Crete, and there were less than three thousand 'first-line' planes available for the Russian attack. When Goering began to get the full picture, Udet offered his resignation, but it was refused. His profile was too high to allow him to be seen as incompetent or disillusioned. Besides, Goering was going to need a scapegoat when Hitler discovered the true chaos. Sick, broken, and chronically depressed, Udet put a bullet through his brain early on the morning of 17th November, 1941. He was forty-five. Within hours, Goebbels had an announcement issued that the popular air ace had perished while testing a new weapon. The Führer ordered a state funeral for 'this fine officer, killed in the execution of his duty.'

Flags throughout Berlin flew at half-mast, and an ashen Goering walked behind the gun carriage beside a grim Hitler. Those who knew the true circumstances of Udet's suicide were sworn to secrecy – his current girlfriend, who had heard the fatal shot over the telephone, was threatened with death if she opened her mouth – but whispers soon began circulating among his closest friends. He was known to have been a crack shot, yet rumour had it Udet muffed this last shooting, remaining alive long enough to write with his finger on the wall, in his own blood, 'It is all the fault of Goering.'[18] The 1956 film, *The Devil's General*, starring Curt Jurgens, was based on Udet's life and disenchantment with Hitler and Nazism. Leni found it an accurate enough portrayal of his character, although its suggestion that the Gestapo had a hand in Udet's suicide she declared no more than an unworthy plot device.

These two had always understood each other, and shared a reckless streak, though Riefenstahl always maintained there was never a whiff of romance between them. Both had enemies, who were happy to make more of their intimacy, and the story goes that Eva Braun, jealous of the Führer's admiration and apparent fondness for Leni Riefenstahl, leaked a rumour (via Himmler) that the roué airman and the ambitious film-maker had an 'interesting arrangement'. According to Glenn Infield, the ruse paid off. Udet fell at once from favour, to be subjected to constant harassment from the Führer over his work. Infield puts this as a critical factor in Udet's downfall and ultimate suicide.[19]

The significant romantic figure in Riefenstahl's life during these war years was an infantry officer she had first encountered on a train coming over the Brenner Pass. Alone in her compartment, she became aware of a man in the corridor outside, staring in at her with his face pressed to the glass. She closed her eyes to avoid the disturbing gaze, but some days later – we are told by coincidence – this same soldier was hired as a stand-in for the ruthless landowner in *Tiefland*. His name was Peter Jacob, and he was a first lieutenant in the mountain infantry, with an Iron Cross for gallantry in the French Campaign. At the time of their meeting, in 1940, he was recuperating from light injuries at Mittenwald barracks in Bavaria. Riefenstahl was taken by his raffish appearance – 'his casually hanging cloak, his cap askew' – but she was wary. For the eleven years since she had parted from Schneeberger, she had avoided deep relationships, preferring short-term flings and warm friendships without the devastating power to hurt. But this was different: Lieutenant Jacob was a man of explosive passions, and profoundly disquieting. By the time he returned to the front, his film work completed, he and Leni had declared their 'great love', though it was not one for which she could hold out much prospect of a happy ending. She agonised as German forces swept through the Balkans to take Athens in April 1941, then heard over the radio that Peter had been awarded the Knight's Cross for bravery as the Metaxes Line collapsed. Later that year, marriage was mooted in their correspondence, though it seemed out of the question with him away and *Tiefland* still unfinished. Like so many couples, they snatched what time together they could: he was granted a short leave before being posted on to Russia. Then she waited and worried once more, burying herself in work and neglecting her family and friends. Her state of health went up and down. Peter, who suffered so badly from cold he had to spend time in hospital, was given a courier job for a few weeks. This secured them a few more happy days together before he left once more for the front. Yet when his ship was held up in port for almost a fortnight because of ice, inexplicably he did not come back to her. She was sure he had spent the time with someone else. Her memoirs include extracts from letters Peter wrote to her from the Russian Front between March and June 1942, imploring her not to desert him. He looked forward to a further few weeks' leave later that summer, he told her.

Meanwhile, she managed to secure temporary studio-space in Babelsberg for some of the wolf scenes she needed for *Tiefland*. A new young animal had been trained, which the shepherd hero, 'Pedro', was supposed to 'strangle' with his bare hands. That went well enough, but the rest of the scene, shot on location, threw up its share of snags. Leni had written it to take place beside a mountain lake, and when no lake or spring could be found in the vicinity, it was decided to construct one. Fifty local inhabitants obligingly formed a human chain to fill it with buckets of water from the valley. After many hours, a beautifully realistic pool had appeared but Pedro's sheep could not be persuaded to browse around it. They streamed on past. Someone came up with the bright idea of providing salt-licks to keep them where they were wanted, but these only had the effect of making them so thirsty the precious lake was drunk dry. Three times, the human chain was pressed into service, and in the end the only way to achieve the idyllic scene, was for every one of the eighty sheep to be tethered in place around the watering hole.

The flock was no more accommodating when it came to registering restiveness as the wolf approached. In vain, the crew leapt about banging saucepans and firing scatter guns. The sheep munched on unperturbed. An explosives expert was called in. He set off a small charge, and in a moment what had been high farce turned to ghastly tragedy. The man blew himself up. No one had the heart to continue shooting for many days.

Peter arrived during this troubled session in the Dolomites, and even when the scenes were complete, there was little time for him and Leni to spend together. Before he returned to his unit, however, the pair were officially engaged.

All that was required now to complete *Tiefland* were some bull-fighting sequences. A distribution deal with Spain had guaranteed sufficient pesetas to cover location work in Salamanca, but the Ministry of Economics forbad any currency being taken abroad: no unnecessary travel was allowed. This time a direct appeal to Martin Bormann paid off and Riefenstahl was granted the approval she needed. How strange, in the middle of war to be able to escape the restrictions and rationings, the bombing and fighting, and experience

216

this blessed, if busy, intermission. Real coffee for breakfast! And chocolate, too. It seemed like a dream, and even more so when Peter showed up unexpectedly, having somehow wangled special leave from the Russian front. Six hundred charging bulls were filmed without accident.

Leni returned to Berlin with the precious footage to find the city badly damaged. Evacuations were in full swing, and she decided to move her company, her staff, all the *Tiefland* material and much of her precious archive to Kitzbühel, where she secured a chalet. Other negatives and prints were stored in two bunkers to the north of the capital. The move was completed in November 1943, when she hoped to embark on the editing, but again illness struck her down.

On the first day of spring, 1944, Leni Riefenstahl and Major Peter Jacob (as he had just become) were married in Kitzbühel. In the week following, flowers and congratulations arrived from the Führer and the couple were invited to meet him at the Berghof on 30th March. It was three years since Leni had seen Hitler, when he had paid her a surprise visit in a Munich clinic. She was appalled by the change in his appearance. He seemed shrunken and palsied, although there was still something of the old fire when he talked. And he did do all the talking, though in a rather abstracted fashion, preoccupied with affairs of war. Leni had supposed the purpose of the summons was for Hitler to take a look at her husband, but he barely paid Peter any attention at all. When the monologue was over, they were dismissed. She looked back over her shoulder to see Hitler standing blankly, watching them go. She wondered then if she would ever see him again.

In Müller's film of Riefenstahl, there is a photograph of her and Peter Jacob taken on the day they visited the Führer. It is one of the prettiest, least posed pictures of her ever to have been published. Relaxed and smiling, if rather thin, she looks as happy as any newly-wed. Within days, however, Peter's leave would be over once more. There was little to smile about for the rest of that year. In July her father died, and within a few days Leni received news that her brother, too, had been killed by a grenade on the Russian front on the same day that a group of Hitler's officers attempted to blow him up in his secret headquarters. Heinz's death was the bitterest of blows, and one to which Leni has never become fully reconciled. From being in a reserved occupation, managing their father's armaments factory, he was transferred to a punishment battalion after being accused by a former colleague of black marketeering and anti-war sentiments. Leni was sure he had been the victim of a vendetta, and

217

it haunted her that for all the pleading and fighting she had done to keep her cameramen out of the conflict, she never once spoke to Hitler or Bormann about Heinz's plight. His marriage had broken down and he was in dispute over custody of his two small children. His estranged wife was known to have close connections with a Gestapo officer and Heinz had been receiving threatening letters from this man. Leni's guilt was compounded by the fact that while she was tidying up the final studio work that autumn in Prague, the children – who had been entrusted to her care, according to her brother's wishes – were snatched from her house in Kitzbühel, and she never managed to regain custody of them.

In retrospect, Leni Riefenstahl found it hard to explain why she and her staff should have worked so diligently to complete *Tiefland* when their world was collapsing about them.[20] It was 'absurd' and 'completely inexplicable', and she put it down to her Prussian sense of duty. Yet she was not alone. As German hopes faded, Goebbels cranked his Dream Factory into even higher gear to lift national morale. The most ambitious production, *Kolberg*, which was nearing completion under the direction of Veit Harlan, told the story of a tiny Prussian town's heroic resistance against the might of Napoleon's army. Besides strengthening morale, this was to be Goebbels' answer to *Gone with the Wind*, and so obsessed was he by it that he diverted over 100,000 men from the Russian front in 1944 for the siege scenes. 'A law of madness prevailed,' Harlan admitted afterwards. They knew as much at the time, 'Hitler as well as Goebbels must have been obsessed by the idea that a film like this could be more useful to them than even a victory in Russia. Maybe they too were now just waiting for a miracle because they no longer believed in victory in any rational way.'[21] The film's leading lady Kristina Soederbaum, who played the heroic village maiden, found the situation so ridiculous she felt 'like a monkey' before the cameras.[22]

In UFA's Babelsberg Studios, southwest of Berlin, work was going ahead on another major production that Goebbels hoped would be the German equivalent of the inspirational *Mrs Miniver* or *This Happy Breed*. Set in 1943, in a residential district of Berlin under Allied bombardment, *Das Leben geht weiter* (*Life Goes On*) was intended to encourage a dispirited populace to stand firm. As such, it had high priority, a massive budget and some of the best movie stars of the day. Many thought Goebbels himself had a hand in writing the screenplay. Precious petrol reserves and colour film stock were made available; and (with echoes of Riefenstahl and her gypsies) a camp-load of Polish prisoners of war were employed as extras. Henry Jaworsky worked on it, filming air-raids. Shooting had been going on for six months, and the reels were hidden in a crypt for safety before the Allies arrived, but no footage was ever found after the war. The director, Wolfgang Liebeneiner, (again, like Riefenstahl) seems to have discerned which way the wind was blowing, and was anxious to protect his workers from being sent to the front. His daughter confirmed that the film was 'a kind of an island'. She saw her father as a minor Oskar Schindler. He was definitely playing for time towards the end. After 1945, everyone concerned with this lost feature film seems to have preferred to forget its existence.[23]

As bombs rained down on German cities, tucked away in the Salzburg mountains, Leni worked on as if possessed. Nobody knew what to expect if the war was lost, and each day brought new fear and terror. Soon, the Red Army was battering Berlin's outer defences, and the Allies forced the Siegfried Line. Auschwitz was liberated, Dresden devastated. Albert Speer offered Leni's mother the last chance of a lift out of Berlin to join her daughter in Kitzbühel. By March the Americans were crossing the Rhine, and in mid-April Schneeberger begged Riefenstahl's help to avoid draft into the territorial army for Berlin's last stand. Even schoolboys and old men were being called up. (The Flea was already over fifty by then.) Leni secured him a short dispensation to help with the *Tiefland* titles, and almost immediately his wife was arrested for berating wounded soldiers on a train. She was demanding to know why they kept fighting for Hitler. More strings were pulled, more officials chatted up, and Gisela Schneeberger walked free.

By the end of the month Hitler was dead. He had committed suicide in the Reichstag bunker along with Eva Braun and the entire Goebbels family. The Russians now had control of Berlin. As the war ended, Riefenstahl followed the Schneebergers to the Tyrol in search of sanctuary. Despite her best efforts, *Tiefland* remained unfinished.

XVI

Alone in the Wilderness

From the moment news came through that hostilities were over, the Schneebergers sought to distance themselves from Leni Riefenstahl. They made their getaway that same night, abandoning her in a small hotel in Mayrhofen at the head of the Zillertal valley. Next day she tracked them down to a family guest-house in hills above the village, but it was only to be sent rudely packing by Gisela.

'Whatever made you think we'd help *you*?' she shrieked at Leni. 'You Nazi slut!'

Even Hans could find no word of kindness; Leni's beloved Snowflea, who in desperation had sought her assistance only weeks before – and received it – could not so much as bring himself to look her in the eye.

This betrayal, as she saw it, on the part of former friends and some of her dearest colleagues was the bitterest element she would find of her new postwar status. One by one, most of Riefenstahl's associates, including Arnold Fanck, would disown her in their personal bids to sever connections with a discredited regime, the obscene excesses of which were only now becoming widely known. Leni was quickly finding she had no one to turn to; doors no longer swung magically open. Miserably, she began making her way through a Tyrol chaotic with returning troops and occupying forces. All that mattered now was to get back to Kitzbühel, where she hoped still to find her mother.

This part of Austria had fallen into American hands and she was picked up several times by the Allies, detained and questioned, but never held so securely as to be unable to escape. Eventually she reached home to find her house requisitioned. Americans billeted there were courteous and helpful, directing her on towards Ribbentrop's nearby property where she was reunited, not only with her mother, but her husband Peter also. Twice more the Americans rearrested her, bringing her on the second occasion first to prison in Salzburg and then to Seventh Army Headquarters for interrogation. There she shared a room with (among others) Hitler's senior secretary, Johanna Wolff, and from the window could recognise many figures from Hitler's immediate circle exercising in the yard: Goering, Dietrich and the Führer's adjutants Schaub and Brückner.

Riefenstahl's questioners sought to establish the degree of her intimacy with the Führer, at the same time probing to discover what she knew of the concentration camps. Like so many Germans, she had been aware of their existence without fully appreciating their infamy, somehow accepting them as internment centres for the indigent and, later, for political prisoners and traitors. The Jews, she had been told – and seems never to have seriously questioned the fact – were similarly being rounded up and held for the security threat they posed in wartime. Now, for the first time, she saw the haunting photographs from Buchenwald and other liberated camps, and was forced to confront the ghastly tangles of bodies and the skeletal survivors, all eyes, more like ghosts than men and women, with their unfathomable expressions . . .

'So, do you believe it, now?' The interrogating officer demanded, but it was all too much to take in just like that.

'It's so . . . so incomprehensible,' was all she managed to stutter in reply, deeply shaken.

'You will come to understand it,' the American told her tautly.[1]

Back in the cell, she and Fraulein Wolff tried to make sense of the horrors. 'The Führer could not possibly have known about these things,' Johanna Wolff asserted stoutly. She had been his secretary for twenty-five years and was quite unable to reconcile her benign employer, who treated all those in the Berghof as his immediate family, with the monstrous fiend that was emerging from this terrible evidence. 'Those fanatics around him must have kept him in the dark about their crimes,' she insisted.

Leni was not yet ready to admit Hitler's fiendishness as an intrinsic part of his nature from the start – for were that so, she would have to accept that she had been deluded. Instead but she sought to understand his apparent 'schizophrenia'. At this juncture, she still preferred to believe that the Führer had been in touch with his Volk in the early years of power and had absorbed their desires and love as a positive charge, seeking only what was best for the Fatherland. Only as his great plans failed and victory slipped from his grasp did he become, as she saw it, 'spiritually anaemic and finally inhumane'.[2]

As her interrogation continued, Leni realised that her captors had done their homework thoroughly: they seemed to know more about her than she knew herself. She was treated well and even invited sometimes to take tea with the commandant and his officers. On the 3rd June, 1945, she was 'released without prejudice' and told that her rehabilitation document would be equally valid with all the occupying powers.

★

Peter, meanwhile, had found work as a driver for one of the American majors, a man they soon counted as a family friend and one who would help Leni to retrieve her *Olympia* material from the Schneebergers. She and her household were allowed back into their Kitzbühel chalet, where she intended to finish the post production work on *Tiefland*. This period of calm, however, ended abruptly as the Americans withdrew from the Tyrol, leaving it under French jurisdiction. Riefenstahl wavered too long over whether or not to transfer herself and her film material into the new American zone, which, in retrospect, would seem to have been her wisest move. Instead, staying on, she heartened herself with fond memories of the French and their appreciation of her two great documentaries before the war. These were an artistic people, her friends, and she foresaw no trouble at their hands. Nonetheless, despite her American papers, she soon found herself arrested once more – as did Peter, too, separately – and this time both treatment and questioning were much harsher. As always under tension, Leni's health broke down and she was racked once more with 'colics'. Several weeks went by before, sick in body and spirit, she was released to join Peter under house arrest in Kitzbühel. The French commanding officer, Major Guyonnet, had satisfied himself that Riefenstahl was no more than a fading 'third-rate movie actress'.[3]

It was during her confinement in Kitzbühel that Budd Schulberg, the screenwriter son of a Paramount studio executive, tracked her down. At the time he was part of an American team collecting pictorial evidence against the major Nazi war criminals for the Nuremberg trials. He had been receiving co-operation from Hitler's friend and photographer Heinrich Hoffmann in identifying thousands of stills photographs, mainly from Hoffmann's own archives for which the index had been lost or destroyed.[4] In order to put together a similar archive of film, Schulberg and his colleagues were anxious to trace all Riefenstahl's documentaries, and at first hoped to enlist her assistance in a similar role to that of Hoffmann. A confiscated copy of *Triumph of the Will* was already in American possession, but the two lesser-known Party rally films were proving elusive. Berlin counter-intelligence provided Schulberg with the address of Leni's bombed-out house in Berlin, where he discovered an undamaged safe in the basement. To his intense disappointment, it yielded up nothing but dirty laundry.

During the last weeks of his military service Schulberg extended his sleuthing to the Salzburg area, where he eventually ran Leni and her Major Jacobs to ground at their 'hunting lodge' in Kitzbühel. He presented himself, and was welcomed by the couple, as a fellow *cinéaste*, interested in Riefenstahl's films. Leni could not know he was a long-term adversary, for this 'rumpled Jewish intellectual',[5] who would go on to write *On the Waterfront*, had by his own admission played a crucial role in organising the Ribbentrop-in-skirts campaign against Riefenstahl during her 1939 visit to Hollywood. So close to 'demob', he was no longer interested in soliciting any co-operation, but he still yearned to get his hands on her two missing films. They had been stored in a tunnel near Bolzano, she confided, but as she was forbidden to travel, she had no means of knowing whether they were still there. It was not enough to help his quest, and once home, Schulberg took the sting out of his disappointment by writing up his visit to Riefenstahl as an interview for the *Saturday Evening Post*. His 'Nazi Pin-up Girl', which appeared towards the end of March 1946, set a tone of mocking condemnation which became the widely accepted form for reporting Riefenstahl stories during the immediate postwar years. The article revealed no new information about her, but drew on the Jaeger series to give a limp flourish to all the usual rumours and allegations.

★

In Austria, the French authorities eventually ordered that Leni's house and all her property in Kitzbühel be seized, including the precious *Tiefland* footage. She, her family and the few members of her staff who had remained with her in the house were removed to dismal accommodation in Breisach, a small town not far from Freiburg which had been battered almost to rubble during the war. Food was scarce, as it was throughout Germany, and twice a week the little group was obliged to report to the French police. During this extremely harsh period Riefenstahl was subjected to more rigorous questioning about colleagues in the film industry and what she knew of concentration camps. At length, her assistants were allowed to go free, but she, her mother and her husband were moved to a two-room apartment in Königsfeld in the Black Forest, with instructions to report weekly to the police in nearby Villingen. There, a few CARE packages from well-wishers in America found her and news and messages from the outside world began trickling in.

One friend told Leni that all her film and personal effects had been carted off to Paris. 'I thought I'd lose my mind,' she wrote later. 'My life's work seemed destroyed.' The war had been over for two years and still there was no prospect of a proper trial, although all her assets, rights and freedom were withheld. Her relationship with Peter was falling apart under the strain, and she initiated divorce proceedings. By now she was suffering acute depression, for which she sought medical treatment and, understanding that she had been booked into a sanatorium, Leni was shocked to be taken away under guard to a closed institution on the orders of the military government. She would remain in this asylum for three months, undergoing electro-compulsive therapy. Of the painful experience she has little to say in her memoirs beyond the fact that her divorce went through during this time. Stressed and disturbed, she clearly was in need of help and rest, but from information that found its way to her later, she came to believe that the order for her confinement was mainly to restrict any intervention on her part while authorities in Paris squabbled over the ownership of her films.

At last she was returned to her mother in Königsfeld, an attractive little resort in deep woods with a warm community and a lively programme of concerts and other cultural events. The days passed more peacefully. Peter, who had resisted the divorce, lived and worked in the town a few miles away, helping them out with money and still hoping for a reconciliation. Leni's mother, too, thought it would be for the best if the pair were to get together again, but on this Leni dragged her feet, made wary by Peter's past infidelities.

That autumn she was sought out by a Franco-German film producer who brought astonishing news. He knew the whereabouts of a print of her *Tiefland* film, and he was prepared to help her recover it, along with her freedom, were she to go into partnership with him. He was asking power of attorney on her behalf, equal shares in any profits she made, exclusive distribution rights over all her films, and the agency for all future film and book contracts for a period of ten years. The prospect of being free and able to work again seemed so remote as to be worth any price, and Leni signed. Early in 1948, when she received official notice that her three-year house arrest was over, she concluded that her benefactor must indeed have the influence in these matters he claimed. His lawyers began the long job of trying to secure release of her confiscated films.

If, as a girl and a young woman, Leni Riefenstahl was accustomed to find success wherever she looked for it, it was a privilege she would never enjoy again. She was forty-two years old when the war ended and, in those first years of peace, tried hard to believe her situation was only temporary. Before too long, and before her powers waned, she *would* work freely again – she had to believe it. Yet, every little improvement in her condition seemed destined to be followed immediately by some devastating and unexpected setback which kept her as far from this goal as ever. In the wake of her release from house arrest, the first blow to fall was publication in Paris of Eva Braun's supposed 'Intimate Diary', with its many and scurrilous references to Leni Riefenstahl. The story was quickly splashed across the gossip pages of Europe, and Riefenstahl's French lawyers found that in the wake of this publicity all the progress they had made towards retrieving her confiscated property was rescinded.

The source of this lurid material was none other than Luis Trenker, who personally vouched for its authenticity. He claimed that Eva Braun herself had entrusted him with the manuscript, but he never produced an original. All anyone ever saw was ninety-six typed pages, bare of handwritten annotations or corrections. It was a frivolous and entertaining concoction, readily swallowed at first by historians and an eager public, painting as it did a picture of Eva-the-courtesan, lounging among silken, swastika-emblazoned sheets and dreaming erotic dreams of her Führer. In real life, it was well enough known by those in her circle that Eva Braun was always insanely jealous of possible rivals to Adolf Hitler's affection, and the 'diary' built upon this torment. In particular, she is shown agonising over the precise nature of Riefenstahl's relationship with her lover. What was the fatal fascination this headstrong film director exerted over him? Not her politics, apparently. Eva has Hitler ridiculing Leni's political pronouncements as well as her 'bitchy' gossip. Yet he is said to have acknowledged her 'beautiful body', even if the fact that she was 'all instinct' repelled him. Frequent reference is made to Leni Riefenstahl dancing naked for Hitler at the Berghof, Leni Riefenstahl 'giving herself airs and graces', Leni Riefenstahl 'wiggling her behind' . . . 'I hate that woman,' Eva is made to say.[6]

France Soir ran the story with relish, speculating that Marlene Dietrich should play Riefenstahl when the diary finally made it to the silver screen. Leni's lawyers warned her that she could kiss goodbye to ever seeing *Tiefland* again, or any of her other assets, unless she could prove the diary a fake. But how could she? Obviously she must confront Trenker, though he was hardly likely to cave in and admit to being a forger, any more than Leni could believe it of him. Despite their past differences, and the many discomfitures she had been put through (she was sure) at Trenker's hand, and despite his irrational jealousy of her successes, she still could not picture him as capable of this outrageous slander. 'Oily goats' were one thing, and even the possible pinching of other people's film ideas, but this was altogether more audacious and spiteful. Could he have sunk so low?

Douglas L. Hewlett, in the publisher's preface to *Le Journal Intime d'Eva Braun*, explained how Luis Trenker had met Eva Braun in Berlin and later in Kitzbühel in the winter of 1944/5, at which time she handed the text of the 'Diary' over to him in a sealed package for safe keeping – a fact which Hewlett claimed was confirmed by Eva Braun's own family. This sealed package, with the initials 'EB' upon it, was opened after Eva's death in the autumn of 1945 in Bolzano in the presence of the notary Max Fieresi. American representatives of the occupying forces were made aware of it and were said to have found nothing in the manuscript to suggest it was not genuine. None the less, the publisher had to admit that the absence of any accompanying explanation in Eva Braun's own hand (although easy to see why such provision might have seemed incautious at the time), made it impossible to verify the document formally.

As public interest in its colourful 'disclosures' grew, and the first doubts began being expressed, Trenker himself remained evasive about the diary's origins. In time, the matter would blow up to embroil him in a damaging scandal, but during those early days after publication, Leni Riefenstahl felt herself pitted against a brick wall. Her letter to Trenker demanding clarification remained unanswered for weeks, and then, when she did hear from him, it brought no answer to any of her questions. Instead, Trenker told her piously that, for having believed the false doctrines of the Führer, she must expect to to go through the purgatory that she and so many others had 'earned'. May it be 'a time of penitence and soul-searching' for her, from which he hoped she would receive 'spiritual recuperation' and an end to all her worries.[7]

German nationals were not permitted to bring lawsuits outside their own country after the War, and in any case Riefenstahl had not the means to conduct any action of her own against the publishers. She soon learned, however, that Ilse Braun, Eva's sister and similarly without resources, was seeking to have a tribunal condemn the diary as a forgery within Germany, where it had been serialised in a weekly magazine. The two women had a prickly first meeting, Ilse unsure whether Riefenstahl was in league with Trenker or no. In the end they agreed to join forces as co-plaintiffs and apply for legal aid.

Meanwhile, Leni made the most of her new-found freedom by spending time on the Wendelstein mountain in the Bavarian Alps, where on her birthday she was visited by Hans Ertl. She had not seen him in a long while, having fallen out after he failed to receive an invitation to the première of *Olympia*. Now they talked and talked, catching up on all the news and gossip, and finally discussing the strange business of the Eva Braun 'diary'. Ertl told Leni how in November 1946 Trenker had been trying to glean information about both her and Eva Braun, 'for an Italian newspaper' he had said. He had written to another mountaineering cameraman, Wolfgang Gorter, requesting specific details of Eva's girlhood and romances, and urging upon him the need for secrecy. This Riefenstahl was able to confirm by visiting Gorter herself, from whom she borrowed Trenker's letter in order to have notarised copies made. Hans Steger also wrote to say Trenker had been sniffing around there, too, trying to dig up scandal about her. In particular he had wanted to get hold of the photograph taken at the time of the Konskie massacre.

'I sent him packing, of course,' her friend assured her.

Someone else Leni met around this time was Michael Musmanno, an American naval aide and an observer at the Nuremberg war crime trials, who went on to become a judge with the Supreme Court of Pennsylvania. Musmanno was investigating the last days of Hitler, about which he would shortly publish a book,[8] and was interviewing everyone he could find who had known the Führer. Riefenstahl was on his list. In the course of their discussions Musmanno told Leni she could take it from him that the diary was a forgery from beginning to end, and Trenker a liar. The American agencies were familiar with the document and, should she need it, she could obtain further information from the War Department in Washington. Among those Musmanno had canvassed on the matter (either personally or through intermediaries) were Frau Winter, Hitler's Munich Housekeeper, and the photographer, Heinrich Hoffmann, who was Eva Braun's employer. It was in Hoffmann's studio that Hitler had first seen the young shop-girl climbing a stepladder.

The German hearing took place in Munich on 10th September 1948, when the court found in favour of Ilse Braun and Leni Riefenstahl. The diary was indeed a forgery, and an injunction was issued against the publishers. No action could be taken against Trenker since at that time he was protected by Italian citizenship.

After the hearing, the intriguing discovery was made that chunks of these apocryphal memoirs had been lifted more or less intact from an old book by Countess Larisch-Wallersee about life in the Viennese imperial court and the tragic love of Rudolf of Hapsburg for Marie Vetsera! What was never cleared up satisfactorily was Trenker's part in the whole mysterious business. Was he the sole perpetrator of the forged diary, or involved in some conspiracy? Even as late as April 1957, the magazine *Stern* was running an article under the headline 'Is Luis Trenker lying?' It attempted to make sense of the confusion of half-truths and prevarications with which the South Tyrolean film actor-director surrounded himself. A few years later, in his own memoirs, Trenker again claimed to have received the diary from Eva, but that a copy was found in a chest with other documents by Italian partisans in South Tyrol immediately after the end of the war. No less than the Prefekt of Bolzano had testified to this fact on 19th August that year. It was this 'second' copy of the diary which found its way to agents of the American press and publication, long before his own packet was opened.

In a recent biography of Trenker, written in conjunction with his son Florian, Stefan König[9] tells how another of Trenker's friends, the Dutch film maker Jan Boon who spent part of the war years in the Kitzbühel area, remembered smuggling a packet at Trenker's request 'backwards and forwards across the "green border" between Germany and Austria.' At first he thought it was a film treatment that Trenker was seeking to protect, but with time on his hands one day, as he hid from the border patrol, Boon took a look inside and quickly ascertained it was no film script. He was protecting a diary, 'obscene, vulgar and pornographic.' As to whether or not he thought Trenker the author of this vulgarity, Boon would not be drawn. The old man hestitated for a moment – not out of embarrassment, König maintains, but merely to accentuate the point – before telling a story of how he had come to win the friendship of the Dalai Lama. Someone sent him a photograph of himself and the Tibetan leader greeting one another warmly as only close friends do: 'I don't know if you will understand what I am saying,' Boon told König. 'But I would never publish that photograph.' The bonds and loyalties of friendship were inviolable to this old Dutchman, whatever the situation. Who was he to question the integrity of a 'Brother of the Snow'?

★

By the end of 1948, a de-Nazification court in Villingen had cleared Leni Riefenstahl of being a member of the Nazi party or any of its affiliated organisations, and in 1949 in Freiburg, the Baden State Commissariat for Political Purging Organisations, upheld this decision against French protest. In its findings, it added that despite the 'rumours and assertions widespread among the public and in the press', there was 'no evidence of a relationship between her and any of those people that did not arise from normal commercial intercourse during the execution of the artistic projects assigned to her.' Not a single witness or document had been found to indicate a close relationship between Frau Riefenstahl and Hitler. On the contrary, a number of affidavits had been secured from members of the Führer's entourage to testify that no such liaison existed.

This court found the *Olympia* film to have been an international project and beyond the limits of incrimination, and it accepted her assertion that *Triumph of the Will* was an assignment from which she had vainly tried to extricate herself. She had treated the task as a documentary and displayed neither the intention nor the awareness to execute it as propaganda for the National Socialist Workers' Party. In the court's opinion, she could not be blamed for any subsequent exploitation of the film for propaganda purposes.

After this judgement, Riefenstahl must have felt her days in the wilderness were over. She had been exonerated on all counts, and the court made a point of recognising her friendly relations with Jews, and the fact that during the Nazi years she had employed those categorised as non-Aryans in her film work. The court spelled out, moreover, that when *Triumph* was made the Jewish laws had yet to be promulgated and Hitler's war preparations were not obvious to outsiders – who were similarly kept in the dark over the true nature of the 'movement'. She had not required her workers to give the Hitler salute.

Nevertheless, the French military government remained dissatisfied, and it protested a second time. As a result, the Baden State

Commissariat reconsidered six months later and this time classified Leni Riefenstahl (in her absence) as 'a fellow traveller' or 'sympathiser', forfeiting the right of election to public office.

In between these de-Nazification hearings, Riefenstahl felt obliged to fight the first of the many libel cases that dogged her postwar years. On 1st May 1949, *Revue* had published its defamatory piece about the gypsy 'film slaves' employed in the making of *Tiefland*. During the hearing that November, the magazine's owner Helmut Kindler shouted out in court, 'The film *Tiefland* must never be screened, for you are the devil's own director!' He failed to impress the judge who, in awarding damages to Riefenstahl, reminded the court that the systematic persecution of gypsies did not begin for another two years after she had employed her extras. Kindler's chief Romany witness was accused of perjury.

Throughout this period, with her assets frozen and no income, Leni Riefenstahl was dependent upon the charity of acquaintances at home and abroad, not just financially but for gifts of food, clothing and medicaments. She had returned to live in Munich in the American zone, where she occupied a small bed-sitting room in the house of friends who ran a modest car repair business. Later, a generous donation from Herr Mainz, the former head of Tobis, enabled her to rent a small apartment in a better part of the city, even if it was immediately necessary to sublet two of its three rooms in order to keep up with the rental payments. Now at least her mother could join her.

In June 1950 the American Motion Picture Branch granted Riefenstahl permission to make an inventory of the archive material which had been stored in a bunker in Berlin and miraculously survived intact. Erna Peters, who had been Riefenstahl's cutting room assistant since 1933, went to Berlin and, under American supervision, catalogued almost one and a half thousand cans of film. Everything was there − all her pre-*Tiefland* films and a quantity of unused *Olympia* material. Some years later, however, when it was finally decided this archive could be released to her, the bunker was all but empty, and it was not until the 1980s that the bulk of this film was traced to the Library of Congress in Washington.

Nothing further had come of the contract Riefenstahl signed with the Franco-German film producer, Monsieur Desmarais, who had meanwhile emigrated to the United States. An Italian producer, Signor Panone, promised work in Rome and accepted her treatment for a ski film in colour. It was to be filmed in Cortina and called *I*

Diavoli Rossi (*The Red Devils*), but this too came to naught when Panone's backers refused finance for any film made by Leni Riefenstahl. Another company launched a rescue bid, which also foundered after its director shot and killed himself. A third Italian venture, which involved setting up a new co-production company with Signor Gramazio, successfully completed its first project, a re-cut version of Riefenstahl's *The Blue Light* film with a new soundtrack. This was premièred in Rome in November 1951 and, under the title *Die Hexe von Santa Maria* (*The Witch of Santa Maria*), was destined for release in Munich the following April. The prospect of a possible revival in her career, however, afforded the media an opportunity for rekindling anti-Riefenstahl stories. Despite losing one libel case to Riefenstahl, *Revue* magazine weighed in again with an inflammatory story about her 'involvement' in the Konskie massacre ('*Leni Riefenstahl hushes it up*'). Once more, hopes were dashed. With the film effectively boycotted in Germany, unlikely ever to recoup its outlay, Leni's relationship with her new partner deteriorated into litigation. Even worse, when a similar article appeared in Paris, the business of getting her confiscated film released to the Austrian embassy, as had just been authorised, was once more halted. She was overwhelmed with debt and the prospect of legal actions, almost without end.

★

Her second de-Nazification trial gave back to Leni Riefenstahl her badly damaged Berlin villa, which had become a squat for homeless Russian refugees since the war. Even more important, her right to work was acknowledged, although the only other offer she had received was from the Scandinavian Olympic Committees, who wanted her to film the 1952 Winter and Summer Olympic Games. Touched by their consideration, Riefenstahl nonetheless turned down the invitation, knowing that she could never improve on her 1936 Olympics film.

While the court could clear her of complicity with Nazi war crimes, it could do nothing to quell the persistent public animosity, fanned by the publication of such new interpretations of film history as Siegfried Kracauer's psychological analysis of German film, *From Caligari to Hitler* (published in 1947) as well as the manner in which her court cases were reported. Leni remained fair game when it came to newspaper coverage. The London *Sunday Chronicle*, for instance, covering the four-hour *Revue* trial, still referred to her as 'red-haired

231

Leni Riefenstahl, Hitler's favourite sultry-voiced film girl', and the court's decision in her favour as 'a victory of slim ankles and the six-inch heels of Leni's strapless Roman sandals over the elegance of a German lance-corporal, who 12 years ago took a photo of her under very different circumstances which last week nearly ruined her career . . .' Under the sub-head *Tulips From Her Fans*, the article described how the picture showed 'the attractive Miss Riefenstahl in slim-hipped, well-cut riding jackboots and a revolver in a Wehrmacht holster' watching as victory-crazed German troops sent volleys of machine-gun bullets ricocheting across cobbled streets to kill thirty men, women and children after they had worked for hours scratching their own graves with their bare hands.

Millions of ordinary Germans, it continued, were bewildered by the court's verdict, remembering the days when pictures of Riefenstahl with the Führer appeared in every newspaper and on every cinema screen. They recalled how she had been given the 'exclusive rights, worth a quarter of a million pounds' to film the Berlin Olympics and how all the cinemas in Germany were 'forced' to show it for a week. In those days, they had watched, half-amused, as Leni 'sprawled around on the ground in front of Hitler for hours at Party rallies, taking "angle shots" of the Führer and trying to catch his eye', but were genuinely shocked to learn 'that the vivacious ex-film star had actually been present at Nazi atrocities, which most of them would now rather pretend never happened.'

In a postwar Germany, struggling to come to terms with the barbarous acts committed in its name, people felt compelled to push others between themselves and what happened. 'We should have known what was going on,' they might say, 'but what about Leni Riefenstahl? She was a friend of Hitler's – she should have known more than we did. She bears more guilt than we do.' It was an understandable attitude, and defied all legal rulings.

★

Armed with the Berlin court's findings, Leni was now in a position to demand the return of her *Tiefland* material from the French authorities, though even this was by no means straightforward. At one stage, tipped off by Otto Lantschner that the film was in imminent danger of destruction, she waylaid the Austrian finance minister on a train to Vienna, begging him to intervene personally on her behalf. At last a boxcar load of film was returned to her and she could barely wait to run it through her fingers once more. As her promising

Italian film plans collapsed in ruins, at least she would have the compensation of finally being able to complete her own wartime epic.

There were still shocks in store as it became clear that the precious material had been tampered with. French film interests, believing it to be war booty, had cut and recut sections of already-edited film. Others were missing or damaged. It seems that the more Riefenstahl had pressed for the return of her film, the more the French agencies determined to prove it legitimately forfeited, anxious to avoid accusations of theft and copyright infringement. Better that it were lost or destroyed than discovered in this state, they must have reasoned. In the circumstances it was miraculous that it survived at all.

Leni soon established that some of the missing reels, if they could not be traced, would require the storyline to be adjusted. On the plus side, she secured a couple of distribution contracts within Germany and Austria, and assistance with editing from Dr Arnold, inventor of the celebrated Arriflex camera, in his Arri studios. She rustled up some capital through the sale of her Berlin house (though not for anything like its value) and within two months of working at full stretch had put a new *Tiefland* together. Herbert Windt, her long-time musical collaborator recorded the film score with the Vienna Symphony Orchestra, and in February 1954 the film finally enjoyed its opening night in Stuttgart, twenty years after work had first begun on the project.

Sinking into her seat in the darkness, Leni Riefenstahl tried to view the film with the fresh eyes of an ordinary film-goer, but with so much of her adult life wrapped up in this picture, it was hard to be objective. What struck her most was that the ill-health she had suffered at times in the shooting seemed reflected in her performance. The figure on the screen was neither the woman she was now nor the one for whom she had originally written the part. She could hardly bear to watch, believing herself seriously miscast in the role. Also, without the missing material the film remained unbalanced in her eyes. The main thread of the story was not affected, but the development of some subsidiary themes had had to be curtailed. In particular, an extended symbolic sequence showing the regeneration of the land after the death of the selfish landowner was lost. She was her own harshest critic, for visually the film was splendid, a far more mature and polished work than *The Blue Light*. Yet it fell short of her dreams and remained too potent a reminder of the tribulations entailed in its production.

The audience was enthusiastic, calling for her to take repeated bows on stage after the credits rolled up. The distributors were delighted. Reviews were mixed, but the film was highly acclaimed in Italy, where Vittorio De Sica was one of its admirers. For a while it had seemed that widespread release might be prevented by a revival of the 'gypsy extras' accusations, but Riefenstahl met with leaders of the Association of Survivors of Concentration Camps, who subsequently issued a press release to say that although they would have preferred the film in question were not screened at the present time, they would take no further action against such showings. Riefenstahl allowed the movie to run for only as long as it took to make a modest return, and then withdrew it from public exhibition. It has remained difficult to view since then, although breathtaking snippets were included in Müller's television biography of Riefenstahl. For an appraisal of the work in its entirety, academic studies, such as that by David Hinton, provide an intelligent assessment of the film's plot and realisation. Hinton found Riefenstahl 'very convincing' in her role of Marta, but would agree with Leni herself that the real star was her ski-slope discovery, Franz Eichberger. This young man turned in a beautifully judged and natural performance with just the right air of innocence and naïveté, and it was everyone's loss that he was never able to develop his acting career further. Hinton felt *Tiefland* showed a humane awareness that went beyond portraying individual failings as *The Blue Light* had done. In its examination of the injustice of a feudal system which allowed one man to benefit from the efforts and suffering of many, Hinton considered Riefenstahl had transformed the American Western genre into European social criticism (cattle-men versus the homesteaders). The battle for water represented the struggles of all commoners against their masters throughout Europe's history, and the story could be seen as much as an allegory of the twentieth century as the eighteenth, which is where Hinton presumes it was set.

It seemed at last as if Riefenstahl's luck was changing. Now was the time to push again for her *Red Devils* film, which she saw almost as a light-hearted skiing version of *Penthesilea*. She had accepted that her original film could never be revived. The devils of the title were the Tyrolean Reds, famous Austrian skiers, pitted against a Norwegian women's team. This was the Greek and Amazon conflict updated, with the team leaders – Michael and Christa, rather than Achilles and Penthesilea – inevitably falling in love during what Leni called (in her treatment) 'the merry warfare'. Good-natured pranks and rivalry give way to a fierce massed race – the 'foxhunt' of Fanck features, but this time in colour and cut to music so that the impression is conveyed of 'actually dancing and gliding on their skis, an effect which will greatly emphasize the beauty of their movements'.[10] Extending techniques she had employed in the editing of *Olympia*, she hoped thus to co-ordinate 'a symphony of colour, music and movement'.

As with her original *Penthesilea,* the pre-production was well advanced before disaster struck. Versions in three languages were planned as well as another in 3-D, this being the latest cinema draw. Big names were bandied about for the lead parts: Jean Marais, Vittorio De Sica, Ingrid Bergman and the young Brigitte Bardot. But once the locations were chosen and finance seemed assured, the Austrian government – goaded by Opposition taunts of misuse of taxpayers' money – withdrew its promised share of the funding. The project was killed stone-dead. After discussion with government representatives in Vienna, Herbert Tischendorf, head of the German studio involved in this proposed tri-national co-production, was convinced Riefenstahl had some very unpleasant facts to face. 'You will never be allowed to make films again for the rest of your life,' he told her.

XVII

In and Out of Africa

O ut of the blue, towards the end of 1952, Leni Riefenstahl received a 'fan letter' from the avant-garde French playwright and film director, Jean Cocteau. It brought her confidence at a time when courage was at an ebb and led to a warm friendship. Two years later, as president of that season's Cannes Film Festival, Cocteau set his heart on *Tiefland* being among the works shown. So strongly did he feel about this film's unparalleled poetry and 'Breughel-like intensity', he offered to write the French subtitles himself. To the West German government, Riefenstahl remained a tainted artist, and Cocteau's request was quickly turned down on the grounds that this film was 'in no way suitable to represent the cinema of the Federal Republic of Germany'. Cocteau saw to it that the picture was screened nonetheless, but unofficially, outside the competition. At the same time, he entertained a desire to act himself under Riefenstahl's direction, and the two collaborated on the treatment for an ambitious piece entitled *Frederick and Voltaire,* which Riefenstahl has described as about the love-hate relationship between Frederick the Great and the celebrated French philosopher. Cocteau envisaged playing both roles, and the film's credibility would depend largely upon the strength of the anecdotal dialogue and historical correctness. Though he and Leni were excited enough not to worry whether they were paid or not, the project was no more successful than the many others Riefenstahl explored in those days. Her French friend's ill health and the impossibility of obtaining finance doomed the delightful pipe dream. As Cocteau remarked sadly, shortly before he died in 1963, they were both artists born out of their time.

As the years passed, it began to look as if Tischendorf's gloomy prediction had been been right. Leni remained a social pariah, to be regularly humiliated, and though she steadfastly refused to believe it, she might well never make another film. Evidence that this rejection stemmed from a concerted policy was provided in 1965 by Arthur L. Mayer in a statement for a 'Riefenstahl issue' of *Film Comment* magazine. Mayer had been in charge of all film activities in the American-occupied zone of Germany after the war, a position requiring close liaison with his counterpart French and English administrators in the other Allied zones. Work permits were denied to all film makers who could be 'identified' with the Nazi regime and Leni Riefenstahl was on this blacklist, he revealed. Personally, he had 'great admiration' for her work and he knew she had been 'vexed' by his decisions, but his hands were tied. He had to comply with 'the law'. It was a misguided policy, he thought, tending only to drive out talent. Many West German film-makers fled to East Germany, where they were able to find work as lip-service Communists – in exactly 'the same way that they were formerly Nazis in name only'. It was Mayer's view that in three decades West German cinema had still not recovered from the loss. True genius was too rare to be wasted, and whether you liked its possessor or not was of no consequence.[1]

In the Spring of 1955, *Olympia*, which had still not seen cinema release in the United States or Britain, was given a private showing at the Museum of Modern Art in New York. Vernon Young was in the audience to review the film for a highbrow quarterly. His claim to have come with no particular preconceptions nor curiosity in the subject may be true as far as it goes, but of course he could see the work only through postwar eyes. No one after 1945 would ever be able to separate the unconscious signals transmitted in the film from the horrors of holocaust reality. The flames in the Olympic brazier could never again symbolise anything but the flames of war and of the death camp. Young was surprised to be so moved by the film's artistry, and he wrestled with profound disquiet in accepting that he had just experienced 'a lyric wrested from the enemies of the lyrical.'

Leaving the auditorium, he overheard one sceptic saying, 'with all those cameras, you couldn't miss!' And he thought, 'The hell you couldn't, and the hell they don't! Try to find an equal five minutes in the billion feet you've seen of Fox Movietone, Pathé and Paramount: The Eyes, Ears, Nose and Throat of the World. You saw nothing like this. *Olympia, 1936* is not a newsreel; it is history, aestheticized.'[2] He wondered if Hitler ever realised that *Olympia* was an act of treason – 'The redemption of the adrenal cortex by the creative eye? The vindication of mass by perspective?' Americans may have 'won' the

Olympic contest, he said[3], but Riefenstahl's film made Germany a winner too. And what if this was the Germany of the Reichsführer? The bust, he reflected, can sometimes outlast the citadel.

Not long afterwards, some eminent Hollywood film directors voted *Olympia* one of the world's ten best motion pictures ever. In Germany, influential film clubs began inviting Leni Riefenstahl to their meetings to discuss this and her other work. For a while it looked as if, at home and abroad, her films could at least be seen on the art-circuit and discussed objectively. In Britain, the National Film Theatre invited her to give one of their Sunday afternoon celebrity lectures in the Spring of 1960. The printed programme which went out to members at the turn of the year announced she would talk on 'My Work in Films' and that other speakers in the series included film director Ivor Montagu, who had worked with Alfred Hitchcock, was winner of the Lenin Peace Prize and author of a history of film in which Riefenstahl's name received no mention, and the actor, Peter Sellers. The media was quick to pick up the story of her proposed visit and almost immediately protests began flooding in to the British Film Institute, some of them violent. Ivor Montagu cancelled his appearance. The film society of St Thomas's Hospital threatened to withdraw its corporate membership, and 'one gentleman went so far as to smash with his fist a photograph of Miss Riefenstahl in the clubroom – a scene which must have astonished that lively but generally amicable meeting place.'[4]

Even the German Embassy chimed in with its own disapproval. Nevertheless, Stanley Reed, who as Controller of the National Film Theatre had issued the provocative invitation, felt strongly that anyone of distinction in the cinema world should be free to be heard, regardless of political affinities. 'Satan himself is welcome at the NFT,' he declared stoutly, 'provided he makes good pictures.' Peter Sellers agreed. He found all the newspaper muck-raking distasteful, and made a point of re-emphasising his willingness to share a bill with Leni Riefenstahl. In a letter to Ivor Montagu, released to the press, he remarked that alongside her brilliant contribution to the art of film making, the efforts of both himself and Mr Montagu appeared very puny indeed, and added, 'A plague on the political views of Miss Riefenstahl and yourself!'

The most visible pestilence to break out was a rash of anti-Semitic graffiti. Giant swastikas were daubed on the gateway to a Jewish cemetery in Bushey Park, while similar devices, with Nazi slogans, appeared in Hampshire, Devon, Bristol, Kingston-upon-Thames and in Manchester. The Film Institute felt compelled to convene a special meeting of its governers to reconsider the position. On 8th January, after more than two hours' deliberation, the invitation to Leni Riefenstahl was withdrawn. The Institute maintained that the decision had been taken only out of concern for public safety. In fact unofficially there was strong feeling against Riefenstahl among some of the governers themselves, who held that the proposed visit had been foisted upon them. Even the fact that *Triumph of the Will* was omitted from the potted biography of Riefenstahl in the Theatre's programme rankled. Failure to mention 'that brilliant, but evil, obsequious and blood-curdling piece of hero-worship' (the words are Ivor Montagu's) could be seen only as the result of inexcusable ignorance or a devious effort to gloss over the unpalatable.

The magazine *Films and Filming* considered the BFI's back-pedalling as the craven act of weak men. Riefenstahl herself, when she learned of it, tried to be philosophical, telling reporters she had no wish to go where she was unwanted. All the same, she was quick to send an affidavit to Britain, backed up by supporting documentation, declaring she never had been a member of the Nazi party, nor active politically in art or writing; she had never held any office or honorary title, had gained no financial benefit from Hitler or the Third Reich and most certainly had never had *intime* relations with the Führer. Her motives for supplying all this material went beyond wounded pride: she had other irons in the fire.

Following the huge international success of *The Red Shoes*, a film starring the ballerina Moira Shearer, a young English entrepreneur was wanting Riefenstahl to remake *The Blue Light* as a fairy tale ballet, and in new *Technirama*. To do so, she needed a British work permit, and when her application was received, the Foreign and Colonial Office sought the views of the appropriate trade unions, in particular the Association of Cinematograph Television and Allied Technicians (ACTT). It was essential to try to repair the damage of her aborted visit, and more especially to refute wilder press allegations made in the wake of a new book about Adolf Eichmann, claiming that she had filmed inside a death camp.[5] However, a press conference organised by her proposed colleague some months later, specifically to allow her to speak in her own defence, backfired badly. The London *Evening Standard* found it 'a profoundly distressing occasion', describing Fraulein Riefenstahl ('at fifty-one still an attractive and vivacious woman') as 'pathetically anxious to win approval'. One reporter declined to shake hands with someone

'whose hands were stained with blood' and others remained un-
convinced by her protestations that what had been written about
her was 'lies, all lies'. Leni was reduced to tears and the event had to be
aborted. Her presence, the *Standard* considered, posed an appalling
problem. 'What can one's attitude be to a woman who was one of the
geniuses of the cinema, and yet who was responsible for one of the
most morally perverted films ever made? Nobody wants to see this
unhappy woman persecuted. Yet she is clearly unwelcome here.
Today's unfortunate scenes need not be repeated if Fraulein
Riefenstahl would go back to Germany and stay there.'[6]

Never, Riefenstahl declared in the heat of the moment, had she
come up against such an atmosphere of prejudice. 'Everywhere else in
the world I am accepted as an artist. But in England, no! In England
any German who did not actually kill Hitler is still regarded as a Nazi
criminal!'[7]

Perhaps the time was still too early, or too inappropriate, for her to
work in Britain, but there is no gainsaying that an orchestrated
campaign against any possible 'rehabilitation' was still in force. Ivor
Montagu, for his stand in the the British Film Institute affair, appears
to have become a focus for correspondence and action towards this
end. On behalf of the Executive Committee of the ACTT, he
consulted war crimes lawyers and the Wiener Library's special files to
prepare a thirteen-page 'Private Opinion' in response to Riefenstahl's
affidavit and associated documents.

His assessment is interesting, but although the British Film Institute
allowed me access to the Montagu report, permission to quote from
it was refused by the trade union for which it was written. Broadly,
Montagu accepts that it could not be assumed Riefenstahl was guilty
of war crimes, nor that she was ever in a position to influence
Nazi policy. The Polish massacre story was not to her discredit and
acts of kindness to individual Jews could not be denied her. Nevertheless he found the West German de-Nazification pronouncement
on Riefenstahl open to question and her own explanations for
making the Hitler-period documentaries overtly self-justifying and un-
satisfactory. Montagu, it appears, could neither dispel nor sanction
the view of someone so lacking in contrition for her past role in
making Nazi propaganda films. She appeared to be unaware of any
fault or mistakes on her part and was content to be evasive over in-
convenient facts that could not be ignored in order to maintain her
stance of innocence. Montagu deplored her toadying to Hitler to
gain prominence.[8]

By contrast, in the United States it was possible throughout much of that year to see even *Triumph of the Will* publicly. Following an eight-month theatrical run in San Francisco, *Triumph* came to the New Yorker Theater in Manhattan at the end of June in the face of all the usual threats and abusive telephone calls. NAZI MOVIE DRAWS THRONG AT THEATRE ran a *New York Times* headline. Trouble was feared from an advertised rally of American Nazis, and one exit door to the cinema was burned, but the screening passed off quietly. Afterwards the organisers were interrogated by the FBI, seeking to know what motivated the showing and to whom the profits were paid. On balance, you could say 1960 had been a year of progress for Riefenstahl on that side of the Atlantic, but that cut no ice nearer home. She was enmeshed in a wrangle with a Swedish film company over the extensive and unsanctioned use of huge chunks of *Triumph* in Erwin Leiser's *Mein Kampf*, a powerful and highly successful indictment of the Nazis.

In Britain, although the plan to remake *The Blue Light* bit the dust, as did other projects, not everyone in the film industry was comfortable about the harassment still being meted out to Riefenstahl fifteen years after the War's end. Following the BFI fiasco, she received outspoken support from John Grierson, a man universally acknowedged as one of the fathers of documentary film.[9] He defended her on television as one of the greatest film-makers in the world and 'certainly the greatest female film-maker in history'. She had produced propaganda for Germany, and he was a propagandist on the other side. He described how in the course of his wartime work he was obliged to take Riefenstahl's films and cut them into strips in order to turn German propaganda against itself. He had never made the mistake of forgetting how great an artist she was,[10] declaring, 'Across the devastation of war, I salute a very great captain of the cinema.' To illustrate his point, several excerpts from *Olympia* were included in his programme, *This Wonderful World*. Riefenstahl was delighted, and doubly so when shortly afterwards the BBC sent Derek Prouse and a camera team to Munich to interview her. Jittery watchdogs of public opinion in London armed themselves to resist what they saw as a renewed campaign for her 'sanitisation'. The Home Secretary was lobbied to ensure that people 'identified with the Nazi movement' did not come into the country. When the interview was screened in February 1961, *The Spectator* was among those to consider that the 'romantic Miss Riefenstahl' had been let off too lightly, challenging the BBC to explain why it had not seen fit to 'temper its admiration for this indiarubber lady of Hitler's Germany, this Ophelia among the storm troopers, with just a modicum of sobering doubt.'[11]

To many, Riefenstahl appeared as irredeemable as ever. The weight of hate was crushing, and the indiarubber lady by this time was seriously in danger of running out of bounce. She felt as if she had barely lived since the end of the War. She had been crawling around in the 'mire of human nastiness'. If no longer imprisoned, she was certainly shackled when it came to following her profession, and there had been no appreciable let up in the interrogations, except that now they were called interviews. Only concern for her ageing mother kept her fighting on. That spirited old lady had such a zest for living, it was truly incredible. Where did she get her courage? Enough that it was there: her daughter had no option but to match it.

Riefenstahl knew now that the hassle and denials would never cease till the day she died. Even so, there were chinks of light appearing. A precious new and parallel life had taken her rather by surprise, offering a welcome refuge and fresh inspiration. She is usually able to trace her directional changes in life back to a single illuminating moment. On this occasion it was a sleepless night in 1955, when she picked up and read Ernest Hemingway's *The Green Hills of Africa* from cover to cover. By morning her sole desire was to get there herself, by hook or crook. The Dark Continent had come to represent for her a place of freedom and light, somewhere she could be happy, as Hemingway had been.

It was shocking, therefore, not long afterwards, to learn from the newspapers that a barbaric trade in African slaves still persisted, despite all efforts to stamp it out. Perhaps as many as fifty thousand people were stolen from their village homes every year, destined – those that survived a horrific journey – for lives of drudgery and despair in the Arab world. A Belgian missionary, after months of dangerous detective work, had found evidence of a huge organisation supplying this illicit trade and his report to the United Nations made chilling reading. Riefenstahl had been casting around for a film idea to take her to Africa, and she saw at once how a fictional drama could be superimposed on the missionary's findings. By setting an original story against an almost documentary background, she would help to open the eyes of the civilised world to this monstrous cruelty.[12] It became more than just another film proposal: it was a cause. She launched into the research with all the zeal of old and, in the way coincidences work, was shortly introduced to a writer who had just completed a book on the same theme. Leni quickly secured from him the film rights, along with the title, and set about producing a treatment for what had now become *Black Freight*.

Touting it around the production companies was discouraging. For a while it looked as if she might to clinch a deal with Gloria Film, where her old colleague Waldi Traut held an important position. At the last minute, just as contracts were about to be exchanged, like so many times before, Gloria's head of distribution refused to sign.

It was bad enough for the film to slip through her fingers, she couldn't lose Africa, too. But what was she to do? The fare was beyond her resources. Then, it was as if fate took a hand. In one account she says a loan was unexpectedly repaid; in another that the money was raised by selling some of her previously confiscated items, returned by the Austrian authorities. Whichever it was, she waved goodbye to her mother on 5th April 1956 and boarded a plane for the Sudan.

Stepping off the aircraft into a Khartoum sunrise and the sudden embrace of warm, moist air, she knew at once this was something special. A group of Sudanese, the first black people she had seen since filming *Olympia*, were walking towards her in the dreamy morning. They seemed to float on a cushion of wobbly air, enlarged by the damp haze, appearing 'detached from the earth like a mirage':

> They moved in slow motion, the sun behind them. Their black faces, swathed in white cloths, the relaxed, walking figures, their wide robes blowing about them, moved towards me as in a profound dream – Africa had drawn me into a vision of beauty, strangeness and freedom.[13]

It was a new love affair, love at first sight. Flying on to Nairobi, she booked a Land Rover with its driver (who turned out to be an Englishman she had met at the Berlin Olympics when he was captain of the British swimming team) and headed off into the grassland. This was one year after the Mau Mau troubles, one year before Independence: she and George Six went off to look at the Tana river, which he told her would make a perfect location if her *Black Freight* film ever got off the ground.

Two hundred and fifty miles north of the Kenyan capital, as they sped towards a dry gully, an antelope suddenly leapt in front of the vehicle. George threw the wheel round in an attempt to swerve, only to skid in the deep red dust. They hit one of the stone buttresses of the bridge and the vehicle left the road, flying through the air to fall upside down in the riverbed below. Leni and George were flung half through the windscreen, where they dangled unconscious, trapped in the wreckage. The young Kenyan boy who had been sitting with the baggage in the back, was pinioned between the boxes and scared out of his wits, but otherwise unhurt. Managing to extricate himself, he pulled George clear, and then, once his boss came round, they both tugged Leni from the wreck, fearful that all the leaking petrol might explode at any moment. By good fortune, although it was a very remote spot, a district officer happened by within the hour and was able to summon help.

Leni was taken to Gorissa, where she was found to have a fractured skull and multiple injuries, including several broken ribs. Drifting between excruciating pain and unconsciousness, she had to wait four days for a light plane to take her to hospital in Nairobi. The one shot of morphia available had to be saved for the flight itself. No one held out much hope for her survival. George was luckier: he had less serious injuries to only one leg.

Coming round at last in a bright, friendly hospital room, Leni's first sense was one of happiness at finding herself still alive. The injuries began to heal although it was clear she would need an operation for the head wound once she got home. George had hastily stitched the flaps of her scalp back together in Gorissa to staunch the bleeding – with a darning needle and without an anaesthetic, she says. Her recovery was set back when one of her lungs collapsed and she was told that only immediate surgery could save her. Both the physician and his deputy were away on leave and Leni was scared. Yet she refused to sign the consent form and resisted all efforts to make her change her mind. Instinct was telling her this was the right course and she hung on grimly. By the time her doctor returned from his vacation, the lung had reinflated on its own, as much to her surprise as anyone's. She was soon able to recuperate at the home of George and his wife in Arusha, and then continued her holiday peregrinations, exploring towards the Tanganyikan border. She was enthralled by the statuesque Masai, but to take their photographs she needed first to gain their confidence, just as she had that of the Sarntalers all those years ago. She would sit quietly in the open, in the same place every day, reading a book, until she was accepted by the tribespeople and invited into their homes.

When she returned to Germany in June, her mother – who had expected to find her weak from her accident – was amazed by how healthy her daughter appeared. Leni was euphoric, reborn. During her last days in Nairobi, she had secured promises of help from her friends if she could come back soon to make her film. There was very little chance of Gloria changing its mind, but so confident was she, and so excited – and so persuasive – that Waldi Traut, remembering all their past successes, dipped deep into his own pocket and invested 200,000 marks in *Black Freight*. Within weeks Leni was back in Africa for the pre-production work.

There were echoes in her plot of *SOS Eisberg!*, as well as *The Blue Light* and *Tiefland*. A determined woman anthropologist takes on her husband's quest after he is lost in Central Africa. Many adventures lead her to the tribal village he was investigating, only to find its inhabitants have been snatched into slavery. Working with a British undercover agent, the heroine frees the captives on their way to Arabia, discovering in the process that it was these same slave-traders who had murdered her husband. Her native friends lead her to a secret cave, where the walls are decorated with mysterious hieroglyphs. This is the priceless clue to the ancient culture of the area, for which her husband had been searching. She had fulfilled his quest.

The Kenyan island of Lamu in the Indian Ocean was perfect for some of the scenes, but for Central African slaves Leni had to search further afield as the locals were too slender for the role. She found likely looking 'actors' among the forest inhabitants near the Ugandan border, but persuading them to go with her was another matter. How were they to know she and her young Arab interpreter were not themselves slave-traders? Even after she had collected a group together, they were all so terrified that every one had fled by the time the train arrived back in Mombasa. More men of similar stature were rounded up from the Mombasa docks and driven through the night to the film camp, but this was by no means an end to all the problems.

Disaster followed disaster, starting with the sudden flaring of the Suez Crisis and a blockade of the Suez Canal. All Leni's photographic material, on its way to them by sea, was forced to take the long route round South Africa with the loss of six precious weeks. Costs rocketed beyond control, while grievances festered among the crew. Somehow the entourage had grown to more than fifty, not perhaps many for a feature film, but a formidable number to feed and move around on a shoestring budget, now that they were bogged down in the rainy season they had hoped to avoid. The working script was stolen from a parked car along with cameras and film stock. Other items also went missing, but eventually a new camp was established in the Queen Elizabeth National Park in the extreme west of Uganda.

Here, at the foot of the Ruwenzori mountains, shooting could at last get under way. Even so, there were days when the weather was unseasonally cold and dull and they could not get the pictures they wanted. Boats sank in the lake or were damaged and the Africans, understandably enough, fought shy of being filmed with crocodiles and charging bull elephants.

Leni's production assistant had been sending lurid reports home to Waldi Traut, who, alarmed, cabled for Leni to return at once to Munich with the rushes. His own pockets were now empty and he hoped she could help him charm more finance out of possible backers. Perhaps Bavarian Film could be persuaded. However, when she arrived in Germany, it was to find Waldi and his woman-friend seriously ill in Innsbruck hospital. Their car had skidded off a Tyrolean mountain road in a spectacular crash. All Leni's efforts to get a cable through to her crew in Africa failed. For three weeks, as she dashed about distractedly, trying to scoop something from the chaos, she agonised over what might be happening on location without her. At last, to her intense sadness but not surprise, she learned that the group had broken up and their safari organisers had seized all the film stock and equipment as security against the money they were owed. The African cast had simply vanished, and there was not enough money to bring all the Europeans home. Her all-too-ambitious project had collapsed utterly, and so too did Leni. The next weeks were spent in a clinic with a nervous disorder, narrowly escaping addiction to the morphine injections she was being given to calm her down.

It is impossible to say whether tighter management or a more cohesive team could have salvaged Leni's dream; neither could have altered political events. Yet, despite the disappointment, Leni's love for Africa remained undimmed. Five years later, with Japanese partners, she planned another film, this time about the Nile. That too crumbled, and again it was in part due to political events that could hardly have been foreseen. She had come to know the Sudanese Director of Tourism well, and was able to secure from him a rare permit to film in the closed southern province of his country. Within days of arriving back in Germany to make the necessary preparations, the Berlin Wall was erected. On a personal level, this meant Leni's mother lost her little house in Zersdorf in East Berlin; the tragedy for the film was that her Japanese business colleagues, with interests on both sides of the border, were ruined.

At least she still had the precious permit, and the following year brought fresh hopes of using it. She was invited to join a small anthropological expedition heading for Kordofan to study the Nuba people. Years before she had clipped a picture from *Stern* magazine, taken by George Rodger and showing two pick-a-back Nuba wrestlers. These magnificent, well-muscled young men with their ash-painted bodies reminded her of a Rodin sculpture, and she had pinned the photograph over her desk for inspiration, never expecting to encounter anything like that herself. Perhaps this was her great chance to get back into films. Giving up on the major studios, this time she approached top industrialists for a loan to make a 35mm travel documentary. In particular Alfried Krupp she knew to have a strong interest in Africa as he had asked to see pictures of her earlier travels but, to her lasting disgust, he and Harald Quandt (Goebbels' step-son, to whom she also wrote) shied off. The sting of this latest rejection can still be sensed decades later in her autobiography. It looked as if Leni would have to trim her ambitions and merely help the expedition with 16mm coverage of its fieldwork. Friends stumped up her airfare, and her ex-husband agreed to help support Leni's mother in her absence. She was off once more.

A long journey on dirt roads brought her party finally to the isolated province of Kordofan in central Sudan, where Riefenstahl showed the local police chief her cut-out photograph. They were looking for Nuba like these, she told him. He shook his head ruefully.

'You are ten years too late,' he said. 'They're not like that now. Everyone wears clothes and they work on plantations.'

Could it be true? Had she come so far . . . so close . . . only to be too late? How tragic — not only for her but, she believed, tragic for the Nuba too. One look at her distraught face prompted the police chief to add more hopefully. 'There may be isolated groups, I suppose. We don't go south of Kadugli; you might find some there.'

They drove on through high grass, deep sand and scoured valleys, climbing steadily into the Nuba Hills. Suddenly, ahead of them, a cluster of little round huts like beehives came into view, huddled among the rocks on the mountainside. A long-legged girl on a rock was twirling a stick. She wore nothing but a string of red beads. Leni had found her 'untouched' Nuba. A little further still, in a large open space surrounded by trees, they came upon as many as two thousand people, milling and swaying and jabbing their spears into the evening sky. The figures were strangely painted, 'like creatures from another planet'. Approaching more closely, Leni could see them forming circles, each enclosing pairs of fighting men. It was a festival, with wrestlers challenging one another, sparring, performing ritual steps and moves, egged on by their fellows. Victors would emerge from the circles on the shoulders of their rivals. This was her picture come to life! Infusing everything and accentuating the excitement was a throb of drums and the high ululating song of the women.

That night the expedition party returned to Kadugli, but within the week they had set up camp not far from this village, where Leni began the patient watching and waiting to be accepted. It didn't take long. These were the Mesakin Quissayr Nuba – a cheerful, guileless people, scrupulously honest and with a lively curiosity. Helped by the children, Leni soon picked up enough words of their language to make simple conversation. She loved their innocence and unspoilt customs, made the more poignant for knowing that this was a doomed existence. Already outside influences were pressing in. Embarrassed by tribal nakedness, the muslim Sudanese government had instigated a policy of distributing clothes to these villages, inevitably at the same time introducing other trappings of so-called civilisation. Within five or six years, self-supporting Mesakin settlements like these would have changed irrevocably.

Leni Riefenstahl spent ten months in Africa during this trip, travelling widely and often alone. Sharing little in common with the anthropological expedition, she soon parted company from her fellows, moving on to visit the Shilluk, the Masai and other tribes. She slept mostly out of doors, without a car or tent. When she met a couple of her countrymen on safari, she talked them into taking her back to the Nuba Hills, though failed to persuade them to stay for more than a couple of weeks. By this time, Leni appears to have been totally accepted as a friend in her village, and was even invited to take part in the funeral rites for one of the young wrestlers who had been killed by a snake. Wherever she went, even when alone, she never felt afraid, and was never molested. After the years of struggle and insult at home, it was a delight to be able to move without fear and be welcomed for herself. When she returned to Germany, the only thing on her mind was how to scrape together enough money to go back again, quickly. Next time, she promised herself, she really would make the film of her beloved Nuba, rather than concentrate on stills photography as she had been obliged to do on this trip. She had exposed more than two hundred rolls, which were sent home for processing. Later, back in Munich, she was horrified to discover that more than half of these had been ruined when a careless assistant removed the undeveloped rolls from their containers and then left them lying around, exposed to the light. At least the Nuba material was safe – and magnificent. A selection from these pictures was published in one of Germany's quality picture magazines to high acclaim. The feature secured her several lecture bookings, but the backing for a new film venture was as difficult as ever to find, although Volkswagen did offer her a couple of specially adapted vehicles.

She was kept on tenterhooks for months, waiting for a visa from the Sudanese authorities. As her planned departure date crept closer, and still no progress had been made, she took up the invitation of a short break in the villa of a friend on Ibiza. There she met a fellow film director, Robert Gardner, who was head of the Film Study Center at Harvard University. His own work in Africa and New Guinea forged a ready bond between them, and soon an animated Leni was pouring out her plans to him and bemoaning the difficulties she faced.

'You should come to America,' Gardner told her. 'You'd find everything a lot easier there. You really *have* to make this Nuba film, you know. Even if it's only in 16 mm.'

Gardner could scarcely believe the coincidence of bumping into her like this. He had just been to Munich trying to reach her. Afterwards, he described how, as they talked, 'Leni became entirely real even as her narrative conjured a history of increasing improbability.' It would not be unfair to describe hers as a 'somewhat lopsided personality', he supposed. It was 'as if the abundance of her creative gift simply obstructed growth in other respects.' Yet he found her immensely charming, if with the eager and intense enthusiasm of a child rather than a woman in her sixties. Clearly she could never accept the prospect that she might never make films again.

'Come and stay with us in Boston,' he found himself saying. 'Stay as long as you like. We'll look after you.'

It was not altogether altruism, for it would be an enormous feather in his cap to secure Leni Riefenstahl as a visiting speaker at the University. It would certainly be instructional for his students. Her plans were suited by it, too – National Geographic and Kodak both wanted to see her Nuba photographs – and as two of Leni's friends were happy to pay the fare, she made a flying visit to New England that fall. With Gardner's help a contract was secured with Odyssey Productions for the Nuba film, while her own brand of pleading and tears coaxed the required filming permit from the Sudanese ambassador in Washington. Unfortunately, it cost her a high profile National Geographic article since, in so doing, she missed the contract-signing appointment set up for her with the journal's executives. It had proved a very expensive permit, but with less than a fortnight before her departure, she was content.

As she had come to expect, efforts to film her African friends did not run smoothly. A Sudanese coup threw up complications and her chief cameraman had to pull out at the last minute through illness. Once in Kordofan, some of her star wrestlers were arrested and sent to prison for goat-stealing. As the expedition drew to an end her own cameras were stolen, but all these were as nothing beside two personally devastating calamities. Her beloved mother died (aged eighty-four) while Leni was in the Nuba Hills. She had received a telegram, somewhat delayed, and dashed home in the middle of the shoot, only to arrive after the funeral. Her natural grief was overlain with a racking sense of guilt. How terrible to think she had not shared her mother's last hours – 'one of the worst blows ever dealt to me by fate,' she said.[14] There was nothing she could do but sadly rejoin the expedition, taking with her a new assistant cameraman.

When she got back to Germany some weeks later, she was told that Geyer laboratories had managed to ruin an entire batch of film shot on the latest highly-sensitive Ektachrome ER-stock. All her precious wrestling footage and that of other ceremonials had turned lettuce-green. To compound the disaster, even otherwise usable stock was printed without edge-numbers, rendering it next to useless. She had nothing to show her American collaborators, and her relations with Odyssey soured irreversibly, as had those with Geyer. Any hope that this film could lead to other feature work in America, as was promised, evaporated. There seemed so little left for her anywhere in the world of cinema. And certainly nothing in Germany. What had these years of struggle achieved?

She seriously considered throwing in the towel and going to live with the Nuba, permanently. Her dream was of a beehive hut of her very own. The prospect of falling ill, or worse, so far from home did not trouble her. 'It would be easier for me to die among my Nuba than here in the big city, where I lead such a solitary life,' she rationalised. There, she knew, each of her neighbours would sacrifice his best cow for her funeral; they had once joked as much. She had laughed more with the Nuba, she remembered with nostalgia, than she had done in all her life. Yet in her heart she knew this primal paradise she pined after would predecease her. It was already vanishing fast.

By one means or another, she scrounged and saved enough money to continue dodging in and out of Africa until the late 1970s. Her biggest stroke of fortune came just before her expedition of November 1968. She had been given a four-wheel drive vehicle by an executive in the motor industry and was hoping (rather against hope) to engage a companion for the journey who could not only shoot film but maintain and repair a Land Rover. Someone in her (new) printing laboratory suggested Horst Kettner, a shy, rather serious young cameraman and a former auto-mechanic, a Sudeten-German who had grown up in Czechoslovakia. He knew nothing about Leni or her work, but as he wanted to see Africa he was only too happy to become her assistant and muscle-man, all expenses paid but without a salary.

He proved his worth almost immediately by travelling to England to pick up the Land Rover, then collecting, sorting and loading stores and equipment. Driving through the night to Genoa to catch their boat, he coped with a tyre change and still got them there just in time. Throughout their months away, he was resourceful, good humoured, good company, and above all a great hit with her Nuba friends. He took over as voluntary medical officer to the village, and in cases too serious for his pills and bandaging, he would drive his 'patients' to the hospital in Kagduli. Leni could not have asked for a better helpmeet; she felt she could count on his loyalty and strength as she had not been able to rely on anyone for years. Other trips followed, always with Horst at her side. He became indispensable. Though forty years separate them in age, they have lived and worked together now for nearly thirty years. There is a touching shot in Müller's film, made when Leni was ninety, showing her and Horst returning at dusk after a day's diving. They approach the camera along a wooden jetty, drained of colour in the dim light – one tall and bulky, the other short and with an air of fragility, two tousled blond heads – lugging the heavy underwater camera lopsidedly between them, tired but still excitedly talking over the highlights of the dive.

One of their most exciting adventures was to the 'Nuba of Kau' – as Leni called them, but known to ethnologists as the South-East Nuba – where they filmed and photographed the gory ritual of knife-wrestling, as well as love dances and the elaborate body-scarring women undergo as part of their sexual development. Although this tribe lived little more than a hundred miles from Leni's Mesakin friends, their language, customs and temperament were quite different. They were wild and passionate – and camera-shy. Leni and Horst had to be extraordinarily patient to get any pictures at all, and sometimes despaired of ever returning home safely. Both of them

251

became so edgy towards the end that they could eat nothing, only drink, and each lost several stone in weight.

By now, Leni's stills photographs were becoming well known. Her first collection of African pictures *The Last of the Nuba* was published in 1974; two years later saw *People of Kau*, and in 1982, after she had made her last visit to the Sudan, came *Leni Riefenstahl's Africa*, followed by *Vanishing Africa*. By then, the Nuba she had known and loved had indeed vanished. What she sees as 'the destructive hand of civilisation' had not only brought them ragged clothes and a challenge to their identity, but money, whisky and locks to their doors. Tourists were finding their way into the Nuba Hills, where the exoticism they sought was fading. Ceremonial fights and dances were as often as not performed for money before a forest of long lenses.

Leni is quick to refute any accusation that her photographs may have played a part in this transformation, or that she is just 'a white romantic'. She deplores the more sinister accusation that her interest in the Nuba is only another manifestation of her known obsession with cults and the body beautiful. Others brought the Nuba to public attention before her eloquent pictures, she says. Her privilege was to be a witness, a recorder of the evanescent moment. She had seen paradise corrupted. 'Before they knew money, they did not steal,' she says. 'They were much happier without civilisation. They were less diseased, not so poor.' When she showed her first book of pictures to the Mesakin they had been ashamed of their nudity. Soon they would be embarrassed by all aspects of their culture – the bizarre face painting and body art (a legacy she believes that dates back to ancient Egypt), the bracelet-knife fighting or the love dancing.'

Riefenstahl's photographs unashamedly glorify the human form at its most perfect – the Nuba believe their own bodies to be the supreme expression of art – and this has led some critics to fall into step behind Susan Sontag when she says in her denigrating article *Fascinating Fascism* that Riefenstahl's portrait of a 'soon-to-be-extinguished' Nuba is 'continuous with her Nazi work':

> Although the Nuba are black, not Aryan, Riefenstahl's portrait of them is consistent with some of the larger themes of Nazi ideology: the contrast between the clean and the impure, the incorruptible and the defiled, the physical and the mental, the joyful and the critical.[15]

The Sudanese government, however, was delighted with the sensitive portrayal she always gave its people and had grown increasingly accommodating of her travel requirements. In 1975 President Nimeiri granted her Sudanese citizenship in recognition for her services to his country, telling her she was the first foreigner to receive such an honour. The following year he presented her with a special medal in appreciation of her books and her love for the country.

By now she was in her seventies and, although still remarkably energetic and sporty, she was finding the long overland expeditions a strain. She and Horst supplied photographs to many top magazines, and laboured away in their cutting room when at home, but the long-awaited Nuba film failed to appear. Nine-thousand feet of hard-won Nuba material was stored in cans in their basement. Something held Leni back from cutting into it. Perhaps, in part, it was that footage shot opportunistically under expedition conditions could not match the exquisite quality of her pre-war films when she had corps of professional cameramen at her command. Nor was it as striking as her extraordinary stills photographs. She still grieved over the early material spoiled in the processing laboratories, for it had proved impossible to replace. In all the later footage (of which clips were included in Müller's film) several of the Nuba wrestlers are seen to be wearing underpants, balaclavas and other incongruous items of clothing. This did not sit well with Leni's ideas of cultural purity. Even so, there was a unique film in there, waiting.

Friends may have thought that now she was slowing down, Leni would be spending more time at home, but they were wrong. As so often before, a timely new obsession arrived in her life to assuage the disillusion she genuinely felt at what was happening to the tribes-people. Recuperating after one of their exhausting photographic trips, she and Horst had spent a few days beside the Indian Ocean, where they tried their hands at snorkelling. It was another of Leni's moments of illumination. The beauty of the corals and fish was staggering. Here was a living palette of iridiscent colour. She must see it again, but not just looking down on it, she wanted to swim with the fish.

That meant learning to dive with an aqualung, but who would teach scuba diving to a septuagenarian? The easy answer would be not to let on about her age. Using the name on her passport, Mrs Helene Jacob, and knocking twenty years off her age – which she could easily get away with, for she was still a lithe and beautiful woman – she signed up for a training course, and passed. As did Horst. To start with, she simply enjoyed the effortless motion and the unrolling pageant of wildlife in this sea-green world. Asking nothing more, she could watch little fish or sea slugs for hours, just as when a child a single beetle might absorb her total attention. When her air gauge told her it was time to head for the surface, it always came as a disappointment.

Soon, watching was not enough; she needed to take pictures of what she saw, and this required learning a completely different technology. As she half-suspected, it proved infinitely more difficult than surface photography. Her first attempts were so disappointing, she almost gave up. But she could not. She and Horst travelled to the Red Sea, the Bahamas, the Virgin Islands and increasingly to the Maldives. Every new dive was an adventure, and their photography improved all the time. Horst took the movies, Leni the stills. Another book of photographs, *Coral Gardens*, was published in 1978.

Still diving in her nineties, she became probably the oldest diver in the world. Her ability to be entranced, her striving towards ever better pictures had not diminished at all. Another memorable vignette from the Müller film was of her gently caressing the back of a giant sting ray which was clearly enjoying the experience as much as she was. Video technology allows her and Horst to view their work the same night, when it is fresh, just as she used to do with her film rushes. Müller's film also shows her and Horst sitting on the end of a bed, glued to a large screen and nudging one another as each fresh image is thrown up. She praises the good shots, ticks him off amiably if she thinks his exposure is wrong. The passion, the impulsive movements, the long slender legs are still those of a girl. She has been saddened by the deterioration in the underwater habitat in the years since she made her first dives. Once more she seems doomed to record a fugitive existence. It has made her an ardent conservationist, a supporter of Jacques Cousteau, and a member of Greenpeace.

If her parallel lives, or escapes, of travelling in Africa and exploring under the sea have given back to Leni Riefenstahl a freedom and integrity denied her at home since the War, they could not erase her past, nor people's response to it. The vilifying articles have continued, as well as the court cases to counter them. She has fought to retrieve copyright of her pre-war films. In all, she says, she has had to fight fifty legal battles. She is tired of fighting. Death will be a blessed relief, she told Ray Müller.

XVIII

The Long Shadow of Shame

'I detest women who dabble in politics,' Hitler is said to have remarked to his aides over his tea and cakes one evening in 1942. He had been thinking about women all day, and how different they were from men, which led him further to observe that it was fortunate he hadn't married. Women were unreasonable and demanding of a man's time, the more so if they were intelligent . . . And yet he had to admit there were some lovely members of the opposite sex in the world. Putzi Hanfstaengl's former wife eclipsed most – indeed, he had known a lot of very attractive women . . . in his youth, in Vienna . . . But now, if you were to ask him who was his ideal, four sprang to mind to whom he would give star roles: Frau Troost (the widow of his first architect) for her talent in matters of interior decoration; Frau Wagner, daughter-in-law of the composer; Frau Scholtz-Klink, who headed his Women's Bureau and instructed the girls and Hausfraus of Germany on their obligations to men and the Third Reich – and Leni Riefenstahl.[1]

The cachet of being 'the Führer's favourite' brought Leni few favours. She did not need Hitler's sponsorship; she was already well known for her own talent, and it should have served her well under any administration. Hitler's unsought blessing (delivered posthumously when *Hitler's Table Talk* was published in 1953) has haunted her ever since. Barely an interview or an article about her over the years has failed to make play of the fact that she was Hitler's ideal of German womanhood. The other three are usually ignored. Conveniently forgotten, too, is that Leni was in fact the opposite of the 'ideal' malleable maiden the Party promoted and Frau Scholtz-Klink brainwashed. The unique privileges her favoured status conferred kept her at arm's length from other film-makers of the Nazi

255

years, as well as guaranteeing that she remained an outsider after the Third Reich had collapsed.

During the 1930s and the war years, when little was publicly known about Eva Braun, Leni Riefenstahl was 'Hitler's Pet' or 'Hitler's Girlfriend' in popular folklore. The myth was perpetuated by Budd Schulberg in his dismissive 1946 *Saturday Evening Post* article. 'Nazi Pin-up Girl' robbed Leni of her reputation as a film-maker at the same time as distorting her relationship with Hitler. Deploring the article's 'leering style' and 'twisted content' Richard Corliss of the New York Museum of Modern Art suggested that even its cheap salacious title and sub-headings were libellous since Leni Riefenstahl had never been a member of the Nazi Party, any more than she was primarily known for 'cheesecakery'.[2] Neverthless, the same 'leering' shorthand continued to characterise newspaper headlines for years.

Siegfried Kracauer, rushing into print with the first politically correct postwar study of German Cinema in 1947, searched zealously for the springs of Nazism. He saw suspicious bubblings in Arnold Fanck's heroic mountain films. To him, the worship of elemental forces signalled a message of disdain for a corrupt civilisation which he found distinctly fascistic in tendency, and he called attention to the groups of Munich students who had flowed into the Bavaraian Alps every weekend from the early years of the century:

> Full of Promethean promptings, they would climb up some dangerous 'chimney', then quietly smoke their pipes on the summit, and with infinite pride look down on what they called 'valley-pigs' – those plebeian crowds who never made an effort to elevate themselves to lofty heights. Far from being plain sportsmen or impetuous lovers of majestic panoramas, these mountain climbers were devotees performing the rites of a cult.[3]

To Kracauer, 'irritated at the mixture of sparkling ice-axes and inflated sentiments', Fanck's glacier worship was 'symptomatic of an anti-rationalism on which the Nazis could capitalise'. The kind of heroism Fanck portrayed was 'rooted in a mentality kindred to Nazi spirit,' Kracauer insisted. 'Immaturity and mountain enthusiasm were one.'

He can be accused of looking down the telescope from the wrong end. Nazi films drew from the imagery of the *Bergfilme*, rather than the latter anticipating the Nazi credo. Trenker is a key figure here, a kind of archeopteryx, in that his *Der Rebell* bridged mountain and nationalistic films. It was far easier to read veiled Nazi messages into his themes than those of the 'scoutish' Fanck. The free-flow of mountain cameramen between Fanck, Trenker and Riefenstahl – with their favoured devices of surging storm clouds, smoke flares, lyrical peaks and high black and white contrast, not to say their concommitant sense of heroism – saw to it that these images passed into the cliché of nationalistic and later Nazi movies.[4]

The mish-mash of ideas concocted by Hitler into his hideous philosophy were drawn from myths and themes, trends and perceived injustices common to many – the *Zeitgeist* brew of his particular moment. Once he commanded power, whatever came before and contributed some influence to his thinking became 'proto-Nazi' in broad definition. But the same elements may well be seen to form intrinsic parts of other philosophies and movements also – extending far beyond the thrusting borders of Germany. Judging ideas or films to be proto-Nazi in retrospect holds little water and to attach a slur to mountain films (and through them to mountaineers) is particularly cruel in the case of Fanck, whose career was blighted by Goebbels' antagonism even before the war.

*

The arts are early targets of any totalitarian regime. If firm control is to be established, not only must free expression be stifled, but the direct channels art offers to popular consciousness have to be usurped for the transmission of whatever ideology is being promoted. Art, in other words, is perceived as a form of power, just as power comes to be expressed through the graphic and plastic arts of the day, and especially through film, sculpture and architecture. The rigidity or sterility of a state is quickly reflected in its art, and nowhere more so than in a dictatorship. The striking similarities that can be found between the art of one dictatorship and another is hardly remarkable, therefore. Monumental edifices, repetitive effigies, blatant posters, romantic images glorifying toil and struggle, all are propagandist motifs to engineer a workforce into compliance and to make deities of state leaders.

That said, the existence of a universal vocabulary of power within art and architecture should not be forgotten. Whatever the regime – democratic, imperial, or totalitarian – there are governmental offices, houses of parliament, presidential and royal palaces all drawing on this vocabulary, whatever the vernacular employed. By the same token, it is altogether too simplistic to dismiss all totalitarian art as worthless and beyond consideration because of its origins or the transparency of its message. Much of the early Soviet art, for instance, was extra-ordinarily vigorous, as too was the poster art of Nazi Germany. Infinitely more was banal beyond description, of course, yet in the case of a discredited regime like that of Hitler's Germany, it has been almost impossible to make a dispassionate assessment. A distaste for what it represents, or the fear of being contaminated by association, or out of respect for those dissenters whose ideas and livelihood (and sometimes even their lives) were snuffed out by such art's ruthless promoters, have conspired to stifle its study almost as effectively as such state art stifled alternative expressions. Any attempts to display works of art of this period, or even to show Leni Riefenstahl's documentaries, met with insuperable opposition until recently. 'Every word about it is too much,' was the verdict of such an objective historian as Nikolaus Pevsner,[5] and it found universal echo.

*

By the late 1960s younger critics were looking at the case against *Triumph of the Will* and its film-maker with fresh objectivity. Kevin Brownlow attempted a revision of all the hackneyed misinformation. 'We all know Leni Riefenstahl!' he said, rehearsing the familiar catchphrases for his readers, 'Director of the propaganda film, *Triumph of the Will*, a worshipper of Hitler, who later became his mistress, an ardent Nazi who filmed in concentration camps under direct orders from Eichmann . . .'

> You may remember the pictures showing Miss Riefenstahl standing by the bodies of dead Poles. You may not, perhaps have noticed the brief apologies which followed, when the supposedly authentic press photos were found to be photo-montage fakes. So the prejudices pour out.[6]

> Such time-honoured adages as 'Art transcends the artist' and 'politics and art should not be confused' are instantly forgotten when Riefenstahl's name is mentioned, and the blame, Brownlow suggested, lay at our own feet. We had fallen victim to insidious propaganda. 'Leni Riefenstahl has become a symbol. While ex-Gestapo men receive comfortable salaries in West German security forces, this great artist is forced to carry on the burden of their crimes. *And it is our fault.*'

Vigorously challenging such an interpretation, the film historian Paul Rotha, author of a survey of world cinema, deplored Kevin

Brownlow's 'idolatry' for Leni Riefenstahl, which was only surpassed, he said, by that lady's own 'unadulterated' idolatry for the
Führer. Uncharitably, he called her a 'film technician with . . . a flair
for engaging the services of other accomplished technicians'. He
subscribed to the Kracauer line:

> Her fascination for the mystique which the Nazis used so subtly and
> so devastatingly was apparent in her close association with the
> Arnold Fanck mountain films and strongly in her own *The Blue
> Light*, both pre-Third Reich. Her work was saturated with that
> hypnotism by the elements which formed such a part of Nazi
> mythology.[7]

If she wasn't a member of the National Socialist Party, her 'white-
heat passion' and her 'ardent fervour' for Hitler and all that Nazism
stood for were indelible in her work. Andrew Sarris disagreed,
proffering the opinion that Leni Riefenstahl emerged from *Triumph*
'more honorably as an artist on a political tightrope than did such
luminaries of the Soviet era as Eisenstein and Dovzhenko.'[8]

In August 1972, the month Leni Riefenstahl turned seventy, the
Sunday Times Magazine (having published already a selection of her
Nuba photographs) commissioned from her a portfolio of stills of
that year's Munich Olympics. To many, particularly representatives
of the World Jewish Congress, it appeared grossly insensitive for
someone so closely 'involved' with the Third Reich to be employed
at a Games taking place within ten miles of Dachau concentration
camp. Their protest was highlighted by the macabre coincidence that
Arab terrorists saw to it at these Games that young Jews of a post-
Holocaust generation were victims once more on German soil.[9]

The *Sunday Times*, as could be expected, was harshly criticised.
Denis Hamilton, the paper's editor-in-chief and architect of its stylish
1970s renaissance, stood by the commission, declaring that pictures
Riefenstahl had delivered demonstrated she was 'the best photographer in the world in this area.' To the charge that the paper sought
to 'deodorise the stench' surrounding the film-maker, he recalled
that the lady had been twice checked and cleared of guilt in German
courts of law, and saw no reason why her earlier link with the
Nazi Party should warrant a constant boycott of her work. While
naturally having great sympathy for Jewish complaints, the London
paper did not find them at all 'logical'. Later, in a further flight of
creative commissioning, its Picture Editor, Michael Rand, hired Leni
to produce a photo-essay on Mick and Bianca Jagger.

Over Labor Day weekend in 1974, Leni was one of the guests of honour at a new festival in Telluride, Colorado. It was a minor watershed in her fight towards rehabilitation. Other guests – who included Gloria Swanson and Francis Ford Coppola – found themselves lobbied to boycott the festival if she put in an appearance, but they stood firm. Police took the precaution of checking all festival-goers for weapons and Leni sat in her box 'trembling' during the screening of *The Blue Light*. Things passed off peacefully, then and for the showing of *Olympia* the following day, and she was presented with a silver medallion in appreciation. She was clearly delighted, yet nevertheless felt it prudent to decline an invitation to a 'Women in Films' festival in Chicago a few days later. She had been warned to expect picketing if she went there. A handful of mainly young protesters at Telluride had paraded outside the theatre with a banner claiming *Triumph of the Will* shared in the guilt for the millions of Jewish dead. Other placards carried such messages as 'Every fine artist knows that the Nazis were anti-art' – 'The greater the artist, the greater the responsibility. When she serves evil, the greater the crime!'[10] These were genuinely-expressed feelings which, counter-pointed by the warmth and recognition she had also been shown, could not fail to move and distress Leni. As such, they were unanswerable.

Even so, in honouring her – as 'the artist, not the individual', explained the town's Jewish mayor – Telluride was reflecting a discernible softening in public attitude, which prompted those opposed to any attempts at a Riefenstahl comeback to step up their campaign. She was no political babe-in-the-woods, they believed, and had placed her talent in the service of incredibly brutal and ferocious racism. The efforts of a small coterie of 'art for art's sake' film critics to laud her an artist were to be strenuously resisted since it was impossible to whitewash Leni Riefenstahl 'without at the same time humanising the monster she idolised.'[11]

The publication in 1974 of *The Last of the Nuba* brought out even bigger guns. Susan Sontag, one of America's foremost critics, analysed it at length for the *New York Review of Books*.[12] Known for her intellect and rigorous enquiry, Sontag has a reputation for making 'thoughts grow', and her assessment of Leni Riefenstahl fixed many of her readers' opinions and proved as damaging to its subject as had Kracauer's remarks almost three decades before.

Perhaps the first thing to mention is that this is a review of two works; Sontag mischievously twins Leni's book of African photographs with one on SS Regalia, under the title *Fascinating Fascism*. After a brief first impression – 126 'splendid' colour photographs, the 'most ravishing' book of recent years, featuring the 'aloof, godlike Nuba' – Sontag addresses the montage of black-and-white photographs of Leni Riefenstahl on the book's jacket. 'A chronological sequence of expressions (from sultry inwardness to the grin of a Texas matron on safari) vanquishing the intractable march of ageing,' she says. This provides the cue for a tart side-swipe at Elisabeth Schwarzkopf and the 'kind of imperishable beauty . . . that only gets gayer and more metallic and healthier looking in old age.' An interesting allusion, this, when you consider the diva stands similarly accused of Nazi taint. It makes you wonder if a master list exists somewhere, with scores to be earned, as in Scrabble, for the most names you can turn over in a single article. Why draw such a comparison at all, unless you have already bracketed the two names together?

Several more column inches are devoted to dissecting the wording of the jacket blurb. Yet Susan Sontag, of all people, as a widely-published author, must know it is nigh-impossible to see in advance, let alone have any influence over the jackets of books appearing in translation.

In the body of her article, it is soon apparent that Sontag wholeheartedly embraces the gospel according to Kracauer. 'The mountain climbing in Fanck's pictures was a visually irresistible metaphor of unlimited aspiration toward the high mystic goal . . . later to become concrete in Führer worship.' Even the 'the valley-pigs' reference is marshalled into line, before we are told that Riefenstahl in *The Blue Light* allegorises 'the dark themes of longing, purity and death', rather than treating them, 'rather scoutishly', as Fanck had.

She muddles Riefenstahl's filmography and some of the minor facts – something which could pass unremarked were it not for Sontag's pedantry over what she sees as false information peddled by and about Riefenstahl on the book's jacket. Also, she seems unable to grasp that 'making films of her own devising' can include projects that do not reach fruition – such as *Penthesilea*.[13]

The main thrust of Sontag's argument, however, is that all four of Leni Riefenstahl's commissioned documentaries celebrate not just the beauty of the body, but 'the rebirth of the body and of community, mediated through the worship of an irresistible leader' and they are all of a piece with her earlier and later work. After the war, Riefenstahl fabricated a vindicating version of events, so Sontag believes.

The fictional mountain films expressed yearning and challenge, and 'ordeal of the elemental, the primitive'; the Nazi films are 'epics of achieved community, in which triumph over everyday reality is achieved by ecstatic self-control and submission.' And the elegiac Nuba photographs, which at first glance represent just one more 'lament for vanishing primitives', can be seen on closer inspection to be the third in her 'triptych of fascist visuals'. Chillingly, Sontag reduces the tribesmen (in the captured image) to 'emblems of physical perfection' who in their 'exhibition of physical skill and courage and the victory of the stronger over the weaker' (in their wrestling) 'have, at least as she sees it, become the unifying symbol of communal culture – where success in fighting is the "main aspiration of a man's life" '.

These are knotty points to argue, with Sontag wanting it all ways! Of course any person's work is continuous, however many apparent changes of direction a career takes. The eye that sees, the artist's personal vision, though it might alter its perspective, remains the same conduit to the same brain. In fact the demeaning of the Nuba – in the way Sontag suggests Riefenstahl achieves – could as easily lie solely in Sontag's interpretation of these images. Associations concerning Riefenstahl in her mind could intrude into her relationship with the pictures. Other artists have taken similar photographs of the Nuba before and since, George Rodger who inspired Riefenstahl, took his wrestling photographs in 1948 and 1949 and, with his different pedigree, they were considered high points of his career. Nobody interpreted them as in any way fascistic.[14]

To try to understand what Sontag has in mind when she describes a 'fascist aesthetic', we gather from the essay that it is an amalgam of Nietzschean straining after an ideal, ecstasy in victory, and submission to a stern leader (or faith) even in the face of death: 'Fascist art glorifies surrender; it exalts mindlessness; it glamorises death.' Cult of beauty comes in there, too, and 'the fetishism of courage and the ideal of life as art'. Since Riefenstahl's representations are never bland and witless, the sin in her case is one of 'aesthetic excess'. The Nuba pictures, Sontag says, though admittedly stunning, would 'not change the way people see and photograph (as has the work of Weston and Walker Evans and Diane Arbus)'. Riefenstahl's two great documentaries, while 'undoubtedly superb' and maybe even 'the two greatest documentaries ever made', could not be considered 'really important in the history of cinema as an art form.' Now, there's a Janus point of view! The photographs failed to move Sontag, clearly, but what should we make of her opinion of the films? Are we to conclude that you cannot progress film further in this direction – and would that mean this is the culminating form, the splitting sporangium as it were, or the dead end of an evolutionary twig?

Michael Tobias, in *Mountain Gazette*, a creative North American broadsheet of the 1970s, saw Sontag's review as an 'inciteful, garrulous attack' on Riefenstahl and her role as an artist, and 'aspew with sticky, blaring phrases'. That Sontag was unable to derive inspiration from the Nuba photographs was wholly astonishing to him – and 'says nothing about Riefenstahl'. Over many years Sontag had advocated a manner of 'interpretation' which she now appeared to violate 'with the same bleak, aggravated tendentiousness that she hearkens us to espie in Riefenstahl'.[15]

As an instinctive artist, Leni was ill-equipped to answer such theorists as Kracauer and Sontag. She may have been very acute, and adept at ducking and weaving when it came to battles of will with Goebbels, or playing one Nazi leader off against another, but she had no defence against this flashing intellectual wordplay. Sontag runs verbal rings around Riefenstahl in ways that have as much to do with propaganda as theory.

'It is a mystery to me how such an intelligent woman can talk such rubbish,' Leni says, explaining that the pictures were taken just as the people lived. For the most part she was the unobserved observer and in no way directed what happened. What can be fascist about that? Yes, she appreciated the body beautiful, and yes, all those in the pictures were strong and healthy. (The old and the sick sit in the huts or the shadows, she explained.) 'I didn't create these people. The Good Lord did that.'[16]

Susan Sontag went on to underline her assessment by republishing it later in a collection of essays, *Under the Sign of Saturn* (1996), disingenuously amending some, but not all, of the factual errors and expanding her line of argument without telling the reader of the later version that it is in any way different from her original published review.

How much more sympathetic – and perceptive – is the realisation by Thomas Elsaesser (in *Sight and Sound*, February 1993) that it is not innate fascism but her 'dance-view' of life which informs Leni Riefenstahl's preoccupation with the human form, leading her to 'instrumentalise the body'. According to Elsaesser, 'a consistent line runs through her life which seems to focus on the body as total expressive fact.'

It is not just her dance-awareness that is so often omitted from serious studies of Riefenstahl's art. Her volatile nature is also ignored, as is how much being a mountaineer and nature-lover has shaped both her and her art. Marrying her love of activity with her need for comradeship, in her younger years at least, wild places have provided not just an escape route and visual inspiration, but a valid alternative universe away from the madnesses of the everyday or 'real' world. Of course her eyes should have been open earlier to what was happening, but a disinterest in politics and other 'boring grown-up things' is not uncommon among the young today in democratic, but media-driven cultures.

★

When considering 'the case' against Leni Riefenstahl, a number of points repeatedly crop up. *Triumph of the Will*, of course, generates the most heat – 'probably the nearest thing to pure *Schrecklichkeit* in celluloid that has ever been seen' (David Platt, 1972[17]). While accepting that it is regarded and has served as Nazi propaganda, we have to decide for ourselves whether it was conceived as such by Riefenstahl. If she had not made this film, and not made it *so well*, other charges against her would pale in significance. Despite the damning caption in the behind-the-scenes book of the Party rally, it is hard – with the evidence of other rallies and Nazi spectaculars – to make a self-standing case for her having been involved in staging this event. We know she was hand-picked by Hitler for the assignment. If we believe that with this film she was actively and knowingly promoting National Socialism and its leader (which is clearly what the Nazis intended), then she was Hitler's handmaiden and as guilty as any other proselytiser of the regime's early days.

Even if we accept that Riefenstahl was blind to the propaganda implications when making *Triumph,* the end result was certainly a propagandist work, and one moreover which has become the standard by which all later propaganda productions are measured. At the same time, it is an artistic film; and that produces difficulties for its appreciation. Can a work of propaganda be art? Artful, certainly. This is a slick, artful, cunning film, but does not its cunning lie in its filmic eloquence? Wasn't Riefenstahl's mastery of the medium rather than the message? The message of *Triumph* itself, for that matter, is not altogether clear. On the face of it, Riefenstahl is celebrating a fervent new religion, outlining the Nazi catechism, chanting a hymn to Hitler. Yet more than one critic has remarked that *Triumph of the Will* can be seen as conscious treachery against the regime it purports to exalt, plainly demonstrating the grotesqueness and overriding insanity of what was happening within Germany. In other words, far from being effective as propaganda, *Triumph of the Will* carried its own antidote for those who had will and wit enough to recognise what they were seeing. The title alone must have provided a cautionary ring for anyone possessing even a residue of individual thought. As many people must have been repelled by the images of mass sub-jugation as were enthused by them. The film was far from a run-away success in the German provinces, and of dubious propaganda value. Levi Riefenstahl's own argument against it being a work of propaganda is that, as a documentary, it was awarded the gold medal at the World's Fair in Paris in 1937, a presentation made by Edouard Deladier, the French Prime Minister. Such an honour would not have been given to a work of Nazi propaganda, she is convinced.

In the popular mind, good art should be on the side of the angels. Part of an artist's role is to reveal the flaws in a society, whatever the personal consequences. We honour (retrospectively, at least) those painters, writers, musicians, film makers of the avant-garde and the underground, who suffer for their art. They are the banned, the subversive, the dissenters and the refugees, resisting overweening force, rather than celebrating it as *Triumph of the Will* appears to do. Where they do document factual events, we look to artists to do so objectively, reflectively. What makes Riefenstahl so problematical is that, on the face of it, she breaks all the basic laws by working from within.

That itself raises further issues for consideration. How much, in 1934, should she have been able to foresee? Her detractors usually ignore the fact that this film dates from the 'honeymoon' period between Hitler and the Germans, and that its editing was completed before the infamous anti-Semitic Nuremberg Laws were proclaimed. It has been said: 'If Hitler had succumbed to an assassination or an accident at the end of 1938, few would hesitate to call him one of the greatest of German statesmen, the consummator of Germany's history.'[18] These words are those of the eminent historian, Joachim C. Fest; others, too, think the tenets expressed in *Mein Kampf* would in those circumstances have been excused as a young man's febrile fantasies. Was Leni Riefenstahl alone to have foretold the future when even leading statesmen abroad failed to read the signs accurately?

In 1993, a 'Without Walls' film on British television, entitled *Good Morning Mr Hitler*, featured an extraordinary and hitherto unknown colour film of the 1939 festival weekend in Munich, taken by amateur enthusiasts of the city's Film Society.[19] This rare footage, shot on 16mm, is of special interest for, unlike newsreels of the same event, it has escaped the editorial hand of Goebbels' propaganda forces. It is an informal and fascinating eye-witness account, showing the extravagant pageantry of the street parades, the Party hierarchy and, above all, the men, women and children of Munich off guard and off duty. And what seems profoundly disquieting, looking at it now, is that with only six weeks to go before Europe is plunged into war, it portrays a carefree, joyful atmosphere of apparent idyllic innocence. Josefa Hammann, who took part in the pageant as an 18-year-old, told the 'Without Walls' film team it had been a wonderful experience which she remembered as freshly now at seventy years old. 'For us, it didn't have anything to do with politics,' she said. 'For us it was just a lovely day, where you met other people and also where we could show ourselves off . . . A lot of fun really, one can say.'

This is by no means an unusual reaction. A sense of belonging and purpose blinded many to what was going on, to the extent that even after the War nostalgia would linger for the good times. A public opinion survey undertaken in 1951 showed that almost half of those citizens of the Federal Republic of Germany questioned described the Hitler years of 1933–1939 as the period in which things had gone best for Germany.[20] The 'Aryan' experience was clearly at complete odds with the Jewish experience. It is also worth remembering the illusion of normality given up to the last minute by the massive preparations for the 1939 Nuremberg Rally, which was only cancelled on 26th August – when the thousand special trains for mustering rally-goers were diverted to take men and munitions into Poland. (Letting the rest of the world believe Nuremberg was going ahead as usual could have been a ruse, of course, to lull opponents and preserve an element of surprise in attack.)

*

How we feel about Riefenstahl's Nuremberg films colours the way her other work is perceived. Would *Olympia*, for instance, have had any difficulty being seen as a sporting document pure and simple were it not for the blight of her Nuremberg trilogy? Perhaps that is too knotty for a simple answer. Today, probably yes – but its two years of post-production launched it at a far more sensitive time that when it was shot. By then the free world had come to realise the evil and dangers inherent in the apparatus of the Third Reich. Anything emanating from Germany with State blessing would have been suspect.

Then there is the contamination of her familiarity with Hitler and with other Party leaders, and her apparent freedom to walk through guarded doors and up and down the corridors of power. She appears to have 'enjoyed' her special privileges in the sense of relishing the thrill, reflected power and publicity these gave her. She was ambitious, opportunistic, impressed by power, and not above having a little swank. On the other hand, as the de-Nazification trials found, she had no practical influence on Nazi policy. She would petition Hitler when it came to film problems; she 'pulled strings' from time to time during the War to keep her cameramen from fighting at the front, but she had not enough influence to save her own brother. There is no evidence that she met Hitler more than a handful of times during the war years, and several clues to suggest that she used Frentz or Hitler's housekeeper Frau Winter as a conduit to discover news and to apprise the Führer of what she was doing. Frau Winter told a Miss Billig, who was interviewing her on behalf of M. A. Musmanno after the war, that Leni Riefenstahl 'loved the Führer deeply' and before her marriage came frequently to Munich. 'She often cried when talking to me,' she said. 'She asked me whether she should marry the Führer or not. She . . . even would have stayed with him as his "friend" but he did not ask her.' Leni knew nothing about Eva Braun, and Frau Winter chose not to enlighten her. 'All of a sudden Leni married this Jacob fellow. I think she still loved the Führer. He liked her but never paid much attention to her.'[21]

There were always plenty of people like Frau Winter ready to interpret Leni's relationship with Hitler. Even so, evidence points to the fact that Hitler began distancing himself from Leni after *Olympia*, although he visited her in hospital in March 1941, when he fantasised on the possibility of them making films together after the war. Then he did not see her again until she visited him with her new husband three years later, by which time he seemed to Leni more of a ghost than a man in touch with reality. Eva Braun's mother remembered Hitler saying 'Leni Riefenstahl is coming with her husband. She wants me to give him a decoration.'[22] Why had the friendship cooled? Perhaps his advisors were urging him to adhere to the propaganda image of the Leader married to his Volk. Maybe he himself found Riefenstahl too unpredictable in her friendships, always the subject of gossip. She was a free spirit of volatile temperament, and made no obvious attempts to rein in what she said or did in public. Her high profile almost guaranteed that scandals followed wherever she went, whether or not of her making.

Hitler is known to have been furious in 1937 when *Paris-Soir* and some other foreign newspapers ran a story that Leni Riefenstahl had been banished from the Fatherland after a row with Goebbels about her 'Jewish ancestory'. The 'fallen angel of the Third Reich' was holed up in Switzerland, the reports ran. To scotch the rumour before it caused a worldwide sensation, Hitler ordered that he, she and Goebbels be photographed informally in the garden of her new Berlin home to demonstrate their cordiality.[23] Later, once he had learned of her 'interesting arrangment' with Udet, myth has it that Hitler renounced Riefenstahl since he could not be seen to share a woman with one of his subordinates. This does not tie in with this supposed recommendation of her as one of his four ideal women, a remark made in 1942 *after* the suicide of Udet.

One damning piece of evidence that is often flourished against Leni is the congratulatory telegram she sent to the Führer in June 1940 when the Germans seized Paris. With 'indescribable joy' and 'deep emotion', she sent warmest thanks to her leader on the occasion of Germany's 'greatest victory', telling him the deeds he accomplished went 'beyond the power of imagination'. Her memory now is that, with the withdrawal of the British Army from Dunkirk and the fall of France, she in common with most of her countrymen believed the war was over: 'We were in a frenzy of joy for three days,' she says. 'Bells rang and people kissed in the streets.'

Perhaps her response to the popular euphoria was extreme, but the sentiment expressed was shared with many. Sending impromptu messages with little thought for consequences had always been Leni's way. The existence of this telegram in public archives lends credibility also to her other claims of being with Hitler (physically or in spirit) at his most dramatic moments. It goes some way to allaying suspicion that in her memoirs she overplays her unlikely assertion of finding her way unerringly to his side at times of national crisis.

The use of the gypsy extras from the Maxglan camp in the making of *Tiefland* during 1940–41 continues to haunt Riefenstahl. Grotesque as the idea seems now, she was not alone in employing internees from labour camps for the crowd scenes in moving pictures. Several of Leni's gypsies spoke out to say they had been treated well and had enjoyed the interlude. Rumours continue to circulate, however, that she made promises that they would come to no harm after the filming, when later in the war they in fact wound up in Auschwitz, where many were slaughtered. A court found no evidence at all that Riefenstahl had made empty promises, nor did it consider she could have known of the gypsies' likely fate. German film maker Nina Gladitz, who included such accusations in a television film in 1985, was ordered to excise them from the programme. Nevertheless, talk continues and the smirch is not as easily removed.

From her memoirs, Luis Trenker appears to have played what appears a treacherous role in spreading a similar rumour. He would talk openly of the 'fate' of a friend of his who, after falling out with Riefenstahl on the set of *Tiefland,* had been denounced by her to the authorities. This man, Moser, was sent to a concentration camp, Trenker alleged, where he died. It was not until years later that Leni and Horst, paying a pilgrimage to the Vajolet Towers where much of *Tiefland* was shot, learned that, far from dying under the Nazis, Moser had spent the war years in the mountains of the Italian Tyrol with his English girlfriend, and had never been interned at all. He died long after the war from eating poisonous fungi. How many times Trenker has appeared as the instrument of blight over Leni's fortunes! Was it professional jealousy that motivated his Machiavellian campaign against her, or did he seek to deflect curiosity from his own activities during the Nazi era? Or was it perhaps that his memory was long, and Hell hath no fury like a he-man scorned?

★

In a sense Leni Riefenstahl kept the world waiting too long for her memoirs. She has said she was holding out until she could tell the truth without fear of retaliation . . . But there is such distance now, with most of the events described, that the passion has ebbed away and delicate detail been lost. We are left with her 'silent film' memory storage and its curious semiology, which seems very often to have been prompted by other people's accounts. Robbed of freshness and immediacy, some of these encounters are rendered absurdly theatrical. 'Goebbels brings out the melodramatist and pulp novelist in her' remarked Thomas Elsaesser in his *Sight and Sound* review of her book.[24]

Pushing from her mind any consideration of uncomfortable fact or rumour, she exhibits a facility for sidestepping awkward questions in interview, on the apparently naive assumption that what you don't face goes away. Since the escape route that presents itself may differ from one interview to the next, this has led to some conflicting evasions over the years, and a few notable ellipses in her memoirs. It is inevitable, however, that in covering the same ground over and again, from one interrogation to the next, some element of rehearsal comes in and spontaneity is lost.

In the days of her involvement with Hitler, she was prepared to believe him an idealist surrounded by gangsters. She can admit now, knowing the ghastly atrocities of his regime, that he was a monster in his own right, probably the most monstrous of the gangsterly bunch. But she finds it as hard as any other German to accept that she should have been able to see this in advance. In one thing, her story never changes: Hitler was charming, hypnotic – and omnipotent of course – and she, like others, was bedazzled. Hearing him for the first time at a public rally was like being struck by lightning. His message was peace and work for all – very idealistic. She 'knew nothing' of politics and was completely swept away. 'All' the young people were, she says, blinded by the promise of a glorious tomorrow. How could it be otherwise?

After 1945, you would have thought it were otherwise. How swiftly all those supporters melted away once the truth was known. Nobody, then, wanted to admit to having been humbugged by Hitler. In this at least, Riefenstahl is unusually truthful: she does not seek to deny the headiness of her former intoxication – even if she claims it more for the man than his message. Jawosky said you had to hand it to her, 'When the war was over [and] she was prosecuted, she said "I believed in Hitler, do what you want, kill me". After the war most Nazis started to disappear. But she said, "I believed in him, okay. Maybe in my shoes you would have, too." I think that's personality, don't you?'[25]

Speer has told how he was too wrapped up in his own work and career to pay sufficient attention to what was going on beyond his own sphere, and the same could be said of Riefenstahl. It was an effective strategy of Hitler's to give the young and gifted important work which not only stretched their talents and fed their ambition but kept them out of the critical mill. He made a policy, too, of compartmentalising. Even within government, people only knew what they needed to know, and were kept guessing about what went on in other compartments. By doubling up some of the responsibilities, Hitler fostered secrecy and competition as his officers tried to guard and extend their personal power bases. Those outside the Nazi hierarchy knew even less. They were overfed on propaganda, like fatted

270

geese. Add to that an all-too-common human willingness to delegate political responsibility, to let the leader carry one's conscience, and it is easy to see how curiosity and dissent can be held at bay.

★

The broad brush strokes of stereotype give the inclination of truth. Take the popular image of Hitler: Hitler ranted, Hitler brooded, he stabbed the air, he transfixed with his pale electric eyes . . . Well, he *did*, but he also slithered through a quicksilver range of emotions in between, and presented himself in a myriad different versions to different people, some invented, some presumably native – although those are the very hardest on which to get a handle, particularly in the harsh light of hindsight.

How can we get between the brushstroke bars in Leni Riefenstahl's reminiscences when in most cases that is all she gives us – is probably in fact all she can remember now? Yes, Hitler was hypnotic – quite apart from his evangelist powers with the masses, he attracted worship from all manner of women – and, yes, she was young when she met him. Not perhaps in years, and certainly not in amorous adventures, but she was undeveloped in her critical mind and supremely disinterested in what did not involve her personally. It left her blind to political events and their consquences. Her life was balanced between escapism and the social whirl in Berlin. She had numerous 'friends' and colleagues, but it is doubtful if she knew many among those who could be called 'ordinary' people. She has always made a point of saying that the everyday, the ordinary held no interest for her. She was happiest in the desert-island context: with a hot-house group of intimates, permutating ideas, and exploring the infinite possibilities of interrelationship.

Before making any documentaries, Riefenstahl spent over a decade in the business of concocting stories. In film and dance, she sought to seduce with these stories, to lead people into make-believe worlds. We know how pyschologically damaging such immersion in artificiality can be. How many survive a showbusiness life intact? The bridges of reality between one make-believe project and the next are flimsy affairs. And when, as in the Hitler years, these spans lead you over another world, more bizarre – and more infernal – than anything anyone could dream up, should we be surprised that appreciation of reality is warped? Or that one day the bridge ultimately collapses to pitch the unprepared traveller into the inferno?

As to whether Riefenstahl is a reliable witness, there are times when

271

one's suspicions are alerted. Dates, perhaps, do not tie up from one person's account to another, or we discover occasions when she seems unnecessarily vague or misleading. An example would be her first trip to the mountains, which she says she undertook with her young brother. Henry Sokal claimed to have been with her. Both may be true, but if so, why suppress Sokal? He is an important character in her story. It prompts the question: what else has she taken out?

Take the historical events of the spring of 1933, when Riefenstahl claims to be cut off from world affairs, filming in the Swiss Alps. There was no television: true. Film sets are islands in time and space: true. But the Alps are not that far from Berlin. Are we to believe that over several intense months, Riefenstahl had no break at all, no day or weekend off to visit parents or friends? Just how isolated was she? Legitimacy is lent to the question by several entries in Goebbels' diaries recording encounters with her during this time. She refutes them energetically. In Müller's film, he lets the narrator ask: who is telling the truth – the Minister for Propaganda or the film director?

With almost every protagonist dead, her claims and our doubts are equally hard to verify. We know that much deliberate misinformation has been spread about her, and sterotypical images peddled. After her Berlin de-Nazification, the presiding judge, Dr Levinsohn, told her always to remember him if she needed help or advice. He had dealt with many cases of libel, but never before had he come up against one in which so many falsifications and lies had been presented.

Closer inspection of the 'conflicting accounts' Riefenstahl is popularly said to have given to the many questions put to her reveals that in fact her statements have been remarkably consistent over the long years. Yes, there are certain sensitive matters and relationships that she usually tries to sidestep. And we may accuse her of being blinkered, self-centred, self-serving and incredibly naïve. On the pivotal issues and stances relating to her career, however, most of the contradictions can be traced back to individual suspect sources. Noteworthy among these is 'her' behind-the-scenes Nuremberg book. Despite the name on the cover, she reiterates that the account was ghosted for her by Ernst Jaeger under the editorial direction of the Party publishers. In any case, it was a propaganda vehicle and, whether or not she saw the approved text (she claims the latter), she almost certainly was in no position to change it.

The consistency in her story could be, as Sontag among others posits, that she settled on a defensive line after the war and stuck to it. It could equally mean she does not shift her ground because that is how she remembers events. That others' recollections do not exactly corroborate her own should not surprise us. This is not an unusual problem facing historians. Even where dates can be made to match, there are several versions to history.

★

Riefenstahl may have been cleared of punishable blame through the courts, but legality and moral culpability are not one and the same. Survivors of the Holocaust have been vigilant in ensuring that Leni Riefenstahl should never be 'forgiven'. There is a parallel to be drawn here with ex-prisoners of the Japanese, who believe their suffering in the Far East, and the ultimate sacrifice demanded of so many of their fellows, was not properly credited at the time and has since been forgotten. For them, forgiveness is impossible to contemplate, certainly without visible signs of contrition and retribution from their captors. And their feelings have to be honoured (along with their dead). We cannot insist that such deep-felt beliefs are ignored. Yet equally, half a century later, a way has to be found for the hurt to be understood and accommodated – without forgetting. There comes a time when old wounds and outrages have to be laid aside for life and normality to go forward.

In Leni Riefenstahl's case, matters might have been easier had she been able to say sorry. Instead, she merely insists, 'Sorry for what?' If one meant, did she regret making *Triumph of the Will*, then, yes, of course she did regret it. In view of its later implications that would be self-evident. She could not regret being alive in that period, any more than she could change it. Ray Müller's biographical film of her concluded with her saying, 'No words of anti-Semitism ever passed my lips. Nor did I write any . . . I was never anti-Semitic and I never joined the Nazi Party. So what am I guilty of? Tell me that. I didn't drop any atom bombs. I didn't denounce anyone. So where does my guilt lie?'

How should her special 'guilt' be pinpointed, when other directors and other actors who were involved in horrific propagandist films against the Jews were not left so long in the wilderness after the war? Was it that she was always an outsider to the film industry – before and during the war – and was thus easily shunned afterwards as well? How much did her own character and personality contribute to her excommunication? Her self-centredness and obsessive single-mindedness had always set her apart; she had made enemies, and her many friends and colleagues were under pressure to renounce ties with her if it linked them too with a tainted regime. Among those who did provide evidence in her support during the various inquistions and de-Nazification procedures, it is surprising to find Ernst Jaeger. Ten years after he 'jumped ship' in America, he wrote spontaneously from Hollywood:

> . . . in 1935, I was expelled for life from the (Nazi) Press Chamber . . . Frau Riefenstahl not only was aware of this expulsion, but defied it for many years . . . not because she expected any advantages from my writing ability, but out of a desire to make some form of protest, in my case as in so many others . . . (She) always induced me to stand up for other similarly censored writers and to help them materially. Frau Riefenstahl spent huge sums towards this end, even though privately she was by no means wealthy in those days.[26]

Not only was Riefenstahl on an unofficial blacklist at home, it cannot be disputed that outside Germany too there was an orchestrated campaign to stop her working again. Many of the activists were Jewish. We should seek to be sure in our minds if this represents a natural and acceptable watchfulness that the memory of the Holocaust is not diminished, or whether it has become polarised into a more specific and personal vendetta.

Perhaps there can never be any resolution to the black or white of this issue. Neither Leni's critics nor her apologists are likely to budge from positions buttressed largely by articles of faith. All we can demand is logical re-appraisal. All we can hope for is to eliminate the inconsistencies. If we take, for instance, one of the most-cited accusations – she was a Nazi to the core and slavishly followed Hitler's will – and set that against her refusal to remove the black gold medallist Jesse Owens from her Olympic film, we must have the grace to acknowledge the difficulty in reconciling the two.

*

When does Leni Riefenstahl say the scales fell from her eyes? She was horrified after her American tour of 1939 to discover from one of Hitler's adjutants that the reports about *Kristallnacht,* as they appeared in the American press, were substantially correct. A prevalent myth in Germany at the time cushioned Hitler from any responsibility. People believed that the Führer was kept in the dark about the misdeeds of his underlings, and was unaware of the just complaints of his Volk. Even after an outrage as grotesque and cautionary as the

Night of Broken Glass, there was still resistance to laying the blame at Hitler's door.

Leni attended the third annual Day of German Art in Munich in July 1939 in more jaundiced mood than she had earlier festivals. With her critical senses attuned, she was prepared to challenge intellectually what she was being shown and told were the ultimate expressions of national art. Hitler, opening proceedings, announced with solemn satisfaction that the 'primitive' areas of painting and sculpture had been cleansed. The whole 'sickening, decadent swindle' of fashionable, modernist 'daubings' was swept away, and 'a new, decent and respectable level of achievement had been secured'. Goebbels added that art was now restored to the masses and no longer existed 'only for the upper ten thousand'. Nor was it 'degraded by Jews'. Leni looked around at the muscle-bulging statuary, the chocolate box nudes, the idealised landscapes and heroic peasantry. She took in the heavy-handed erotic symbolism of Padua's Leda and the Swan,[27] the sensation of that year's show – and she saw kitsch. Her own passion, for which she had been rebuked by Hitler, was for the impressionists and modern artists like Käthe Kollwitz. Forbidden works now. If Hitler, who claimed to be the arbiter of good taste, could be *so* wrong about art, she thought, could he not be making political mistakes as well?

She did not contemplate leaving Germany. It was too late for that, and in any case her love of Heimat and family prevented her going. (Even for a couple of years after making *Triumph*, she could probably have emigrated to Hollywood if she had cut herself off vociferously enough from her Nazi past, but by 1939 it was definitely too late.) When war came, and she found she had no stomach for chronicling the front line events, she resolutely kept herself out of the propaganda machine, which should have counted in her favour. Nevertheless she was in a privileged position in having that option. And although the limited financial independence she enjoyed, and which enabled her to execute her own projects, came from the success *Olympia* had given her, it was not free from being seen as Nazi patronage, given the convoluted funding of that film.

The end of the war was a period of awakening for all Germans that almost beggars description. 'It was so sad, so dreadful – all our ideals were shattered,' Leni has said. 'You could hardly comprehend the horrors. It was a terrible fall into the abyss.' Though it irritates non-Germans to hear it, the overwhelming sense in the Fatherland as elsewhere was horror that human beings had done such monstrous things, not in the heat of war, but by chilling, meticulous design. And these inhuman things had been done on Hitler's orders and in the name of the German people. The Volk and the youth had been betrayed by their leader.

'It was quite a time before I could believe it, and when I did my life fell apart because I had believed in Hitler,' Leni said. 'It was so shattering that one's own life was unimportant. There were only two possibilities: either to live with this appalling burden of guilt weighing us down, or to die. It was a constant dilemma – live or die.'[28]

Sixty million lives had been lost. Of course that made a difference to how she viewed her own work. Now she could perceive how sequences in *Triumph* would not be uplifting, as she had thought at the time, but seen through the eyes of the victims would arouse quite different emotions. 'How awful for them to see the swastikas, the SS and SA and those people on screen – people we had never thought of as criminals. It was a breakdown that has actually been permanent. I've never recovered from that horror.' She feels like Junta, the outcast in *The Blue Light*, loved and hated, and doomed when the illusionary crystal shattered.

People say she is blind, she doesn't want to know. They say she's still a Nazi, and always will be. To all of which she replies, wearily, 'None of this applies to me . . . I condemn all that happened, but it doesn't help. They don't believe me.'

★

In condemning Leni Riefenstahl, insufficient weight has been given to what society may have lost by hobbling her talent. Maybe her romanticised vision could never have survived into a pragmatic postwar world. There is some evidence that by the time *Tiefland* was eventually released, the appetite for such entertainment was already fading. We cannot know if she could have adapted her talent to new directions, re-invented herself as she had so many times before. The stifling of her career was a personal tragedy, but it is worth venturing that posterity too is the poorer. Original talent is a rare gift.

Whether you belong to those who believe she was an honourable witness and only ever interested in her art, or whether you think she wilfully traduced that art in the glorification of a barbarous ideology – or, indeed, if you think the truth lies somewhere in between (that she herself was exploited) – society owes her a debt. Without *Triumph of the Will*, our understanding of the Nazi phenomenon, and its power through myth and pageantry to bind millions of free-thinkers to a single purpose, would be much diminished, particularly half a century after the event. In a cynical world, knowing it happened does not of itself assist comprehension. Far from restricting showings of this profoundly disturbing film, there is a strong case for making it required viewing for young people.

Roy Fowler, Chairman of the History Project of the cinematographers' union BECTU, suggests an analogy can be made between Leni Riefenstahl and the Russian film-maker Sergei Eisenstein, another 'surpassing genius, much of whose work was debased by a foul regime'. Eisenstein he points out 'has never been vilified within or without his country'. Fowler ponders the question: 'Undoubtedly Riefenstahl is a victim, but in what measure, at whose hand, and for what reason are the mysteries.'[29]

In his film, Ray Müller suggested to her that the world was still waiting for her to say she was sorry. Leni Riefenstahl shrugged. 'Being sorry isn't nearly enough,' she sighed, 'but I can't tear myself apart or destroy myself. It's so terrible. I've suffered anyway for over half a century and it will never end until I die. It's such an incredible burden that to say sorry is inadequate. It expresses so little.'

Notes and References

Chapter I The Woman in White

1. Padraic King, 'The Woman Behind Hitler', *Detroit News,* 21st February, 1937.
2. 'Loving Hitler', Gitta Sereny meets Leni Riefenstahl, *The Independent on Sunday – The Sunday Review,* 13th September, 1992.
3. Fanck's *Das Weisse Stadion* – The White Stadium – over-hastily edited with the assistance of Walter Ruttman. 'Although the photography has been described as interesting, the film was a bore and was almost instantly forgotten' – David Hinton.
4. Henry Jaworsky, interviewed by Gordon Hitchens and others in *Film Culture,* Spring 1973.
5. 'Interview with a Legend' by Gordon Hitchens in *Film Comment,* Winter 1965.
6. *Goebbels Tagebuch*
7. Riefenstahl's memoirs only mention Zielke being committed to the asylum *after* the filming of *Olympia,* although she acknowledges his behaviour could be bizarre on occasions. Reference to his being found guilty of damaging German reputation comes from Cooper C. Graham in his *Leni Riefenstahl and Olympia* 1986. Graham had interviewed Zielke.
8. Henry Jaworsky interviewed by Gordon Hitchens and others in *Film Culture,* Spring 1973.
9. *Welt am Sonntag* (Berlin), 12th January 1969.
10. Albert Speer, *Inside the Third Reich,* 1970 (Ch. 6).
11. André G. Poplimont *Berlin 1936, Bulletin du Comité international olympique,* No. 56 (October 15, 1956 pp. 19–20) and reported by R. D. Mandell in *The Nazi Olympics,* 1971.

Chapter II Mountains of Destiny

1. Perhaps we should not be surprised at such an extreme response: Riefenstahl's eye for the dramatic and her fascination with musculature and

278

movement is evident to anyone who has seen even the stills from her Olympia film, as it is in her later work with the Nuba people of Africa. But at this stage in her youth, she herself was conscious only of how the forms and images she encountered in her daily life related to dance – in the same way that all the music she heard was heard solely through the ears of a dancer.

2. Leni Riefenstahl, *The Sieve of Time*, 1992.
3. Leni Riefenstahl, *Kampf in Schnee und Eis*, 1933.
4. Ibid.
5. Source: Piero Zanotto, *Luis Trenker lo schermo verticale*. Trento: Manfrini, 1982.
6. This date could be earlier. Fanck's film was released in 1921; Trenker would have been working on *Mountain of Destiny* at some time in 1923.
7. Luis Trenker, 'Mountains are more than beautiful scenery', a chapter in *The Big Book of Mountaineering*, edited by B. Moravetz, 1980.
8. Riefenstahl, *Kampf in Schnee und Eis*.

Chapter III   The Father of Mountain Films

1. Arnold Fanck, 'Wie ich dazu kam die ersten Hochgebirgsfilme zu drehe', article in *Jahrbuch des Deutscher Alpenvereins, 1957*.
2. Ibid.
3. Ibid.
4. Ibid.
5. Ibid.
6. H. H. Wollenberg, *Fifty Years of German Film*, 1948 (p. 22).
7. Leni Riefenstahl, *Kampf in Schnee und Eis*, 1933.
8. In her memoirs – written as an old lady of eighty-five – Riefenstahl recalls that sending Froitzheim away was the most painful decision she was ever called upon to make. Though she had known how to project her sexuality from an early age, and was accustomed to having a string of admirers – one young man, she tells us, cut his wrists for love of her (and was pushed under a couch till morning) – Froitzheim had been her first lover and she had hero-worshipped him for his rakish good looks for two years before getting to know him.
9. Riefenstahl, *Kampf in Schnee und Eis*.
10. Arnold Fanck article, 'Wie ich dazu kam . . .'
11. Leni Riefenstahl, *The Sieve of Time*, 1992.

Chapter IV   Climbing the Heights

1. Leni Riefenstahl, *Kampf in Schnee und Eis*, 1933.
2. David B. Hinton, *The Films of Leni Riefenstahl*, 1978.
3. Riefenstahl, *Kampf in Schnee und Eis*.
4. Hannes Schneider (1890–1955) of St Arlberg was arrested by the Nazis after the Anschluss and subsequently allowed to emigrate to the United States where he set up the Eastern Slope Ski School in North Conway, NH.

5. It brought her to the attention of Max Reinhardt, who engaged her for his Deutsches Theater in Berlin.
6. There is suspicion that, in her memoirs, Riefenstahl is economical with the truth when it comes to Sokal. He told Glenn Infield (author of *Leni Riefenstahl, The Fallen Film Goddess*, 1976) he had once been her fiancé, and far from finishing with her in Zurich, spent 'several weeks' in her company at a fashionable hotel in the Dolomites in the summer of 1924. This would be on her mountain-discovery tour. Thus, Sokal may very well have met Trenker when Riefenstahl introduced herself to him. He mentions attending a presentation of one of Fanck's pictures starring the South Tyrolean actor (although his memory supplies the wrong name for the film.) Sokal also says his liaison with Riefenstahl was over by the time *The Holy Mountain* was being filmed, but on this Riefenstahl disagrees. His presence on the film set, and the fact that he subsequently took an adjacent apartment to her own in Berlin, is proof, she maintains, with some credibility, that he was still interested in her.
7. G. O. Dyhrenfurth, article in *Mitteilungen des Deutschen und Österreichischen Alpenverein*, 1926 (p. 286)
8. Riefenstahl, *Kampf in Schnee und Ice.* (Same source for all climbing description here.)
9. David Gunston, 'Leni Riefenstahl' in *Film Quarterly 14,* 1960 (pp. 4–19).
10. Stephen Bach, *Marlene Dietrich, Life and Legend,* 1992 (pp. 167–8).
11. Riefenstahl, *Kampf in Schnee und Eis.*
12. Ibid.

Chapter V   White Hell and Black Despair

1. The film of *All Quiet on the Western Front* (1929–30) would soon give the lie to this assumption – and would be made, ironically, by Universal in America.
2. Marc Sorkin, 'Six Talks on G. W. Pabst' in *Cinemontages 3*, New York, 1955.
3. David Gunston, 'Leni Riefenstahl', *Film Quarterly*, Fall 1960.
4. *Close Up*, Vol. V, December 1929, No. 6.
5. When *The Holy Mountain* was released to English-speaking audiences, the title must have seemed blasphemous to distributors, as in London it was changed to *The Wrath of the Gods*. It was a silent film, of course, with titles, and for some reason, an introductory caption had been inserted claiming it to be 'an enterprise by the Alpine Club and its members.' Red rag to bullish Strutt, who was quick to acquit the Club of any participation whatsoever in such an 'atrocity'.
6. It was barred, too, in Zurich, though exhibited in Zermatt during a visit there by Whymper's adoptive daughter until the personal intervention of a spokesman of the Swiss Alpine Club. In retrospect, Dr Fanck was unwise to have associated himself with this film. Besides its patent inauthenticity, it exploited national prejudicies and set many against him, who might

otherwise have come to be more sympathetic to his individual cinematography. As it was, remembrance of the episode coloured the views of many people against him (besides Strutt) – and, by association, against Trenker and indeed Riefenstahl who was in no way involved. Such views were quickly converted into folklore.

7. E. L. Strutt, in *Alpine Journal* Vol. 42 (pp. 121–2).
8. *Piz Palü*, like many of the later silent films, would soon be reissued with post-synchronised sound.
9. Leni Riefenstahl, *The Sieve of Time*, 1992.
10. Ibid.

Chapter VI   The Blue Light

1. This film's original title was *Über den Wolken* (*Above the Clouds*), it was also known as *Avalanche*.
2. Siegfried Kracauer, *From Caligari to Hitler*, 1947 (pp. 257–8).
3. Leni Riefenstahl, *Kampf in Schnee und Eis*, 1933.
4. Ibid.
5. Michel Delahaye 'Leni et le loup', article in *Cahiers du Cinema,* September 1965.
6. Riefenstahl, *Kampf in Schnee und Eis*.
7. Others have remarked upon similarities with the romantic novel *Bergkristal*, by Gustav Renker, published around 1930.
8. Originally entitled *Sonne über dem Arlberg* (*Sunshine over the Arlberg*).
9. Equivalent to 'hare and hounds', a recurrent theme in Fanck's work (in 1923 he had made *Fox-Hunt in the Engadine*, also with Schneider), and one which Riefenstahl too hoped to re-employ after the war.
10. Riefenstahl, *Kampf in Schnee und Eis*.
11. Ibid.
12. *Film Culture,* Spring 1973 (Henry Jaworsky interviewed by Gordon Hitchens).
13. Riefenstahl, *Kampf in Schnee und Eis*.
14. Ibid.
15. Ibid.
16. Ibid.
17. Ibid, and Leni Riefenstahl, *The Sieve of Time*, 1992.
18. Ibid.

Chapter VII   SOS Eisberg!

1. Leni Riefenstahl, *Kampf in Schnee und Eis*, 1993, and retold in *The Sieve of Time*, 1992.
2. E.L. Strutt, writing in the *Alpine Journal* Vol. 45, May 1933.
3. The source for this Trenker story is said to be Tabori's *The Private Life of Adolf Hitler*, 1947. This author found it quoted in Infield's, *Leni Riefenstahl, the Fallen Film Goddess*, 1976.
4. There is an interesting reference in Ernst Jaeger's sensational articles in the

Hollywood Tribune in 1939 (in which truth is known to have been lavishly embellished, though it is not so clear where it actually stops). Jaeger, who prompted Riefenstahl to attend this recruiting rally, says her presence did not go unnoticed. 'The city room of the Berlin Nazi paper, *Der Angriff* was buzzing with quips about it. And the ever-suspicious Dr Goebbels kept asking what business had Leni Riefenstahl at a Hitler meeting? She was intrusive – trying to catch Hitler's eye.' Hard to do, if she really could not see his face.

5. Riefenstahl, *The Sieve of Time*.
6. Riefenstahl, *Kampf in Schnee und Eis*.
7. Hans Ertl, *Meine wilden dreissiger Jahre*, 1982. Note: Leni Riefenstahl (in correspondence with the author) holds Ertl's as unreliable memoirs.
8. Ibid.
9. Ibid.
10. Riefenstahl, *The Sieve of Time*.
11. Dr Ernst Sorge (later to become a Russian spy, according to Jaworsky), *With Plane, Boat, and Camera in Greenland*, 1933.
12. Sepp Rist, 'Als erster Mensch auf einem Eisberg', in *Alpinismus*, December 1974.
13. Sorge, *With Plane, Boat, and Camera in Greenland*.
14. Ibid, pp. 137–8.
15. Riefenstahl, *Kampf in Schnee und Eis*.
16. Ertl, *Meine wilden dreissiger Jahre*.
17. Riefenstahl, *Kampf in Schnee und Eis*.
18. Ibid.

Chapter VIII   Burning Questions

1. Alan Bullock, *Hitler, A Study of Tyranny*, revised edn. 1954 (pp. 199–200).
2. In his *Hitler*, Joachim Fest puts the total number of unemployed, including the 'invisible' jobless, in October 1932 as 8.75 million (p. 353 in Penguin edition).
3. Dr Ernst Sorge, *With Plane, Boat, and Camera in Greenland*, 1933 (p. 203).
4. By the end of the war Goering was commander of the elite 'Flying Circus'.
5. Hermann Rauschning, *Hitler Speaks*, 1939.
6. Ernst ('Putzi') Hanfstaengl, *Hitler, the Missing Years*, 1957 (pp. 193–4).
7. Leni Riefenstahl, *The Sieve of Time*, 1992.
8. Ibid.
9. Josef Goebbels, *Tagebuch*, 9th December 1932.
10. Ibid.
11. Strasser's intimations proved correct: he found death among the victims of the Night of the Long Knives less than two years later when Hitler settled many outstanding scores.
12. Riefenstahl, *The Sieve of Time*.
13. Untranslated into English at the time, though incorporated with some changes into her memoirs: *The Sieve of Time*, 1992.
14. Alan Bullock, *Hitler, a Study of Tyranny* revised edn. 1954 (p. 245.).

15. Riefenstahl, *The Sieve of Time*.
16. *Die Tagebücher von Joseph Goebbels: Sämtliche Fragmente*. Edited by Elke Fröhlich for the Institut für Zeitgeschichte, Munich, in collaboration with the Bundesarchiv. At least nine volumes to date.

Chapter IX   Into the Whirlpool

1. Viktor Reimann, *Joseph Goebbels, the Man who Created Hitler*, 1977 (p. xi in the Sphere paperback edition).
2. Friedrich Lessing, *Hamburgische Dramaturgie* (According to Rudolf Semler, Press Officer to the Propaganda Ministry, and quoted in *The Great German Films* by Frederick W. Ott, 1986.)
3. Figures taken from Viktor Reimann's *Joseph Goebbels, the Man who Created Hitler*. Originally published in *Der Deutsche Film, 1932*, journal of the Party's own film section.
4. Infuriated by the way in which Goebbels was appropriating *Battleship Potemkin*, and holding it up as an example to Nazi film-makers, Sergei Eisenstein published a searing open letter to the German Propaganda Minister in an emigré German newspaper, which was copied in translation by the *New York Times* on 30th December, 1934: 'How do you dare to talk about "life",' he demanded, 'you, who are bringing death and banishment to everything living and everything good in your country with the executioner's axe and the machine gun. You, who are executing the best sons of the German proletariat and are scattering to the four corners of the earth all those constituting the pride of real German science and of the cultured people of the whole world! How do you dare to ask your film artists to give truthful pictures of life without enjoining them, first of all, to trumpet forth to the world the torments of the thousands who are being tortured to death in the catacombs of your prisons . . . ?'
5. The scene was imitated that same year in *Hans Westmar*, directed by Franz Wenzler and based on the Horst Wessel story, and Hans Steinhoff's *Hitlerjungen Quex*. Later, its echoes would also be seen in Leni Riefenstahl's *Triumph of the Will*.
6. Quotes in this and adjacent paragraphs taken from Frederick W. Ott's *The Great German Films*, 1986.
7. Adolf Engls and Arnold Raether, newly-appointed officials in the theatre and fine arts branches of Goebbels' Ministry spoke out bluntly in support of Goebbels, saying, 'the Friedrichstrasse crowd was finished' (a reference to Jewish film producers); German films must be made by Germans; 'only the Aryan could understand the spirit of the German *Volk* – their purpose was to educate the people and to propagandise' – Source: F. W. Ott, *The Great German Films*, 1986.
8. Quoted in F. W. Ott, *The Great German Films,* 1986 (p. 141). The incident is described more fully in Mark Shivas' interview with Fritz Lang in *Movie No 2*, September 1962, and collected in Andrew Sarris, *Interviews with Film Directors*, 1967.

9. David Stewart Hull, *Film in the Third Reich*, 1969 (p. 66).
10. 'What a pity that the film *The Emperor of America* did not end by pointing the moral lesson! Trenker has produced two films which are masterpieces of their kind – *Mountains in Flames* and *The Rebel*. In these he was beholden to no man; but in his other films he was financed by Catholic interests' – *Hitler's Table Talk*, edited by H. R. Trevor-Roper, 1953 (p. 646).
11. This letter is quoted in David Stewart Hull's *Film in the Third Reich*, 1969 (p. 26).
12. 'I tried to carry out my assignment with due deference for Schinkel's interior. But Goebbels thought what I had done insufficiently impressive. After some months he commissioned the Vereinigte Werkstätten (United Workshops) in Munich to redo the rooms in "ocean-liner" style' – Albert Speer, *Inside the Third Reich* (p. 59 in 1958 Sphere paperback edition).
13. Hans Ertl, *Meine wilden dreissiger Jahren*, 1982. (Riefenstahl disputes the Ertl version.)
14. By 1934, every film had to be licensed before work could begin, and approved again before it could be released. Where it was considered important, the RFK dictated which actors were to take part. The Film Credit Bank – formed through an alliance between finance capital, the largest film companies and government – had the object of simplifying and controlling the budgets of sanctioned projects. This, too, would later be absorbed into the Chamber of Film.
15. In 1927 Ruttman had been responsible for the acclaimed *Berlin, the Symphony of a Great City*.

Chapter X   Nuremberg Rallies

1. Amber Blanco White: *The New Propaganda*, 1939. He emphasised his rather extreme opinion by drawing attention to the encouragement of passionate devotion to a leader, purges of dissentients and subjection of the rank and file – albeit on a small scale.
2. Adolf Hitler, *Mein Kampf*.
3. Stephen H. Roberts, *The House that Hitler Built*, 1937 (p. 135).
4. UFA did have close links with the Party, however, through its controller, the press baron Hugenberg.
5. Philip Gibbs, *Across the Frontiers*, 1938 (p. 227).
6. Albert Speer, *Inside the Third Reich* (p. 51 in Sphere paperback edition, 1978).
7. The host of new members who joined the party after the September 1930 election.
8. Leni Riefenstahl, *Hinter den Kulissen des Reichsparteitag-Films*, 1935.
9. Alan Wykes, in his book *Nuremberg Rallies* (1969), claims that Julius Streicher, the sadistic and anti-Semitic Gauleiter of Franconia, had evicted a Jewish sculptor and his family from this large house to provide the film team headquarters. Riefenstahl in her memoirs acknowledges the help of Gutterer, a government official, in furnishing an 'empty house'.

10. Evidence points to Ernst Jaeger, former editor of *Film-Kurier*, having ghost-written this publicity book. This would have been under the supervision of a representative from the Propaganda Ministry. Riefenstahl herself may never have seen the final proofs. (This now is her recollection.)
11. Albert Speer, *Inside the Third Reich* (pp. 100–101 in Sphere paperback edition, 1978).
12. Ibid.
13. All quotations in this and previous two paragraphs from William L. Shirer, *Berlin Diary*, 1941.
14. Leni Riefenstahl, *The Sieve of Time*, 1992.

Chapter XI   Triumph of the Will

1. Keith Reader, *The Cinema, a History*, 1979 (p. 53).
2. Bardèche/Brasillach, *Histoire du Cinema*, 1964.
3. Steve Neal, *Triumph of the Will: Notes on Documentary and Spectacle*, in *Screen XX: 1 (Spring 1979)*. The Museum of Modern Art in New York has also published a detailed outline, see *Film Comment 65*.
4. First appeared in *Cahiers du Cinéma, No. 170*, September 1965, reprinted with an English translation in the same journal No. 5, 1966; incorporated (in English) also in *Interviews with Film Directors*, edited by Andrew Sarris, 1967.
5. Ibid.
6. Siegfried Kracauer, *From Caligari to Hitler*, 1947 (p. 290).
7. David B. Hinton, *The Films of Leni Riefenstahl*, 1978 (p. 41).
8. Ibid (p. 42).
9. From the *Illustrierte Film-Kurier* programme for the film, as translated in David Welch, *Propaganda and the German Cinema 1933–1945*, 1971.
10. William L. Shirer, *Berlin Diary 1934–1941*, 1941 (p. 25).
11. Richard Meran Barsam, *Filmguide to Triumph of the Will*, 1975.
12. David B. Hinton, *The Films of Leni Riefenstahl*, 1978 (p. 46).
13. Richard Meran Barsam, *Filmguide to Triumph of the Will*, 1975 (p. 47).
14. A 'Cathedral of Light' is illustrated at the end of Riefenstahl's *Olympia*; it is possible that Speer was simply confused about the date his light fantastic first appeared; or maybe the feature evolved to its final form. Gitta Sereny was told by Riefenstahl that the idea was hers not Speer's, and by Walter Frentz that it was his. In particular Frentz claimed credit for angling the searchlight beams into a dome, rather than having them point straight up into the sky as Speer wanted.
15. Barsam, *Filmguide to Triumph of the Will* (pp. 54–5).
16. Hinton, *The Films of Leni Riefenstahl* (p. 51).
17. Shirer, *Berlin Diary* (p. 27).
18. William K. Everson, essay in *The Documentary Tradition* (edited by L. Jacobs), 1971.
19. John Grierson, *Grierson on Documentary*, ed. Forsyth Hardy, 1947, and quoted also in Barsam, *Nonfiction Film, a Critical History*, 1974.

20. World Union of Documentary 1948 definition of documentary film: '... all methods of recording on celluloid any aspect of reality interpreted either by factual shooting or by sincere and justifiable reconstruction, so as to appeal either to reason or emotion, for the purpose of stimulating the desire for, and the widening of human knowledge and understanding, and of truthfully posing problems and their solutions in the spheres of economics, culture, and human relations.' (Quoted in Richard Meran Barsam, *Nonfiction Film, a Critical History*, 1974, Revised 1992).

21. Actually read for him by Gauleiter Wagner of Bavaria. As he got older, Hitler found the almost constant speechifying of the annual congresses a terrible strain and the long standing a torture. 'It's because of the superhuman effort which that demands of me that I was already obliged to have the opening proclamation read out,' he explained (in *Hitler's Table Talk*, edited by Hugh Trevor-Roper, 1953 (p 242).

22. Müller's television film, *The Wonderful, Horrible Life of Leni Riefenstahl*, 1993.

23. The *Observer*, London, 30th, March 1935.

24. August 1934 plebiscite gave Hitler 88.1% of votes; that held on German foreign policy in March 1936 rose to 98.5% of eligible voters (figures given in Henry Lichtenberger's *The Third Reich*, 1937 (repr. 1969).

25. A quotation from S. Kracauer, *From Caligari to Hitler*, 1947 (p. 303).

26. Paul Rotha, *The Film Till Now* (revised and enlarged edition) 1949 (p. 591).

27. Ken Kelman, 'Propaganda as Vision – Triumph of the Will' in *Film Culture*, Spring 1973.

Chapter XII   Goebbels' Dream Factory

1. Leni Riefenstahl, *The Sieve of Time*, 1992.

2. '... the entire "play" is idiotic to such a degree that, at the end of the film, one finds difficulty in recalling the few pictures of mountain scenery which should have proved the delight of all mountaineers ... the most inane tale ever invented' – Hans Lauper, writing in *The Alpine Journal*, May 1935.

3. David Stuart Hull, *Film in the Third Reich*, 1969 (p. 44).

4. Julian Petley, *Capital and Culture, German Cinema 1933–45*, 1979 (pp. 1–4).

5. At first some films, not deemed suitable for German audiences, could obtain finance to be made for export only, but that anomoly did not last long. An intriguing reversal brought about in world cinema by the Nazi-induced dynamics was that while emigrant German film-makers like Fritz Lang and Friedrich Murnau took their quality expressionistic ideas to Hollywood, Germany was being forced to ape Hollywood's more frivolous concoctions.

6. *New York Times*, 30th November, 1934.

7. Goebbels abolished criticism at a meeting of the Culture Chamber on 27th November 1936. The following year Captain Weiss, head of the Reich Press Association, attempted to clarify the situation, 'The newspapers make a serious mistake when they believe that the prohibition of criticism means

praising everything,' he said. 'The art of observation does not differ from the criticism of the arts. Everything does not have to be accepted as good.' (*New York Times*, 16th March 1937.)

8. Figures taken from H. H. Wollenberg, *Fifty Years of German Film*, 1948 (p. 38).
9. Frederick W. Ott, *The Great German Films*, 1986 (p. 149).
10. Reference and translation from Erwin Leiser, *Nazi Cinema*, 1974 (p. 35).
11. Ralf Georg Reuth, *Goebbels: the life of Joseph Goebbels the Mephisthophelean Genius of Nazi Propaganda*, 1993 (p. 195).
12. In a television programme, *We Have Ways of Making You Think* (written and produced by Laurence Rees in 1992), Lida Baarova spoke of her relationship with Goebbels. She particularly liked his wittiness and sarcasm, she said. They laughed a lot and in her own way she loved him – or at least she loved being loved by him. She was only twenty-two; the affair lasted two years.
13. *The Emperor of California* was based on Blaise Cendrars' novel *L'Or*, which was originally to have been a Hollywood project for Eisenstein.
14. 'How the Nazis Created a Dream Factory in Hell' by Tom Reiss, the *New York Times*, 6th November 1994.
15. D. D. Shipman, *The Story of Cinema*, 1982 (p. 298).
16. According to Henry Jaworsky, Goebbels used two of his own children as stars in one of the infamous 'killing films', probably *Victim of the Past* made by the Propaganda Ministry in conjunction with the Racial and Political Office. They would have been the examples of 'racial purity' – the wanted children – not the 'hereditory ill' to be put down. An ironically meaningless distinction, as it turned out.
17. Louis Marcorelles, 'The Nazi Cinema (1933–1945)', article in *Sight and Sound*, Autumn 1955.

Chapter XIII   Olympiad, 1936

1. Howard Smith, *Last Train from Berlin*, 1942 (p. 6).
2. Martha Gellhorn, *The Face of War*, 1959; 3rd revised edition, paperback, 1986 (p. 19).
3. *Völkischer Beobachter*, 19th August 1932 (translated and quoted in Cooper C. Graham *Leni Riefenstahl and Olympia*, 1986).
4. The 2nd Maccabiah was held in Tel Aviv in April 1935.
5. Dr Theodor Lewald had been head of the German Olympic Commission since 1924. Before the First War he helped to organise the German Olympic teams.
6. Reprinted as frontispiece in *Preserve the Olympic Ideal: A Statement of the Case Against American Participation in the Olympic Games in Berlin*, New York: the Committee on Fair Play in Sports, 1935.
7. Julian Petley, *Capital and Culture, German Cinema 1933–45*, 1979 (p. 53).
8. Tobis was the German branch of a Dutch company, largely owned by a consortium of Dutch banks. Financial difficulties played into Nazi hands and by the end of 1937, Tobis had come under German ownership.

9. The Reichs Kredit Anstalt offered to finance the Olympic film privately but were turned down by the Propaganda Ministry. Whether 'Reich funds' implies official Propaganda Ministry finance is unclear [to this writer], but Goebbels is known to have operated a 'slush fund' which could be tapped for his more devious cinematic dealings.

10. One source not quoted in Cooper C. Graham's work is Glenn B. Infield's *Leni Riefenstahl, The Fallen Film Goddess*, 1976. Infield had also been to Koblenz and other European archives, and reached slightly different conclusions.

11. *Goebbels Tagebuch*, 1935, Bundesarchiv. (There are various published versions of Goebbels' diaries, including volumes edited by Elke Fröhlich for the Institut für Zeitgeschichte, Munich.)

12. *Reichsfinanzministerium*, Abt. 1, R2, vol. 4788 (pp. 429–30, BA), quoted in Cooper C. Graham, *Leni Riefenstahl and Olympia*, 1986. The latter is the source for all Cooper C. Graham quotations in this chapter.

13. There is a confusion in the English translation at least of *The Sieve of Time* whereby her 1935–6 Christmas-holiday visit to Hitler in Munich appears on one page to be on Christmas Eve or before and, later in the passage, after Christmas Eve. A further discrepancy appeared in an earlier testimony (not repeated in her memoirs): referring to Goebbels trying to wrest the editing of *Olympia* from her in November 1936, she claimed to have sought an audience with Hitler, with whom she 'had not spoken alone for a period of one and a half years'.

14. Recognising the paper as a propaganda instrument, any 'news items' in the *Völkischer Beobachter* should be treated with caution. Goebbels would hardly be expected to announce that Riefenstahl had been hired by any-one but himself, any more than that she was not his first choice for the task.

15. This particular quotation from Glenn B. Infield, in his *Leni Riefenstahl, the Fallen Film Goddess*, 1976 (pp. 114–5).

16. Captured documents show Riefenstahl recommended several of her and Fanck's most experienced men to Weidemann: a 'Hans Weidemann' file among captured German Propaganda Ministry Documents was seen by Cooper C. Graham at the National Archives, Washington DC (Serial 125, Item RFK 12).

17. James P. Cunningham, 'Hitler Makes U.S. Olympics Films Advertise Germany,' *Motion Picture Herald*, 8th August 1936 (quoted in Cooper C. Graham).

18. Ernst Jaeger, 'Fackellauf durch Griechenland', *Film-Kurier* special feature, July 1936 (quoted in translation in Cooper C. Graham *Leni Riefenstahl and Olympia*, 1986).

19. Ernst Jaeger, 'How Leni Riefenstahl Became Hitler's Girlfriend' in *Hollywood Tribune*, 19th May 1939.

20. The altercation and finals took place on 3rd August; the row with Goebbels and apology on 6th August.

21. Goebbels Diaries, 6th August 1936.

22. 'Frau' denotes a more mature woman than 'Fraulein', not that a woman is married necessarily – it isn't a straight translation of 'Mrs'.

23. Ernst Jaeger, 'Die Kamera kämpft mit', *Film-Kurier*, 8th August 1936.
24. Frederick T. Birchall in *New York Times*, 14th August 1936.
25. Interview with Henry Jaworsky in *Film Culture*, Spring 1973.
26. Hans Ertl, *Meine wilden dreissiger Jahre*, 1982.
27. On the first day of the Games, Hitler had shaken hands with the victors, only to be told by Count Baillet-Latour that this broke Olympic protocol. It wasn't just Owens who did not get congratulated after that; still there is a suggestion that in his case the Reich Sports Leader and the Hitler Youth Leader thought 'the interests of sport' would be served if the Führer were to meet the American star performer. Hitler emphatically refused.
28. Leni says after this near miss, they had to fill it in, as well as some of the others, but Jaeger records there were still pits in the vicinity of the finish during the final.
29. Ernst Jaeger, 'Die Kamera kämpft mit – Marathon Sonntag' in *Film-Kurier*, 10th August 1936 (translated by Cooper C. Graham in his *Leni Riefenstahl and Olympia*), 1986.
30. Graham says eight 'searchlights' not enough, four light trucks were also brought in. A few hundred people lingered in the stands when they noticed something interesting going on.
31. *Ambassador Dodd's Diary, 1933–1938*, 1941 (p. 349).
32. Willy Zielke has long felt he was never given the credit he deserved for his work on the *Olympia* prologue. He gave a lengthy interview to Cooper C. Graham in 1983, from which it emerged his understanding was that he should shoot and edit the prologue, and his preference was for long dreamy dissolves rather than Riefenstahl's swift, short cuts, which were crude to his eyes. 'When I looked at what she had made of it,' he said, 'I got a toothache'. He had to remind himself, 'It was not my film – right?'
33. Their location work here at the Kuhrischer Nehrung, besides offering a light-hearted interlude in a hectic summer, proved inspirational in her later *Penthesilea* thinking. Rumours persist that one of the naked-maiden shots is of Riefenstahl herself, although the oblique camera angle protects her anonymity. In any case, the assumption must be that she herself choreographed this erotic little dance which symbolises the birth of the Olympic flame.
34. Goebbels Diaries, 25th October 1936.
35. Cooper C. Graham, *Leni Riefenstahl and Olympia*, 1986.
36. This figure includes the several foreign-language versions – each a separate film in its own right inasmuch as footage was individually tailored and its own commentary recorded – and the twelve short sports films made by Riefenstahl's company from the out-takes.
37. In *The Sieve of Time*, Riefenstahl gives the meeting with Hitler as on 11th November; an earlier report issued by her had the consultation taking place 'in December 1936', at which time she said she had not spoken alone with the Führer for eighteen months.
38. Herman Weigel, 'Interview mit Leni Riefenstahl', *Film-Kritik*, August 1972 (translation provided by Graham C. Cooper.)

Chapter XIV   The Door Begins to Close

1. Leopold's father King Albert I had been a keen mountaineer, regularly climbing with the Stegers, Hans and his wife Paula Wiesinger. Albert died in a climbing accident in 1934. Leopold inherited his enthusiasm.

2. Anderl Heckmair, *My Life as a Mountaineer*, 1975 (p. 78). (Geoffrey Sutton's impeccable translation imparts a sophistication to Heckmair's account which may not be in the Bavarian original.)

3. Ibid (p. 80).

4. Ibid (pp. 80–81).

5. Ibid (p. 82).

6. The seeds of the successes in these interwar years were sown before the turn of the century in a surge of guideless climbing activity associated with the major European universities. By 1907 the *D.u.Ö.A.V* (German and Austrian Alpine Club) could boast an unprecedented 70,000 members.

7. Othmar Gurtner, 'The Eiger Myth', article in *The Mountain World 1958/59*, 1958 (pp. 20–41).

8. Gitta Sereny, 'Blind Eyewitness', article in *The Independent on Sunday*, 13th September 1992.

9. Gitta Sereny, *Albert Speer, his battle with Truth*, 1995 (p. 133).

10. At the Winter Games the British team had agonised over what they should do if Nazi salutes were expected of them. They compromised with a shoulder high 'Olympic salute' but came in for flak at home, since to the uninitiated this was not sufficiently distinguishable from the fascist variety.

11. 'Leni Riefenstahl, Hitler's honey, will get a chilly reception out here' – Ed Sullivan forecast in his syndicated column *Looking at Hollywood*, 7th November 1938.

12. Jaeger has quoted Inez Robb of the *Daily News* reporting 'The child is charming!' She checked in at the Hotel Pierre and set out determinedly to explore the city's smart night spots – the Stork Club and El Morocco – earning the mention in Walter Winchell's Broadway tattle column (in the *Daily Mirror*, 9th November 1938) that she was 'as pretty as a swastika'.

13. William L. Shirer, *The Rise and Fall of the Third Reich*, 1959 (p. 433).

14. As a journalist, Jaeger was not above turning out a sycophantic piece when the occasion demanded. On the other hand, he had had his knuckles rapped by Goebbels' Ministry after a previous visit to Hollywood when he wrote too enthusiastically of the successes of such German-Jewish exiles as Max Reinhardt.

15. The Hollywood Anti-Nazi League (which was non-sectarian and claimed a membership of 100,000, according to Cooper C. Graham) campaigned on behalf of other left-wing causes and was frequently suspected of being a front for Communist activists. Graham: 'After the Hitler-Stalin Pact in August of 1939, when many [US Communist Party] members became pro-German, the Hollywood Anti-Nazi League collapsed.'

16. According to Cooper C. Graham, Riefenstahl had three different versions of *Olympia* in her luggage. At an improvised theatre in the California Club she screened the Hitler-free version, fearing that 'if the projectionist were too leftist, he might set fire to the [original] film.'

17. Cooper C. Graham, relying on Jaeger's evidence, says Riefenstahl's friend, Maria Jeritza, poisoned her against Jaeger with her 'spy' stories; Riefenstahl chose to believe Jeritza and fired him (*Leni Riefenstahl and Olympia*, p 225).
18. As told by Riefenstahl in *The Sieve of Time*, 1992.

Chapter XV   Leni's War

1. Article in *Film Culture*, Spring 1973, and quoted in David Hinton's *The Films of Leni Riefenstahl*, 1978.
2. Ibid.
3. Interview in *Sight and Sound*, Winter 1965/66.
4. Ibid.
5. Towards the end of the war (November 1944) Riefenstahl did wander around the Italian Front searching the casualty stations for her husband, from whom she had not heard for some time.
6. Feature in *Revue* (Munich), 19th April, 1952, under the headline LENI RIEFENSTAHL HUSHES IT UP, claimed her to be 'one of the few German women not only to have known but also witnessed with her own eyes' the terrible crimes for which Germany's international reputation still suffered.
7. Dr Goebbels still hoped Riefenstahl would collaborate with him on his proposed film about the press, *Victory of Power* (according to an interview she gave to Michel Delahaye in 1965).
8. It is true she had contemplated filming *Penthesilea* in muted colour, but for *Tiefland* there was never a question in her mind but it should be monochrome. So much artistry in the cinema was being lost by the near-universal switch to colour, she believed. Black and white filming was a special kind of art, more like a graphic art in her view, and some of its effects simply could not be achieved in colour.
9. Of the 30,000 gypsies living in Germany in 1939, only 5,000 survived the war.
10. David Stewart Hull, *Film in the Third Reich*, 1969 (p. 138).
11. Riefenstahl employed an assortment of temporary drama directors to supervise her acting scenes. For a short while Pabst became available, but to Leni's intense disappointment, Hollywood seemed to have extinguished the great director's spark; she could see nothing remaining of what had been such a good eye for visual matters; he was dour and perfunctory and despotic. Everyone on set, she said, felt relief when Goebbels moved him on yet again, and his scenes were later reshot.
12. Interview with Henry Jaworsky, *Film Culture*, Spring 1973.
13. Fanck's Berlin-model film, and another on the work of the monumental sculptors Breker and Thorak have been seen in recent years on British television and within the Council of Europe's *Art and Power* exhibition. In the first, occasional plays of light, particularly in a fountain sequence, reveal hints of his mastery even within the constraints of the subject. David Hinton has pointed out that the slow tracking style evident in the sculpture films are definitely in the Riefenstahl style, indicating 'the teacher had become the student of the pupil'.

14. Jaworsky claimed he refused to work on *Triumph of the Will* on political grounds. In fact, film work on *The Wonders of Flying* would appear to have overlapped the rally shooting and could explain his and Schneeberger's absence from this particular Riefenstahl film.

15. Putzi Hanfstaengl names a 'Jaworsky' as the photographer in the plane when the macabre joke was played on him 'to bring him to heel'. Putzi, however, fled the country immediately, and made his way to America.

16. Hans Ertl, *Als Kriegs Berichter 1939–1945*, 1985.

17. Jaworsky says of Zielke: 'He was very clever. When the war started he went insane and went to an asylum and was completely schizophrenic. When the war was over he was good again . . . He was a great artist, but he didn't want any part of the Nazis' – *Film Culture*, Spring 1973.

18. This is the rumour, as told by Jaworsky. Leonard Mosley, in his biography of Goering, *The Reich Marshal*, 1974, describes two scrawled messages behind the bed, not in blood but red crayon. The first: 'Iron Man, you have forsaken me!' (Iron Man was one of the nicknames of Goering.) The second trailed away, but asked, 'Why did you put me in the hands of Milch . . .' (His jealous career rival).

19. Glenn B. Infield, *Leni Riefenstahl, the Fallen Film Goddess*, 1976. (Infield also implies that Riefenstahl was the 'girlfriend' who had to be warned off after Udet's suicide.)

20. 'Absurd' as it may have been to continue with her film as the Third Reich crumbled – she put it down to her Prussian sense of duty – Riefenstahl was not alone. In UFA's Babelsberg Studios, southwest of Berlin, work was going ahead on a major production that Goebbels had hoped would be the German equivalent of the inspirational *Mrs Miniver* or *This Happy Breed*. Set in 1943, in a residential district of Berlin under Allied bombardment, *Das Leben geht weiter* (*Life Goes On*) was intended to encourage a dispirited populace to stand firm. As such, it had high priority, a massive budget and some of the best movie stars of the day. Many thought Goebbels himself had a hand in writing the screenplay. Precious petrol reserves and colour film stock were made available; and (with echoes of Riefenstahl and her gypsies) a camp-load of Polish prisoners of war were employed as extras. Shooting had been going on for six months, but no footage was ever found after the war. The director, Wolfgang Liebeneiner, (again, like Riefenstahl) seems to have discerned which way the wind was blowing, and was anxious to protect his workers from being sent to the front. His daughter confirmed that the film was 'a kind of an island', and her father a minor Oskar Schindler. Liebeneiner was definitely playing for time towards the end. Although the reels were hidden in a crypt for safety before the Allies arrived, everyone concerned with this lost feature film seems to have preferred to forget its existence after the war. (Source: 'The last Nazi film', article by Lee Marshall in the *Sunday Telegraph*, 26th February, 1995.)

21. Veit Harlan, quoted in Erwin Leiser, *Nazi Cinema*, 1974 (p. 129).

22. Kristina Soederbaum in the television film *We Have Ways of Making You Think* (Laurence Rees, 1992). One of the first prints of *Kolberg* was flown to the beleaguered fortress of La Rochelle to inject spirit into the defending

forces. In fact La Rochelle surrounded soon after the preview, and the print fell into Russian hands. On 17th April 1945, Goebbels summoned his Ministry staff together for an emotive showing of the film. 'Gentlemen,' he beseeched those present, 'in a hundred years' time they will be showing a fine colour film of the terrible days we are living through. Wouldn't you like to play a part in that film? Hold out now, so that a hundred years hence the audience will not hoot and whistle when you appear on the screen.' (Variously reported, in Hugh Trevor-Roper's introduction to *The Goebbels Diaries, the Last Days*, 1978.

23. 'The last Nazi film', article by Lee Marshall in the *Sunday Telegraph*, 26th February, 1995.

Chapter XVI   Alone in the Wilderness

1. Based on information in Leni Riefenstahl's *The Sieve of Time*, 1992.
2. Riefenstahl, *The Sieve of Time*.
3. In conversation with Budd Schulberg and described in Schulberg's *Saturday Evening Post* article, 30th March 1946.
4. Hoffmann was father-in-law to Baldur von Schirach – Reich Leader of the Hitler Youth and later Gauleiter of Vienna – he doubtless hoped his co-operation would count in von Schirach's favour (sentenced to twenty years at Nuremberg).
5. *An Empire of Their Own: How the Jews invented Hollywood*, by Neil Gabler, 1989, describes how Schulberg – who as a youthful left-wing idealist had visited Russia in 1934 and been a committed Communist since 1937 (to be known as the 'Hollywood Party's Stalin') – offended both the Jews and Communists of Hollywood in 1941 with his exposure of amorality in the film industry in the novel *What Makes Sammy Run?*
6. Extracts from the spurious Eva Braun diary, published in Paris in 1948, and quoted in Riefenstahl's *The Sieve of Time*.
7. Quoted by Leni Riefenstahl in *The Sieve of Time*.
8. Michael A. Musmanno, *Ten Days to Die*, 1950. 'The Musmanno Archives' comprising transcripts of his interviews etc. were deposited on his death with the Supreme Court of Pennsylvania, and were extensively quoted in Glenn Infield, *Eva and Adolf*, New York: Grosset and Dunlap, 1974.
9. Stefan König and Florian Trenker, *Bera Luis, das Phänomen Luis Trenker – Eine Biographie*, 1992.
10. From Leni Riefenstahl's treatment, as quoted in David Hinton, *The Films of Leni Riefenstahl*.

Chapter XVII   In and Out of Africa

1. *Film Comment*, Winter 1965, and quoted again in *Film Culture* in Spring 1973, both in connection with Gordon Hitchens' interviews with Leni Riefenstahl. She contests Mayer's recollection of this in the belief that her documents from the American Zone, exonerating her from being a Nazi, freed her to work. 'Blacklisting' was not a word she would enter-

tain, it must have been a private kind of boycott. (It is not clear if she appreciated the word could have any unofficial interpretation.)

2. This and later quotes in this paragraph fromVernon Young, ' "Hardly a Man is Now Alive": Monologue on a Nazi Film', leading article in *Accent* (a quarterly of new literature), Spring 1955.

3. The Americans did not 'win' actually – the Olympic Spirit resists the notion of an overall winner. With twelve first places, the Americans dominated the track and field events; but Germany, by its own system of reckoning and taking all disciplines into account, earned more medals and points than any other nation at the Summer Games.

4. From *To Encourage the Art of the Film, The Story of the British Film Institute*, by Ivan Butler, 1971 (p. 36).

5. In the book *Six Million Dead,* published in Paris, claims were made that Leni Riefenstahl, on Eichmann's instructions, had filmed within an extermination camp.

6. London *Evening Standard*, 13th December 1960.

7. London *Sunday Dispatch*, 18th December 1960.

8. Ivor Montagu, 'Opinion' for Executive Committee, ACTT, May 1960 (Copy in British Film Library).

9. John Grierson's work with the Empire Marketing Board and the GPO Film Units, and subsequently with the Films Division of the Ministry of Information during the war encouraged many new talents and pioneered quality.

10. The American cameraman Willard Van Dyke has also told how during the war at the Office of War Information, he and his colleagues tried to find a way of using captured German film material to make anti-Nazi films. 'We had a fine-grain of all Leni Riefenstahl's work,' he wrote afterwards, 'and we used to sit night after night screening this material, trying to discover how to turn it against the Nazis. But we never could . . . it was all spectacle, and there was simply no way to make it unattractive.'

11. Robert Muller, 'The Romantic Miss Riefenstahl', *The Spectator,* 10th February 1961.

12. From her film treatment, *Black Freight* or *Black Cargo* (as it is sometimes translated), as quoted by David B. Hinton.

13. *Leni Riefenstahl's Africa*, 1982, 1981.

14. From chapter by Leni Riefenstahl in the book *Visions of Paradise,*1981.

15. Susan Sontag's *Fascinating Fascism* was first published in *The New York Review of Books*, 6th February 1975. It has most recently been reprinted – with considerable adjustment – in her collection of essays, *Under the Sign of Saturn*, 1996.

Chapter XVIII   The Long Shadow of Shame

1. Ed. Trevor-Roper, *Hitler's Table Talk 1941–1944*, 1955 (pp. 246–52).

2. Richard Corliss, 'Leni Riefenstahl: A Bibliography', *Film Heritage* 5, 1969 (pp. 27–36).

3. Siegfried Kracauer, *From Caligari to Hitler, a Psychological History of the*

German Film, 1947 (p. 111) There is no acknowledgement in his *Notes* or *Bibliography* that he owed anything to, or was even aware of the writings of E. L. Strutt in the *Alpine Journal*, but he clearly hated mountain films and had absorbed similar disquiet over climbing development during the early years of this century.

4. The free use of *Bergfilme*-inspired stylisation in such euthanasia films as the Propaganda Ministry's *Erbkrank* (*Victim*, 1936, premiered 1937) was a particularly distasteful source of retrospective taint.

5. Quoted in Peter Adam *The Arts of the Third Reich*, 1992 (p. 7).

6. Kevin Brownlow, 'Leni Riefenstahl', *Film 47*, Winter 1966 (pp. 14–19).

7. Paul Rotha, 'I deplore . . .' Note in *Film 48*, Spring 1967. (Reprinted in Rotha's book *The Film Till Now, a Survey of World Cinema*, first published in 1930 and updated with Richard Griffith in 1949.)

8. Andrew Sarris, 'Films' review of *Olympia* in *The Village Voice*, New York 4th May 1967.

9. All eleven Israeli Olympic sportsmen taken hostage from the Olympic Village by Arab terrorists: two were shot in the raid, and the remainder slaughtered during a bungled rescue bid at Munich airport.

10. Reported in the *Denver Post*, 3rd September 1974.

11. 'Nazi Film Expert attempts Comeback', article by David Platt in *Morning Freiheit*, 8th September 1972.

12. Susan Sontag, 'Fascinating Fascism' in *The New York Review of Books*, 6th February 1975. The article (with some revisions) is incorporated in a new collection of Sontag's essays, *Under the Sign of Saturn*, 1996.

13. One error is to credit Riefenstahl with an amateurish home movie of Hitler's *Berchtesgaden over Salzburg*, which was almost certainly taken by Eva Braun (who had once worked in a photographic studio). James Manilla who inadvertently launched the story later conceded the mistake in *Film Library Quarterly*, Summer 1972.

14. In February 1994 a Channel 4 documentary by John Bulmer caught the fleeting nature of a village culture in Ethiopia. The Surma stick-fighters practise similar ritualised aggression and 'living art' (body painting and decorative scarring or cicatrisation) as the Nuba; they are similarly under pressure to wear clothes and adapt to a 'more modern' way of life. It was not suggested in any reviews that focusing on these aspects of their lives bore fascist overtones.

15. Michael Tobias, 'The Last of the Nuba' (Book Review), *Mountain Gazette 34*, June 1975.

16. In Müller's film, some of the Nuba stills are juxtaposed with images from the prologue of *Olympia* with striking concordance. One comparison does emphasise Riefenstahl's vision of the body beautiful. It glistens. And we remember the vaseline applied with some tomfoolery to her 'Grecian' athletes on the Baltic beach. In Kau the warriors and young women traditionally burnish themselves with oil, and Riefenstahl saw to it that when she brought them gifts, plenty of oil was included.

17. 'Nazi Film Expert Attempts Comeback', article by David Platt in *Morning Freiheit*, 8th September 1972.

18. Joachim C. Fest, *Hitler*, 1973 (Penguin paperback edition, p. 9).
19. The 1939 'Weekend in Munich' film was shot by members of the Munich Amateur Film Society and put together by the talented Hans Feierabend. *Good Morning, Mr Hitler!* was shown on Channel 4 on 18th May 1993. A book, *Weekend in Munich* by Robert S. Wistrich, 1995, expands on the film and art, propaganda and terror in the Third Reich.
20. Ulrich Herbert, 'Good Times, Bad Times: Memories of the Third Reich', essay collected in *Life in the Third Reich*, edited by Richard Bessel, 1987 (p. 97).
21. Quoted in Glenn Infield, *Eva and Adolf*, 1974 (p. 261).
22. Ibid (p. 286).
23. 'La Disgrâce de Leni Riefenstahl', *Paris-Soir*, 14th June 1937. Newspapers were told at a Propaganda Ministry press briefing to strongly emphasise the complete fabrication of this story, and not to shrink from using such expressions as 'filth pedlar' or 'gutter press' when alluding to the paper(s) responsible.
24. 'Leni Riefenstahl: the body beautiful, art cinema and fascist aesthetics' by Thomas Elsaesser in *Sight and Sound*, February 1993; and reprinted in *Women Direct*, edited by Pam Cook and Philip Dodd, Scarlet Press.
25. In an interview with Gordon Hitchens, *Film Culture*, Spring 1973.
26. Ernst Jaeger's letter, dated 11th July 1948, is quoted in Leni Riefenstahl's *The Sieve of Time*, 1992.
27. Paul Mathias Padua's daring painting was the erotic sensation of the 1939 Great German Art Exhibition, or 'beerotic' if you read *Time* magazine that month. It was snapped up by the Führer.
28. Quote from the Müller film, *The Wonderful, Horrible Life of Leni Riefenstahl*, 1993.
29. Letter to the author, 4th March, 1996.

Select Bibliography

Book publications.

Acker, Ally, *Reel Women, Pioneers of the Cinema 1896 to the Present,* NewYork: Continuum, 1991.

Adam, Peter, *The Arts of the Third Reich,* London: Thames & Hudson, 1992.

Ades, Dawn (and others), *Art and Power, Europe under the Dictators 1930–45.* London: Hayward Gallery, 1995.

Bach, Stephen, *Marlene Dietrich, Life and Legend,* London: HarperCollins, 1992.

Barsam, Richard, *Filmguide to Triumph of the Will,* Bloomington/London: Indiana University Press, 1975.

——*Non-fiction Film, A Critical History,* London: Allen and Unwin, 1974; revised and expanded, Indiana University Press, 1992.

—— (ed), *Life in the Third Reich,* Oxford: Oxford University Press, 1987.

Bleuel, Hans Peter, *Strength Through Joy: Sex and Society in Nazi Germany,* London: Secker & Warburg, 1973.

Bullock, Alan, *Hitler, A Study in Tyranny,* London: Odhams, 1951; Companion Book Club (revised edition) 1954.

Burden, Hamilton T., *The Nuremberg Party Rallies: 1923–39,* London: Pall Mall Press, 1967.

Butler, Ivan, '*To Encourage the Art of the Film: the Story of the British Film Institute*', London: Robert Hale, 1971.

Christmann, Sepp & Erwin Huber, *Lauf, Sprung und Wurf,* Berlin: Cigaretten Bilderdienst, 1941.

Cook, Pam & Dodd, Philip (eds), *Women and Film, A Sight and Sound Reader,* Scarlet Press, updated 1993 or 1994.

Craig, Gordon, A., *Germany 1866–1945,* Oxford: Clarendon/Oxford University Press, 1978/1981.

Dodd, William E. Jr., & Martha Dodd (eds) *Ambassador Dodd's Diary 1933–1938,* London: Gollancz, 1941.

Eisner, H. Lotte, *The Haunted Screen: Expressionism in the German Cinema and the Influence of Max Reinhardt,* London: Thames & Hudson, 1965; Berkeley, 1977.

Ertl, Hans, *Meine wilden dreissiger Jahre,* Munich: Herbig, 1982.
——(See also: Schmidkunz).
Fairlie, G., *Flight Without Wings* (Biography of Hannes Schneider), London: Hodder & Stoughton, 1958.
Fanck, Arnold, *Der Kampf Mit Dem Berge,* Berlin: Verlag Reimar Hobbing, 1931.
——*SOS Eisberg!: Mit Fanck und Ernst Udet in Grünland – Die Grünland-expeditian des Universals-Films,* Munich: Bruckmann Verlag, 1933.
——*Stürme über dem Mont Blanc: Ein Filmbildbuch,* Basel, 1931.
——*Regie mit Gletschern, Stürmen und Lawinen,* Munich: Nymphenburger Verlag, 1973.
Fest, Joachim C., *Hitler,* New York: Harcourt Brace, 1974 (also London: Penguin Books, 1982).
Gabler, Neal, *An Empire of Their Own: How the Jews Invented Hollywood,* London: W. H. Allen, 1989.
Gellhorn, Martha, *The Face of War* (Revised edn), London: Virago, 1986.
Gill, Anton, *A Dance Between Flames* (Berlin between the Wars), London: John Murray, 1993.
Goebbels, Joseph, *The Goebbels Diaries* (translated and edited by Louis P. Lochner), London: Hamish Hamilton, 1948.
——*The Goebbels Diaries, 1939–1941* (Translated and edited by Fred Taylor), London: Hamish Hamilton, 1982; Sphere, 1983.
——*The Goebbels Diaries, the Last Days* (Edited and introduced by Hugh Trevor-Roper), London: Secker & Warburg, 1978.
——*Die Tagebücher von Joseph Goebbels: Sämtliche Fragmente.* (Edited by Elke Fröhlich for the Institut für Zeitgeschichte, Munich, in collaboration with the Bundesarchiv.) Several volumes variously dated.
Graham, Cooper C., *Leni Riefenstahl and Olympia,* Metuchen, NJ & London: The Scarecrow Press, 1986.
Granta (editor: Ian Jack) *Granta 51: Big Men (and L.A. women),* London: Penguin, 1995. (Articles on Hitler and women, and on Speer by Gitta Sereny).
Grierson, John, *Grierson on Documentary,* edited by Forsyth-Hardy, New York: Harcourt Brace 1947/London: Faber & Faber, 1966.
Grunberger, Richard, *A Social History of the Third Reich,* London: Weidenfeld & Nicolson, 1971; Pelican, 1974; Penguin 1991 (Important chapter on the Cinema).
Halliwell, Leslie, *Halliwell's Film Guide,* London: Paladin/Grafton, 5th ed. 1986, and republished regularly. (Gives TRIUMPH OF THE WILL 4 stars, OLYMPIA 3, and THE BLUE LIGHT 1).
Hanfstaengl, Ernst ('Putzi'), *Hitler, the Missing Years,* London: Eyre & Spottiswoode, 1957.
Hart-Davis, Duff, *Hitler's Games,* London: Century, 1986; Coronet paperback, 1988.
Heckmair, Anderl, *My Life As A Mountaineer,* London: Gollancz, 1975.
Heck-Rabi, Louise, *Women Filmmakers, A Critical Reception,* Metuchen, NJ/London: The Scarecrow Press, 1984.

Select Bibliography

Hinton, David B., *The Films of Leni Riefenstahl*, Metuchen, NJ/London: The Scarecrow Press, 1978.

Hinz, Berthold, *Art in the Third Reich*, New York, Random House, 1979.

Hitler, Adolf, *Mein Kampf,* London: The Paternoster Library, 1933; 'Unexpurgated edition' London: Hurst and Blackett, 1939 (and frequent reprints).

——*Hitler's Table Talk 1941–1944*, edited by Hugh Trevor-Roper, London: Weidenfeld & Nicolson, 1953, (Reprinted by the Oxford University Press.).

Hoffmann, Heinrich, *Hitler Was My Friend*, London: Burke, 1955.

Hull, David Stuart, *Film in the Third Reich,* London & Los Angeles: University of California Press, 1969.

Infield, Glenn, *Eva and Adolf,* New York/London: Grosset & Dunlap 1974; New English Library, 1975.

——*Leni Riefenstahl, the Fallen Film Goddess*, New York: Thomas Y. Crowell, 1976.

Killen, John, *The Luftwaffe*, London: Muller, 1967; Sphere, 1969.

König, Stefan (with Florian Trenker), *Bera Luis*, Velag J. Berg, 1992.

Koonz, Claudia, *Mothers in the Fatherland: Women, the Family and Nazi Politics,* London: Jonathan Cape, 1987.

Kracauer, Siegfried, *From Caligari to Hitler, a psychological history of the German film*, NewYork: Princeton University Press; London: Dennis Dobson, 1947.

Leiser, Erwin, *Nazi Cinema*, London: Secker & Warburg, 1974.

Lloyd, A. & Robinson, D. (eds), *Movies of the Thirties*, London: Orbis, 1983.

Mandell, Richard D., *The Nazi Olympics*, London: Souvenir Press, 1971.

Manvell, Roger & Fraenkel, Heinrich, *Dr Goebbels,* London: Heinemann, 1960.

——*The German Cinema,* London/New York: Praeger, 1971.

Mosley, Leonard, *The Reich Marshal, a Biography of Hermann Goering*, New York: Doubleday, 1974.

Noyce, Wilfrid, *Scholar Mountaineers,* London: Dobson, 1950 (Chapter on Nietsche and modern mountaineering).

Ott, Frederick W., *The Great German Films*, Secaucus, NJ:Citadel, 1986.

Owings, Alison, *Frauen, German Women recall the Third Reich*, Rutgers University Press, 1993; London: Penguin, 1995.

Petley, Julian, *Capital and Culture, German Cinema 1933–45*, London: British Film Institute, 1979.

Peukert, Detlev J. K., *Inside Nazi Germany: Conformity, Opposition and Racism in Everyday Life*, London: Batsford, 1987; Penguin, 1993.

Powell, Dilys (and others), *Since 1939: Ballet, Films, Music, Painting*, London: Readers Union, 1948.

Pronay, Nicholas & Spring, D.W. (eds), *Propaganda, Politics and Film, 1918–45*, London: Macmillan, 1982. (Collection of papers from seminar by contemporary luminaries).

Read, Anthony & Fisher, David, *Berlin, the Biography of A City,* London: Pimlico, 1994.

Reimann, Viktor, *Joseph Goebbels, the Man who Created Hitler*, London: Kimber, 1977; Sphere, 1979.

Select Bibliography

Riefenstahl, Leni, *Kampf in Schnee Und Eis*, Leipzig: Hesse & Becker, 1933.
——*Hinter Den Kulissen Reichspartei-Tag-films*, Munich: Franz Eher, 1935
(Behind-the-Scenes Picture Book, Some Background Information.
Ghost-written by Ernst Jaeger).
——*Schönheit Im Olympischen Kampf*, Berlin: Im Deutschen Verlag, 1937.
(Large folio-size picture collection of film stills and 'on location' shots).
——*Last of the Nuba*, New York: Harper & Row, 1974.
——*People of Kau*, London: Collins, 1976.
——*Leni Riefenstahl's Africa*, London: Collins/Harvill, 1982.
——Essay in *Visions of Paradise*, Edited by Bernhard Grzimek, London: Hodder
& Stoughton, 1981.
——*Memoiren* (Autobiography), 1987. Translated as *The Sieve of Time*, London:
Quartet, 1992; and published in the USA as *Riefenstahl, A Memoir*, New
York: St Martin's Press, 1993.
Rotha, Paul, *The Film Till Now*, London: Jonathan Cape, 1930; revised edition
with Richard Griffith, London: Vision, 1949.
Rutherford, Ward, *Hitler's Propaganda Machine*, London: Bison, 1978.
Sarris, Andrew (ed) *Interviews with Film Directors*, New York: Bobbs Merrill,
1967 (Reprints the Delahaye article in English).
Schmidkunz, Walter, *Bergvagabunden, Ein Hans-Ertl Buch*, Frankfurt: Guten-
berg, 1937.
Sereny, Gitta, *Albert Speer, his Battle with Truth*, London: Macmillan, 1995.
Shipman, David, *The Story of Cinema I – From the Beginnings to 'Gone with the
Wind'*, London: Hodder & Stoughton, 1982.
Shirer, William L., *Berlin Diary*, London: Hamish Hamilton, 1941.
——*The Rise and Fall of the Third Reich. A History of Nazi Germany*, London:
Secker & Warburg, 1959.
Sontag, Susan, *Under the Sign of Saturn*, London: Vintage, 1996 (Collection of
essays, including 'Fascinating Fascism' from the *New York Times Book
Review*).
Sorge, Dr Ernst, *With 'Plane, Boat and Camera in Greenland*, London: Hurst &
Blackett, 1935.
Speer, Albert, *Inside the Third Reich,* London: Weidenfeld & Nicolson, 1970;
Sphere, 1971; Cardinal, 1978. (The definitive account of Hitler's Nazi
Germany by Hitler's Armaments Minister.).
Spender, Stephen, *World Within World*, London: Hamish Hamilton, 1953
Taylor, A. J. P., *The Origins of the Second World War*, London: Hamish Hamilton
1961; Penguin 1964.
Toland, John, *Adolf Hitler*, Garden City, NY: Doubleday 1976.
Welch, David, *Propaganda and the German Cinema 1933–1945*, Oxford: Oxford
University Press, 1983.
Wistrich, Robert S., *Weekend in Munich – Art, Propaganda and Terror in the Third
Reich,* London: Pavilion, 1995.
Wollenberg, H. H., *Fifty Years of German Film*, London: Falcon, 1948.
Wykes, Alan, *Nuremberg Rallies*, (Purnell Campaign Book), London: Macdon-
ald, 1969.
Zanotto, Piero, *Luis Trenker – Lo Schermo Verticale*, Trento: Manfrini, 1982.

Select Bibliography

A selection of articles from magazines and journals:.

Alpine Journal, 'The mountaineer and the mountain film', article in No. 243, November 1931 Editor's note on Mountaineering Films (*Das blaue Licht*) in No. 246, May 1933.

Alpinismus, September 1966 issue is devoted to mountain films and filming with articles by and about Fanck, Trenker etc.

Barsam, Richard 'Leni Riefenstahl, Artifice and Truth in A World Apart', article in *Film Comment*, November 1973.

Berson, Arnold 'The Truth About Leni', *Films and Filming*, April 1965

——'Shame and Glory in the Movies', *National Review*, 14th January 1964.

Blobner, Helmut & Holba, Herbert, 'Jackboot Cinema', *Films and Filming*, December 1962.

Brownlow, Kevin, 'Leni Riefenstahl', *Film*, Winter 1966.

——'Reply to Paul Rotha', *Film*, Spring 1967.

Close Up, Reviews of *The White Hell of Piz Palu* (December 1929), *Sonne über dem Arlberg* and *White Frenzy* (March 1932), *The Blue Light* (June 1932).

Clough, Patricia, 'It was all for art, not Hitler', article in *The Times*, 21st August 1982.

Corliss, Richard, 'Leni Riefenstahl: A Bibliography', *Film Heritage*, 5/1969,.

Davis, Victor, 'Leni Riefenstahl At Ninety, Unlocks Her Nazi Secrets', article in *Mail on Sunday*, 23 August 1992.

Delahaye, Michel, 'Leni Et Le Loup: Entretien Avec Leni Riefenstahl', *Cahiers du Cinema* No. 170, September 1965.

Elaesser, Thomas, 'The body beautiful, art cinema and fascist aesthetics', in *Sight and Sound*, February 1993.

Estes, Jim, 'Nazi Film – A Triumph of Evil Genius', *San Francisco Chronicle*, 28.7.59, p. 35.

Fanck, Arnold, 'Wie ich dazu kam die ersten Hochgebirgsfilme zu drehen', *Jahrbuch, Deutscher Alpenverein*, 1957.

Film Comment, Winter 1965 Biographical Sketch of Leni Riefenstahl.

Film Culture, Spring 1973 Several articles on and interview with Leni Riefenstahl.

Filmfestival Internazionale Montagna Esplorazione 'Citta di Trento', Retrospettiva Arnold Fanck (in the Programme for Trento 1984).

——Omaggio A Luis Trenker – Cinquant'anni Di Regia Cinematografica in Alta Montagna: 1931–1981 (in the Programme for 1981; 1980 and 1982 programmes also include Trenker Features).

——Mostra Richard Angst (Catalogue of exhibition celebrating Angst's 50 years of camerawork, largely with Fanck, a side-event to Trento 1984).

Film Review 1978–79, the Feminine Angle – Women Film Directors.

Films, 'an Ambassador for Nazi Germany', April 1982 (pp. 12–14).

Films and Filming, 'Directors of the Decade: the Thirties – Leni Riefenstahl', March 1983.

Fischer, Heinrich, 'The Theatre and Film in Nazi Germany', *Tricolor* (New York), July-August 1945.

Gardner, Robert, 'Can the Will Triumph?' in *Film Comment*, Winter 1966.

Gregor, Ulrich, 'A Comeback for Leni Riefenstahl?', *Film Comment*, Winter 1965.

Gunston, David, 'Leni Riefenstahl', *Film Quarterly* 14 (1960).

Hitchens, G., 'An Interview with a Legend', *Film Comment*, Winter 1965.

——Leni Riefenstahl Interviewed, *Film Culture*, Spring 1973.

Kellman, K., 'Propaganda A Vision – Triumph of the Will', in *Film Culture*, Spring 1973.

Mancini, Marc, 'Camp Movie?' in *American Film*, March 1984. (*Tiefland*).

Manilla, James, 'Review of A Lesser Riefenstahl Work' in *Film Comment*, Winter 1965, (Report of showing of *Berchtesgaden über Salzburg*, shown on 4th November 1958 at Raymond Rohauer's Coronet Theater, Los Angeles (not a Riefenstahl work at all.).

Mannheim, L. Andrew, 'Leni', in *Modern Photography*, February 1974.

Marcorelles, Louis 'The Nazi Cinema', *Sight and Sound*, Autumn 1955.

McLemore, Henry, 'Propaganda? Not in this Film' in *Los Angeles Evening News*, 1938 (November or December).

Phillips, M. S., 'The Nazi Control of the German Film Industry' *Journal of European Studies*, 1, 1971.

Reiss, Tom, 'How the Nazis Created a Dream Factory in Hell', *New York Times*, 6th November 1994.

Richards, Jeffrey, 'Leni Riefenstahl: Style and Structure', *The Silent Picture 8* (Autumn 1970).

Rickmers, W. R., Note on Mountain Films in *Alpine Journal* No. 243, November 1931.

Riefenstahl, Leni, 'Reply to Paul Rotha', *Film*, Spring 1967.

——Riefenstahl Statement on Sarris/Gessner Quarrel About Olympia, *Film Comment*, Fall 1967.

Schiff, Stephen, 'Leni's Olympia', *Vanity Fair*, September 1992.

Schulberg, Budd, 'Nazi Pin-up Girl, Leni Riefenstahl, Hitler's no. 1 movie actress, explains away – with a professional smile – her former status in Nazi Germany', *Saturday Evening Post*, 30th March 1945.

Sereny, Gitta, 'Loving Hitler', *Independent on Sunday*, 13th September 1992.

Sontag, Susan, 'Fascinating Fascism', *New York Review of Books*, 6th February 1975.

Tobias, Michael, 'The Last of the Nuba by Leni Riefenstahl', Review in *Mountain Gazette*, June 1975.

Winston, Brian, 'Was Hitler There?' (Reconsidering 'Triumph of the Will'), *Sight and Sound*, Spring 1981.

Young, Vernon, 'Hardly A Man is Now Alive: Monologue on A Nazi Film', *Accent*, Spring 1955.

Riefenstahl Filmography

Acting Roles

The Holy Mountain (*Der Heilige Berg*; also known as *Peaks of Destiny*), directed by
   Arnold Fanck for UFA, released 1926.
The Great Leap (*Der Grosse Sprung*; also known as *Gita, the Goat Girl*), directed by
   Arnold Fanck for UFA, released 1927.
Fate of the House of Hapsburg (*Die Vetsera*; also known as *The Tragedy of
   Mayerling* or *Das Schicksal derer von Habsburg*), directed by Rolf Raffe,
   released 1928.
The White Hell of Piz Palü (*Die Weisse Holle von Piz Palü*), directed by Arnold
   Fanck and G.W. Pabst for Sokal, released 1929.
Storm over Mont Blanc (*Stürme über dem Mont Blanc*; also known as *Avalanche*),
   directed by Arnold Fanck, released 1930.
The White Frenzy (*Sonne über dem Arlberg*; also known as *Der Weisse Rausch*),
   directed by Arnold Fanck for Sokal, released 1931.
SOS Iceberg! (*SOS Eisberg!*), directed by Arnold Fanck and Tay Garnett for
   Universal, released 1933.

Riefenstahl as Director

The Blue Light (*Das Blaue Licht*), in which Leni Riefenstahl also played the
   leading role, released 1932.
Mademoiselle Docteur, unrealised film project with Arnold Fanck, in which
   Riefenstahl also planned to play the star part, 1933.
Victory of Faith (*Sieg des Glaubens*), 1933.
Triumph of the Will (*Triumph des Willens*), 1935.
Day of Freedom – Our Armed Forces (*Tag der Freiheit*), 1935.
The Camera Goes Too (*Die Kamera Fährt Mit*), 1937.
Olympia (in two parts: *Fest der Volker* and *Fest der Schönheit*), 1938.

Penthesilea, unrealised film project, 1939.
Van Gogh, abandoned, 1943.
Lowland (Tiefland), finally released 1954.
The Last of the Nuba, unfinished, 1973.

Also attributed to Leni Riefenstahl are a number of unrealised film projects in the 1950s, including *Three Stars in the Robe of the Madonna*, *Eternal Summit*, *Sun and Shadow*, *Frederick and Voltaire*, and *Black Cargo* which was never finished.

Index

Index

Index

Index

Index